Modernization of European Company Law and Corporate Governance

European Company Law Series

VOLUME 6

The CECL-book series on European company law is closely linked to the bimonthly journal *European Company Law* ('ECL'), also published by Kluwer Law International. The persons comprising the ECL's editorial board and the editors of the CECL-book series are one and the same. The aims and objectives of CECL can be found at <www.cecl.nl>. The series covers subjects of company law in a broad sense, including insolvency, co-determination and securities law. The editorial board ensures that all parts of this series are well written, of sufficient scientific depth and, at the same time, useful for legal practitioners and academics alike. The board's credo is that international and comparative law should never degenerate into a theoretical *l'artpour l'art*-exercise, but must always be subservient to the requirement of practical applicability and a further development of the law.

Kluwer Law International

Modernization of European Company Law and Corporate Governance

Some Considerations on its Legal Limits

Gert-Jan Vossestein

Wolters Kluwer
Law & Business

AUSTIN BOSTON CHICAGO NEW YORK THE NETHERLANDS

Published by:
Kluwer Law International
PO Box 316
2400 AH Alphen aan den Rijn
The Netherlands
Website: www.kluwerlaw.com

Sold and distributed in North, Central and South America by:
Aspen Publishers, Inc.
7201 McKinney Circle
Frederick, MD 21704
United States of America
Email: customer.service@aspenpublishers.com

Sold and distributed in all other countries by:
Turpin Distribution Services Ltd.
Stratton Business Park
Pegasus Drive, Biggleswade
Bedfordshire SG18 8TQ
United Kingdom
Email: kluwerlaw@turpin-distribution.com

Printed on acid-free paper.

ISBN 978-90-411-2592-7

Printed in Great Britain.

Table of Contents

List of Abbreviations

AA	*Ars Aequi*
AG	Advocate General, also *(die) Aktiengesellschaft*
Am. J. Comp. L.	*American Journal of Comparative Law*
BB	*Betriebs-Berater*
Bull. EU (EC) (EG)	Bulletin of the European Union (Bulletin of the European Communities) (Bulletin van de Europese Gemeenschappen)
Bus.L.R.	*Business Law Review*
C. com.	Code de commerce
CDE	*Cahiers de droit européen*
CML Rev.	*Common Market Law Review*
COM	Commission documents (proposals for directives, regulations or decisions of the Council and/or European Parliament, Green Papers, White Papers, political communications, reports and working documents)
Cornell L. Rev.	*Cornell Law Review*
EBLR	*European Business Law Review*
EBOR	*European Business Organization Law Review*
EC	European Community *and* Treaty establishing the European Community
ECFR	*European Company and Financial Law Review*
ECHR	European Court of Human Rights
ECL	*European Company Law*
ECR	European Court Reports (Reports of Cases before the Court of Justice and the Court of First Instance)

EEC	European Economic Community
EESC	European Economic and Social Committee
E.For.Aff.Rev.	*European Foreign Affairs Review*
EJCL	*Electronic Journal of Comparative Law*
ELJ	*European Law Journal*
ELRev.	*European Law Review*
ERCL	*European Review of Contract law*
ERPL	*European Review of Private Law*
EU	European Union *and* Treaty on European Union
EuR	*Europarecht*
Eur. J. of L. and Econ.	*European Journal of Law and Economics*
EuZW	*Europäische Zeitschrift für Wirtschaftsrecht*
fn.	footnote
Fordham Int'l L.J.	*Fordham International Law Journal*
German L.J.	*German Law Journal*
Harv. L. Rev.	*Harvard Law Review*
ICCLJ	*International and Comparative Corporate Law Journal*
ICLQ	*International and Comparative Law Quarterly*
IFLR	*International Financial Law Review*
IP	Commission press release
J. Bus.	*The Journal of Business*
JCP	*Journal of Consumer Policy*
J.L. Econ. & Org.	*Journal of Law, Economics & Organization*
J. of Pol. Econ.	*Journal of Political Economy*
JOR	*Jurisprudentie Onderneming & Recht*
LIEI	*Legal Issues of Economic Integration*
LQR	*Law Quarterly Review*
MEMO	Commission memorandum
MJ	*Maastricht Journal of European and Comparative Law*
NIPR	*Nederlands Internationaal Privaatrecht*
NJB	*Nederlands Juristenblad*
n.y.r.	not yet reported
OJ	Official Journal of the EU (before 1 February 2003: Official Journal of the EC)
Ondernemingsrecht	*Ondernemingsrecht* (forming the continuation of *De NV* and *TVVS*)
Oxf. Rev. Econ. Policy	*Oxford Review of Economic Policy*
QJE	*The Quarterly Journal of Economics*
RabelsZ	*Rabels Zeitschrift für ausländisches und internationales Privatrecht*
RDUE	*Revue du Droit de l'Union Européenne*
Rev.trim.dr.eur.	*Revue trimestrielle de droit européen*
RIW	*Recht der internationalen Wirtschaft*

RMCUE	*Revue du Marché commun et de l'Union européenne*
SEW	*Sociaal-Economische Wetgeving. Tijdschrift voor Europees en economisch recht*
SPEECH	Commission speech
TPR	*Tijdschrift voor Privaatrecht*
TVR	*Tijdschrift voor rechtspersoon en vennootschap*
TVVS	*TVVS. Maandblad voor ondernemingsrecht en rechtspersonen*
UL Rev.	*Utrecht Law Review*
WPNR	*Weekblad voor Privaatrecht, Notariaat en Registratie*
Yale L.J.	*Yale Law Journal*
YEL	*Yearbook of European Law*
ZGR	*Zeitschrift für Unternehmens- und Gesellschaftsrecht*
ZHR	*Zeitschrift für das Gesamte Handelsrecht und Wirtschaftsrecht*
ZIP	*ZIP Zeitschrift für Wirtschaftsrecht*

Treaties, (Preparatory) Acts and Reports, Cited in Abbreviated Form

Action Plan	Communication from the Commission to the Council and the European Parliament. Modernising Company Law and Enhancing Corporate Governance in the European Union – A Plan to Move Forward, COM (2003) 284 final of 21 May 2003
EC/EC Treaty	Treaty establishing the European Community
EEC Treaty	Treaty establishing the European Economic Community
EU Treaty	Treaty on European Union
High Level Group Report I	Report of the High Level Group of Company Law Experts on Issues Related to Takeover Bids of 10 January 2002, available at the Commission's Internal Market website: <http://ec.europa.eu/internal_market/>
High Level Group Report II	Report of the High Level Group of Company Law Experts on a Modern Regulatory Framework for Company Law in Europe of 4 November 2002, available at the Commission's Internal Market website: <http://ec.europa.eu/internal_market/>

Case-law Cited in Abbreviated Form

Cartesio	Case C-210/06 *CARTESIO Oktató és Szolgáltató bt*, judgment of 16 December 2008, not yet reported
Centros	Case C-212/97 *Centros Ltd v. Erhvervs- og Selskabsstyrelsen* [1999] ECR I-1459
Daily Mail	Case 81/87 *The Queen v. HM Treasury and Commissioners of Inland Revenue, ex parte Daily Mail and General Trust plc.* [1988] ECR 5483
Inspire Art	Case C-167/01 *Kamer van Koophandel en Fabrieken voor Amsterdam v. Inspire Art Ltd* [2003] ECR I-10155
Sevic	Case C-411/03 *SEVIC Systems Aktiengesellschaft v. Amtsgericht Neuwied* [2005] ECR I-10805
Überseering	Case C-208/00 *Überseering BV v. Nordic Construction Company Baumanagement GmbH (NCC)* [2002] ECR I-9919

Textbooks Referred to Throughout

Barents & Brinkhorst	R. Barents & L.J. Brinkhorst, *Grondlijnen van Europees Recht*, Deventer: Kluwer 2006
Craig & de Búrca	P. Craig & G. de Búrca, *EU Law*, Oxford: Oxford University Press 2008
Edwards	V. Edwards, *EC Company Law*, Oxford: Oxford University Press 1999
Grundmann	S. Grundmann, *European Company Law*, Antwerp/Oxford: Intersentia 2007
Habersack	M. Habersack, *Europäisches Gesellschaftsrecht*, Munich: C.H. Beck 2006
Kapteyn & VerLoren van Themaat	P.J.G. Kapteyn et al. (eds), *Kapteyn & VerLoren van Themaat. The Law of the European Union and the European Communities*, Austin/Boston/Chicago/New-York: Wolters Kluwer 2008
Lauwaars & Timmermans	R.H. Lauwaars & C.W.A. Timmermans, *Europees recht in kort bestek*, Deventer: Kluwer 2003
Lenaerts, Arts & Maselis	K. Lenaerts, D. Arts & I. Maselis, *Procedural Law of the European Union* (R. Bray ed.), London: Sweet & Maxwell 2006
Lenaerts & Van Nuffel	K. Lenaerts & P. Van Nuffel, *Constitutional Law of the European Union* (R. Bray ed.), London: Sweet & Maxwell 2005
Lutter	M. Lutter, *Europäisches Unternehmensrecht* (ZGR-Sonderheft 1), Berlin/New-York: Walter de Gruyter 1996

Rickford	J. Rickford (ed.), *The European Company. Developing a Community Law of Corporations*, Antwerp: Intersentia 2003
Schermers & Waelbroeck	H.G. Schermers & D.F. Waelbroeck, *Judicial Protection in the European Union*, The Hague/London/New-York: Kluwer Law International 2001
Schwarz	G.C. Schwarz, *Europäisches Gesellschaftsrecht*, Baden-Baden: Nomos 2000
Timmermans	C.W.A. Timmermans, *Company Law as Ius Commune?* (First Walter van Gerven Lecture), Antwerp: Intersentia 2002
Tridimas	T. Tridimas, *The General Principles of EU Law*, Oxford: Oxford University Press 2006
Usher	J.A. Usher, *General Principles of EC Law*, London/New-York: Longman 1998
Weatherill & Beaumont	S. Weatherill & P. Beaumont, *EU Law*, London: Penguin Books 1999
Wouters	J. Wouters, *Het Europese vestigingsrecht voor ondernemingen herbekeken* (vol. I–IV), Leuven: Katholieke Universiteit Leuven 1996–1997

Foreword by Peter Dortmond

It gives me great pleasure to contribute a foreword to this particular addition to the Kluwer European Company Law Series, which Series is published under the aegis of the Centre for European Company Law (CECL).*

In May 2003, the European Commission presented its well-known Action Plan *Modernising Company Law and Enhancing Corporate Governance in the European Union*. The European regulatory framework for company law and corporate governance needed to be modernized – emphasized the Commission – in view of: the growing trend for European companies to operate cross-border in the internal market; the continuing integration of European capital markets; the rapid development of new information and communication technologies; the (then) forthcoming enlargement of the EU to ten new Member States; and, finally, the damaging impact of – recent – financial scandals. The Action Plan is prioritized over the short term (2003–2005), medium term (2006–2008) and long term (2009 onwards), and indicates which type of regulatory instrument should be used for each proposal, with approximate timescales. The Action Plan is based on a comprehensive set of legislative and non-legislative proposals, under the following headings: corporate governance; capital maintenance and alteration; groups and pyramids; corporate restructuring and mobility; the European private company; the European cooperative society and other EU legal forms of enterprise; and enhancing the transparency of national legal forms of enterprise. The main – policy – objectives of the Action Plan are, first, to strengthen shareholders' rights and protection for employees, creditors, and the other parties with which companies deal; and second, to foster the efficiency and competitiveness of business, with special attention to some specific cross-border issues (e.g., cross-border merger or transfer of seat).

---

* For information on the aims and activities of this Centre, see <www.cecl.nl>.

It may be concluded now, six years after its launch, that the Action Plan (at least the first two implementation phases thereof) has been a real success. Since May 2003, nearly all measures scheduled for implementation in the short term and medium term have been adopted (or are in the process of adoption). Among the results achieved are the Directive on cross-border mergers (2005) and the Directive on shareholder rights (2007). A notable exception, of course, is the Directive on cross-border transfer of the registered office ('conversion'). Regrettably, the Commissioner for the Internal Market, Charlie McCreevy, decided not to proceed with this Directive in October 2007. It cannot be excluded, however, that this initiative will be reanimated after the coming European Parliament elections and, subsequently, a new Commission (and Commissioner for the Internal Market) will have taken office.

The modernization process certainly has not come to a halt. The proposal for a European Private Company, which was submitted in June 2008, is in progress, and a consultation on a possible European Foundation Statute was launched in February 2009. Moreover, already implemented modernization initiatives may be updated. An example of this is the 2004 Recommendation on the remuneration of directors of listed companies, which – within the context of the financial crisis – was complemented by a new Recommendation in April 2009.

As the author points out, the Action Plan does not reveal any close attention being paid to the issue of legislative competence as regards such Community action. So far, there has been relatively little attention for this subject in academic literature, too; this literature is predominantly concerned with issues such as how specific EC company law directives and regulations should look like ideally (from a company law perspective) or how EC company law influences the company law of specific, individual Member States.

This book now offers a thorough, comprehensive examination of the issue of Community competence in the field of company law modernization (and the related issue of requirements for the lawful exercise of this competence). The relevant legal bases (by which Community competences are conferred) are dealt with extensively. It appears from this that the Community has far-reaching powers in the field of company law modernization. However, as an analysis of various EC company law directives and regulations makes clear, the Community legislature frequently fails to explain how an act based on a specific Treaty Article meets the terms of that provision. Problematic to a certain extent, moreover, appears to be the issue of the choice of the correct legal basis (as in the case of the Directive on shareholder rights).

I warmly recommend this book to anyone who works or does research in the field of (EC) company law: to academics, practitioners, those involved in the legislative process, as well as students.

Peter Dortmond,
May 2009

List of Cases

European Court of Justice

32/62	*Alvis v. Council EEC* [1963] ECR 101
9 and 11/71	*Compagnie d'approvisionnement, de transport et de crédit a.O. v. Commission* [1972] ECR 391
21–24/72	*International Fruit Company a.O. v. Produktschap voor Groenten en Fruit* [1972] ECR 1219
8/73	*Hauptzollamt Bremerhaven v. Massey Ferguson* [1973] ECR 897
2/74	*Reyners v. Belgium* [1974] ECR 631
17/74	*Transocean Marine Paint Association v. Commission* [1974] ECR 1063
Opinion 1/75	'Draft OECD Understanding on a Local Cost Standard' [1975] ECR 1355
3–4/76 and 6/76	*Cornelis Kramer a.O.* [1976] ECR 1279
15 and 16/76	*France v. Commission* [1979] ECR 321
46/76	*Bauhuis* [1977] ECR 5
71/76	*Thieffry v. Conseil de l'Ordre des Avocats de la Cour de Paris* [1977] ECR 765
123/77	*UNICME v. Council* [1978] ECR 845
155/79	*AM & S v. Commission* [1982] ECR 1575
66/80	*International Chemical Corporation v. Amministrazione delle finanze dello Stato* [1981] ECR 1191
15/83	*Denkavit Nederland* [1984] ECR 2171
37/83	*Rewe-Zentrale* [1984] ECR 1229

112/83	*Produits de Maïs v. Administration des douanes et droits indirects* [1985] ECR 719
182/83	*Fearon v. Irish Land Commission* [1984] ECR 3677
270/83	*Commission v. France* ('Avoir Fiscal') [1986] ECR 273
205/84	*Commission v. Germany* [1986] ECR 3755
79/85	*Segers v. Bedrijfsvereniging voor Bank- en Verzekeringswezen, Groothandel en Vrije Beroepen* [1986] ECR 2375
89, 104, 114, 116–117 and 125–129/85	*Åhlström v. Commission* [1988] ECR 5193
45/86	*Commission v. Council* [1987] ECR 1493
46/87 and 227/88	*Hoechst v. Commission* [1989] ECR 2859
81/87	*Daily Mail* [1988] ECR 5483
374/87	*Orkem v. Commission* [1989] ECR 3283
69/88	*Krantz v. Ontvanger der Directe Belastingen* [1990] ECR I-583
322/88	*Grimaldi v. Fonds des maladies professionnelles* [1989] ECR 4407
331/88	*The Queen v. Ministry of Agriculture, Fisheries and Food, ex parte FEDESA a.O.* ('Fedesa') [1990] ECR I-4023
C-63/89	*Assurances du Crédit v. Council and Commission* [1991] ECR I-1799
C-221/89	*The Queen v. Secretary of State for Transport, ex parte Factortame* ('Factortame') [1991] ECR I-3905
C-300/89	*Commission v. Council* ('Titanium dioxide') [1991] ECR I-2867
C-340/89	*Vlassopoulou* [1991] ECR I-2357
C-19/90 and C-20/90	*Karella a.O. v. Ypourgio a.O.* [1991] ECR I-2691
C-286/90	*Anklagemindigheden v. Poulsen and Diva Navigation* [1992] ECR I-6019
C-369/90	*Micheletti a.O. v. Delegación del Gobierno en Cantabria* [1992] ECR I-4239
C-267/91 and C-268/91	*Criminal proceedings against Keck and Mithouard* [1993] ECR I-6097
C-330/91	*The Queen v. Inland Revenue Commissioners, ex parte Commerzbank AG* [1993] ECR I-4017
C-19/92	*Kraus* [1993] ECR I-1663
C-292/92	*Hünermund a.O. v. Landesapothekerkammer Baden-Württemberg* [1993] ECR I-6787
C-350/92	*Spain v. Council* [1995] ECR I-1985
C-51/93	*Meyhui v. Schott Zwiesel Glaswerke* [1994] ECR I-3879

C-280/93	*Germany v. Council* [1994] ECR I-4973
C-415/93	*Union royale belge des sociétés de football association a.O. v. Bosman* [1995] ECR I-4921
C-427/93, C-429/93 and C-436/93	*Bristol-Myers Squibb a.O. v. Paranova* [1996] ECR I-3457
C-470/93	*Verein gegen Unwesen in Handel und Gewerbe Köln v. Mars* [1995] ECR I-1923
C-479/93	*Francovich v. Italy* [1995] ECR I-3843
Opinion 1/94	'Competence of the Community to conclude international agreements concerning services and the protection of intellectual property' ('GATS and TRIPS') [1994] ECR I-5267
Opinion 2/94	'Accession by the Communities to the Convention for the Protection of Human Rights and Fundamental Freedoms' [1996] ECR I-1759
C-44/94	*The Queen v. Minister of Agriculture, Fisheries and Food, ex parte Fishermen's Organisations a.O.* [1995] ECR I-3115
C-55/94	*Gebhard v. Consiglio dell'Ordine degli Avvocati e Procuratori di Milano* [1995] ECR I-4165
C-193/94	*Skanavi and Chryssanthakopoulos* [1996] ECR I-929
C-233/94	*Germany v. Parliament and Council* ('Deposit Guarantees') [1997] ECR I-2405
C-271/94	*Parliament v. Council* [1996] ECR I-1689
C-57/95	*France v. Commission* [1997] ECR I-1627
C-70/95	*Sodemare a.O. v. Regione Lombardia* [1997] ECR I-3395
C-265/95	*Commission v. France* ('Spanish strawberries') [1997] ECR I-6959
C-284/95	*Safety Hi-Tech v. S. & T.* [1998] ECR I-4301
C-341/95	*Bettati v. Safety Hi-Tech* [1998] ECR I-4355
C-97/96	*Verband deutscher Daihatsu-Händler v. Daihatsu Deutschland* [1997] ECR I-6843
C-108/96	*Mac Quen a.O.* [2001] ECR I-837
C-114/96	*Criminal proceedings against Kieffer and Thill* [1997] ECR I-3629
C-122/96	*Saldanha and MTS Securities Corporation v. Hiross* [1997] ECR I-5325
C-212/97	*Centros* [1999] ECR I-1459
C-222/97	*Trummer and Mayer* [1999] ECR I-1661
C-234/97	*Fernández de Bobadilla* [1999] ECR I-4773
C-255/97	*Pfeiffer* [1999] ECR I-2835
C-307/97	*Saint-Gobain* [1999] ECR I-6161
C-44/98	*BASF* [1999] ECR I-6269

C-168/98	*Luxembourg v. Parliament and Council* [2000] ECR I-9131
C-172/98	*Commission v. Belgium* [1999] ECR I-3999
C-190/98	*Graf* [2000] ECR I-493
C-251/98	*Baars* [2000] ECR I-2787
C-281/98	*Angonese* [2000] ECR I-4139
C-367/98	*Commission v. Portugal* [2002] ECR I-4731
C-376/98	*Germany v. Parliament and Council* ('Tobacco Advertizing') [2000] ECR I-8419
C-377/98	*Netherlands v. Parliament and Council* ('Biotechnology Directive') [2001] ECR I-7079
C-397/98 and C-410/98	*Metallgesellschaft a.O.* [2001] ECR I-1727
C-169/99	*Schwarzkopf* [2001] ECR I-5901
C-306/99	*Banque internationale pour l'Afrique Occidentale SA* ('BiAO') [2003] ECR I-1
C-393/99 and C-394/99	*Inasti v. Claude Hervein a.O.* [2002] ECR I-2829
C-483/99	*Commission v. France* [2002] ECR I-4781
C-503/99	*Commission v. Belgium* [2002] ECR I-4809
Opinion 2/00	'Cartagena Protocol on Biosafety' [2001] ECR I-9713
C-86/00	*HSB-Wohnbau* [2001] ECR I-5353
C-208/00	*Überseering* [2002] ECR I-9919
C-463/00	*Commission v. Spain* [2003] ECR I-4581
C-469/00	*Ravil* [2003] ECR I-5053
C-56/01	*Inizan* [2003] ECR I-12403
C-79/01	*Payroll a.O.* [2002] ECR I-8923
C-98/01	*Commission v. United Kingdom* [2003] ECR I-4641
C-103/01	*Commission v. Germany* [2003] ECR I-5369
C-108/01	*Consorzio del Prosciutto di Parma and Salumificio S. Rita* [2003] ECR I-5121
C-167/01	*Inspire Art* [2003] ECR I-10155
C-211/01	*Commission v. Council* ('Carriage of Goods') [2003] ECR I-8913
C-313/01	*Morgenbesser* [2003] ECR I-13467
C-338/01	*Commission v. Council* ('Directive on mutual assistance between Member States in the recovery of public-law claims') [2004] ECR I-4829
C-491/01	*British American Tobacco (Investments) and Imperial Tobacco* ('British American Tobacco') [2002] ECR I-11453
C-9/02	*de Lasteyrie du Saillant* [2004] ECR I-2409
C-299/02	*Commission v. Netherlands* [2004] ECR I-9761
C-434/02	*Arnold André* [2004] ECR I-11825
C-435/02 and C-103/03	*Springer* [2004] ECR I-8663
C-442/02	*CaixaBank France* [2004] ECR I-8961

C-40/03 P	*Rica Foods v. Commission* [2005] ECR I-6811
C-41/03 P	*Rica Foods v. Commission* [2005] ECR I-6875
C-94/03	*Commission v. Council* [2006] ECR I-1
C-140/03	*Commission v. Greece* [2005] ECR I-3177
C-178/03	*Commission v. Parliament and Council* [2006] ECR I-107
C-210/03	*Swedish Match* [2004] ECR I-11893
C-244/03	*France v. Parliament and Council* [2005] ECR I-4021
C-380/03	*Germany v. Parliament and Council* ('Tobacco Advertizing II') [2006] ECR I-11573
C-411/03	*Sevic* [2005] ECR I-10805
C-436/03	*Parliament v. Council* ('SCE Regulation') [2006] ECR I-3733
C-446/03	*Marks & Spencer* [2005] ECR I-10837
C-533/03	*Commission v. Council* [2006] ECR I-1025
C-66/04	*United Kingdom v. Parliament and Council* ('Regulation on smoke flavourings') [2005] ECR I-10553
C-154/04 and C-155/04	*Alliance for Natural Health a.O.* [2005] ECR I-6451
C-174/04	*Commission v. Italy* [2005] ECR I-4933
C-217/04	*United Kingdom and Northern Ireland v. Parliament and Council* ('Regulation establishing ENISA') [2006] ECR I-3771
C-282/04 and C-283/04	*Commission v. Netherlands* ('KPN/TPG') [2006] ECR I-9141
C-346/04	*Conijn* [2006] ECR I-6137
C-374/04	*Test Claimants in Class IV of the ACT Group Litigation* [2006] ECR I-11673
C-452/04	*Fidium Finanz AG* [2006] ECR I-9521
C-453/04	*Innoventif* [2006] ECR I-4929
C-463/04 and C-464/04	*Federconsumatori a.O.* [2007] ECR I-10419
C-470/04	*N. v. Inspecteur van de Belastingdienst Oost/ Kantoor Almelo* [2006] ECR I-7409
C-112/05	*Commission v. Germany* ('Volkswagen') [2007] ECR I-8995
C-231/05	*Oy AA* [2007] ECR I-6373
C-341/05	*Laval un Partneri* [2007] ECR I-11767
C-383/05	*Talotta* [2007] ECR I-2555
C-402/05 P and C-415/05 P	*Kadi a.O. v. Council and Commission*, judgment of 3 September 2008, not yet reported
C-438/05	*The International Transport Workers' Federation and the Finnish Seamen's Union* ('Viking') [2007] ECR I-10779

C-210/06	*Cartesio*, judgment of 16 December 2008, not yet reported
C-301/06	*Ireland v. Parliament and Council* ('Data retention'), judgment of 10 February 2009, not yet reported
C-500/06	*Corporación Dermoestética*, judgment of 17 July 2008, not yet reported
C-13/07	*Commission v. Council* ('Accession of Vietnam to WTO'), Opinion of AG Kokott delivered on 26 March 2009
C-155/07	*Parliament v. Council* ('Decision 2006/1016/EC – Community guarantee to the European Investment Bank'), judgment of 6 November 2008, not yet reported

European Court of First Instance

T-102/96	*Gencor v. Commission* [1999] ECR II-753
T-306/01	*Yusuf and Al Barakaat International Foundation v. Council and Commission* [2005] ECR II-3533
T-47/02	*Danzer v. Council* [2006] ECR II-1779
T-184/04	*Sulvida v. Commission* [2005] ECR II-85

European Court of Human Rights

30417/96	*Olczak v. Poland*, decision of 7 November 2002 (Reports of Judgments and Decisions ECHR 2002-X)
48553/99	*Sovtransavto Holding v. Ukraine*, judgment of 25 July 2002 (Reports of Judgments and Decisions ECHR 2002-VII)
56400/00	*Cēsnieks v. Latvia*, decision of 12 December 2002 (not published in the Reports)

Introduction

This book is about the modernization of European company law and corporate governance. More particularly, it addresses two main questions: (1) to what extent does the European Community (or its institutions[1]) enjoy legislative competence in the field of company law and corporate governance and, once this competence has been established; (2) which – legal – requirements apply to the exercise of this competence.

Immediate cause for raising these two questions is the European Commission's *Action Plan to Modernise Company Law* of May 2003.[2] The Action Plan aims, in the short, medium, and long term,[3] to bring about thoroughgoing, especially legislative changes concerning a broad range of subjects: corporate governance; capital maintenance and alteration; groups and pyramids; corporate restructuring and mobility; the European private company; the European cooperative society and other EC legal forms of enterprise; and, finally, the transparency of national

1. The EC Treaty's enabling norms are usually so formulated that they do not empower the Community as such, but rather name the institution(s) that are so empowered (A. von Bogdandy & J. Bast, 'The European Union's vertical order of competences: The current law and proposals for its reform', *CML Rev.* 39 (2002): 235). See further Ch. 1. Legal scholars (nevertheless) distinguish occasionally between the competences of the Community as such ('vertical' competences), and the distribution of competences among its institutions ('horizontal' competences). The issue of vertical competences then concerns the vertical relationship between the Member States and the Community, whereas the issue of horizontal competences concerns the horizontal relationships between the EC's different institutions and therefore the internal division of powers. See von Bogdandy & Bast, just cited, 235–236. So as to leave no doubt, both competence issues are covered by the first question referred to in the main text.
2. Communication from the Commission to the Council and the European Parliament, 'Modernising Company Law and Enhancing Corporate Governance in the European Union – A Plan to Move Forward', COM (2003) 284 final of 21 May 2003.
3. Namely, 2003–2005, 2006–2008 and 2009 onwards, resp.

legal forms of enterprises.[4] Implementation of this comprehensive, legislative programme can only take place, as I will argue, to the extent that there is a (Community) competence to act and that there is compliance to the requirements for the lawful exercise of this competence.

The Action Plan does not reveal any close attention being paid to the issue of legislative competence as regards such Community action. There is relatively little attention for the subject in academic literature too[5] (this literature is predominantly concerned with issues such as how specific EC company law directives and regulations should look ideally (from a company law perspective[6]) or how EC company law influences the company law of specific, individual Member States). On the whole, this also holds true for the issue of requirements for the lawful exercise of Community competence (in the field of company law).[7]

In case a specific EC company law instrument is in breach of the above limits ('competence' or 'requirement for the lawful exercise of the competence'), its legality may be challenged under Article 230 EC before the Court of Justice and it may subsequently be annulled; the Court also may, in a preliminary procedure under Article 234 EC, declare such an act invalid.[8] In fact, in the past few years, the Court of Justice has indeed given rulings in cases in which the lawfulness of instruments of company law was challenged.[9]

4. The Action Plan is discussed in more detail in Ch. 2.
5. I dealt with the subject referred to in the main text in G.-J. Vossestein, 'De bevoegdheid van de Europese Gemeenschap tot regeling van het vennootschapsrecht', *WPNR* (2002): 247–253.
6. The term 'company law' will be dealt with presently.
7. In common with the issue of competence, the subsidiarity principle, which is a prominent requirement for the lawful *exercise* of Community competence (about these requirements: Ch. 5), is not given proper attention in the Action Plan. See further Ch. 5, which contains, *inter al.*, an analysis of the Action Plan in view of the principle of subsidiarity. (As to the prominent position of the subsidiarity principle it is noted that in respect of this principle various 'motivation' requirements apply (which, for the most part or generally, do not apply in respect of the observance of other requirements for the lawful exercise of Community competence). E.g., Art. 4 *Protocol on the application of the principles of subsidiarity and proportionality* and Art. 253 EC. See, to this effect, also C.W.A. Timmermans, 'Subsidiarity and Transparency', *Fordham Int'l L.J.* 22 (1999): 118). As regards the other requirements for the lawful exercise of Community competence, it is noted that, occasionally, company law specialists contend in respect of certain specific provisions of EC company law that they are in breach of Art. 43 EC. This, the observance of Art. 43 EC, is a requirement for the lawful exercise of Community competence which is thus dealt with in the literature. The contentions at issue will be examined in Ch. 5, within the context of a more general discussion of the observance of Art. 43 EC as a requirement for the lawful exercise of Community competence (in the field of company law).
8. The issue of judicial review is discussed in more detail in Ch. 1.
9. Joined Cases C-435/02 and C-103/03 *Springer* [2004] ECR I-8663, concerned the validity of a 1990 Directive amending the Fourth and Seventh Directives. Case T-47/02 *Danzer* v *Council* [2006] ECR II-1779, was a case ex Art. 288 EC, in which the Court of First Instance 'for the sake of completeness' entered into the validity of the First and Fourth Directives. Finally, in Case C-436/03 *Parliament* v *Council* ('SCE Regulation') [2006] ECR I-3733, the Court of Justice ruled on an inter-institutional conflict between the European Parliament and the Council. The European Parliament in this case sought annulment of the Council Regulation on the Statute

The main purpose of this book is – in short – to offer a general framework for examining the above limits. With a view to a clear understanding of the matter and to elucidate the practical relevance of this abstract framework, specific EC company law instruments (or provisions thereof) will be tested for compatibility with the EC Treaty. In this context, the focus is on the EC company law instruments that have been adopted in implementation of the 2003 Action Plan. More generally, the book hopes to initiate further investigation of the interface between company law and EC law.

In connection with the main purpose of this book, one final remark should be made. Notwithstanding that the analyses presented here are geared towards EC company law, the analyses may be helpful for further research on the limits at issue to other fields of law as well, such as EC contract law and EC securities law.[10]

In the remainder of this Introduction, first, the term 'EC company law' is defined; then, the structure of this book is described in broad outline, and finally the system of citation is explained.

What does 'EC company law' mean? As regards first, the aspect 'company law' of the notion EC company law, I note that the EC Treaty does not deal with 'company law' as such. There are, however, various Treaty Articles, to be discussed below,[11] which enable the EC to regulate certain aspects of 'company law' and, in fact, a substantial body of Community 'company law' has been built up over the years.

It will not be attempted to present an abstract or theoretical definition of company law,[12] with all the associated difficulties in determining dividing lines

---

for a European Cooperative Society (SCE). In none of these three cases, incidentally, the Court of Justice annulled or declared invalid the above instruments of EC company law.

10. In the field of EC contract law there has been more attention for the limits at issue than in the field of EC company law. Weatherill in particular, has done important pioneering work. See e.g., S. Weatherill, 'The European Commission's Green Paper on European Contract Law: Context, Content and Constitutionality', *JCP* 24 (2001): 364; S. Weatherill, 'The Commission's Options for Developing EC Consumer Protection and Contract Law: Assessing the Constitutional Basis', *EBLR* (2002): 506. See further (on private law): J. Strese, *Die Kompetenzen der Europäischen Gemeinschaft zur Privatrechtsangleichung im Binnenmarkt* (Baden-Baden: Nomos, 2006). See, finally (on securities law): N. Moloney, 'New Frontiers in EC Capital Markets Law: From Market Construction to Market Regulation', *CML Rev.* 40 (2003): 833–842; N. Moloney, *EC Securities Regulation* (Oxford: OUP, 2008), *inter al.*: 6–10, 247–248, 345–346, 563–566, 735–738, 897–900, 941–944, and 1031–1033.
11. See Chs 3 and 4.
12. The question of what constitutes company law is occasionally asked in legal literature. It is being answered by identifying core features of company law, such as the creation of separate legal personality for the company; the conferment of limited liability on the company's shareholders and managers; the provision of centralized management; the allocation of control rights over the company; and the creation of transferable shares. See: P.L. Davies, *Introduction to Company Law* (Oxford: OUP, 2002), in particular Ch. 1 ('The Core Features of Company Law'); H. Hansmann & R. Kraakman, 'What is Corporate Law?', in *The Anatomy of Corporate Law. A Comparative and Functional Approach*, ed. R. Kraakman et al. (Oxford: OUP, 2004), 1–19. Usually, the description of company law serves an analysis of so-called agency problems of the business firm or – more generally – of the functions of 'company law'.

with other bodies of law, such as capital market law,[13] employee involvement law[14] and insolvency law.[15] Another approach, which focuses on concrete EC company law instruments, is chosen here. Two categories of instruments, which together make up EC company law, are discerned. First, the instruments which existed or had been proposed in May 2003, when the Commission published its *Action Plan to Modernise Company Law.* The Action Plan itself, conveniently, contains a list of these 'old' instruments. Second, the company law instruments which are part of the Action Plan.[16] A survey of the various EC company law

13. About the delineation of company law and capital market law, *inter al.*: K.J. Hopt & E. Wymeersch (eds), *Capital Markets and Company Law* (Oxford: OUP, 2003), in particular the preface by the editors on v–vi. See also in this connection: J. Garrido, 'Company Law and Capital Markets', in Rickford, 95–111; Habersack, 2–4.
14. About the delineation of company law and employee involvement law, *inter al.*: S. Grundmann, *Europäisches Gesellschaftsrecht* (Heidelberg: C.F. Müller, 2004), 64–66.
15. About the delineation of company law and insolvency law, *inter al.*: B. Wessels, 'The Insolvency Regulation: Three Years in Force', *ECL* (2005): 50–58; P.J. Omar, 'The Convergence of Company and Insolvency Initiatives within the European Union', *ECL* (2005): 59–65.
16. For convenience, it is briefly referred to EC company law (instruments), instead of EC company law and corporate governance (instruments). It should be realized, however, that the issue of corporate governance could, in principle, be singled out from the (rest of the) Action Plan (and the definition of EC company law). In this connection, it can first be referred to the full title of the Action Plan, which is: 'Modernising Company Law and Enhancing Corporate Governance in the European Union – A Plan to Move Forward'; furthermore, the 2003 programme is based on a comprehensive set of legislative and non-legislative proposals, under various headings, including that of 'corporate governance'. The term EC *company law* as defined here, however, does (as indicated) include EC *corporate governance.*

    The Action Plan, furthermore, refers to various 'related initiatives': The Financial Services Action Plan (1999), the Financial Reporting Strategy (2000), the Communication on Corporate Social Responsibility (2002), the Communication on Industrial Policy in an Enlarged Europe (2002) and the Communication 'Reinforcing statutory audit in the EU' (2003). These initiatives (and the concrete instruments they may underlie) do not fall within the scope of EC company law as defined here, and will not be dealt with (further). (The Action Plan (see 3–4) explicitly states that these initiatives are 'not part' of the Action Plan).

    One may wonder why the Action Plan refers to the 2000 *Financial Reporting Strategy* separately; the initiative was (already) part of the 1999 Financial Services Action Plan (FSAP, the initiative listed first by the Action Plan as being outside its – the Action Plan's – scope). See FSAP, 21 *jo.* 23. A further issue is that the *Financial Reporting Strategy's* main aim was adoption of a Regulation on the application of international accounting standards. This Regulation however, was already adopted in 2002, well before the Action Plan was published. Finally, it is somewhat ambiguous that whereas the *Strategy* itself is outside the scope of the Action Plan, the Regulation just referred to, which is the main component of this *Strategy,* is presented as an instrument of EC company law. It would have been more logical to not include the Regulation in the list of existing EC company law instruments.

    Let me further note that the Action Plan, as mentioned, also considers to be outside its scope the FSAP. The Directives on cross-border mergers and on cross-border transfer of the registered office – which are part of this FSAP – however, are in fact explicitly part of the Action Plan (as well). See Action Plan, *sub* 3.4. (Corporate restructuring and mobility) and 25. There are, incidentally, also EC company law instruments which are not part of the Action Plan (i.e., the 'old' company law instruments – only – listed in the Action Plan), but which do belong to the FSAP, namely: (1) the Regulation on the Statute for a European company (SE) and the

instruments is included in two (corresponding) annexes to this book: Annex I (Pre-Action Plan company law instruments) and Annex II (Action Plan company law instruments).

As regards second, the aspect 'EC' of the notion EC company law, some clarification might be in place, as the term which is regularly used by company law specialists is 'EU' company law.

The directives, regulations, and other instruments which constitute European company law, are all based on the (E)EC Treaty. The EC Treaty was signed originally as the Treaty establishing the European Economic Community or EEC Treaty in Rome in 1957, which entered into force on 1 January 1958. The Treaty has been amended, *inter alia*, by the Single European Act (signed in 1986) and by the Treaty on European Union or EU Treaty, commonly known as the Maastricht Treaty (signed in 1992). This latter Treaty extended the sphere of action of the Community to such an extent that the original title 'European Economic Community' was replaced by 'European Community'.[17] Further amendments to the – by then – EC Treaty entailed the Treaty of Amsterdam (signed in 1997) and the Treaty of Nice (signed in 2001).[18]

Apart from the EC Treaty, primary Community law also comprises the Treaty establishing a European Atomic Energy Community or EAEC Treaty. This Treaty was signed at the same time as the EEC Treaty, in 1957.[19] Primary Community law furthermore comprised the Treaty establishing the European Coal and Steel Community or ECSC Treaty. This Treaty, however, was signed for a period of fifty years; the ECSC Treaty entered into force in July 1952 and ended in July 2002.[20]

Community law may not be identified with European Union law.[21] The European Union was established by the EU Treaty.[22] The European Union is 'founded on'[23] or encompasses: (1) the European Communities (i.e., the European Community, the European Atomic Energy Community and the – meanwhile inoperative – European Coal and Steel Community); (2) a common foreign and security policy, which is governed by Title V of the EU Treaty; and (3) police and judicial cooperation in criminal matters which is governed by Title VI of the EU Treaty.[24]

accompanying Directive supplementing the Statute for a European company with regard to the involvement of employees (2001); (2) the Regulation on the application of international accounting standards (2002); and (3) the Directive on takeover bids (2004). To be sure, the major part of the instruments of the FSAP do fall outside the scope of the ACTION PLAN on company law and do not belong to EC company law as it is defined here.

17. See Art. 8 EU (Art. G EU pre-Amsterdam).
18. For these Treaty amendments, see Lenaerts & Van Nuffel, 8–10.
19. See further Lenaerts & Van Nuffel, 7.
20. *Ibid.*, 3.
21. See in particular Lenaerts & Van Nuffel, Ch. 18 ('Non-Community acts of the Union').
22. Article 1, first para. EU.
23. Article 1, third para. EU.
24. Before the Treaty of Amsterdam, Title VI read: 'Provisions on cooperation in the fields of justice and home affairs.' The Treaty of Amsterdam led to the incorporation in the EC Treaty of a number of issues relating to justice and home affairs. As a result, only police and judicial

These three elements constitute the so-called first, second, and third pillars of the European Union.[25] So, even though Community law is part of EU law (first pillar), EU law (second and third pillar) is not always Community law.[26]

As European company law was built up exclusively on the basis of the (E)EC Treaty and not the other Community Treaties, let alone on the basis of the second and third pillars of the European Union, I use the designation 'EC' company law and not 'EU' company law.

The structure of this book is as follows. Chapter 1 is about the place of EC company law in the EC Treaty. Chapter 2 sketches the historical development of EC company law. In addition, the objectives of EC company law policy are discussed. Finally, it will refer to the current EC company law *acquis.* Chapter 3 and Chapter 4, then, are about the competence of the EC in the field of company law: Chapter 3 concerns Article 44 EC, whereas Chapter 4 is about the other EC Treaty Articles which enable the EC to regulate certain aspects of company law. Chapter 5 is about the requirements for the lawful exercise of this competence. More specifically, it is about the principle of subsidiarity and the observance of Article 43 EC. To distinguish between the competence itself and the – lawful – exercise thereof is common practice in legal doctrine.[27] Chapter 6, finally, contains concluding remarks.

As regards, finally, the system of citation of the book let me note this. Throughout this work, standard abbreviations are used. They are included in three separate lists: 'List of Abbreviations', 'Treaties, (Preparatory) Acts and Reports, cited in abbreviated form' and 'Case-law cited in abbreviated form'. In addition, textbooks which are regularly referred to are cited in abbreviated form. They are included in the list 'Textbooks referred to throughout'.

As to the system of citation of the Articles of the Treaty on European Union and the Treaty establishing the European Community, the method adhered to by the EC Court of Justice will be followed.[28] So, where reference is made to an Article of a Treaty as it stands after 1 May 1999 (coming into force of the Treaty of Amsterdam), the number of the Article is immediately followed by two letters indicating the Treaty concerned: EU for Treaty on European Union and EC for EC Treaty.

Sources referred to in footnotes are presented in chronological order. Otherwise, the system of citation is self-explanatory.

Law is stated as at 1 January 2009. Wherever possible, subsequent developments have been taken into account.

---

cooperation in criminal matters fell within the field of application of Title VI of the EU Treaty. See Lenaerts & Van Nuffel, 60.

25. Schermers & Waelbroeck, 8 and Craig & de Búrca, 15.
26. See further Lenaerts & Van Nuffel, 708.
27. For the distinction between competence and the exercise thereof, see Ch. 5.
28. See 'Note on the Citation of Articles of the Treaties in the Publications of the Court of Justice and the Court of First Instance'. This 'Note' is published on the Court's website: <http://curia.europa.eu>.

Chapter 1

EC Company Law within the Framework of the Treaty: A General Survey

I. INTRODUCTION

This chapter is about the place of EC company law in the EC Treaty. It sets out the basic principles of this field of law that are of relevance for a proper understanding of the issues involved in this book. (While the issues involved will be rather familiar to lawyers in the field of European law, they may be less known to national company lawyers and helpful in this respect). After this introduction, section II concerns the general framework within which EC company law operates. First, it deals with the objectives of the European Community (subsection A). Next, subsection B concerns the EC company law actors and acts. In order to attain its objectives, the EC Treaty provides for various institutions and acts. Insofar as they are relevant to EC company law, they are addressed in this section. Subsection C deals with powers and limits. In order to act, institutions are entrusted with powers. As will be shown, within Community law, institutions do not have all-encompassing powers: they can act only where the EC Treaty equips them with competence; the exercise of their competence is (frequently) bound by the principle of subsidiarity; further, they are bound by the general principles of Community law; and they have to adhere to the basic prohibitions on restrictions to the free movement, particularly – in the area of EC company law essential – the freedom of establishment. Subsection D on judicial review makes some observations on the legal procedures in which it can be determined that EC institutions have acted outside their powers and the consequences if the EC institutions did so. In section III of this chapter, some relevant future developments are briefly indicated.

II. EC COMPANY LAW WITHIN THE FRAMEWORK OF THE TREATY

A. OBJECTIVES OF THE EUROPEAN COMMUNITY

1. Articles 2 EC and 3 EC

Article 2 EC sets out in general terms the objectives of the Treaty[1] and the instruments by which they are to be achieved:

> The Community shall have as its task, by establishing a common market and an economic and monetary union and by implementing common policies or activities referred to in Articles 3 and 4, to promote throughout the Community a harmonious, balanced and sustainable development of economic activities, a high level of employment and of social protection, equality between men and women, sustainable and non-inflationary growth, a high degree of competitiveness and convergence of economic performance, a high level of protection and improvement of the quality of the environment, the raising of the standard of living and quality of life, and economic and social cohesion and solidarity among Member States.

To achieve the stated, long-term, 'political' objectives, Article 2 EC distinguishes three instruments. First, the establishment of a common market. Second, the establishment of an economic and monetary union. Third, the implementation of certain common policies or activities. These three instruments are worked out at great length in Articles 3(1) EC and 4 EC,[2] which read:

> [Article 3] 1. For the purposes set out in Article 2, the activities of the Community shall include, as provided in this Treaty and in accordance with the timetable set out therein:
>
> (a) the prohibition, as between Member States, of customs duties and quantitative restrictions on the import and export of goods, and of all other measures having equivalent effect;
> (b) a common commercial policy;
> (c) an internal market characterised by the abolition, as between Member States, of obstacles to the free movement of goods, persons, services and capital;
> (d) measures concerning the entry and movement of persons as provided for in Title IV;
> (e) a common policy in the sphere of agriculture and fisheries;
> (f) a common policy in the sphere of transport;
> (g) a system ensuring that competition in the internal market is not distorted;

---

1. Article 2 EC uses the word 'task', whereas Art. 3(1) EC refers to 'the purposes set out in Article 2'.
2. See Lenaerts & Van Nuffel, 82. See also Kapteyn & VerLoren van Themaat, 120–122.

(h) the approximation of the laws of Member States to the extent required for the functioning of the common market;
(i) the promotion of coordination between employment policies of the Member States with a view to enhancing their effectiveness by developing a coordinated strategy for employment;
(j) a policy in the social sphere comprising a European Social Fund;
(k) the strengthening of economic and social cohesion;
(l) a policy in the sphere of the environment;
(m) the strengthening of the competitiveness of Community industry;
(n) the promotion of research and technological development;
(o) encouragement for the establishment and development of trans-European networks;
(p) a contribution to the attainment of a high level of health protection;
(q) a contribution to education and training of quality and to the flowering of the cultures of the Member States;
(r) a policy in the sphere of development cooperation;
(s) the association of the overseas countries and territories in order to increase trade and promote jointly economic and social development;
(t) a contribution to the strengthening of consumer protection;
(u) measures in the spheres of energy, civil protection and tourism.

[Article 4]

(1) For the purposes set out in Article 2, the activities of the Member States and the Community shall include, as provided in this Treaty and in accordance with the timetable set out therein, the adoption of an economic policy which is based on the close coordination of Member States' economic policies, on the internal market and on the definition of common objectives, and conducted in accordance with the principle of an open market economy with free competition.
(2) Concurrently with the foregoing, and as provided in this Treaty and in accordance with the timetable and the procedures set out therein, these activities shall include the irrevocable fixing of exchange rates leading to the introduction of a single currency, the ecu, and the definition and conduct of a single monetary policy and exchange-rate policy the primary objective of both of which shall be to maintain price stability and, without prejudice to this objective, to support the general economic policies in the Community, in accordance with the principle of an open market economy with free competition.
(3) These activities of the Member States and the Community shall entail compliance with the following guiding principles: stable prices, sound public finances and monetary conditions and a sustainable balance of payments.

The activities mentioned in Article 3(1)(a) to (d), (g) and (h) EC are assumed to relate to the first instrument, that is, the common market;[3] Article 4 EC should be

3. See Kapteyn & VerLoren van Themaat, 120.

regarded as building upon the second instrument, that is, the establishment of an economic and monetary union,[4] and the remaining elements of Article 3(1) EC finally, namely those laid down *sub* (e), (f), and (i) to (u), should be characterized as more specific forms of the third instrument, which embraces common policies or common activities.[5]

Each of the concrete activities of the EC set out in Articles 3(1) EC and 4 EC is developed more specifically in Part three of the Treaty (Articles 23 EC to 181a EC inclusive).[6]

The second and third instrument (the economic and monetary union, and the common policies or activities respectively) lack relevance to the issue of EC company law and will not be dealt with any further.[7] The concept of the common market, by contrast, is of importance[8] and is elaborated upon in the next section.

2. Establishment and Functioning of a Common Market

a. Establishment

The establishment of a common market is, as stated, one of the instruments to attain the objectives of the EC Treaty. The term 'common market' of Article 2 EC is used in the EC Treaty without being explicitly defined;[9] it is, however, argued[10] that it encompasses, apart from the elimination of obstacles to the free movement of goods, persons, services and capital, also, *inter alia*, a system of undistorted

4. *Ibid.*, 121.
5. *Ibid.*, 120.
6. *Ibid.*, 117 and 120. It should be noted however, that 'the association of the overseas countries' of Art. 3(1)(s) EC is dealt with in Part four of the Treaty. With respect to the 'measures in the spheres of energy, civil protection and tourism' of Art. 3(1)(u) EC, Declaration no. 1 of the 'Declarations annexed to the final act of Maastricht' on civil protection, energy, and tourism is of relevance. In it, it is declared that: 'the question of introducing into the Treaty establishing the European Community Titles relating to the spheres referred to in Article 3(t) [now Art. 3(u) EC] of that Treaty will be examined.' So far, specific Titles have not been introduced; see in this connection Lenaerts & Van Nuffel, 83.
7. An exception is Art. 137 EC, which provides a legal basis to adopt directives in the field of, *inter al.*, the information and consultation of workers and codetermination. Art. 137 EC is part of Title XI (of Part three of the Treaty) on 'Social policy, education, vocational training and youth'. This article will be dealt with in Ch. 4.
8. Article 44 EC, which is an important legal basis for Community action in the field of company law, is part of the Treaty provisions on freedom of establishment, which freedom in turn is an important aspect of the common market. To give another example, Art. 94 EC, empowers the Community legislature to adopt directives: 'for the approximation of such laws, regulations or administrative provisions of the Member States as directly affect the establishment or functioning of the *common market*'. (emphasis added).
9. K. Mortelmans, 'The common market, the internal market and the single market: What's in a market?', *CML Rev.* 35 (1998): 107; L.W. Gormley, 'Competition and Free Movement: Is the Internal Market the Same as a Common Market?', *EBLR* (2002): 517.
10. See e.g., Lenaerts & Van Nuffel, 139–141.

competition.[11] The Single European Act of 1987 inserted the term 'internal market' into the (now) EC Treaty (Article 3(1)(c)EC).[12] As opposed to the concept of the common market, the internal market is defined in the Treaty. Article 14(2) EC provides:

> The internal market shall comprise an area without internal frontiers in which the free movement of goods, persons, services and capital is ensured in accordance with the provisions of this Treaty.

It has been advanced that the 'internal market' has a more limited scope than the 'common market', which arguably also encompasses a system of undistorted competition.[13] Others, however, have argued that at least the Court of Justice seems to see no distinction between the two market concepts and appears to treat the common market and the internal market as if they were interchangeable concepts.[14] For the purposes of our investigation, however, this discussion is generally not (too) relevant. Both the 'common market' and the 'internal market' encompass free movement of persons, which includes the freedom of establishment (Articles 43–48 EC);[15] this (latter) freedom in particular, is of relevance to the issue of EC company law.

The internal market is, according to Article 3(1)(c) EC, established through the abolition, as between Member States, of obstacles to the free movement of goods, persons, services, and capital. To abolish those obstacles, the EC Treaty provides for two instruments which are complementary in their operation.[16]

a. First, there are the so-called basic prohibitions of restrictions to free movement. These 'basic prohibitions' are laid down in Article 28 EC (prohibition of quantitative restrictions between Member States); Article 39 EC (freedom of movement for workers);[17] Article 43 EC (prohibition of restrictions on the freedom of establishment); Article 49 EC (prohibition of restrictions on freedom to provide services); and finally, Article 56 EC (prohibition of restrictions on the movement of capital).

---

11. Part of this system are the rules on competition which are directed to undertakings (Art. 81 EC et seq.). On the relationship between the rules on free movement and the rules on competition: J. Stuyck, 'Libre circulation et concurrence: les deux piliers du Marché commun', in *Mélanges en hommage à Michel Waelbroeck* (vol. II), ed. M. Dony & A. De Walsche (Brussels: Bruylant, 1999), 1485 and 1496; K. Mortelmans, 'Towards convergence in the application of the rules on free movement and on competition?', *CML Rev.* 38 (2001): 634.
12. See Art. 13 of the Single European Act, OJ 1987 L 169, 1.
13. Lenaerts & Van Nuffel, 143.
14. See: Gormley, just cited, 519 and 520; Barents & Brinkhorst, 289.
15. Part three, Title III of the EC Treaty is titled 'Free movement of persons, services and capital'. The free movement of persons in this Title encompasses the freedom of movement for workers and the right of establishment. See further Ch. 4 (on the subject of the relationship between Article 94 EC and 95 EC).
16. Opinion of AG Geelhoed in Case C-491/01 *British American Tobacco* [2002] ECR I-11453, pt. 103.
17. According to Art. 39(2) EC, this freedom entails the abolition of any discrimination based on nationality between workers of the Member States as regards employment, remuneration, and other conditions of work and employment.

The basic prohibitions of restrictions to free movement are addressed to the Member States.[18] The case-law of the Court of Justice has shown a development toward convergence between the prohibitions.[19] In this context, it can be referred to the Court's ruling in *Gebhard*.[20] In this case, the Court held that:

> It follows (...) from the Court's case-law that national measures liable to hinder or make less attractive the exercise of *fundamental freedoms guaranteed by the Treaty* must fulfil four conditions: they must be applied in a non-discriminatory manner; they must be justified by imperative requirements in the general interest; they must be suitable for securing the attainment of the objective which they pursue; and they must not go beyond what is necessary in order to attain it (...).[21] (emphasis added).

The basic prohibitions curtail Member States' powers in a range of areas of law, including the field of national company law.[22] Article 43 EC, concerning freedom of establishment, for instance, precludes national legislation such as the Netherlands Law on Formally Foreign Companies which, in short, imposed on the exercise of freedom of establishment in the Netherlands by a foreign company certain conditions provided for in Netherlands law in respect of company formation relating to minimum capital and directors' liability.[23] Article 56 EC, concerning free movement of capital, to give another example, prohibits Member States to maintain in force or introduce certain types of so-called golden shares.[24] In advance of

18. K. Mortelmans, 'The relationship between the Treaty rules and Community measures for the establishment and functioning of the internal market – towards a concordance rule', *CML Rev.* 39 (2002): 1338. As to whether the prohibitions referred to also apply to the Community institutions, see s. C.3, *infra* and further Ch. 5.

    Let me note here that with respect to the provisions on free movement of persons, the Court of Justice has held that these can also be invoked against organizations not governed by public law (Case C-415/93 *Union royale belge des sociétés de football association a.O.* v *Bosman* [1995] ECR I-4921, paras 82–84) and private persons (Case C-281/98 *Angonese* [2000] ECR I-4139, paras 30–36). See further Case C-438/05 *The International Transport Workers' Federation and the Finnish Seamen's Union* ('Viking') [2007] ECR I-10779; and, Case C-341/05 *Laval un Partneri* [2007] ECR I-11767.

    Finally, as appears from Case C-265/95 *Commission* v *France* ('Spanish strawberries') [1997] ECR I-6959, paras 30–32, Member States may not only be found to have infringed their Treaty obligations for having adopted measures contrary to the provisions on free movement, but also for abstaining from taking action.
19. See K. Mortelmans, 'Towards convergence in the application of the rules on free movement and on competition?', *CML Rev.* 38 (2001): 617–619.
20. Case C-55/94 *Gebhard* v *Consiglio dell'Ordine degli Avvocati e Procuratori di Milano* [1995] ECR I-4165.
21. *Ibid.*, para. 37.
22. The term 'company law' is used here rather informally. For a brief discussion of what constitutes company law, see the introductory chapter of this book.
23. *Inspire Art*, para. 105.
24. Case C-367/98 *Commission* v *Portugal* [2002] ECR I-4731; Case C-483/99 *Commission* v *France* [2002] ECR I-4781; Case C-503/99 *Commission* v *Belgium* [2002] ECR I-4809; Case C-463/00 *Commission* v *Spain* [2003] ECR I-4581; Case C-98/01 *Commission* v *United Kingdom* [2003] ECR I-4641; Case C-174/04 *Commission* v *Italy* [2005] ECR I-4933; Joined

Chapters 3 and 5, where its scope is extensively addressed, it should be added, that Article 43 EC (or Article 56 EC for that matter) not only may apply to measures which make a distinction between national and foreign companies, but also to measures which do not make such a distinction (so-called indistinctly applicable measures);[25] furthermore, the latter measures may be justified, not just under the exceptions explicitly laid down in the Treaty, but also in case of 'imperative requirements in the general interest', the so-called 'rule of reason'.[26]

The basic prohibitions contribute greatly to the establishment of the common market. The market integration brought about by these prohibitions is described as 'negative integration'.[27]

b. The *second* instrument is the Community legislature's power, under various harmonization provisions,[28] to remove the obstacles to the free movement which remain – or which are created – by virtue of the fact that the national legislature applies one of the derogations from the basic prohibitions (i.e., the justifications explicitly laid down in the Treaty or the imperative requirements in the general interest).[29] It is through the complementary application of the basic prohibitions and the Community action just referred to that an internal market is established.[30]

This, however, still does not provide any guarantee that the market thus established can also *function* as a common market; additional harmonization measures will frequently be needed for that end.[31] The significance of harmonization, therefore, is not limited to the *establishment* of the internal market. Harmonization – as

---

Cases C-282/04 and C-283/04 *Commission* v *Netherlands* ('KPN/TPG') [2006] ECR I-9141; Case C-112/05 *Commission* v *Germany* ('Volkswagen') [2007] ECR I-8995; and Joined Cases C-463/04 and C-464/04 *Federconsumatori a.O.* [2007] ECR I-10419.

The literature on golden shares includes: E. Szyszczak, 'Golden Shares and Market Governance', *LIEI* (2002): 255–284; G.-J. Vossestein, 'Gouden aandelen', *WPNR* (2002): 807–812; H. Fleischer, 'Case note' [on the first three golden share judgments mentioned above], *CML Rev.* 40 (2003): 493–501; S. Grundmann & F. Möslein, 'Die Goldene Aktie. Staatskontrollrechte in Europarecht und wirtschaftspolitischer Bewertung', *ZGR* (2003): 317–366; U. Klinke, 'European Company Law and the ECJ: The Court's Judgements in the Years 2001 to 2004', *ECFR* (2005): 270–321; and G.-J. Vossestein, 'Volkswagen: The State of Affairs of Golden Shares, General Company Law and European Free Movement of Capital', *ECFR* (2008): 115–133.

25. See K. Mortelmans, 'Towards convergence in the application of the rules on free movement and on competition?', *CML Rev.* 38 (2001): 617–618. For an in-depth examination of the scope of the basic prohibitions in the field of free movement of persons, see E. Spaventa, 'From Gebhard to Carpenter: Towards a (non-)economic European constitution', *CML Rev.* 41 (2004): 743–773.
26. See Mortelmans, just cited, 618. In this connection Mortelmans, however, refers to: 'the still unsettled case law on the possibility of invoking rule of reason exceptions in respect of discriminatory measures'.
27. See: Weatherill & Beaumont, 554 and 599; Lauwaars & Timmermans, 179 and S. Weatherill, *Cases and Materials on EU law* (Oxford: OUP, 2007), 289.
28. See, in particular: Art. 40 and Art. 42 EC (relating to workers); Art. 44 EC (relating to establishment); Art. 52 EC (relating to services) and the general harmonization provisions of Art. 94 and Art. 95 EC.
29. Opinion of AG Geelhoed in *British American Tobacco*, just cited, pt. 103.
30. *Ibid.*, pt. 147.
31. *Ibid.*

Article 3(1)(h) EC explicitly makes clear – is also required for the *functioning* of the internal market.[32] The issue of harmonization and its relevance to the functioning of the internal market is elaborated upon in the next section.

b. Functioning

In the view of the drafters of the Treaty, integration would, apart from the elimination of obstacles through the basic prohibitions, be further achieved by common policy-making;[33] by creating Community rules. Market integration through acts adopted by the Community institutions,[34] is called 'positive integration'.[35] The concept of positive integration has a broad scope. It includes harmonization of national legislation – already briefly dealt with in the previous section – as well as the adoption of uniform legislation.[36]

The essence of harmonization is to bring divergent national laws more in line with each other.[37] Harmonization performs two functions. Its first function relates to the *establishment* of the common market, and was dealt with above. As to harmonization's second function, Article 3(1)(h) EC makes clear that harmonization is also prescribed whenever – divergent – national laws directly affect the *functioning* of the common market.[38]

Harmonization measures may be adopted by the Community institutions under a wide range of Treaty provisions. The specific legal bases for the attainment of free movement, particularly in the field of EC company law, are discussed in depth in Chapters 3 and 4.

Finally, it must be emphasized that the term harmonization here may also include what the Court of Justice regularly calls 'coordination', which relates to Community rules that try to resolve conflicts or disparities between national legal systems.[39]

Positive integration may, besides measures of harmonization (and coordination), also include what are called *uniform* Community measures (uniform

---

32. Kapteyn & VerLoren van Themaat, 308.
33. Part III of the Treaty is titled 'Community policies'. It covers Art. 23 EC to Art. 181a EC inclusive.
34. Rulings of the Court of Justice that apply the free movement prohibitions, however, are aspects of negative integration in that they may achieve uniformity between Member States, but only by the negative process of holding national laws incompatible with these prohibitions. See Weatherill & Beaumont, 599.
35. See: Weatherill & Beaumont, 554–555; Lauwaars & Timmermans, 179; S. Weatherill, *Cases and Materials on EU law* (Oxford: OUP, 2007), 289–290 and 585; and Kapteyn & VerLoren van Themaat, 307.
36. The term uniform legislation – as a category of Community measures to be distinguished from harmonization – is taken from Kapteyn & VerLoren van Themaat, 579.
37. See: P.J. Slot, 'Harmonisation', *ELRev.* 21 (1996): 378–387; Lenaerts & Van Nuffel, 267–268.
38. See Kapteyn & VerLoren van Themaat, 308.
39. For this method of harmonization, see: Timmermans, 6; K. Mortelmans, 'The relationship between the Treaty rules and Community measures for the establishment and functioning of the internal market – towards a concordance rule', *CML Rev.* 39 (2002): 1310.

legislation). The main or predominant purpose of these uniform measures is not to bring divergent national laws more in line with each other; instead, these uniform measures are aimed at offering genuine Community facilities, such as Community legal forms for doing business.[40] The legal basis for this type of Community action is discussed in Chapter 4.

B. EC Company Law Actors and Acts

In order to attain its objectives, the EC Treaty provides for various institutions and empowers them to issue certain acts. The composition of these institutions, and the specific differences between the various acts, are part of general institutional European law and will not be entered into; I refer to the extensive literature on these topics.[41] I will, however, make a few general observations on some of these topics as far as they concern the EC company law issues involved in this book.

1. Actors

a. Institutions

Principal actors in the field of EC company law are the Commission, Council, and the European Parliament. Which of these institutions[42] (and particularly in what role) is involved in the adoption of an act, depends on the legal basis which is provided for in the Treaty.[43] Some of these legal bases, which are discussed extensively in Chapters 3 and 4, provide for example for a consultative role for the European Parliament (as Article 308 EC), others provide for codecision by it (as Article 44 EC and Article 95 EC). This is the source of a growing number of inter-institutional conflicts. Recently, this type of conflict concerned for the first time the lawfulness of an EC company law instrument: Council Regulation No. 1435/2003 on the Statute for a European Cooperative Society.[44]

Two bodies are further active in the field of EC company law: The *European Corporate Governance Forum* and the *Group of Non-Governmental Experts on Corporate Governance and Company Law*. As their legal status is less known, I will briefly address their status.[45]

---

40. For these legal forms, see Annex I.
41. See e.g., H. von der Groeben & J. Schwarze (eds), *Kommentar zum Vertrag über die Europäische Union und zur Gründung der Europäischen Gemeinschaft* (Baden-Baden: Nomos, 2003); Lenaerts & Van Nuffel. As to the differences between directives and regulations (with further references): S. Prechal, *Directives in EC Law* (Oxford: OUP, 2005), 14–15.
42. The institutions in the sense of the EC Treaty are the European Parliament, the Council, the Commission, the Court of Justice and the Court of Auditors (see Art. 7(1) EC). For a detailed discussion of the institutions, see Lenaerts & Van Nuffel, 383–458.
43. See further below, s. C.1, on the principle of conferred powers.
44. Case C-436/03 *Parliament* v *Council* ('SCE Regulation') [2006] ECR I-3733.
45. An issue that will not be examined in this book, however, is the lawfulness of the constitutive acts by which these Community bodies are set up. These acts are of a purely institutional nature

b. *European Corporate Governance Forum*

In October 2004, the Commission set up, by decision[46] *sui generis,*[47] the *European Corporate Governance Forum* (hereinafter: 'Forum') to coordinate corporate governance efforts of Member States. The creation of this Forum was one of the short-term initiatives (2003–2005) of the 2003 *Action Plan to Modernise Company Law.*[48] Notwithstanding doubts expressed by the European Parliament on this subject,[49] the Commission set up the Forum anyway.

This subsidiary Community body comprises fifteen members.[50] They are appointed by the Commission[51] for a three-year period (which can be extended).[52] The Forum meets, under the chairmanship of the Commission,[53] two to three times a year[54] and delivers a yearly report to the Commission.[55] The Forum is specifically established to enhance the convergence of national codes of corporate governance and to provide advice to the Commission, either at the Commission's request or on its own initiative, on policy issues in the field of corporate governance.[56]

c. *Group of Non-Governmental Experts on Corporate Governance and Company Law*

In April 2005, the Commission, by a further decision[57] *sui generis,* set up the *Group of Non-Governmental Experts on Corporate Governance and Company Law* (hereinafter: 'Group'). The creation of this group is an initiative not explicitly laid down in the *Action Plan to Modernise Company Law.* The Group has been

---

and are not to be considered as – substantive – instruments of company law. As a consequence, the lawfulness of the establishment of these bodies or – in other words – of the 'committee architecture', is considered outside this book's scope.

46. Commission Decision 2004/706/EC of 15 Oct. 2004 establishing the European Corporate Governance Forum, OJ 2004 L 321, 53.
47. It can in particular be referred to Lenaerts & Van Nuffel, 784, who observe that: 'the institutions adopt various such decisions [*sui generis*] (. . .) to adopt the statutes of other bodies'.
48. Action Plan, 24. The Action Plan is discussed *in extenso* in Ch. 2.
49. See European Parliament Resolution on the communication from the Commission to the Council and the European Parliament: Modernising company law and enhancing corporate governance in the European Union – a plan to move forward, P5_TA-PROV(2004)0346 (texts adopted at the sitting of 21 Apr. 2004), in particular pt. 13, which reads as follows: 'Expresses doubts about the point of the setting up by the Commission of a European Corporate Governance Forum, as harmonisation of corporate governance codes is not being proposed and coordination of work on national codes already takes place at association level (e.g., Unice).'
50. Article 3, para. 1 Decision.
51. Article 3, para. 1 Decision.
52. Article 4 Decision.
53. Article 3, para. 3 Decision.
54. IP/04/1241 of 18 Oct. 2004 (Corporate governance: Commission creates European Forum to promote convergence in Europe).
55. Article 7 Decision.
56. Article 2 Decision.
57. Commission Decision 2005/380/EC of 28 Apr. 2005 establishing a group of non-governmental experts on corporate governance and company law, OJ 2005 L 126, 40.

established in view of the fact that 'the Action Plan recognises the importance of expert and public consultation as an integral part of the development of company law and corporate governance at Community level'.[58] Consultation of the Group will supplement, not replace, public consultations.[59]

This subsidiary Community body comprises a maximum of twenty members.[60] They are appointed by the Commission[61] for a three-year period (which can be extended).[62] The Commission will regularly consult the Group,[63] chair the Group meetings[64] and establish the calendar for meetings.[65] The role of the Group is to provide technical advice to the Commission on the Commission's initiatives in the field of corporate governance and company law at the Commission's request. The chairman of the Group may suggest that the Commission consults the Group on any related matter.[66] The 'technical work' of the Group should be complementary to 'the more strategic role' in the convergence of corporate governance in Europe, carried out by the European Corporate Governance Forum.[67]

It cannot be excluded that both the Forum and the Group, might – eventually – adopt new company law instruments, such as an EC corporate governance code, for example.[68]

2. Acts

EC company law is mainly built up of regulations and directives. Whereas a regulation has general application, is binding in its entirety, and is directly applicable in all Member States,[69] a directive is binding, as to the result to be achieved, upon each Member State to which it is addressed, but it leaves to the national authorities the choice of form and methods.[70] Some EC company law instruments have taken the form of a (non-binding) recommendation[71] or communication.[72]

58. See the second recital in the preamble to the Decision.
59. IP/05/500 of 28 Apr. 2005 (Corporate Governance: new group to advise the Commission on strengthening shareholders' rights and modernising company law).
60. Article 3, para. 1 Decision.
61. *Ibid.*
62. Article 4 Decision.
63. IP/05/500, just cited, and Art. 7, para. 1 Decision.
64. Article 6, para. 1 Decision.
65. IP/05/500, just cited.
66. Article 2 Decision.
67. IP/05/500, just cited.
68. The Forum has issued various statements (and a recommendation), including the 'Statement of the European Corporate Governance Forum on the comply-or-explain principle', 22 Feb. 2005, all available at the Commission's Internal Market website: <http://ec.europa.eu/internal_market/>.
69. Article 249, para. 2 EC.
70. Article 249, para. 3 EC.
71. Article 249, para. 5 EC.
72. E.g., the ACTION PLAN itself.

The use of these measures is elaborated upon in the next chapter.[73] A full survey of EC company law instruments is included in Annex I and II.

C. EC Company Law Powers and Limits

1. The Principle of Conferred Powers

The principle of conferred powers signifies, in short, that the Community can act only where the EC Treaty equips it with competence. Community competences are conferred by specific provisions of the EC Treaty, known as legal bases. There is no legal basis which confers a general, comprehensive competence with respect to company law as such. There are, however, various Treaty Articles which enable the Community to regulate certain aspects of company law. It is these Treaty Articles which have been used for the EC company law *acquis* which is dealt with in the next chapter.[74]

The principle of conferred powers is laid down in Article 5, first paragraph EC, which provides that:

> The Community shall act within the limits of the powers conferred upon it by this Treaty and of the objectives assigned to it therein.

This principle is pivotal to the relationship between the EC and its Member States: where the Community is not empowered to act, such action falls within the residuary competence of the Member States.[75] The EC's competences are subject to the limits imposed by the terms of the grant made by way of the Treaty.[76]

Community competences, as just mentioned, are conferred by specific provisions of the EC Treaty, known as legal bases. A legal basis will define the competence *ratione materiae*:[77] it authorizes action in pursuance of a designated purpose. It will furthermore indicate what institutions (e.g., European Parliament, Council, Commission) are to be involved in the adoption of the act, the decision-making procedure to be followed, including the relevant voting rule for the institution(s), and it may also prescribe the type of instrument that may be used, for example only directives.[78]

---

73. On the effectiveness and suitability of various of these instruments to harmonize national company laws, see e.g., R.M. Buxbaum & K.J. Hopt, *Legal Harmonization and the Business Enterprise* (Berlin/New York: De Gruyter, 1988), 226–249; C. Timmermans, 'Methods and Tools for Integration', in *European Business Law. Legal and Economic Analyses on Integration and Harmonization*, ed. R.M. Buxbaum et al. (Berlin/New York: De Gruyter, 1991), 129–166; Edwards, 9–11.
74. A survey of EC company law instruments is included in Annex I and II.
75. Lenaerts & Van Nuffel, 87.
76. A. Dashwood, 'The relationship between the Member States and the European Union/European Community', *CML Rev.* 41 (2004): 357.
77. Lenaerts & Van Nuffel, 87.
78. See: Dashwood, just cited, 358; Lenaerts & Van Nuffel, 87–88.

With respect to the division of competences between the EC institutions themselves,[79] brought about by this drafting technique,[80] Article 7(1) EC provides that:

> (...) Each institution shall act within the limits of the powers conferred upon it by this Treaty.

If the Treaty provision, which is stated as being the legal basis for the act, is substantively insufficient to support its content, the institution which adopted the act in question will have exceeded its powers. This is even the case if the institution could have adopted the same measure on the basis of some other Treaty provision.[81] In advance of this chapter's section on judicial review[82] it is noted, that if indeed a Community institution exceeds its powers like this, the act concerned can, depending on the procedure, be declared void for lack of competence (under Article 230 EC) or invalid (under Article 234 EC).

2. The Principle of Subsidiarity and General Principles of Community Law

a. Principle of Subsidiarity

The principle of subsidiarity is set out in the second paragraph of Article 5 EC, according to which, in areas which do not fall within its exclusive competence, the Community is to take action only if and in so far as the objectives of the proposed action cannot be sufficiently achieved by the Member States and can therefore, by reason of the scale or effects of the proposed action, be better achieved at Community level.[83]

According to this article, subsidiarity must be considered only in relation to areas which do not fall within the exclusive competence of the Community. The expression 'exclusive competence' is used to make the distinction between the situation where the Community alone has jurisdiction and the situation where it

---

79. As was mentioned in the Introduction of this book, it can be distinguished between the competences of the Community as such ('vertical' competences), and (of relevance here) the distribution of competences among its institutions ('horizontal' competences). The issue of vertical competences then concerns the vertical relationship between the Member States and the Community, whereas the issue of horizontal competences concerns the horizontal relationships between the EC's different institutions and therefore the internal division of powers. See A. von Bogdandy & J. Bast, 'The European Union's vertical order of competences: The current law and proposals for its reform', *CML Rev.* 39 (2002): 235–236. For a further discussion of the distinction between the vertical and horizontal division of competences, see R.H. van Ooik, *De keuze der rechtsgrondslag voor besluiten van de Europese Unie* (Deventer: Kluwer, 1999), 22 and 40–43.
80. For a more elaborate treatment of the drafting technique of specific and detailed attribution of competences, see Dashwood, just cited, 357–362.
81. Lenaerts, Arts & Maselis, 291–292.
82. See s. D, *infra*.
83. See also Case C-491/01 *British American Tobacco* [2002] ECR I-11453, para. 177.

shares it with the Member States.[84] Most Community powers are considered to be non-exclusive.[85] However, two exclusive competences have been recognized by the Court of Justice.

> First, the power pursuant to Article 133 EC to conduct a common commercial policy vis-à-vis third countries with respect to trade in goods.[86] Second, the competence pursuant to Article 102 of the 1972 Act of Accession[87] to determine conditions for fishing with a view, *inter alia*, to ensuring protection of fishing grounds.[88] It is furthermore assumed that Article 26 EC, which states that Common Customs Tariff duties shall be fixed by the Council, precludes a parallel competence on the part of the Member States and, finally, that the competence conferred on the Community in relation to Economic and Monetary Union is exclusive in character.[89]

The question whether other Community competences, particularly those in the field of company law,[90] are (non-)exclusive is dealt with (in more detail) in Chapter 5.

b. General Principles

Article 220 EC provides that the EC Court of Justice ensures that in the interpretation and application of Community law 'the law is observed'. This article is said to be the most important of the founding Treaties.[91] Its importance lies in that it mandates the Court to work out a system of legal principles in accordance with which the legality of Community action must be determined.[92]

In formulating general principles, the Court draws inspiration from the constitutional traditions common to the Member States and – furthermore – from international treaties on which the Member States have collaborated or of which they are signatories.[93] A third source of general principles is the EC Treaty itself.[94] Where the same concept is expressly stated in a number of different provisions in different parts of the Treaty, the Court may find that such a concept is an

84. Lenaerts & Van Nuffel, 87.
85. *Ibid.*, 97.
86. Opinion 1/75 'Draft OECD Understanding on a Local Cost Standard' [1975] ECR 1355, 1363–1364.
87. Act concerning the Conditions of Accession and the Adjustments to the Treaties – Accession to the European Communities of the Kingdom of Denmark, Ireland and the United Kingdom of Great Britain and Northern Ireland, OJ 1972 L 73.
88. Joined Cases 3-4/76 and 6/76 *Cornelis Kramer* [1976] ECR 1279, paras 39–41.
89. See: Lenaerts & Van Nuffel, 97–98; Kapteyn & VerLoren van Themaat, 141.
90. See also W. Schön, 'Gesellschaftsrecht nach Maastricht – Art. 3b EGV und das europäische Gesellschaftsrecht', *ZGR* (1995): 1–38.
91. See Tridimas, 19.
92. Tridimas, 20. General principles of Community law may be invoked not only as a ground of review, but also in interpreting written rules of Community law and in actions for damages under Art. 288 EC. For these functions of the general principles, see: A. Arnull, *The European Union and its Court of Justice* (Oxford: OUP, 1999), 192; Tridimas, 29–35.
93. Arnull, just cited, 191. See also Usher, 12.
94. See Arnull, just cited, 191.

underlying general principle of Community law.[95] The prime example of this is the principle of non-discrimination.[96]

The general principles of Community law may be divided into constitutional and administrative principles.[97] Constitutional principles must be complied with by the institutions even when issuing legislative measures.[98] They include, *inter alia*, the principle of non-discrimination, the principle of legal certainty, the principle of proportionality, and the principle of respect for fundamental rights.

The administrative principles,[99] such as the right to a fair hearing,[100] the confidentiality of communications between lawyer and client ('legal professional privilege'),[101] the right to be assisted by a lawyer[102] and the right against self-incrimination (in a qualified form),[103] apply to Community administrative proceedings.[104] At present, such proceedings (with the exercise of Community powers in individual cases, in an individual manner) do not play a part in EC company law and it is unlikely that this will change in the near future.

---

95. Usher, 12.
96. *Ibid.* See also Arnull, just cited, 192.
97. Lenaerts & Van Nuffel, 704 and 711–712.
98. *Ibid.*, 712.
99. These principles are also called 'principles of good administration' (Usher, 100–120) or 'principles of administrative law' (Lenaerts & Van Nuffel, 711).
100. Case 32/62 *Alvis* v *Council* EEC [1963] ECR 101, about which Tridimas, 370–371; Case 17/74 *Transocean Marine Paint Association* v *Commission* [1974] ECR 1063, para. 15, about which Tridimas, 372. See also Lenaerts & Van Nuffel, 717. For an elaborate examination of the content of this right, see Tridimas, 378–383.
101. Case 155/79 *AM & S* v *Commission* [1982] ECR 1575, para. 27, about which Tridimas, 372–373. See also Lenaerts & Van Nuffel, 717.
102. Joined Cases 46/87 and 227/88 *Hoechst* v *Commission* [1989] ECR 2859, para. 16, about which Tridimas, 373. See also Lenaerts & Van Nuffel, 717.
103. Case 374/87 *Orkem* v *Commission* [1989] ECR 3283, paras 32–42, about which Tridimas, 374–376. See also Lenaerts & Van Nuffel, 717.
104. About the element of 'Community' proceedings, see Usher, 100. See also K. Lenaerts & J. Vanhamme, 'Procedural rights of private parties in the Community administrative process', *CML Rev.* 34 (1997): 531–569. It is advocated that a person may invoke the administrative principles not only against the Community administration, but also against the national administration where it (i.e., national authorities) acts (act) within the scope of Community law. See e.g., Tridimas, 415.

    About the element of 'administrative' proceedings, see Lenaerts & Van Nuffel, 704 and 711, where it is noted that administrative legal principles 'apply only to the execution of Community law' and furthermore that administrative legal principles 'afford guidance for the administration where it encounters ambiguities or *lacunae* in Community legislation which it has to apply'. Administrative acts, may be defined as acts by which the administration applies general rules *in individual cases* or otherwise exercises its powers *in an individual manner*. For this definition, see P. Craig & G. de Búrca, *EU Law*, Oxford: OUP 2003, 558. It must further be noted that the EC Treaty did not set up separate legislative and executive institutions: The legislative function is spread over the Council, the European Parliament and the Commission, whilst the Commission and the Council also perform executive functions. See Lenaerts & Van Nuffel, 570. Finally, notwithstanding that administrative principles 'apply only to the execution of Community law', these principles cannot be excluded or restricted by Community legislation, see Tridimas, 379.

Closely related to the general principles of Community law are – certain – rules of international law. In interpreting and applying Community law within the meaning of Article 220 EC, the Court also takes customary international law[105] and principles of international law, such as the territoriality principle,[106] into account.[107]

3. Basic Prohibitions

Finally, a word on the basic prohibitions of restrictions to free movement. It was noted above that these prohibitions are addressed to the Member States. It should be added, however, that also the Community legislature is bound by these basic prohibitions. This is, for example, settled case-law as regards Article 28 EC (the free movement of goods).[108] The question whether, as to the provisions of freedom of establishment, which are key to EC company law, the Community legislature is bound by Article 43 EC is further dealt with in Chapter 5.

D. Judicial Review

1. Introduction

This section is about the protection against unlawful action by the Community institutions. This issue is part of general procedural EC law and it will therefore not be entered into in detail. I shall, however, make a few general observations on the two main remedies available. First, the so-called action for annulment is dealt with (s. 2). Subsequently, the preliminary rulings procedure as a means of raising the question of the validity of acts of the institutions is considered (s. 3).

2. The Action for Annulment

The action for annulment is provided for in Article 230 EC.[109]

All measures adopted by the institutions 'whatever their nature or form, which are intended to have legal effects' are susceptible to review under

105. Case C-286/90 *Anklagemindigheden* v *Poulsen and Diva Navigation* [1992] ECR I-6019, paras 9–11, 13–16 and 25–29.
106. Joined Cases 89, 104, 114, 116–117 and 125–129/85 *Åhlström* v *Commission* [1988] ECR 5193, para. 18; Case T-102/96 *Gencor* v *Commission* [1999] ECR II-753, paras 89–108.
107. See also Lenaerts & Van Nuffel, 754.
108. Case 15/83 *Denkavit Nederland* [1984] ECR 2171, para. 15; Case C-51/93 *Meyhui* v *Schott Zwiesel Glaswerke* [1994] ECR I-3879, para. 11; Case C-114/96, *Criminal proceedings against Kieffer and Thill* [1997] ECR I-3629, para. 27; Joined Cases C-154/04 and C-155/04 *Alliance for Natural Health* [2005] ECR I-6451, para. 47.
109. For more detailed treatments of the action for annulment, see: Weatherill & Beaumont, 245–305; Lauwaars & Timmermans, 147–155; Barents & Brinkhorst, 229–233; Craig & de Búrca, 502–528.

Article 230 EC.[110] The binding acts of Article 249 EC (regulations, directives and decisions) are therefore covered, but other acts which are *sui generis* ('of its own kind') can also be reviewed (provided they are intended to have legal effects).[111]

While the Member States, the European Parliament, Council, and Commission[112] have unrestricted *locus standi* ('standing') to bring an action under Article 230 EC before the Court of Justice, natural and legal persons ('individuals') have restricted *locus standi*.[113] The action for annulment must be instituted within two months, in short, of the publication of the measure.[114]

Annulment proceedings can be instituted on grounds of: (1) lack of competence; (2) infringement of an essential procedural requirement; (3) infringement of the EC Treaty or of any rule of law relating to its application;[115] or (4) misuse of powers. The grounds of illegality have, it is said, gradually lost their individual importance.[116] Recent annulment proceedings indicate that the Court is not concerned with the specific ground of illegality.[117] Anyway, most causes of illegality come under the heading of 'infringement of this Treaty or of any rule of law relating to its application'.

As to the intensity of legal review, a distinction may be made between questions of law and questions of exercise of discretion.

A typical 'question of law' concerns the meaning to be ascribed to a term in the enabling Treaty provisions,[118] such as the legal bases discussed in Chapters 3 and 4. The Court's general approach is simply to substitute judgment on these questions of law for that of the initial decision-maker (legislature).[119]

As regards 'questions of exercise of discretion' it must be noted that it follows from the case-law of the Court of Justice, in the field of legality of Community acts,

110. Case C-57/95 *France* v *Commission* [1997] ECR I-1627, para. 7.
111. Craig & de Búrca, 503.
112. Article 230(2) EC. For actions brought by the Court of Auditors and by the European Central Bank ('ECB'), see Art. 230(3) EC.
113. See Art. 230(4) EC. According to Art. 225(1) EC in conjunction with Art. 51 of the Statute of the Court of Justice, the Court of First Instance is the court of first resort for individual applicants.
114. Article 230(5) EC.
115. Article 230(2) EC. 'Any rule of law relating to its [the EC Treaty's] application' encompasses: (1) (higher) 'secondary Community law', in particular the binding acts of Art. 249 EC; (2) general principles of Community law; (3) international agreements concluded by the Community and (rules of customary) international law. See: Weatherill & Beaumont, 283; Lauwaars & Timmermans, 155; Barents & Brinkhorst, 231; Craig & de Búrca, 543–544.
116. Schermers & Waelbroeck, 360.
117. *Ibid.*
118. Craig & de Búrca, 569.
119. *Ibid.* For the issue of 'judicial review of compliance with the proper legal basis' (cf. Case C-376/98 *Germany* v *Parliament and Council* ('Tobacco Advertizing') [2000] ECR I-8419, para. 84), the Court's case-law relating to the choice of the legal basis is of fundamental importance. This case-law is dealt with specifically in Ch. 4. In disputes concerning the legal basis, the third ground for annulment ('infringement of the EC Treaty') is considered to be 'the most important'; if the Court establishes that an incorrect legal basis has been used, the act in question is usually annulled on that, third, ground. See R.H. van Ooik, *De keuze der rechtsgrondslag voor besluiten van de Europese Unie* (Deventer: Kluwer, 1999), 339.

that the Community legislature has a broad discretionary power of a 'political nature' (in the application of the various legal bases).[120] The attribution of this power is justified by the fact that the Community legislature is to balance various diverging interests. This issue has been formulated clearly by Advocate General Léger:

> In the light of the case-law, it seems to me that it is possible to draw a distinction between two categories of 'discretion'. The first category is one which could be called discretion of a 'political' nature. The institutions are generally recognised as having such a discretion where they act in their capacity as 'political' authorities and, in particular, where they legislate in a given field or where they lay down guidelines for a Community policy. In that case, recognition of such a discretion is justified by the fact that the institutions must generally reconcile divergent interests and thus select options within the context of the policy choices which are their responsibility. Discretion which is 'political' in nature thus corresponds to the political responsibilities which a Community provision confers upon an institution. (footnotes omitted).[121]

It is settled case-law that in such areas of complex policy choices where the Community legislature enjoys a broad discretionary power, substantive judicial review of legislative acts is limited.[122] The restricted nature of substantive judicial review of legislative acts stems primarily from the fundamental principle of institutional equilibrium and separation of powers.[123] It is inherent in this equilibrium

120. Cf. Opinion of AG Léger in Case C-40/03 P, and 41/03 P *Rica Foods* v *Commission* [2005] ECR I-6811 and [2005] ECR I-6875, pt. 42. The Court of Justice has consistently held, for instance, that in the exercise of the powers conferred upon them by the Treaty, the institutions have a discretion (in particular) with regard to the possibility of pursuing partial harmonization or harmonization in stages. See: Case C-479/93 *Francovich* v *Italy* [1995] ECR I-3843, para. 25; Case 37/83 *Rewe-Zentrale* [1984] ECR 1229, para. 20; and Case C-193/94 *Skanavi and Chryssanhtakopoulos* [1996] ECR I-929, para. 27.
121. Opinion of AG Léger in *Rica Foods*, just cited, pt. 45. In this connection the AG refers, *inter al.*, to: Case C-280/93 *Germany* v *Council* [1994] ECR I-4973, paras 90 and 91; and Case C-44/94 *Fishermen's Organisations a.O.* [1995] ECR I-3115, para. 37. In pt. 46, the AG discusses the second category of discretionary powers: 'The second category would cover what might be called discretion of a "technical" nature. Such discretion is generally allowed to the institutions where they act in their capacity as "administrative" authorities and, in particular, where they adopt individual decisions in competition or State aid matters, and also where they take specific protective measures against dumping. In that case, the discretion allowed to the institutions is justified by the complexity of the technical, economic and legal situations they have to examine and of the assessments which they have to make.' (fn. omitted). AG Léger subsequently concludes in pt. 49: 'That said, it seems to me that the intensity of judicial review varies according to whether the nature of the discretion is political or technical. Indeed, even though, in both situations, judicial review is clearly restricted to "manifest error", it seems to me, in the light of the case-law, that judicial review is less exhaustive where the measure at issue is the result of an institution's exercise of discretion of a political nature.'
122. Opinion of AG Geelhoed in Case C-244/03 *France* v *Parliament and Council* [2005] ECR I-4021, pt. 90.
123. *Ibid.*, pt. 91.

that the Court should respect the 'political responsibilities'[124] conferred by the Treaty on the Community legislature, and should refrain from substituting its judgment on such policy matters.[125] This limited review is shown to be of relevance to Chapter 5 in particular, where the principle of subsidiarity[126] and the issue of observance of Article 43 EC are dealt with.[127]

If an action for annulment is well founded, the Court declares the act concerned void.[128] Such a declaration has retroactive effect: once a Community act is annulled under Article 230 EC, it is void *ab initio* ('from the beginning'). Moreover, it has effect *erga omnes* ('towards everyone').[129]

3. The Preliminary Rulings Procedure

The preliminary rulings procedure[130] is laid down in Article 234 EC.

This procedure provides a form of protection for individuals in that it offers them a way to challenge Community acts.[131] Where a Community act has achieved application by means of a national measure, it is possible to claim before a national

124. See e.g., Case C-331/88 *Fedesa* [1990] ECR 4023, para. 14; Case C-280/93 *Germany* v *Council* [1994] ECR I-4973, para. 89.
125. Opinion of AG Geelhoed in *France* v *Parliament and Council*, just cited, pt. 91. The AG notes that: 'This can be distinguished from the rationale underlying restricted judicial review of administrative decisions taken by the Commission, i.e., the economic and technical complexity of the analysis leading to the act.'

    AG Geelhoed has noted further in this connection (pt. 92): 'In my view, it follows from this principle of institutional equilibrium, as from the democratic principle itself, that the Court should be particularly cautious in reviewing the legality of a legislative act promulgated jointly by the Council and Parliament by way of the co-decision procedure. The Court should be especially slow to annul on substantive grounds the legislative policy decisions of a directly and democratically elected body representing the Community's citizens. I would add that this concern for maximum respect for democratic principles has been a feature of the Court's jurisprudence on numerous other occasions.'
126. For judicial review of observance of the principle of subsidiarity, see C.W.A. Timmermans, 'La justiciabilité de la subsidiarité', in *Festskrift til Claus Gulmann. Liber Amicorum*, ed. B. Vesterdorf, N. Fenger & K. Hagel-Sørensen (Copenhagen: Forlaget Thomson, 2006), 450–459.
127. See in this connection also Craig & de Búrca, 569, who note that: 'It is however clear that the intensity with which this standard of review has been deployed has varied over time and in relation to different subject-matter.'
128. Article 231(1) EC. Art. 231(2) EC contains a special provision for regulations. It reads as follows: 'In the case of a regulation, however, the Court of Justice shall, if it considers this necessary, state which of the effects of the regulation which it has declared void shall be considered as definitive.' For the (analogical) applicability of Art. 231(2) EC to directives and ('general') decisions, see: Barents & Brinkhorst, 232; Craig & de Búrca, 572, fn. 231.
129. See: Lauwaars & Timmermans, 155; Barents & Brinkhorst, 231; Craig & de Búrca, 572.
130. For more detailed treatments of the preliminary rulings procedure, see: Lauwaars & Timmermans, 163–172; S. Prechal & R.H. van Ooik, 'Het institutionele recht van de Europese Unie en de Nederlandse rechter: het acquis in een notendop', *SEW* (2003): 348–352; Barents & Brinkhorst, 255–266; Craig & de Búrca, 460–501 and 528–530.
131. See Case 123/77 *Unicme* v *Council* [1978] ECR 845. The *Unicme* case concerned the contesting of a regulation. It must be noted in addition that Art. 234(1)(b) EC lays down no limitation

court[132] that the relevant Community act upon which the national measure is based is invalid. Using a reference to the Court of Justice under Article 234(1)(b) EC,[133] this claim can then be determined.[134]

The grounds of review under Article 234 EC are the same as those laid down in Article 230 EC.[135] Consequently, all grounds for appeal of the annulment procedure (see s. 2, *supra*) may be invoked.

If the Court of Justice rules that a Community act is invalid, the act concerned will be treated as void for all purposes.[136] So, as a basic rule, the finding of invalidity has both a retroactive effect and an effect *erga omnes*.[137]

III. FUTURE DEVELOPMENTS

The paragraphs above dealt with the place and the limits of EC company law within the framework of the *current* EC Treaty. Let us have a look into the future now.

In 2001, an initiative started to amend, *inter alia*, the current EC Treaty. As the origins of this initiative and the events that followed, are well-known, I only deal briefly with them. Under the title 'Towards a Constitution for European citizens', the Laeken Declaration on the future of the European Union, adopted by the Heads of State or Government on the occasion of the Laeken European Council of December 2001,[138] called for a reorganization and simplification of the present Treaties.[139] To that end, the Laeken Declaration convened a 'Convention'

as to the Community acts which may be challenged. See Case C-322/88 *Grimaldi* v *Fonds des maladies professionnelles* [1989] ECR 4407, paras 8–9.

132. Provided of course that according to national law individuals have a legal remedy against the national measure concerned. See J. Tillotson & N. Foster, *Text, Cases and materials on European Union Law* (London: Cavendish Publishing, 2003), 531.
133. Of the two Community Courts, the Court of Justice has jurisdiction to give preliminary rulings under Art. 234 EC; however, according to Art. 225(3) EC, the Court of First Instance may give preliminary rulings in specific areas laid down by the Statute of the Court of Justice.
134. See Tillotson & Foster, just cited, 511 and 531. See also: Lauwaars & Timmermans, 164; Barents & Brinkhorst, 257–258.
135. See Joined Cases 21–24/72 *International Fruit Company a.O.* v *Produktschap voor Groenten en Fruit* [1972] ECR 1219 in which the Court held at para. 5, that 'the jurisdiction of the Court cannot be limited by the grounds on which the validity [of acts of the institutions of the Community] may be contested', and in this connection: Lauwaars & Timmermans, 165; Craig & de Búrca, 538.
136. See Tillotson & Foster, just cited, 214.
137. As to the retroactive effect, it must be mentioned that the Court of Justice has applied the principle of Art. 231(2) EC to cases arising under Art. 234 EC imposing temporal limits on the effects of a declaration that an act is invalid (Case 112/83 *Produits de Maïs* v *Administration des douanes* [1985] ECR 719). See further: Case 66/80 *International Chemical Corporation* v *Amministrazione delle finanze dello Stato* [1981] ECR 1191 (with regard to the *erga omnes* effect), and Barents & Brinkhorst, 266; Craig & de Búrca, 572–573.
138. This Declaration is published on the Council's website: <www.consilium.europa.eu>. See further Bull. EU 2001 (12), pts. I.1 and I.2 to I.29.
139. See K. Lenaerts & M. Desomer, 'New models of constitution-making in Europe: The quest for legitimacy', *CML Rev.* 39 (2002): 1217–1218.

composed of representatives of the Heads of State or of Government and the parliaments of the (candidate) Member States,[140] the European Parliament and the Commission, together with observers from the European Economic and Social Committee, the Committee of the Regions, the European Ombudsman and the European Social Partners.[141]

In February 2002, the 'Convention on the future of Europe' started its work under the chairmanship of Valéry Giscard d'Estaing. Ultimately, in June–July 2003, the Convention adopted a draft Treaty establishing a Constitution for Europe.[142]

In view of the fact that the Treaty establishing a Constitution for Europe intended to amend the existing Treaties, it had to be adopted in accordance with the procedure for the amendment of the Treaties laid down in Article 48 EU.[143] As a result, the changes had to be approved by the representatives of the national governments meeting in an Intergovernmental Conference (IGC) and had to be ratified by all Member States in accordance with their respective constitutional requirements.[144]

Within the framework of the European Council held in Brussels in June 2004, the IGC reached agreement on the Treaty establishing a Constitution for Europe.[145] The Treaty was signed by the representatives of the Member States in October 2004. The Treaty establishing a constitution for Europe was published in the *Official Journal* in December 2004.[146] In 2005, both France and the Netherlands rejected the Constitution, after holding a referendum on ratification of the Treaty. At the Brussels European Council of 16–17 June 2005, it was subsequently decided to have a 'period of reflection', which should be used 'to enable a broad debate to take place' in each of the Member States. The Heads of State or Government furthermore agreed to come back to this matter later to make an overall assessment of the national debates and to agree on how to proceed.[147]

The 'impasse' was overcome in June 2007, when the European Council agreed to convene another IGC (with a view to amending the existing Treaties).[148]

---

140. Ten mainly Central European countries joined the EU as of 1 May 2004. See the Treaty between Belgium, Denmark, Germany, Greece, Spain, France, Ireland, Italy, Luxembourg, the Netherlands, Austria, Portugal, Finland, Sweden, the United Kingdom (Member States of the European Union) and the Czech Republic, Estonia, Cyprus, Latvia, Lithuania, Hungary, Malta, Poland, Slovenia and Slovakia, concerning the accession of the latter group of states to the European Union, OJ 2003 L 236, 17.
141. Chapter III of the Laeken Declaration, just cited. See also Bull. EU 2001 (12), pt. I.1.
142. Draft Treaty establishing a Constitution for Europe (Adopted by consensus by the European Convention on 13 Jun. and 10 Jul. 2003), 18 Jul. 2003, OJ 2003 C 169, 1.
143. Lenaerts & Van Nuffel, 69.
144. *Ibid.*
145. See Bull. EU 2004 (6), pt. I.1.
146. OJ 2004 C 310, 1.
147. See the Declaration by the Heads of State or Government of the Member States of the European Union on the ratification of the Treaty establishing a Constitution for Europe (European Council, 16 and 17 Jun. 2005). The Declaration is published on the Council's website: <www.consilium.europa.eu>.
148. European Council Presidency Conclusions, Brussels 21–22 Jun. 2007, Council doc. no. 11177/07 of 23 Jun. 2007, pt. 10, which document can be found on the Council's website: <www.consilium.europa.eu>.

The IGC was to carry out its work in accordance with a detailed mandate.[149] The IGC began its work in July 2007.[150] The *Treaty of Lisbon* drawn up by the IGC was approved at the informal European Council on 18–19 October 2007.[151] The Treaty was then signed by the representatives of the Member States in December 2007.[152] That same month, the Treaty was published in the *Official Journal.*[153]

At present, the Treaty of Lisbon is in the process of being ratified by the Member States. All Member States must ratify, as mentioned. In June 2008, Ireland, however, rejected the Treaty.[154] Even though it cannot be ruled out that eventually, at some point in the future, all twenty-seven Member States (including Ireland) will have ratified, for now, it is still uncertain whether this will actually happen. For this reason, the Treaty of Lisbon will, apart from some incidental references, be left aside in subsequent chapters. Moreover, it should be realized that the legality of an act is reviewed in the light of the facts and the state of the law at the time when it was adopted ('tempus regit actum').[155] In view of this, the Treaty of Lisbon, even if it would be ratified by all Member States (and become effective), would still not be of relevance to the legality of the by then (already) existing EC company law instruments.[156]

---

149. European Council Presidency Conclusions, just cited, pt. 11. The mandate is attached to these Conclusions, Annex I. See further MEMO/07/283 of 10 Jul. 2007 (Questions and Answers on the IGC mandate for a Reform Treaty).
150. See MEMO/07/284 of 10 Jul. 2007 (Intergovernmental Conference – procedural aspects).
151. Informal European Council, Lisbon, 18–19 Oct. 2007, Presidency Press Release, <www.eu2007.pt>. See also IP/07/1922 of 13 Dec. 2007 (Commission welcomes signature of the Treaty of Lisbon and calls for its swift ratification).
152. IP/07/1922, just cited.
153. Treaty of Lisbon amending the Treaty on European Union and the Treaty establishing the European Community, OJ 2007 C 306, 1. See also the Commission's Treaty of Lisbon website: <http://europa.eu/lisbon_treaty>.
154. See further, Editorial Comments, 'Direct democracy and the European Union... is that a threat or a promise?', *CML Rev.* 45 (2008): 929–940.
155. See e.g., Joined Cases 9 and 11/71 *Compagnie d'approvisionnement a.O.* v *Commission* [1972] ECR 391, para. 39; Joined Cases 15 and 16/76 *France* v *Commission* [1979] ECR 321, para. 7, and Lenaerts, Arts & Maselis, 289. See also Schermers & Waelbroeck, 378.
156. In addition, most (if not all) provisions relevant for EC company law would under the Treaty of Lisbon in fact remain unchanged (albeit renumbered). This holds particularly true for the provisions on freedom of establishment (Arts 43–48 EC; cf. Arts 49–55 of the Treaty on the Functioning of the European Union (TFEU)), the rules on approximation of laws (Arts 94–95 EC; cf. Arts 114–115 TFEU) and Art. 308 EC (cf. Art. 352 TFEU). See further Annex III for a table of equivalence. Do note that under the Treaty of Lisbon, the European Union would replace the European Community. *EU* company law would then become the appropriate designation.

Chapter 2

EC Company Law: Development, Instruments and Objectives

I. INTRODUCTION

This and subsequent chapters will specifically deal with the intervention of the EC in the area of company law. The next chapters focus on the issue of compatibility of this intervention with the EC Treaty: what are the appropriate legal bases and the limits for EC company law action? To discuss this issue in concrete terms, this chapter first explores the intervention itself: its development, objectives, and scale. More particularly, this chapter sketches in broad lines the historical development of EC company law since its early days in the 1960s to its present status (s. II). It will then address the objectives for which the EC legislature considers, or has considered, action necessary (s. III). It will finally refer to the current *acquis* and progress of the Commission's modernization actions (s. IV).

II. A COMPENDIOUS SURVEY OF THE DEVELOPMENT OF EC COMPANY LAW

Over the years, the Community institutions have taken numerous initiatives in the area of company law, particularly based on Article 54(3)(g) of the EEC Treaty (now Article 44(2)(g) EC).[1] As early as the 1960s, the Commission expressed its

1. On the historic development of EC company law e.g., C. Villiers, *European Company Law: Towards Democracy?*, Aldershot: Ashgate Publishing 1998, 28–51; J. Wouters, 'European Company Law: *Quo Vadis?*', *CML Rev.* 37 (2000): 268–276; S. Deakin, 'Regulatory Competition versus Harmonization in European Company Law', in *Regulatory Competition and Economic Integration*, ed. D.C. Esty & D. Geradin (Oxford: OUP, 2001), 192–195; C. Timmermans, 'Harmonization in the Future of Company Law in Europe', in *Capital Markets and Company*

vision on this article, regarding it as a broad task to harmonize national company laws.[2] Since then, it initiated a wide range of legislative measures, with apparent success: between 1968 (First Directive) and 1989 (Twelfth Directive), nine Directives and one Regulation have been adopted.[3] From this perspective, this period has aptly been described as the 'golden age' of company law harmonization.[4] It should be noted, however, that although the quantity of the measures adopted may typify it as a success, during this age the scope of the harmonization programme and the Commission's attitude towards harmonization has changed in comparison with the early days, scaling down its ambitions. Whereas the First Directive still covered *all* limited liability companies, priority was later given to the public company,[5] with the exception, in particular, of the accountancy Directives.[6] And whereas the early Directives arguably laid emphasis on uniformity and had a prescriptive character,[7]

Law, ed. K.J. Hopt & E. Wymeersch (Oxford: OUP, 2003), 623–626; P.L. Davies, *Gower and Davies' Principles of Modern Company Law* (London: Sweet & Maxwell, 2003), 111–114.

2. See *Rapport fait au nom de la Commission du marché intérieur, par M. Berkhouwer*, European Parliament Session 1966–1967 of 9 May 1966, Document 53 (the 'Berkhouwer report', named after its rapporteur C. Berkhouwer; English version not available; *Rev.trim.dr.eur* (1966): 441: 'la coordination ne peut avoir qu'une étendue très vaste. En fait l'article 54, paragraphe 3 g) vise les garanties exigées des sociétés pour protéger les intérêts *tant des associés que des tiers*; ainsi toutes les dispositions relatives à la structure et aux organes de la société, à la formation et au maintien de son patrimoine, à la formation des bilans et des comptes de pertes et profits, aux émissions de valeurs mobilières, à la fusion, à la transformation, à la liquidation, aux garanties exigées, en matière de groupe de sociétés etc.... doivent faire l'objet de la coordination prescrite à cet article'. (original emphasis; fn. omitted).
3. These company law instruments are dealt with Annex I.
4. Davies, just cited, 111.
5. Timmermans, just cited, 624–625 (referring in particular to the Second, Third, and Sixth Directives (all concerning public companies) and noting that apart from the Twelfth Directive on 'one member companies', very little has been achieved on private companies). See in particular the proposal for a Fifth Directive on the Structure of Sociétés Anonymes, Bull. EC Supp. 10/72, fifth recital: 'Whereas (. . .) the coordination of laws relating to sociétés anonymes (i.e., die Aktiengesellschaft, la société anonyme, la società per azioni, de naamloze vennootschap) must be given priority because these companies much more than others carry on cross-frontier activities' (fn. omitted); and the Explanatory Memorandum to this proposal, *ibid.*, 32 (after noting that coordination began with the First Directive and that a proposal for a Fourth Directive had been submitted to the Council, adding: 'Continuing its work of coordination of the law relating to companies and firms, the Commission has turned its attention to sociétés anonymes. This is the most important type of company from the economic point of view and the most developed from the legal point of view. The coordination effected in respect of it will make it easier to coordinate at a later stage the safeguards required for other types, adding that it has submitted to the Council the following proposals for the coordination of the safeguards of sociétés anonymes: proposals for the Second, Third and Fifth Directive' (fn. omitted). The latter never became a Directive).
6. Timmermans, just cited, 625 (referring to the Fourth, Seventh, and Eleventh Directives, where the global approach of covering all limited liability companies was maintained).
7. J.A. McCahery & E.P.M. Vermeulen, 'Does the European Company prevent the "Delaware Effect"?', *TILEC Discussion Paper*, Mar. 2005, 12–13; see also Deakin, just cited, 193 (referring to the First and Second Directives).

this soon gave way to more flexible approaches which placed greater stress on Member State autonomy.[8]

From its initial 'grand design' on company law harmonization in the Eu(ro)-phoric period of the 1960s, the Commission had changed to pragmatism by the 1980s.[9] Following then the blockages with respect to the SE and the Draft Fifth Directive and the failure to create legislation on groups of companies, harmonization 'degenerated' into a kind of 'muddling through'.[10] From 1989 until 2001, no company law instruments were brought about.[11] European harmonization was said to have lost much of its dynamism.[12]

> Various reasons have been advanced to explain this loss of dynamism: (1) the difficulties in obtaining the necessary level of Member State support for the more controversial proposed harmonization measures. This holds true for the proposed *Fifth Directive* (key questions being: should the board be a one-tier structure like in the UK, or a two-tier-one, consisting of separate supervisory and management boards?; should employee participation on the board be mandatory?), the *European Company* (similar employee issues), and the *Ninth Directive* on Groups (most Member States dealing with groups through general mechanisms of corporate law, whereas Germany has developed a separate regime); (2) the style of harmonization which was criticized as overly interventionist, at least as far as the early Directives were concerned; (3) criticism that, once a policy has been embodied in Community legislation, it is more difficult to change it than in case of domestic legislation.[13] Partly in the same vein it has been referred to: (4) intrinsic difficulties of company law harmonization

8. Deakin, just cited, 193 (referring to the Fourth, Seventh and Eighth Directives). Villiers, just cited, 28–51, describes the successive company law directives as four 'generations' of company law directives. See also: McCahery & Vermeulen, just cited, 12–18; Deakin, just cited, 193–194. The *first generation* of 'heavily prescriptive' directives leaving little discretion to the Member States as to their implementation, comprising the First and Second Directives; the *second generation* having a more flexible approach by the use of options and alternative formulae, though still with some relative precise objectives and requirements, comprising the Third, Fourth, Sixth, Seventh, and Eighth Directives; the *third generation* directives reflecting the so-called 'new approach' to harmonization, being relatively short, containing little detail and offering more discretion to Member States, comprising the Eleventh and Twelfth Directives; the *fourth generation*, finally, following the move towards proportionality and subsidiarity in the early 1990s, having the features of a 'framework directive' and effectively being watered down legal measures to almost statements of objectives, leaving the Member States to choose their own way of giving practical effect to those statements, comprising the draft Thirteenth Directive on takeover bids of 1997 (Villiers, just cited, 49; Deakin, just cited, 194).
9. Wouters, just cited, 271.
10. *Ibid.*, referring to C.W.A. Timmermans, 'Methods and Tools for Integration', in *European Business Law*, ed. R.M. Buxbaum et al. (New York: Walter de Gruyter, 1991), 129.
11. The Commission did, however, organize a 'Conference on Company Law and the Single Market'. It was held in Dec. 1997. The Commission's purpose was to determine what its role should be in the debate on corporate governance and in the adaptation and simplification of company law in the various Member States. See further 'Acts of the Conference on Company Law and the Single Market', published on the Commission's Internal Market website: <http://ec.europa.eu/internal_market/>.
12. See Wouters, just cited, 257.
13. See Davies, just cited, 112–113.

(e.g., worker participation and a large number of Member States participating in decision-making); (5) the completion of the internal market (and the merger boom of the end of 1980s, as well as the increase in cross-border direct investment in the 1990s), apparently not hampered by the incomplete state of company law harmonization; and (6) the quest for subsidiarity.[14]

Admittedly, there was the 1999 Report of the so-called SLIM working group on Company Law[15] on the simplification of the First Directive (on disclosure)[16] and Second Directive (on formation and capital),[17] but key initiatives, such as the proposal for a Regulation on the European Company and the proposal for a Directive on cross-border mergers, remained blocked during this period. Employee participation issues, as is well-known, had led to the deadlock.[18] On top of this, a proposal for a Directive on takeover bids was rejected by the European Parliament in July 2001, after twelve years of negotiation. A conciliation procedure between Parliament and Council had produced a compromise text, but when this was put to the vote at a plenary sitting of Parliament, there was no majority (273 MEPs voted for it and 273 MEPs voted against it).[19]

---

14. See C. Timmermans, 'Harmonization in the Future of Company Law in Europe', in *Capital Markets and Company Law*, ed. K. J. Hopt & E. Wymeersch (Oxford: OUP, 2003), 626–628.
15. This working group issued in Sep. 1999, as part of the fourth phase of the SLIM process (SEC (1998) 1944 of 16 Nov. 1998), its report. The SLIM initiative – Simpler Legislation for the Internal Market – was launched by the Commission in May 1996 with the objective of identifying ways in which Single Market legislation could be simplified. See Communication from the Commission to the Council and the European Parliament, 'Simpler Legislation for the Internal Market (SLIM): a pilot project', COM (1996) 204 of 8 May 1996, about which Bull. EU 1996 (5), pt. 1.3.7. The full text of the Report can be found at the Commission's Internal Market website: <http://ec.europa.eu/internal_market/>. See also Report from the Commission, Results of the fourth phase of SLIM, COM (2000) 56 final of 4 Feb. 2000.
16. The main recommendations relating to the First Directive covered: (1) the need to accelerate the filing and disclosure of company documents and particulars by the use of modern technology and (2) the need to improve cross-border access to company information by allowing their voluntary registration in additional languages. The First Directive has been amended along the lines set out in the recommendations. See: Directive 2003/58/EC of the European Parliament and of the Council of 15 Jul. 2003 amending Council Directive 68/151/EEC as regards disclosure requirements in respect of certain types of companies, OJ 2003 L 221, 13; IP/03/828 of 11 Jun. 2003 (Company law: Commission welcomes Council adoption of a Directive simplifying and modernising the provision of company information), 2.
17. The main recommendations relating to the Second Directive were as follows: removal of the requirement for an expert opinion on contributions in kind in defined circumstances; introduction of no par value shares; simplification of the rules applicable to withdrawal of shares; simplification of the rules applicable to acquisition of own shares; reduction of the scope of the prohibition of financial assistance; simplification of the rules applicable to pre-emptive rights (see also ACTION PLAN, 17). The ACTION PLAN regarded a proposal to amend the Second Directive along the lines set out in the recommendations as a priority for the short term (2003–2005). See ACTION PLAN, *sub* 3.2 (Capital Maintenance and Alteration) and 24.
18. MEMO/03/233 of 18 Nov. 2003 (Commission proposal for a Directive on cross-border mergers – frequently asked questions), 3.
19. IP/01/943 of 4 Jul. 2001 (Commission regrets rejection of Takeovers Directive by the European Parliament). See also IP/02/1402 of 2 Oct. 2002 (Company law: Commission proposes a transparent framework for takeover bids), 3. The European Parliament's decision was (said

In reaction to this rejection, the Commission, in September 2001, set up a High Level Group of Company Law Experts chaired by Jaap Winter. The High Level Group was to advise the Commission in the first instance (by the end of 2001) on a new proposal for a Directive on takeover bids and subsequently (by mid-2002) on priorities for modernizing company law in the EU.[20] After the High Level Group had presented its first report on issues related to takeover bids in January 2002,[21] it turned to its mandate to provide recommendations for modernizing company law.[22]

This mandate was extended by the Commission following the Council of Economic and Finance Ministers in Oviedo on 12–14 April 2002, specifically to review a number of issues related to corporate governance.[23] Later that month, the High Level Group launched an open consultation,[24] for which it published a Consultative Document.[25] The consultation closed in June 2002.[26] In November 2002, the High Level Group delivered its report on a modern regulatory framework for company law.[27]Just prior to the release of this report (in September 2002), the Competitiveness Council had invited the Commission to

to be) motivated by three considerations: (1) rejection of the principle whereby, in order to take defensive measures in the face of a bid, the board of the offeree company must first obtain the approval of shareholders once the bid has been made, and this until such time as a level playing field is created for European companies facing a takeover bid; (2) regret that the protection which the Directive would afford employees of companies involved in a takeover bid was insufficient; (3) the failure of the proposal to achieve a level playing field with the United States (see the Explanatory Memorandum to the Proposal for a Directive of the European Parliament and of the Council on Takeover Bids, COM (2002) 534 of 2 Oct. 2002, 2).

20. IP/01/1237 of 4 Sep. 2001 (Company law: Commission creates High Level Group of Experts). On the creation of the High Level Group: L. Timmerman, 'Kleine gebeurtenissen', *Ondernemingsrecht* (2001): 413.
21. Report of the High Level Group of Company Law Experts on Issues Related to Takeover Bids of 10 Jan. 2002 (High Level Group Report I). The full text of the group's report is available at the Commission's Internal Market website: <http://ec.europa.eu/internal_market/>. See also IP/02/24 of 10 Jan. 2002 (Company Law: Commission welcomes experts' report on takeovers).
22. Press Release High Level Group of Company Law Experts of 4 Nov. 2002, which is available at the Commission's Internal Market website: <http://ec.europa.eu/internal_market/>.
23. MEMO/02/72 of 11 Apr. 2002 (Preparation of the informal meeting of EU Economics and Finance Ministers, Oviedo, Spain, 12–14 Apr. 2002), 3. See also Press Release High Level Group, just cited.
24. IP/02/625 of 25 Apr. 2002 (Company law: expert group launches online consultation on possible reforms).
25. The full text of this document can be found at the Commission's Internal Market website: <http://ec.europa.eu/internal_market/>.
26. IP/02/625, just cited. A summary of the main comments received on the Consultative Document is included in a (second) High Level Group Report, see *infra*, in an Annex 3.
27. Report of the High Level Group of Company Law Experts on a Modern Regulatory Framework for Company Law in Europe of 4 Nov. 2002 (High Level Group Report II). The full text of the group's report can be found at the Commission's Internal Market website: <http://ec.europa.eu/internal_market/>. See also IP/02/1600 of 4 Nov. 2002 (Commission welcomes experts' report on company law and corporate governance).

organize an in-depth discussion on the (then) forthcoming report and to develop an action plan for company law.[28]

In May 2003, the Commission presented its Action Plan 'Modernising Company Law and Enhancing Corporate Governance in the European Union'.[29] The main – policy – objectives of the Action Plan were: (1) to strengthen shareholders' rights and protection for employees, creditors and the other parties with which companies deal; (2) to foster the efficiency and competitiveness of business, with special attention to some specific cross-border issues (e.g., cross-border merger or transfer of seat).[30]

The European regulatory framework for company law and corporate governance needed to be modernized – according to the Commission – for the following reasons: (1) the growing trend for European companies to operate cross-border in the internal market; (2) the continuing integration of European capital markets; (3) the rapid development of new information and communication technologies; (4) the (then) forthcoming enlargement of the EU to ten new Member States; and (5) the damaging impact of recent financial scandals.[31]

28. Council document 12523/02 of 17 Oct. 2002 (2451st Competitiveness Council meeting (Internal Market, Industry and Research), held in Brussels on 30 Sep. 2002), item 14 and Annex II. This document can be found on the Council's website: <www.consilium.europa.eu>. See also ACTION PLAN, 4. The invitation referred to in the main text was endorsed by the Council of Economic and Finance Ministers and by Heads of State and Government at the European Council on 20 and 21 Mar. 2003. See IP/03/716 of 21 May 2003 (Company law and corporate governance: Commission presents Action Plan), 4; see also Council document 8410/03 of 5 May 2003 (Brussels European Council 20 and 21 Mar. 2003 presidency conclusions), pt. 24. For this document, see the Council's website: <www.consilium.europa.eu>.

29. Communication from the Commission to the Council and the European Parliament, 'Modernising Company Law and Enhancing Corporate Governance in the European Union – A Plan to Move Forward', COM (2003) 284 final of 21 May 2003 (ACTION PLAN). See also: IP/03/716 of 21 May 2003 (Company law and corporate governance: Commission presents Action Plan); MEMO/03/112 of 21 May 2003 (Commission Action Plan on 'Modernising Company Law and Enhancing Corporate Governance in the European Union'. Frequently Asked Questions).

The Communication is addressed to the European Parliament and the Council, it has also been transmitted to the European Economic and Social Committee and the Committee of the Regions. See ACTION PLAN, 23. See for further documentation in this connection: (1) European Parliament Resolution on the communication from the Commission to the Council and the European Parliament: Modernising company law and enhancing corporate governance in the European Union – a plan to move forward, P5_TA-PROV(2004)0346 (texts adopted at the sitting of 21 Apr. 2004); (2) Council conclusions on modernising company law and enhancing corporate governance in the European Union, Bull. EU 2003 (9), pt. 1.3.27; Council Press Release 12339/03 (Presse 259), 2525th Council meeting (Competitiveness – Internal market, industry and research) of 22 Sep. 2003, 9–10; MEMO/03/181 of 23 Sep. 2003 (Results of the Competitiveness Council of Ministers, Brussels, 22 Sep. 2003), 3; and (3) Opinion of the European Economic and Social Committee on the 'Communication from the Commission to the Council and the European Parliament Modernising company law and enhancing corporate governance in the European Union – A plan to move forward', adopted at its 404th plenary session of 10 and 11 Dec. 2003 (meeting of 10 Dec.), OJ 2004 C 80, 12.

30. ACTION PLAN, 8–9. The objectives of EC company law policy are further dealt with in s. III, *infra*.

31. ACTION PLAN, 6–7.

The Action Plan is prioritized over the short term (2003–2005), medium term (2006–2008) and long term (2009 onwards), and it indicates which type of regulatory instrument should be used for each proposal, with approximate timescales.[32] The Action Plan is based on a comprehensive set of legislative and non-legislative proposals, under the following headings: corporate governance; capital maintenance and alteration; groups and pyramids; corporate restructuring and mobility; the European private company; the European cooperative society and other EU legal forms of enterprise; enhancing the transparency of national legal forms of enterprises. A list of the individual actions concerned is attached to the Action Plan.[33] The Action Plan was open to public consultation until August 2003.[34] The comments would be given 'adequate consideration' in implementing the Action Plan.[35] In December 2005, the Commission launched another consultation on (future priorities for) the Action Plan.[36] All interested parties were invited to reply to a series of questions by the end of March 2006.[37] The consultation concluded with a public hearing in May 2006.[38] In July 2006, the Commission published a summary report of the reactions received during the whole consultation,[39] which confirmed the continued relevance of the Action Plan.[40]

---

32. *Ibid.*, 4.
33. *Ibid.*, Annex 1.
34. See ACTION PLAN, 23. The Commission published a synthesis of the comments received in Nov. 2003. See Synthesis on the responses to the Communication of the Commission to the Council and the European Parliament, 'Modernising Company Law and Enhancing Corporate Governance in the European Union – A Plan to Move Forward', COM (2003) 284 final of 21 May 2003, A Working Document of DG Internal Market, 15 Nov. 2003. The full text of the Synthesis can be found at: <http://ec.europa.eu/internal_market/>. See also IP/03/1581 of 21 Nov. 2003 (Corporate Governance and Company Law: Commission announces results of consultation on Action Plan).
35. See ACTION PLAN, 23.
36. See IP/05/1639 of 20 Dec. 2005 (Company law and corporate governance: consultation on future priorities for Action Plan). In this connection, the Directorate General for Internal Market and Services published a separate document: 'Consultation on future priorities for the Action Plan on Modernising Company Law and Enhancing Corporate Governance in the EU', see the Commission's Internal Market website: <http://ec.europa.eu/internal_market/>.
37. The consultation's fourteen questions aimed to clarify and evaluate the following: (1) the overall aim and context for future priorities; (2) the continued relevance of the medium- and long-term measures in light of the Lisbon agenda; (3) the added value of modernizing and simplifying European Company Law, with particular regard to the Better Regulation initiative.
38. See IP/06/574 of 4 May 2006 (Company law and corporate governance: public hearing on future priorities for the Action Plan).
39. Directorate General for Internal Market and Services, 'Consultation and hearing on future priorities for the Action Plan on modernising company law and enhancing corporate governance in the European Union (summary report)', Jul. 2006, available at the Commission's Internal Market website: <http://ec.europa.eu/internal_market/>.
40. For the continued relevance of the ACTION PLAN and, in particular, the measures proposed, see the summary report, just cited, 2, 6–7. Since the publication of the summary report, the Commission itself has not set out any (possible) consequences for the ACTION PLAN in response to the consultation. In the autumn of 2006, a few months after conclusion of the 2005/2006 consultation, Internal Market Commissioner McCreevy, in a speech before the European Parliament Committee on Legal Affairs, addressed various issues of company law. However, he did not

The issue of progress on the individual actions of the 2003 Action Plan is dealt with below (and further in Annex II).[41] In advance of this, it is pointed out here, that now, five and a half years after its adoption, many initiatives of the Action Plan have been realized; the Action Plan may be said to have reactivated the whole process of company law harmonization. The adoption of the European Company Regulation and its accompanying Directive on the involvement of employees in October 2001[42] has made this reactivation considerably easier.[43] The fact is, the Directive was able to establish some standard principles for worker participation;[44] an issue – worker participation – which, as stated, had not only blocked the European Company itself for many years,[45] but other key EC company law instruments as well,[46] such as the Directive on cross-border mergers, for example.[47] Other factors – interrelated or otherwise – which contributed to the reactivation of the harmonization process have been drawn attention to in the literature. They include the development of capital markets and their regulation, and a series of corporate scandals (e.g., Enron and Parmalat).[48]

Let me make brief remark, at the end of this section, on a separate Commission initiative (which, as such, is not part of the Action Plan) but which, nonetheless, has, to some extent, impacted upon EC company law, namely the reduction of

---

refer in that connection to the consultation or to any amendment of the ACTION PLAN. See SPEECH/06/720 of 21 Nov. 2006 (Charlie McCreevy speaks to the European Parliament JURI Committee). It was this speech, I presume, the European Corporate Governance Forum referred to where it stated that: 'Commissioner McCreevy will announce his future priorities for the Action Plan on 21 November [2006].' See European Corporate Governance Forum, Minutes of the meeting of 9 Nov. 2006, pt. 6.2. The Community legislature continues to refer to implementation of the ACTION PLAN, that means also *after* the consultation at issue was concluded. See, for instance, recital 1 in the preamble to Directive 2007/36/EC of the European Parliament and of the Council of 11 Jul. 2007 on the exercise of certain rights of shareholders in listed companies, OJ 2007 L 184, 17–24.

41. See s. IV.
42. For these EC company law instruments, see Annex I.
43. Opinion of the European Economic and Social Committee on the 'Proposal for a Directive of the European Parliament and of the Council on cross-border mergers of companies with share capital', adopted at its 408th plenary session of 28 and 29 Apr. 2004 (meeting of 28 Apr.), *sub* 1.2, OJ 2004 C 117, 43.
44. I.e., participation in the decision-making bodies of a company. Art. 2 *sub* k of the SE Directive contains a definition of employee 'participation' for the purposes of the Directive.
45. See: IP/00/1495 of 20 Dec. 2000 (European Company Statute: European Commission welcomes political agreement); and MEMO/03/233 of 18 Nov. 2003 (Commission proposal for a Directive on cross-border mergers – frequently asked questions), 3.
46. See, in this connection, the so-called Davignon-report, Group of Experts 'European Systems of Worker Involvement' (with regard to the European Company Statute and the other pending proposals), Final Report of May 1997, which can be found at the Internal Market website: <http://ec.europa.eu/internal_market/>.
47. See, in this respect, ACTION PLAN, 20.
48. These reasons, being outside the scope of this book, will not be elaborated upon any further here. For in-depth discussions, see: J. Rickford, 'Foreword', in Rickford, 4–7; J. Winter, 'The Need for a Regulatory Framework. EU Company Law at the Cross-Roads', in *Reforming Company and Takeover Law in Europe*, ed. G. Ferrarini et al. (Oxford: OUP, 2004), 4 and 19.

administrative burdens. In November 2006, the Commission presented a *Strategic Review of Better Regulation in the European Union*, including a proposal for a target to reduce the administrative burdens on businesses by 25% by 2012.[49] Ten concrete proposals for 'fast track action' were thereupon identified in the January 2007 *Action Programme for reducing administrative burdens in the EU*.[50] One of these 'fast track action' proposals concerned EC company law, more particularly, the Third and the Sixth Directive. In March 2007, an official proposal for a Directive amending these Directives was made,[51] and this Directive was adopted in November 2007.[52] In March 2008, then, the Commission presented a list of eleven new fast track actions,[53] the so-called 'second package of fast track actions'.[54] One month later, the Commission approved (two) official proposals for four of these actions aiming to abolish requirements in company law.[55] The first proposal concerns the First and Eleventh Directive;[56] the second proposal the Fourth and Seventh Directive.[57] In September 2008, finally, the Commission made a proposal for a Directive containing further simplification of the EC rules on mergers and divisions.[58] The proposal, as the Commission put it,

49. See 'A strategic review of better regulation in the European Union' (Commission communication to the European Parliament, the Council, the European Economic and Social Committee and the Committee of the Regions), COM (2006) 689 of 14 Nov. 2006. On this Communication: Bull. EU 2006 (11), pt. 1.2.1.
50. See 'Action Programme for Reducing Administrative Burdens in the European Union' (Communication from the Commission to the Council, the European Parliament, the European Economic and Social Committee and the Committee of the Regions), COM (2007) 23 of 24 Jan. 2007.
51. Proposal for a Directive of the European Parliament and of the Council amending Council Directive 78/855/EEC concerning mergers of public limited liability companies and Council Directive 82/891/EEC concerning the division of public limited companies as regards the requirement for an independent expert's report on the occasion of a merger or a division, COM (2007) 91 of 6 Mar. 2007.
52. Directive 2007/63/EC of the European Parliament and of the Council of 13 Nov. 2007 amending Council Directives 78/855/EEC and 82/891/EEC as regards the requirement of an independent expert's report on the occasion of merger or division of public limited liability companies, OJ 2007 L 300, 47–48.
53. See MEMO/08/152 of 10 Mar. 2008 (European Commission proposals for fast track administrative burden reductions in 2008).
54. See IP/08/598 of 17 Apr. 2008 (Commission cuts unnecessary administrative burdens in EU company law).
55. See IP/08/598, just cited.
56. Proposal for a Directive of the European Parliament and of the Council amending Council Directives 68/151/EEC and 89/666/EEC as regards publication and translation obligations of certain types of companies, COM (2008) 194 final of 17 Apr. 2008.
57. Proposal for a Directive of the European Parliament and of the Council amending Council Directives 78/660/EEC and 83/349/EEC as regards certain disclosure requirements for medium-sized companies and obligation to draw up consolidated accounts, COM (2008) 195 final of 17 Apr. 2008.
58. Proposal for a Directive of the European Parliament and of the Council amending Council Directives 77/91/EEC, 78/855/EEC and 82/891/EEC and Directive 2005/56/EC as regards reporting and documentation requirements in the case of merger and divisions, COM (2008) 576 of 24 Sep. 2008.

'complements the two packages of "fast track" measures' (just referred to).[59] These 'fast track' actions aim at reducing administrative burdens on businesses through minor legislative changes without challenging the level of protection or the original purpose of the legislation.[60] The just referred to 2007 amendment of the Third and Sixth Directive, which was also aimed at by the Commission in the 2003 Action Plan,[61] is entered into further below.[62]

III. THE OBJECTIVES OF EC COMPANY LAW POLICY

This section is about the objectives of EC company law policy.[63] More in particular, it looks at the goals the Community legislature since its early days generally has advanced for its company law action to attain and their relationship to the present modernization objectives. In doing so, it seeks to give some insight or perspective on the nature of modern EC company law objectives.[64]

As indicated at the start of the previous section (s. II), the Commission from an early beginning has taken a broad view on why harmonization of (aspects of) company law was needed. In fact, when in 1965 the Commission for the first time in a general way expressed its view on the objectives of the EEC in the field of company law, it identified the following four objectives,[65] which over

---

59. IP/08/1407 of 25 Sep. 2008 (Company law: Commission proposes further simplification of EU rules on mergers and divisions).
60. See COM (2007) 91, just cited, 2, which concerns the first package of fast track action. With respect to the second package of fast track action something similar applies, see 'Second progress report on the strategy for simplifying the regulatory environment' (Commission Working Document), COM (2008) 33 final of 30 Jan. 2008, 2: 'whenever a way is found to make life easier for businesses *without affecting the underlying policy goals* or proposing other *significant changes to the regulatory framework*, the Commission will make use of the so-called fast-track actions mechanism'. (emphasis added). See also '2008 Fast Track Actions to reduce administrative burdens in the European Union' (Communication from the Commission to the Council, the European Parliament, the European Economic and Social Committee and the Committee of the Regions), COM (2008) 141 final of 10 Mar. 2008: 'in order to produce concrete results in the short-term, the Action Programme [2007, just cited] also covers immediate measures that are likely to generate significant benefits through *technical changes in existing rules*. Because of the nature of the changes required, these measures can be adopted fairly quickly. They are therefore called "Fast Track Actions" (FTA)'. (emphasis added). See, finally, MEMO/08/152, just cited: 'These immediate measures are likely to generate significant benefits (. . .) through *technical changes in existing rules*'. (emphasis added).
61. See ACTION PLAN, 21 and 26.
62. See Ch. 3.
63. The term 'EC company law policy' is taken from the ACTION PLAN, 8.
64. In advance of the next chapters it is already noted here that – from an *ex ante* perspective – consideration of the objectives the Community legislature wants to achieve is, as Timmermans remarks, 'a legal necessity in terms of the available legal base under the Treaty'. See Timmermans, 5. The legal bases for EC action in the field of company law are entered into in Chs 3 and 4.
65. The Commission presented, more specifically, its view on 6 May 1965 to the Commission for the internal market of the European Parliament. See *Rapport fait au nom de la Commission du marché intérieur, par M. Berkhouwer*, Eur. Parliament Session 1966–1967 of 9 May 1966, Doc. 53

the years indeed were (largely) advanced, combined or individually, by the Community legislature as goals in its measures based on Article 44(2)(g) EC:

(a) facilitating the exercise of the freedom of establishment;
(b) preventing establishment on account of the severity of national company laws;
(c) ensuring certainty in the law; and
(d) reinforcing protection of members and third parties.

Later on, the Community's power in the field of company law was also viewed in function of:

(e) making European companies more competitive, by facilitating transnational European companies.[66]

Let me make some observations on the above objectives, and their relation to the modernization objectives. (As already noted in the previous section, the main policy objectives of the Commission's modernization efforts as expressed in its Action Plan are two-fold: (1) to strengthen shareholders' rights and protection for employees, creditors, and the other parties with which companies deal; (2) to foster the efficiency and competitiveness of business).

a. The first objective advanced by the Commission is facilitation of freedom of establishment of companies.[67] The Commission's Action Plan does not mention facilitation of freedom of establishment of companies as a policy objective.[68] Harmonization for the purpose of freedom of establishment, incidentally, will be examined in detail in the next chapter.

The next objectives (*b – d*, below) are closely tied with the Commission's early view, derived from the history of Treaty negotiations, on harmonization as a counterbalance to the liberal granting of the right of establishment by the EEC Treaty.[69] In this view, the purpose of harmonization is (also) to offset various difficulties ensuing from freedom of establishment.

('Berkhouwer report'); English version not available; *Rev.trim.dr.eur* 1966: 441. For the debate in those early days on the objectives of the EEC in this field, see Edwards, 6 with further references.

66. See Commissie van de EG (Secretariaat-Generaal), 'De Industriepolitiek van de Gemeenschap. Memorandum van de Commissie aan de Raad' ('Colonna Memorandum'), 18 Mar. 1970, Bull. EG, supp. 4/70, 19.

67. Berkhouwer report, just cited, pt. 11-12a of the Commission's response ('[l]a coordination des droits des sociétés [Art. 54(3)(g)] est prescrite (...) pour *faciliter*, par la réalisation d'une certaine uniformité législative, l'exercice de ce droit d'établissement' (the coordination of company laws is prescribed in order to *facilitate*, through realization of a certain legislative uniformity, the exercise of this right of establishment; own translation; emphasis added)). See particularly: Eleventh Directive, fifth recital; Wouters, just cited, 269.

68. Nonetheless, some of its remarks still relate to this objective: it notes as one of the reasons for new initiatives that the growing trend of European companies to operate cross-border calls for common European company law mechanisms, *inter alia*, to facilitate freedom of establishment and cross-border restructuring (ACTION PLAN, 6).

69. Berkhouwer report, just cited, pt. 11. The explanation why harmonization of (aspects of) company law was provided for in the original EEC Treaty seems to have been the fear, expressed by France in particular, that opening up the borders for trade and investment from

b. The second, traditional objective of the Commission is then preventing establishment on account of severity of national company laws.[70] This is closely linked with the idea of preventing a race to the bottom in company law.[71] The race to the bottom theory (more on this later) claims that competition between Member State legislatures in company law harms shareholders by driving these States to adopt company law rules that are too lax with respect to managers and controlling shareholders.[72]

The approach of the Community legislature prior to the Commission's Action Plan is broadly understood as directed primarily towards protecting members and third parties, *in order to prevent a race to the bottom.*[73] The modernizations focus

---

other Member States would entail unacceptable risks because of the fairly low standards of protection granted to shareholders and creditors by the company law system of some of those States (Timmermans, 5). France feared in particular that, in its eyes, the very lax Netherlands company law of those days would attract massive incorporation by foreign business in the Netherlands as a home base from which to penetrate the common market. Harmonization would then be required to bring standards of protection granted by the national company law systems to equivalent levels as a precondition, or at least an accompanying measure, to counterbalance the liberal granting of the right of establishment by the EC Treaty (Timmermans, 5).

70. Berkhouwer report, pt. 12b ('Lors de la réalisation du droit d'établissement, il est à éviter que des transferts d'activités et de capitaux se produisent non pas sur la base des éléments classiques de l'économie, mais plutôt à raison du degré de sévérité plus ou moins grand de chaque législation nationale en matière des sociétés' (In realizing the right of establishment, it is necessary to prevent that the transfer of activities and of capital occurs on account of the more or less strict nature of national company laws and no longer according to the regular economic rules of the game; own translation)).
71. On the issue of a race to the bottom in the field of consumer law, see J. Stuyck, 'European Consumer Law after the Treaty of Amsterdam: Consumer Policy In or Beyond the Internal Market?', *CML Rev.* 37 (2000): 389.
72. The issue of regulatory competition is elaborated upon in particular in Ch. 5.
73. High Level Group Report II, 29 ('The [harmonization] exercise has been much more driven by establishing a proper level of protection – throughout the Union – for those who are involved in and affected by the affairs of the company, in particular shareholders and creditors, *with a view to preventing a "race to the bottom"* by Member States'; emphasis added); See also: A Modern Regulatory Framework for Company Law in Europe: A Consultative Document of the High Level Group of Company Law Experts, 2002, 4; J. Winter, 'EU Company Law on the Move', *LIEI* 31 (2004), 97–114, 97 and 107; E. Wymeersch, 'Modern Company Law-Making – About Techniques of Regulating Companies in the European Union', in: *Reforming Company and Takeover Law in Europe*, ed. G. Ferrarini, K.J. Hopt, J. Winter & E. Wymeersch, (Oxford: OUP, 2004), 145–182, 162 ('By imposing similar rules in each of the states, this policy [indirectly] aimed at avoiding the risk of regulatory arbitrage and the much feared race for laxity, referred to as the "Delaware effect" '); J. Winter, 'Corporate governance regulation and enforcement in the US and the EU', in: *Topics in Corporate Finance – The Quality of Corporate Law and the Role of Corporate Law Judges*, ed. L. Bouchez, M. Knubben, J.A. McCahery & L. Timmerman, (Amsterdam: Amsterdam Center for Corporate Finance, 2006), 19–37, 26; C. Villiers, *European Company Law: Towards Democracy?* (Aldershot: Ashgate Publishing, 1998), 17). This broad understanding is in line with the early expressed objective by the Commission of preventing establishment on account of the severity of national company laws. Nevertheless, Directives in the field of company law have rarely, if at all, been *explicitly* argued in terms of preventing a race to the bottom or preventing establishment on account of the severity of company laws. (But see the Explanatory Memorandum to proposal for the Fourth Directive,

of the Commission to 'meeting company needs'[74] would then denote a distinct shift in the approach the EC could take to company law.[75] Now indeed, the Commission in its Action Plan does not (any longer) mention preventing a race to the bottom or preventing establishment on account of the severity of company laws as an objective, as it did in its early days.[76] It even expressly holds that 'some competition between national rules may actually be healthy for the efficiency of the single market'.[77]

The idea of a race to the bottom in company law presupposes a certain freedom of choice of company law, in case of initial incorporations and for existing companies through reincorporation abroad. Such freedom was for a long time generally believed to be present only to a limited extent, in particular as a result of the real seat approach with regard to the recognition of foreign companies.[78] Things have changed, however, in the past few years. Both the case-law of the Court of Justice[79] and Community instruments[80] have contributed, at least de iure, to this freedom of choice of company law. The freedom of choice of company law incidentally, is discussed in detail below.[81] As a result of this freedom, for the first time, the risk of a race to the bottom could become real.[82] These recent developments might give an impetus to company law harmonization for this policy objective.[83]

c. A third aim of EC company law has traditionally been the promotion of legal certainty in intra-Community commercial relations.[84] A number of common safeguards for the persons involved with the company is considered to be key for the

---

which as a reason for action, *inter alia*, notes that the existing divergences between the national laws on financial accounting may also be a reason for companies, *when choosing a place of establishment, to prefer countries with little requirements in this regard*).

74. Mandate given by the Commission to the High Level Group of Company Law Experts to provide 'recommendations for a modern regulatory European company law framework designed to be sufficiently flexible and up-to-date *to meet companies' needs* (. . .)' (emphasis added). See IP/01/1237 of 4 Sep. 2001 (Company Law: Commission creates High Level Group of Experts).
75. High Level Group Report II, 29; see also 'A Modern Regulatory Framework for Company Law in Europe: A Consultative Document of the High Level Group of Company Law Experts' (of April 2002), 4. The full text of this document can be found at the Commission's Internal Market website: <www.ec.europa.eu/internal_market/>.
76. Berkhouwer report, just cited, pt. 12b.
77. Action Plan, 9.
78. See in this connection S. Rammeloo, *Corporations in Private International Law: A European Perspective* (Oxford: OUP, 2001), in particular Ch. 2 (Recognition Theories: Private International Law Treaties and EC Law).
79. See in particular: *Centros, Überseering, Inspire Art, Sevic* and *Cartesio.*
80. See in particular: the SE Regulation and the Directive on cross-border mergers.
81. See Ch. 5.
82. See also Timmermans, 13, who foresaw this development already in 2001 (Timmermans' lecture dates from 14 Dec. 2001, see fn. 1 of his lecture).
83. Timmermans, however, considers the prospects for such harmonization 'fairly remote'. See Timmermans, 14.
84. Berkhouwer report, just cited, pt. 12c ('La sécurité juridique dans les transactions intra-communautaire doit être assurée (. . .)' (Certainty in the law in intra-Community transactions

creation of trust in cross-border economic relationships.[85] The Action Plan on company law builds on this. But, while in the past, ensuring legal certainty and enhancing trust by protecting shareholders and third parties was seen in function of intra-Community transactions, this is now more phrased in function of business efficiency and competitiveness.[86] In this connection, the Action Plan states:

> Ensuring effective and proportionate protection of shareholders and third parties must be at the core of any company law policy. A sound framework for protection of members and third parties, *which properly achieves a high degree of* ***confidence*** *in business relationships*, is a fundamental condition for ***business efficiency and competitiveness***. In particular, an effective regime for the protection of shareholders and their rights, protecting the savings and pensions of millions of people and strengthening the foundations of capital markets for the long term in a context of diversified shareholding within the EU, is essential if companies are to raise capital at the lowest cost.[87] (emphasis added).

d. A fourth related objective, advanced by the Community legislature is reinforcing protection of members and third parties.[88] A large part of the *acquis* covers measures expressly concerned with this objective. Sometimes protection is explicitly provided for in order to safeguard the exercise of the right of establishment.[89] On other occasions, such an explicit link with freedom of establishment is absent. Various recitals in these directives may suggest that the purpose of harmonization here more lies in (equivalent) protection of the interests of members in its own right.[90] As stated above, the Commission in its Action Plan now sees protection as a function of efficiency and of competitiveness of a business.

---

has to be ensured; own translation)). Cf. various provisions of the First, Third, and Sixth Directive limiting, in view of this objective, cases in which nullity may arise. See also Case 32/74 *Haaga* [1974] ECR 1201, para. 6.

85. Grundmann, p. 21–22; Cf. Action Plan, 6. Cf. the policy objective to increase consumer confidence, which is central to European consumer law harmonization since the so-called 1992 Sutherland Report. See in this connection J. Stuyck, E. Terryn & T. Van Dyck, 'Confidence through Fairness? The New Directive on Unfair Business-to-Consumer Commercial Practices in the Internal Market', *CML Rev.* 43 (2006): 107–152.
86. Action Plan, 8.
87. *Ibid.*
88. Berkhouwer report, just cited, pt. 12c ('la protection des associés et des tiers doit être, le cas échéant, renforcée' (protection of members and third parties needs, as the occasion arises, to be reinforced; own translation)).
89. E.g., the Eleventh Directive (fifth recital). See further Ch. 3 (s. IV in particular).
90. See, e.g., the preamble to the Second Directive (second recital), Third Directive (third recital: 'Whereas the *protection of the interests of members and third parties requires* that the laws of the Member States relating to mergers of public limited liability companies be coordinated and that provision for mergers should be made in the laws of all the Member States'; emphasis added), Fourth Directive (first recital), Sixth Directive (fifth recital) and Seventh Directive (first and third recital). See J. Wouters, 'European Company Law: Quo Vadis?', *CML Rev.* (37) 2000, 270 (remarking 'the emphasis [of these Directives] is entirely on legislative policy aims of equivalent protection for shareholders and creditors in the common market').

e. Finally, EC company law is regarded as an instrument of European industrial policy. This has a long history. Already according to the Colonna memorandum of 1970, unification or harmonization of company law rules should contribute to making European companies more competitive by offering them instruments and rules facilitating cross-border mergers and cooperation, in order to form 'transnational European companies'.[91] In fact, the Council Regulations on the EEIG (1985), the SE (2001), and the SCE (2003) may be seen in this light.

It may further be referred to the 2002 Communication on Industrial Policy in an Enlarged Europe.[92] According to this Communication, improving framework conditions for enterprise will remain the core of EU industrial policy.[93] As part of this policy, the Commission underlines the importance of rules that set the general market framework, such as company law,[94] and recognizes a sound corporate governance framework as one of the key prerequisites for the efficient and sustainable development of competitive businesses.[95]

The Action Plan on company law fits in with this. Its second of two key policy objectives[96] is fostering efficiency and competitiveness of business. Business efficiency and competitiveness should be promoted, *inter alia*, through EC initiatives addressing a number of specific cross-border issues (e.g., cross-border merger or transfer of seat and cross-border impediments to the exercise of shareholder rights).[97]

In academic literature, too, the industrial policy objective of EC company law has been identified for a long time.[98] It is in particular the removal of obstacles to the 'free movement' of companies within the internal market and the facilitation of operations of structuring and restructuring international groups of companies (international mergers, transfer of seats) which are regarded as crucial components of this policy.[99]

In sum: in the past, EC company law action had a variety of goals (particularly facilitation of freedom of establishment, preventing a race to the bottom, ensuring legal certainty, protection of members and others, and industrial policy).[100] It was

91. See Commissie van de EG (Secretariaat-Generaal), 'De Industriepolitiek van de Gemeenschap. Memorandum van de Commissie aan de Raad' ('Colonna Memorandum'), 18 Mar. 1970, Bull. EG, supp. 4/70, 19.
92. Communication from the Commission to the Council, the European Parliament, the Economic and Social Committee and the Committee of the Regions, 'Industrial Policy in an Enlarged Europe', COM(2002) 714 final of 11 Dec. 2002.
93. Communication, just cited, 3; IP/02/1884 of 16 Dec. 2002 (Commission puts industrial policy at the core of its agenda).
94. Communication, just cited, 21.
95. *Ibid.*, 22–23.
96. The first key policy objective was just dealt with, and also in s. II.
97. Action Plan, 9.
98. On the industrial policy foundation of EC company law, above all: C.W.A. Timmermans, 'De tweede golf: de Europese onderstroom', *TVVS* (1983): 166–169; C.W.A. Timmermans, 'Die europäische Rechtsangleichung im Gesellschaftsrecht', *RabelsZ* 48 (1984): 12–13.
99. See Timmermans, 6.
100. This is not to say that emphasis and scope of the EC company law harmonization programme in the past has not varied (see the previous section) and that occasionally also some other goal

seen to be conducive to freedom of establishment and was further viewed as needed to counterbalance difficulties ensuing from freedom of establishment (e.g., establishment on account of severity of company laws). In contrast, modern EC company law objectives as presented by the Commission in its Action Plan emphasize business efficiency and competitiveness, and emphasize less, if at all, freedom of establishment or difficulties ensuing from the exercise of this freedom. Its focus is on two particular goals. First, to foster the efficiency and competitiveness of business. Second, and in function of the first goal, to strengthen shareholders' rights and protection for employees, creditors, and the other parties with which companies deal. (The compatibility of various modernization actions with the EC Treaty, is discussed in the next chapters).

IV. EC COMPANY LAW INSTRUMENTS

EC company law consist of a great number of instruments. A discussion of each of these instruments falls outside the scope of this book. However, an overview of these instruments is included in two annexes to this book. For the purposes of this section, note that two categories of EC company law instruments (which together make up EC company law, as defined in this book)[101] may be discerned: the pre-Action Plan company law instruments on the one hand and the company law instruments (which are part of the Action Plan) on the other. The annexes will provide a (largely) enumerative description of these instruments.

Annex I (pre-Action Plan company law instruments) contains an overview of the instruments which already existed or had been proposed at the time of publication of the Commission's Action Plan.[102] The Action Plan itself, conveniently, contains a list of these 'old' instruments. Since publication of the Action Plan, the proposed company law instruments just referred to have been adopted. As a consequence, this Annex I – which aims to present an up-to-date review – is exclusively about existing EC company law instruments.

Annex II provides an overview of company law instruments which are part of the Action Plan. It contains two sections. First, in section I, the instruments which have been adopted are dealt with. At the end of this section, initiatives are included for company law instruments with respect to which the Commission has decided that there is no (further) action. Second, section II contains an examination of the still remaining actions for which implementation has begun but is not yet completed.

(e.g., SME-policy in the Twelfth Directive) has not played a role (see further J. Wouters, 'European Company Law: Quo Vadis?', *CML Rev.* (37) 2000, 272 et seq.).

101. See the Introduction of this book.

102. For a discussion of these pre-ACTION PLAN company law instruments (with further references), see: Lutter; C. Villiers, *European Company Law – towards Democracy?* (Aldershot: Ashgate Publishing, 1998); Edwards; Schwarz; J. Wouters, 'European company law: *Quo vadis?*', *CML Rev.* 37 (2000): 257–307; Habersack; K.J. Hopt & E. Wymeersch (eds), *European Company and Financial Law. Texts and Leading Cases* (Oxford: OUP, 2007); and Grundmann.

Chapter 3

EC Competence in the Field of Company Law (I): Article 44 EC

I. INTRODUCTION

The two now following chapters are about the competence or powers – the two terms will be used interchangeably – of the EC in the field of company law. Both chapters are closely linked with the principle of conferred powers. As stated in Chapter 1, this principle signifies, in short, that the Community can act only where the EC Treaty equips it with competence. Community competences are conferred by specific provisions of the EC Treaty, known as legal bases. There is no legal basis which confers a general, comprehensive competence with respect to company law as such. There are, however, various Treaty Articles which enable the Community to regulate certain aspects of company law. It is these Treaty Articles which have been used for the EC company law *acquis* as described in the previous chapter.[1]

This and the next chapter are dedicated to these legal bases. They deal extensively with the conditions for the use of these legal bases and analyze whether, in view of their respective used legal bases, various Directives and Regulations satisfy these conditions. It should be added that the choice of the correct legal basis is of considerable practical and institutional, indeed 'constitutional importance'.[2] It determines not only the legislative procedure applicable (rights of the European Parliament to participate, unanimity or qualified majority in the Council), but it may also prescribe the type of instrument that may be used – for example, only

1. A survey of the EC company law *acquis* is included in Annex I and Annex II to this book.
2. Opinion of AG Kokott in Case C-94/03 *Commission* v *Council* [2006] ECR I-1, pt. 24. See also Opinion of AG Kokott in Case C-178/03 *Commission* v *Parliament and Council* [2006] ECR I-107, pt. 29.

directives. It should further be repeated that acts which are based on an incorrect legal basis can be declared void (under Article 230 EC) or invalid (under Article 234 EC).[3]

As to the delineation of both chapters, it is to be noted that the present Chapter 3 deals with Article 44 EC, concerning freedom of establishment. This article is of such importance to EC company law (I shall return to this directly) that it will be dealt with first and (also for easy reference) in a separate chapter. Chapter 4, then, is about the other legal bases which also play a role in the field of EC company law. First, Article 95 EC and Article 308 EC will be examined, and then: Article 61(c) EC *juncto* Article 67 EC; Article 137 EC; Article 211 EC; and Article 293 EC. Finally, in Chapter 4, some 'combined' concluding remarks (i.e., relating to both Chapters 3 and 4) are made.

Turning now to the present chapter, Article 44 EC may be characterized as the *Magna Charta* of EC company law.[4] All the numbered company law Directives are based on this provision.[5] The Directive on takeover bids and the Directive on cross-border mergers have also been adopted on the basis of this provision; the Directive on shareholder rights is partly based on Article 44 EC; the (now withdrawn) draft proposal for a Directive on cross-border transfer of the registered office of limited companies (conversion), finally, also mentioned Article 44 EC as the legal basis for this Directive.[6]

The structure of this chapter is as follows. First, it will focus on the scope of the Treaty provisions on freedom of establishment (Articles 43–48 EC), in section II. Then the power under Article 44 EC to attain freedom of establishment will be examined: section III will deal with Article 44(1) EC; section IV with Article 44(2)(g) EC. Section V, then, concerns the specific issue of whether the Community legislature has the authority to include in directives on the basis of Article 44 EC provisions relating to the treatment of nationals or companies of non-member countries. Section VI, finally, will briefly examine the topic of regulatory competition, as it is sometimes argued in academic literature that freedom of establishment should be interpreted as guaranteeing regulatory competition in the field of company law. The topic of regulatory competition is also dealt with (more extensively) in Chapter 5.

---

3. See Ch. 1.
4. Cf. Lutter, 36; Schwarz, 75.
5. See Annex I. The words 'company law', incidentally, do not appear in the official name of any of the numbered Directives (with the exception of the Twelfth Directive); it is referred, however, to 'safeguards' or to Art. 54(3)(g) EC Treaty (with the exception of the Eleventh and Twelfth Directive).
6. For other Directives that have been based on Art. 44 EC, in implementation of the ACTION PLAN, see Annex II.

II. THE SCOPE OF THE TREATY PROVISIONS ON FREEDOM OF ESTABLISHMENT (ARTICLES 43–48 EC)

A. INTRODUCTION

The freedom of establishment provided for in Articles 43 EC to 48 EC is conferred both on natural persons who are nationals of a Member State and on legal persons within the meaning of Article 48 EC. Subject to the exceptions and conditions specified, it includes the right to take up and pursue all types of self-employed activity in the territory of any other Member State, to set up and manage undertakings, and to set up agencies, branches, or subsidiaries. These two sentences conveniently summarize the general scope (*ratione personae* and *ratione materiae*) of freedom of establishment.[7]

This general scope is articulated in particular in the Court's preliminary rulings on the interpretation of the prohibition of Article 43 EC. In various of these rulings, the Court, before it examines the question whether a national measure constitutes a 'restriction'[8] on this freedom and whether such a restriction is 'justified', first determines 'whether the Treaty provisions on freedom of establishment apply'.[9] In so doing, the Court has examined and defined the scope of the Treaty provisions on freedom of establishment in more detail.

This section, first, deals with the scope *ratione personae* (the beneficiaries) of the freedom of establishment and, subsequently, with its scope *ratione materiae* (the substantive scope).

B. SCOPE *RATIONE PERSONAE*

The freedom of establishment provided for in Articles 43 EC to 48 EC is conferred, as just mentioned, both on natural persons who are nationals of a Member State and on companies or firms within the meaning of Article 48 EC. Before discussing companies and firms, natural persons will be dealt with.

---

7. The Court of Justice did so e.g., in: Case C-55/94 *Gebhard* v *Consiglio dell'Ordine degli Avvocati e Procuratori di Milano* [1995] ECR I-4165, para. 23; Case C-255/97 *Pfeiffer* [1999] ECR I-2835, para. 18; Case C-79/01 *Payroll a.O.* [2002] ECR I-8923, para. 24.
8. This means, restriction within the meaning of Art. 43, para. 1 EC.
9. See e.g., *Überseering*; Case C-9/02 *de Lasteyrie du Saillant* [2004] ECR I-2409; *Sevic*; Case C-470/04 *N.* v *Inspecteur van de Belastingdienst Oost/Kantoor Almelo* [2006] ECR I-7409; Case C-524/04 *Test Claimants in the Thin Cap Group Litigation* [2007] ECR I-2107; Case C-231/05 *Oy AA* [2007] ECR I-6373; (and with respect to Art. 56 EC: e.g., Joined Cases C-463/04 and C-464/04 *Federconsumatori a.O.* [2007] ECR I-10419). For the first two stages (the issue of applicability and the existence of a restriction) of this three-part sequence, see also *Cartesio*, para. 109.

1. Natural Persons

All natural persons who are nationals of a Member State are within the scope of freedom of establishment.[10] This is standard case-law.[11] The question whether a natural person is indeed a national of a Member State (and thus entitled to enjoy the right of establishment), then, is resolved by the applicable national law.[12] Also within the scope are those who are nationals of a Member State and of a third country at the same time[13] and those who are nationals of a Member State who reside outside the EC.[14]

2. Companies and Firms: The Nationality Criteria of Article 48, paragraph 1 EC

Besides natural persons, 'companies or firms' may be within the scope of the Treaty provisions on freedom of establishment. Article 48 EC reads as follows:

> Companies or firms formed in accordance with the law of a Member State and having their registered office, central administration or principal place of business within the Community shall, for the purposes of this Chapter, be treated in the same way as natural persons who are nationals of Member States.

---

10. For a discussion of the concept of natural person in the civil codes of the Member States, see G. Alpa, 'The Meaning of "Natural Person" and the Impact of the Constitution for Europe on the Development of European Private Law', *ELJ* (10) 2004, 734–750.
11. See e.g., *Payroll a.O.*, just cited, para. 24, where the Court ruled: 'the freedom of establishment provided for in Articles 43 EC to 48 EC, is conferred (. . .) on natural persons who are nationals of a Member State'. In the literature, this is also deduced from Art. 43, para. 1, EC.
12. See *Cartesio*, para. 109: 'the question whether Article 43 EC applies to a company which seeks to rely on the fundamental freedom enshrined in that article – *like the question whether a natural person is a national of a Member State, hence entitled to enjoy that freedom* – is a preliminary matter which, as Community law now stands, can only be resolved by the applicable national law'. (emphasis added). In this connection, the Court could have referred to its judgment in Case C-369/90 *Micheletti* [1992] ECR I-4239, para. 10, where it observed that 'it is for each Member State (. . .) to lay down the conditions for the acquisition and loss of nationality'.
13. In Case C-369/90 *Micheletti* [1992] ECR I-4239, paras 10 and 15, the Court has ruled that: 'it is not permissible for the legislation of a Member State to restrict the effects of the grant of the nationality of another Member State by imposing an additional condition for recognition of that nationality with a view to the exercise of the fundamental freedoms provided for in the Treaty'. Against this background, the Court decided that: 'the provisions of Community law on freedom of establishment preclude a Member State from denying a national of another Member State who possesses at the same time the nationality of a non-member country entitlement to that freedom on the ground that the law of the host State deems him to be a national of the non-member country'. This ruling, of course, bears a strong resemblance to the *Überseering* and *Inspire Art* judgments of the Court, to be discussed below, which concern companies and firms (as opposed to natural persons).
14. See Kapteyn & VerLoren van Themaat, 721. For the applicability of freedom of establishment to third country nationals, see Lenaerts & Van Nuffel, 174, 180 and 212. See further W. Weiss, 'The Chapter II on Establishment in the Europe Agreements', *E.For.Aff.Rev.* 6 (2001): 234–281.

> 'Companies or firms' means companies or firms constituted under civil or commercial law, including cooperative societies, and other legal persons governed by public or private law, save for those which are non-profit-making.

Companies or firms (which, hereinafter, for convenience, are referred to as 'companies')[15] are therefore within the scope of the Treaty provisions on freedom of establishment when they: (1) are formed in accordance with the law of a Member State; and (2) have their registered office, central administration, or principal place of business within the Community. In the doctrine, these two conditions are referred to as the 'nationality requirements';[16] they will be dealt with, successively, in sections *a* and *b*. (In section *c* then, the so-called 'real and continuous link requirement' of the 1961 General Programme for the abolition of restrictions on the freedom of establishment, will be examined. Section *d*, finally, deals with 'brass plate companies' and the question whether they may benefit from freedom of establishment).

Before dealing with all this, it should be underlined that the scope *ratione personae* is not limited further by nationality requirements concerning the persons holding the share capital (in the company) or members of the management or supervisory organs (of the company).[17]

a. First Requirement: 'Formed in Accordance with the Law of a Member State'

According to the *First Requirement*, the Company must be 'formed in accordance with the law of a Member State'. This requirement consists of two elements, which will be discussed successively. First, the company must be formed in accordance with the law of a *Member State*, so it must be an 'EC company'; next, the company – still in order to be within the personal scope of freedom establishment – must be *formed in accordance with the law* of such a State.

As regards this first element, it is argued in the literature, that occasionally also companies formed in accordance with the law *of a third country* could enter the scope of freedom of establishment. In this regard, it has been advanced that Belgium, for example, allows a company incorporated under the law of a third country, after transfer of its central administration to Belgium and conformation of its articles of association to the mandatory provisions of Belgian (company) law, a continued existence as a company recognized under Belgian law.[18] The company in question obtains a 'double nationality'[19] and can – so it is argued – from that

15. 'The concept of companies and firms' is dealt with below, in s. 3.
16. See Wouters, 126.
17. For a discussion of the so-called theory of control, according to which (also) the nationality of the persons referred to in the main text should be decisive for the scope of the Treaty provisions on freedom of establishment (*ratione personae*), see Wouters, 127–133.
18. See Wouters, 138.
19. For a detailed description of this operation of cross-border transfer of seat and the double nationality, see Wouters, 632–635 and 640–641.

moment on (also) be regarded as an EC company.[20] The view that such a company may be considered as an EC company, however, is not undisputed.[21] Leaving aside these rather exceptional 'double nationality' companies, the first requirement under consideration here makes clear, in any event, that companies formed under the law of third countries are outside the personal scope of freedom of establishment.

May Community legal forms, that is, the EEIG, the SE and SCE, be regarded as beneficiaries of the freedom of establishment? It could, in my view, be argued that when companies formed in accordance with the law of a *Member State* are within the scope of the Treaty provisions on freedom of establishment, this goes *a fortiori* for Community legal forms, which have been formed in accordance with (secondary) *Community* law.[22] The opinion that Community legal forms are to be regarded as beneficiaries of the freedom of establishment seems to be the prevailing view in academic literature indeed.[23] The issue of Community legal forms as beneficiaries of the freedom of establishment is returned to in Chapter 5 in particular.[24]

The second element is that the company – in order to qualify as a beneficiary of the right of establishment – must be *formed in accordance with the law* of a Member State.

In legal literature, this element is defined as carrying with it: 'the fulfilment of company law requirements which are inherent to the legal structure of (. . .) [the] company, that is, to the 'standard contract' between different participants, for example, the existence of shareholders and directors, the drafting of a company

20. This point of view is held by Wouters, 137–138.
21. Wouters, 138 refers to an opposite view held by J.G. Renauld, *Droit européen des sociétés* (Brussels: Bruylant, 1969), 2.28–2.29, no. 37.
22. See already e.g., Schwarz, 100; W.-G. Ringe, *Die Sitzverlegung der Europäischen Aktiengesellschaft* (Tübingen: Mohr Siebeck, 2006), 51.
23. See Ringe, just cited, 55 with further references. Already in 1988, when there was only one Community legal form, the EEIG, Timmermans took the view that EEIGs are beneficiaries of Art. 52 EEC (now Art. 43 EC). See C.W.A. Timmermans, 'Europeesrechtelijke erkenning van pseudo-buitenlandse vennootschappen', in *Tot vermaak van Slagter*, ed. J.H. Christiaanse et al. (Deventer: Kluwer, 1988), 331.
24. Both the second element (of the first requirement) '*formed in accordance with the law* of a Member State' and the second requirement 'registered office, central administration or principal place of business within the Community' for Community legal forms to be beneficiary of the right of establishment, may be argued to be much less problematic (than the first element of the first requirement, briefly discussed in the main text). (The second requirement, specifically, should be satisfied where Community legal forms are concerned. See: Art. 12 EEIG Regulation; Art. 7 SE Regulation; Art. 6 SCE Regulation). These requirements, laid down in Art. 48 EC will (as far as the Community legal forms are concerned) not be entered into any further here (i.e., in the specific context of the beneficiaries of freedom of establishment). The requirements in question will be returned to below, however, where they will be shown to be of relevance to the issue of compatibility of (provisions of the statutes for) Community legal forms with Art. 43 EC. This issue is dealt with in Ch. 5.

statute, the raising of legal capital or the registration of the company'.[25] Defined rather similarly, the incorporation of the company and its basic structure ('*Grundstruktur*') must emanate from the law of a certain Member State.[26]

In this connection, it can further be referred to the Court's case-law (which is in line with the long standing doctrinal interpretation (of the element '*formed in accordance with the law* of a Member State') just dealt with). First, in *Daily Mail*, the Court held:

> it should be borne in mind that, unlike natural persons, companies are creatures of the law and, in the present state of Community law, creatures of national law. *They exist only by virtue of the varying national legislation which determines their incorporation and functioning.*[27] (emphasis added).

Subsequently, in *Überseering*, the Court observed:

> Überseering, which is validly incorporated in the Netherlands and has its registered office there, is entitled under Articles 43 EC and 48 EC to exercise its freedom of establishment in Germany as a company incorporated under Netherlands law. It is of little significance in that regard that, after the company was formed, all its shares were acquired by German nationals residing in Germany, since that has not caused Überseering to cease to be a legal person under Netherlands law.
>
> Indeed, its very existence is inseparable from its status as a company incorporated under Netherlands law since, as the Court has observed, *a*

25. See W. Schön, 'The Mobility of Companies in Europe and the Organizational Freedom of Company Founders', *ECFR* (2006): 136.
    In the literature, this element is also – similarly – defined as meaning that a company comes into existence as part of a specific legal order, that on formation the requirements of this legal order are complied with (the statutes/articles of association for instance, must meet the requirements), that the necessary entries in the central register, commercial register, or companies register take place according to the provisions of this legal order, and so forth. See P. Troberg & J. Tiedje, 'Artikel 48 EG', in *Kommentar zum Vertrag über die Europäische Union und zur Gründung der Europäischen Gemeinschaft*, ed. H. von der Groeben & J. Schwarze (Baden-Baden: Nomos, 2003), 1598 (no. 7): 'Die Gründung nach den Rechtsvorschriften eines Mitgliedstaates bedeutet, daß eine Gesellschaft (. . .) im Rahmen einer ganz bestimmten Rechtsordnung entsteht, daß bei der Gründung die Voraussetzungen dieser Rechtsordnung beachtet sind, daß zum Beispiel die Satzung deren Anforderungen entspricht und daß Registereintragungen nach den Bestimmungen eben dieses Rechts vorgenommen werden.' The authors add that the moment for testing whether a company is formed in accordance with the law of a Member State is that in which the company wants to exercise its right of establishment: 'Dabei ist von der Situation in demjenigen Zeitpunkt auszugehen, in dem von der Niederlassungsfreiheit Gebrauch gemacht werden soll.'
26. See J. Bröhmer, 'Artikel 48', in *Kommentar des Vertrages über die Europäische Union und des Vertrages zur Gründung der Europäischen Gemeinschaft – EUV/EGV –*, ed. C. Calliess & M. Ruffert (Neuwied/Kriftel: Luchterhand, 2002), 809: 'Art. 48 erfaßt nur solche Gesellschaften, die nach den Rechtsvorschriften eines Mitgliedstaates gegründet worden sind, d.h. die Existenz der Gesellschaft und ihre Grundstruktur müssen sich aus dem nationalen Recht eines Mitgliedstaates herleiten.'
27. *Daily Mail*, para. 19.

> *company exists only by virtue of the national legislation which determines its incorporation and functioning* (see, to that effect, Daily Mail and General Trust, paragraph 19).[28] (emphasis added).

Article 48 EC, so it could be argued in conclusion, leaves it thus, in principle, to the Member States to lay down rules for the incorporation and functioning of their own (national) companies. If a company does not respect these (mandatory) rules, it has no access to freedom of establishment. Moreover, forming a precondition for a company to have access to freedom of establishment, the rules at issue cannot be in breach of that company's right of establishment.[29] The Court's recent judgment in *Cartesio* may be argued to confirm this conclusion. The case which gave rise to this judgment concerned in particular the so-called connecting factor for companies; this issue will be dealt with in the next section, but in advance of that, it is already noted that the Court observed in *Cartesio*, in rather broad terms:

> in accordance with Article 48 EC, (...) the question whether Article 43 EC applies to a company which seeks to rely on the fundamental freedom enshrined in that article (...) is a preliminary matter which, as Community law now stands, can only be resolved by the applicable national law. In consequence, the question whether the company is faced with a restriction on the freedom of establishment, within the meaning of Article 43 EC, can arise only if it has been established, *in the light of the conditions laid down in Article 48 EC*, that the company actually has a right to that freedom.[30] (emphasis added).

This does not imply, in my view, that legislation on the incorporation and functioning of companies enjoys immunity from the rules of the EC Treaty on freedom of establishment.[31] It cannot be excluded, after all, that this legislation may be in breach of *other persons'* right of establishment (notably companies from other Member States).[32]

To conclude this subsection, let me make two final remarks as to the relevance of the requirement '*formed in accordance with the law* of a Member State' to the issue of the Community powers in the field of EC company law. First, notwithstanding that the Court of Justice in the case-law just dealt with accepted

28. *Überseering*, paras 80–81. See also, in this connection, T. Körber, *Grundfreiheiten und Privatrecht* (Tübingen: Mohr Siebeck, 2004), 292–293.
29. Even though Art. 43 EC prohibits not only restrictions on the freedom of establishment (in another Member State) on the part of *the host State*, but also those restrictions which are attributable to *the State of origin* (see *Daily Mail*, para. 16, and further G.-J. Vossestein, 'Exit restrictions on Freedom of Establishment after Marks & Spencer', *EBOR* 7 (2006): 863–878), the Treaty rules on freedom of establishment just do not apply; the company is not within the personal scope of those rules.
30. *Cartesio*, para. 109.
31. Cf. also *Cartesio*, paras 110–113.
32. The question which *Member State* legislation (on the incorporation and functioning of companies) precisely would be in breach of Art. 43 EC, as being – in itself – outside this book's scope, will not be pursued here. The issue of compatibility with Art. 43 EC of *Community legislation* (also on the incorporation and functioning of companies) is dealt with in Ch. 5.

that national law determines the incorporation and functioning of a company, it must be emphasized, I would argue, that the Court has not recognized, in some way, that Article 48 EC would constitute a reserve of legislative competence vested in the Member States which would preclude Community legislation in respect of incorporation and functioning of companies. Now, where the incorporation and functioning of a company are concerned, I would argue, Article 44(2)(g) EC in particular, may constitute a proper legal basis. In this context, it can be referred to, for instance, the First Company Law Directive, which contains, *inter alia*, provisions relating to the incorporation of a company.[33]

Second, the requirement, that a company must be 'formed in accordance with the law of a Member State' will be shown to be of relevance to the issue of compatibility of (provisions of the statutes for) Community legal forms with Article 43 EC. This is elaborated upon in Chapter 5.

b. Second Requirement: 'Registered Office, Central Administration or Principal Place of Business within the Community'

The *Second Requirement* for companies to be within the scope of the Treaty provisions on freedom of establishment is that they have their registered office, central administration, or principal place of business within the Community.[34]

In its case-law, the Court of Justice has referred to the registered office also as *siège statutaire*,[35] and to the central administration also as *siège réel*,[36] 'actual centre of administration'[37] or 'real head office'.[38] The Court has not further defined the principle place of business of Article 48 EC. In legal doctrine, however, the principle place of business is generally described as the place where the core of the company's economic, industrial, or commercial activity is situated and where the main part of the employees are deployed.[39]

33. See Art. 10–12 First Company Law Directive.
34. For a discussion of the varying interpretations these connecting factors are given in the Member States, see J. Rickford, 'Current Developments in European Law on the Restructuring of Companies: An Introduction', *EBLR* (2004): 1228–1231.
35. See *Cartesio*, para. 108.
36. *Ibid.*, paras 105 and 108.
37. See *Überseering*, para. 70.
38. See *Daily Mail*, para. 20. See also *Cartesio*, para. 105. For difficulties concerning the determination of the central administration which result from the use of modern communication technologies, such as videoconferencing, see e.g., U. Noack, 'Moderne Kommunikationsformen vor den Toren des Unternehmensrechts', *ZGR* (1998): 615–616; E. Wymeersch, 'The Use of ICT in Company Law Matters', in *Capital Markets in the Age of the Euro. Cross-Border Transactions, Listed Companies and Regulation*, ed. G. Ferrarini, K.J. Hopt & E. Wymeersch (The Hague: Kluwer Law International, 2002), 473–474 and 501; L. Enriques, 'Schweigen ist Gold: Die Europäische Aktiengesellschaft als Katalysator für regulative Arbitrage im Gesellschaftsrecht', *ZGR* (2004): 740.
39. Wouters, 147, with further references. See also Schwarz, 100–101. Stein describes the principal place of business similarly as: 'the place where the company maintains (. . .) the most important

The Court's long-standing explanation of the requirement under consideration is that the legislation of the Member States varies widely in regard to both the factor providing a connection to the national territory required for the incorporation of a company and the question whether a company incorporated under the legislation of a Member State may subsequently modify that connecting factor.[40] The EC Treaty, so says the Court, has taken account of that variety in national legislation. In defining, in Article 48 EC, the companies which enjoy the right of establishment, the Treaty places on the same footing, as connecting factors, the registered office, central administration, and principal place of business of a company.[41]

In its *Cartesio* judgment of December 2008, the Court has provided further clarifications on the requirement at issue, i.e., the condition of Article 48 EC that companies must have their registered office, central administration, or principal place of business within the Community. Being a judgment of exceeding importance, it merits particular attention. The facts and the dispute in the main proceedings will be dealt with first.

> Cartesio is a limited partnership under Hungarian law. It has two partners (both of whom are natural persons having Hungarian nationality): a limited partner, whose only commitment is to invest capital, and an unlimited partner, with unlimited liability for the company's debts. Cartesio is active, *inter alia*, in the field of human resources, secretarial activities, translation, teaching, and training. Cartesio's seat is established in Baja (Hungary). Cartesio is registered in the Hungarian commercial register. In November 2005, Cartesio filed an application with the Regional Court of Bács-Kiskun, sitting as a commercial court, for registration of the transfer of its seat to Gallarate (Italy) and, consequently, for amendment of the reference to its seat in the commercial register. That application was rejected on the ground that, under Hungarian law, a company incorporated in Hungary may not transfer its seat, as defined by the Law on the commercial register (i.e., the place where the company's central administration is situated),[42] abroad while continuing to be subject to Hungarian law as the law governing its articles of association.[43] Such a transfer would require, first, that the company cease to exist and then, that the company re-incorporate itself in compliance with the law of the country where it wishes to establish its new seat.[44] Cartesio lodged an appeal against that decision with the Court of Appeal of Szeged. In April 2006, then, the Court of Appeal asked the Court of Justice

portion of material means whereby it pursues its purpose'. See E. Stein, *Harmonization of European Company Laws. National Reform and Transnational Coordination* (Indianapolis: The Bobbs-Merrill Company, 1971), 28 (fn. 17).

40. *Daily Mail*, para. 20.
41. *Ibid.*, para. 21.
42. See *Cartesio*, para. 17.
43. *Ibid.*, para. 102. At para. 24 (in a similar context, discussing the dispute in the main proceedings), the Court had (still) referred to 'Hungarian law as its [the company's] *personal law*'. (emphasis added). The Court does not explain its changed choice of words in para. 102, but it may be related to the fact that Cartesio is a limited partnership.
44. *Cartesio*, paras 102–103. Obviously, this two-stage procedure would not result in '*such* a transfer'. The fact is, the company would not be a Hungarian company anymore (even though the firm's seat would have been transferred).

> whether Articles 43 EC and 48 EC are to be interpreted as precluding legislation of a Member State under which a company incorporated under the law of that Member State may not transfer its seat to another Member State whilst retaining its status as a company governed by the law of the Member State of incorporation.

In answering this preliminary question – in short: whether a Member State may preclude a transfer of the central administration (or 'seat') to another Member State – the Court emphasizes in particular the wording of Article 48 EC.[45] Because of their profound importance, the relevant paragraphs of the judgment are reproduced here *ad verbum*:

> [109] Consequently, in accordance with Article 48 EC, in the absence of a uniform Community law definition of the companies which may enjoy the right of establishment on the basis of a single connecting factor determining the national law applicable to a company, the question whether Article 43 EC applies to a company which seeks to rely on the fundamental freedom enshrined in that article – like the question whether a natural person is a national of a Member State, hence entitled to enjoy that freedom – is a preliminary matter which, as Community law now stands, can only be resolved by the applicable national law. In consequence, the question whether the company is faced with a restriction on the freedom of establishment, within the meaning of Article 43 EC, can arise only if it has been established, in the light of the conditions laid down in Article 48 EC, that the company actually has a right to that freedom.
> [110] Thus a Member State has the power to define both the connecting factor required of a company if it is to be regarded as incorporated under the law of that Member State and, as such, capable of enjoying the right of establishment, and that required if the company is to be able subsequently to maintain that status. That power includes the possibility for that Member State not to permit a company governed by its law to retain that status if the company intends to reorganise itself in another Member State by moving its seat to the territory of the latter, thereby breaking the connecting factor required under the national law of the Member State of incorporation.

So, *in the absence of a uniform Community law definition* in Article 48 EC *of the companies which enjoy the right of establishment* on the basis of a single connecting factor determining the national law applicable to a company, the question whether Article 43 EC applies to a company (which seeks to rely on that article) is a preliminary matter which, as Community law now stands, can only be resolved by the applicable national law. In the light of this, and in particular the Member State power of paragraph 110 (just quoted), the answer to the preliminary question is as follows. Articles 43 EC and 48 EC do not preclude legislation of a Member State under which a company incorporated under the law of that Member State may not transfer its 'seat' to another Member State whilst retaining its status as a

45. *Cartesio*, para. 108.

company governed by the law of the Member State of incorporation.[46] The fact that the power of the Member States at issue (in short, to preclude a transfer of seat) is closely related to the personal scope of freedom of establishment (does a company have the right of establishment?), as the Court emphasizes now so explicitly, had incidentally already been brought up by some in the literature.[47]

Now, to conclude this subsection, let me make two final remarks as to the relevance of the above to the issue of the Community powers in the field of EC company law. First, I would like to emphasize (again, as I did in the previous section with regard to the *first requirement* for companies to be within the scope of freedom of establishment), that the Court has not recognized that Article 48 EC would constitute some reserve of legislative competence vested in the Member States which would preclude Community legislation with respect to cross-border transfer of seat (with no change as regards the law which governs the company involved). Quite the opposite, according to the Court, the EC Treaty regards the differences in the legislation of the various Member States as regards the question whether – and, if so, how – the seat may be transferred from one Member State to another (as just described, so with retention of the status as a company under the law of the Member State of incorporation) as *a problem* which is not resolved by the rules concerning the right of establishment, but *which must be dealt with by future legislation.*[48] Where cross-border transfer of the seat is concerned, the initiative for the development of the integration process should therefore come from the Community legislature. The Court, however, observes in *Cartesio* that the legislation on the basis of Article 44 EC has not yet addressed the differences between the legislation of the various Member States as regards transfer of the seat and, accordingly, has not yet eradicated those differences.[49] As the Court

46. *Ibid.*, para. 124. What does the Court exactly mean by the word 'seat' in this connection? It includes, in any case, the central administration or real head office. After all, the dispute in the main proceedings concerned a transfer of the seat thus described (i.e., the place where a company's central administration is situated). Does it also include a transfer of the *registered office with retention of the status as a company governed by the law of the Member State of incorporation*? The answer to this question should in my view be affirmative. The fact is that the Court refers at para. 110 in broad terms to transfer of the 'seat' (not just the central administration); at para. 107 the transfer of the *registered office* of a company ('without losing its legal personality *under the law of the Member State of incorporation*') is equated with such a transfer of the central administration; and the grounds on which the Court bases its answer referred to in the main text seem to apply equally to a transfer of the *registered office* (see particularly, paras 107–109). For the Italian phenomenon of a transfer of the *registered office* with retention of the status as a company under the law of the Member State of incorporation, see F.M. Mucciarelli, 'The Transfer of the Registered Office and Forum-Shopping in International Insolvency Cases: an Important Decision from Italy – Case Note on the Decision "B & C" of the Italian Corte di Cassazione', *ECFR* (2005): 512–533; cf. M. Lamandini, 'Report from Italy', *ECL* (2006): 31–32.
47. See C.W.A. Timmermans, *Neue Rechtsprechung des Gerichtshofs der EG zum Europäischen Gesellschaftsrecht* (Zentrum für Europäisches Wirtschaftsrecht. Vorträge und Berichte, no. 132), Bonn: The members of the Zentrum 2003, 17; G.-J. Vossestein, 'Exit restrictions on Freedom of Establishment after Marks & Spencer', *EBOR* 7 (2006): 871–874.
48. *Cartesio*, para. 108 with references to earlier case-law.
49. *Ibid.*, para. 114.

further correctly observes, the absence of Community legislation in this field is not remedied in any way by the Community rules governing the transfer of the company seat to another Member State, laid down in the Regulations on the EEIG, on the SE or on the SCE. Such transfers necessarily entail a change as regards the national law applicable to the entity making such a transfer. In case of a cross-border transfer of seat of a company governed by the law of a Member State (with retention of its status as a company under the law of the Member State of incorporation), by contrast, there is no change as to the national law applicable. At present, there are no Community legislative initiatives to end the differences – existing or future – in the legislation of the various Member States as regards the question whether – and, if so, how – the seat may be transferred from one Member State to another (with retention of the status as a company under the law of the Member State of incorporation).

My second remark (as to the relevance of this section to the issue of Community legislation) is that the prohibition of Article 43 EC functions not only as a limit to national legislation, but also to EC company law, as will be shown below. It is in this connection that the Court's (above) interpretation of Article 43 EC (*juncto* Article 48 EC) is also of relevance to EC company law. The Court's *Cartesio* judgment may in particular be argued to be of importance to the lawfulness of the so-called real seat arrangement of the SE Regulation. This specific issue, as well as an analysis of various other provisions of EC company law in view of Article 43 EC, is dealt with in Chapter 5.

c. *Real and Continuous Link*

It is sometimes contended,[50] that the (second) requirement dealt with in the foregoing section (that companies must have their registered office, central administration, or principal place of business within the Community) has been modified by the 1961 General Programme for the abolition of restrictions on the freedom of establishment.[51] In this contention, Article 48 EC would require a company, in order to be capable of being considered in another Member State as a company entitled to freedom of establishment, to also have its actual centre of administration there (i.e., in the Member State of incorporation). Title I, Beneficiaries, of this General Programme provides:

> the persons entitled to benefit from the abolition of restrictions on freedom of establishment (. . .) are:
>
> – (. . .)
> – companies and firms formed under the law of a Member State (. . .) and having either the seat prescribed by their statutes, or their centre of

50. See the Spanish Government in *Überseering*, paras 32–33.
51. General Programme for the abolition of restrictions on freedom of establishment of 18 Dec. 1961, OJ Special Edition, Second Series, Jan. 1974 (IX Resolutions of the Council and of the Representatives of the Member States), 7–15.

administration, or their main establishment situated within the Community or in an overseas country or territory,
who wish to establish themselves in order to pursue activities as self-employed persons in a Member State;

- (...)
- companies and firms as above, provided that, where only the seat prescribed by their statutes is situated within the Community or in an overseas country or territory, *their activity shows a real and continuous link with the economy of a Member State* or of an overseas country or territory; such link shall not be one of nationality, whether of the members of the company or firm, or of the persons holding managerial or supervisory posts therein, or of the holders of the capital, who wish to set up agencies, branches or subsidiaries in a Member State. (emphasis added).

The Court rejects the above contention: it is apparent from the wording of the General Programme that it requires a 'real and continuous link' in a case in which a Member State company (that wants to set up agencies, branches, or subsidiaries) only has its registered office (but not its centre of administration or main establishment) within the Community.[52]

How does this real and continuous link requirement relate to Article 43 EC? Article 43 EC (*juncto* Article 48 EC) prohibits restrictions on the setting-up of agencies, branches, or subsidiaries 'by companies *established* in the territory of any Member State' and the General Programme makes clear what '*established*' means in this connection, namely, the presence of a 'real and continuous link'.[53] Instead of modifying the ('second') requirement, which was the subject of the previous section (i.e., that companies must have their registered office, central administration or principal place of business within the Community), the requirement of a real and continuous link, therefore, is rather a separate requirement. It is of relevance to the personal scope of freedom of establishment in that it further defines the persons entitled to benefit from *Article 43 EC*.[54] (The real and

52. The Court, to be precise, has held that: 'It is apparent from the wording of the General Programme that it requires a real and continuous link solely in a case in which the company has nothing but its registered office within the Community.' See *Überseering*, para. 75. The requirement thus defined obviously cannot be met; if a company has 'nothing but its registered office within the Community', there cannot be a real and continuous link either. In view of the system of the General Programme, in particular the second and fourth indent quoted in the main text, the Court's remarks can reasonably only be interpreted as they are in the main text. Überseering BV, incidentally, had both its registered office and actual centre of administration within the Community. See para. 75. The Court, however, left unresolved the question whether Überseering's centre of administration was situated in the Netherlands or in Germany. See para. 64.
53. In Case 71/76 *Thieffry* v *Conseil de l'Ordre des Avocats de la Cour de Paris* [1977] ECR 765, para. 14, the Court held that: 'In the context of the abolition of restrictions on freedom of establishment, that [General] Programme provides useful guidance for the implementation of the relevant provisions of the Treaty'. Here the 'useful guidance' relates to the term 'established' of Art. 43 EC. See also Wouters, 151; see further Edwards, 341.
54. Title I of the General Programme, as was mentioned, is 'Beneficiaries'.

continuous link requirement is entered into in more detail in Chapter 5, where the issue of how Article 43 EC functions as a limit to EC company law, is dealt with).

d. Brass-Plate Companies

With respect to the beneficiaries of the freedom of establishment, it should, finally, be noted that even so-called brass-plate companies may be within the scope *ratione personae* of this freedom.

A brass-plate company – as defined by the Court of Justice – is a company (formed under the law of a Member State) which lacks any real connection with the State of formation.[55]

The Court of Justice has consistently recognized that brass-plate companies may be within the scope of the Treaty provisions of freedom of establishment. It held, for example, in *Inspire Art*, that:

> it is immaterial, having regard to the application of the rules on freedom of establishment, that the company was formed in one Member State only for the purpose of establishing itself in a second Member State, where its main, or indeed entire, business is to be conducted.[56]

In this connection, the Court underlined that the reasons for which a company chooses to be formed in a particular Member State (including that of a more favourable legislation)[57] are irrelevant with regard to application of the rules on freedom of establishment.[58]

Finally, the fact that brass-plate companies lack any real connection *with the State of formation* does not mean that they cannot comply with the 'real and continuous link requirement' of the previous section, as this requirement only demands that the company in question has a certain link with the economy of 'a' Member State, not necessarily the State of formation.[59]

---

55. For this definition, see *Inspire Art*, para. 102.
56. *Inspire Art*, para. 95. Similarly Case 79/85 *Segers* v *Bedrijfsvereniging voor Bank- en Verzekeringswezen* [1986] ECR 2375, para. 16, and *Centros*, para. 17.
57. For this particular reason, see: *Centros*, para. 18 and *Inspire Art*, para. 96.
58. See: *Centros*, para. 18; *Inspire Art*, para. 95. The question of the application of the Treaty provisions on freedom of establishment is different from the question whether or not a Member State may adopt measures in order to prevent attempts by certain of its nationals improperly to evade domestic legislation by having recourse to the possibilities offered by the Treaty. See: *Centros*, para. 18 and *Inspire Art*, para. 98. Whereas the first question relates to the scope of the Treaty provisions on freedom of establishment, the latter question concerns the justification of a national measure which restricts the freedom of establishment. In *Inspire Art*, the latter question was even dealt with under a separate heading: 'Whether there is any justification'. See the text of the Court's ruling immediately preceding para. 106. See also, in this connection, the standard approach the Court of Justice has adopted in preliminary rulings concerning the interpretation of Art. 43 EC *jo.* 48 EC, which approach was described in s. A, *supra*.
59. See the italics in the quote of the 1961 General Programme (main text, s. c, *supra*).

3. The Concept of Companies and Firms: Article 48, paragraph 2 EC

A definition of the type of company and firm which may be beneficiaries of the right of establishment is contained in the second paragraph of Article 48 EC, which reads as follows:

> 'Companies or firms' means companies or firms constituted under civil or commercial law, including cooperative societies, and other legal persons governed by public or private law, save for those which are non-profit-making.

Excluded from the freedom of establishment are therefore legal persons which are non-profit-making. The Court confirmed in 1997, in *Sodemare*, that non-profit-making companies are excluded from the benefit of the chapter relating to the right of establishment.[60] With respect to the meaning of the words 'non-profit-making' *Commission v Belgium* of 1999[61] is of relevance, which now briefly deal with.

This infringement proceeding concerned a Belgian law which required the presence of a Belgian member in the administration of an association or a certain number of members of Belgian nationality in order for the legal personality of an association to be recognized. According to the Commission, this law was in breach of Article 6, paragraph 1 of the EC Treaty (now Article 12, paragraph 1 EC). Article 12, paragraph 1 EC reads as follows:

> Within the scope of application of this Treaty, and without prejudice to any special provisions contained therein, any discrimination on grounds of nationality shall be prohibited.

The Commission stated that:

> the national legislation at issue clearly falls within the scope of the EC Treaty [as required by Article 12 EC] even though it relates to non-profit-making associations. While those associations do not have the objective of maximising or redistributing profits, they may provide services in return for payment or receive income, thus participating in economic life. They are therefore governed by the Community rules on freedom of establishment.[62]

Advocate General Cosmas agreed with the Commission. He observed that:

> The second paragraph of Article 58 of the EC Treaty [now Article 48 EC], could be set against the above approach [i.e., the approach of the Commission]. Under that provision, the companies or firms covered by the right of establishment,

60. Case C-70/95 *Sodemare a.O.* v *Regione Lombardia* [1997] ECR I-3395, para. 25. In this connection the Court refers to Case 182/83 *Fearon* v *Irish Land Commission* [1984] ECR 3677, para. 8. This para. 8 (or other paras of *Fearon* for that matter), however, does not concern the issue of non-profit-making.

61. Case C-172/98 *Commission* v *Belgium* [1999] ECR I-3999.

62. See Opinion of AG Cosmas in *Commission* v *Belgium*, pt. 11. See also the *Commission* v *Belgium* ruling itself, para. 9.

> which is set out in Article 52 [now, after amendment, Article 43 EC], are not to be understood as including those which 'are non-profit-making'. However, in accordance with the prevailing view in Community law, the notion of a profit-making objective, as a purely Community law concept, must be construed broadly. Even legal persons whose main objective is not to increase their profits are covered by the right of establishment in so far as they participate in economic life.[63]

The Court subsequently ruled:

> It should be noted first of all that, under the first paragraph of Article 6 of the Treaty, any discrimination on grounds of nationality within the scope of application of the Treaty is prohibited.
>
> The Belgian Laws at issue regulate the right to form, in Belgium, associations with legal personality and nationals of the other Member States are among the persons to whom they apply. Those Laws thus affect *one of the fundamental freedoms* guaranteed by the Treaty and accordingly fall within its field of application.[64] (emphasis added).

Although the Court's words 'one of the fundamental freedoms guaranteed by the Treaty', are not elaborated upon further in the judgment, they apparently (in view of the Commission's and Advocate General's remarks) relate to 'freedom of establishment'. In my view, it may therefore be assumed that the Court adopted the view that even legal persons whose main objective is not to increase their profits are covered by the right of establishment insofar as they participate in economic life.

C. Scope *Ratione Materiae*

1. Introduction

The freedom of establishment provided for in Articles 43 EC to 48 EC includes, subject to the exceptions and conditions specified, the right to take up and pursue all types of self-employed activity in the territory of any other Member State,[65] to set up and manage undertakings, and to set up agencies, branches, or subsidiaries. As was mentioned above,[66] this is how the Court regularly summarizes the substantive scope of the Treaty provisions on freedom of establishment.[67]

63. Opinion, pt. 12. The Commission's and the AG's interpretation of 'non-profit-making' as only requiring the participation in economic life had, incidentally, already been pleaded by Wouters, 88–89.
64. *Commission* v *Belgium*, just cited, paras 11–12.
65. The right to take up and pursue all types of self-employed activity may be regarded as not so much concerning the establishment as such, but rather the exercise of a profession or business in connection with it. Cf. Lauwaars & Timmermans, 223.
66. See s. II.A, *supra*.
67. See e.g., Case C-79/01 *Payroll a.O.* [2002] ECR I-8923, para. 24, where it is referred to: Case C-55/94 *Gebhard* v *Consiglio dell'Ordine degli Avvocati e Procuratori di Milano*

The Court's summary is clearly based on Article 43 EC, which reads as follows:

> Within the framework of the provisions set out below, restrictions on the freedom of establishment of nationals of a Member State in the territory of another Member State shall be prohibited. Such prohibition shall also apply to restrictions on the *setting-up of agencies, branches or subsidiaries* by nationals of any Member State established in the territory of any Member State.
>
> Freedom of establishment shall include the right to take up and pursue activities as self-employed persons and *to set up and manage undertakings*, in particular companies or firms within the meaning of the second paragraph of Article 48, under the conditions laid down for its own nationals by the law of the country where such establishment is effected, subject to the provisions of the chapter relating to capital. (emphasis added).

Below, I will more closely look at various issues involving the scope *ratione materiae*.

I will first focus on the methods of exercise of the freedom of establishment for companies (s. 2). These methods are, as will be shown below, of great importance to EC company law. The right of establishment does not only concern the methods as such, but also all the aspects which are linked in any way in complementary or functional terms with them and thus the exercise in full of the freedom of establishment.[68] Two of these (related) aspects are the so-called right to leave (which concerns the – home – State of origin) and the subject of recognition of companies (which concerns the – host – State of establishment). These issues will be dealt with as well (in s. 3 and 4, respectively).

Before dealing with all this, let me remove a possible source of misunderstanding. It is regularly referred to a 'free movement of companies' in the literature,[69] apparently after the example of the free movement of natural persons. Natural persons – nationals of the Member States – do indeed enjoy such free movement. Union citizenship is the

---

[1995] ECR I-4165, para. 23; Case C-255/97 *Pfeiffer* [1999] ECR I-2835, para. 18. See further Case C-442/02 *CaixaBank France* [2004] ECR I-8961, para. 9.

68. Cf. Opinion of AG Tizzano in *Sevic*, pt. 32. See also pt. 29, where the AG notes that: 'in order to guarantee full enjoyment of the right of establishment, (...) the Court subjected to Articles 43 EC and 48 EC not only the national rules and practices relating directly and specifically to the pursuit of the economic activity in question but also all those "relating to the various general facilities which are of assistance in the pursuit of those activities"'. (fn. omitted).

69. See e.g., M. Andenas, 'Free Movement of Companies', *LQR* 119 (2003), 221–222; P. Dyrberg, 'Full free movement of companies in the European Community at last', *ELRev.* 28 (2003): 528–537; E. Wymeersch, 'The transfer of the company's seat in European company law', *CML Rev.* 40 (2003): 677, referring to 'free movement of legal entities' and 'free movement of legal persons'; S.F.G. Rammeloo, 'Vrij verkeer van rechtspersonen [free movement of legal persons; GJV] in Europa na HvJ EG Inspire Art Ltd.: zetelleercontroverse beslecht!', *NIPR* (2004): 283–295.

fundamental status of nationals of the Member States when they exercise their right of free movement (and residence).[70] Article 18(1) EC provides: 'Every citizen of the Union[71] shall have the right to move and reside freely within the territory of the Member States, subject to the limitations and conditions laid down in this Treaty and by the measures adopted to give it effect.' (footnote added). By contrast with natural persons, however, companies cannot rely on citizenship of the Union[72] and therefore do not have the (resultant) *right of free movement.*[73] This, incidentally, is also 'overlooked' by the Community legislature in the preamble to the SE Regulation, where it seems to assume that companies (too) are within the personal scope of Article 18 EC.[74] The *citizen's* free movement, in conclusion, does not add (anything) to *companies'* freedom of establishment.[75]

---

70. Recital 3 in the preamble to Directive 2004/38/EC of the European Parliament and of the Council of 29 Apr. 2004 on the right of citizens of the Union and their family members to move and reside freely within the territory of the Member States amending Regulation (EEC) No 1612/68 and repealing Directives 64/221/EEC, 68/360/EEC, 72/194/EEC, 73/148/EEC, 75/34/EEC, 75/35/EEC, 90/364/EEC, 90/365/EEC and 93/96/EEC, OJ 2004 L 158, 77–123. For a discussion of this Directive, see M.K. Bulterman & P.J. Slot, 'Harmonisatie van wetgeving betreffende migrerende EU-burgers en derdelanders: op weg naar een uniform toetsingskader?', *SEW* (2005): 346–362.
71. Article 17(1) EC provides, *inter al.*, that: 'Every person holding the nationality of a Member State shall be a citizen of the Union.' For a discussion of the Court's case-law on the Union citizen's right to move and reside freely (and the right to travel under the US Constitution as interpreted by the US Supreme Court), see C.W.A. Timmermans, 'Lifting the Veil of Union Citizen's Rights', in *Une communauté de droit. Festschrift für Gil Carlos Rodríguez Iglesias*, ed. N. Colneric et al. (Berlin: Berliner Wissenschafts-Verlag, 2003), 195–206.
72. Opinion of AG Kokott in Case C-470/04 *N.* v *Inspecteur van de Belastingdienst Oost/Kantoor Almelo* [2006] ECR I-7409, pt. 41. I agree with the AG that citizenship is assigned to natural persons only. This is clear from the rights conferred on citizens, e.g., the right to vote at municipal elections. I observe also that where Chapter V of the Charter of Fundamental Rights (which is about citizens' rights) confers rights on legal persons, these legal persons are explicitly mentioned besides citizens. See e.g., Art. 42 Charter which provides: 'Any citizen of the Union, and any natural or legal person residing or having its registered office in a Member State, has a right of access to European Parliament, Council and Commission documents.' I observe finally, that the Dutch text version of Art. 18(1) EC, refers to 'het recht vrij op het grondgebied van de lidstaten te *reizen*' (emphasis added), which may be translated as 'the right to travel freely within the territory of the Member States' instead of 'the right to move'.
73. This right of free movement is neither granted to companies in Directive 2004/38/EC, just mentioned. Further, Art. 43–48 EC which are concerned with rights of companies do not speak in terms of such a right.
74. See recital 4 in the preamble to the SE Regulation. It reads as follows: 'The legal framework within which business must be carried on in the Community is still based largely on national laws and therefore no longer corresponds to the economic framework within which it must develop if the objectives set out in Article 18 of the Treaty are to be achieved. That situation forms a considerable obstacle to the creation of groups of companies from different Member States.'
75. To the extent that 'free movement of companies' would link up with the heading of Part Three, Title III of the EC Treaty, above the Art. 39–48 EC, it can only refer to companies' *freedom of establishment* under Art. 43–48 EC.

2. Methods of Exercise of the Freedom of Establishment for Companies

a. Overview

Article 43, first paragraph EC mentions three methods of exercise of the freedom of establishment: the *setting-up* of *agencies*, *branches* and *subsidiaries*.[76] Two (additional) methods are laid down in Article 43, second paragraph EC:[77] the *setting up* and the *management* of *undertakings* (in particular *companies*).[78] The methods of exercise of the freedom of establishment given above are not defined in the Treaty.

As regards the methods of Article 43, first paragraph EC ('agencies', 'branches' and 'subsidiaries') the *opinio communis* is that subsidiaries have legal personality, whereas agencies and branches have not.[79] Agencies and branches are considered to differ in particular in that the management of the first has less autonomy than the management of the second.[80]

As to the (additional) methods of establishment of Article 43 EC, second paragraph EC ('the setting up and management of undertakings, in particular companies') it may be noted that, according to the doctrine, the 'management of undertakings or companies' may take place either directly (in case the laws of the host Member State allow the appointment of legal persons as a director) or indirectly (by means of a natural person who performs acts of management within the managed undertaking on behalf and account of the company which makes use of this form of establishment).[81] The 'setting up of undertakings or companies', then, is considered to overlap with the setting up of subsidiaries; the exact dividing line between the two methods of establishment is open to discussion.[82]

---

76. See, in this connection, *Daily Mail*, para. 17: 'In the case of a company, the right of establishment is generally exercised by the *setting-up of agencies, branches or subsidiaries*, as is expressly provided for in the second sentence of the first paragraph of Article 52 [now, after amendment, Art. 43 EC].' (emphasis added).
77. As was mentioned above, the right to take up and pursue all types of self-employed activity may be regarded as not so much concerning the establishment as such, but rather the exercise of a profession or business in connection with it.
78. See, in this connection, *Sevic*, para. 17: 'In accordance with the second paragraph of Article 43 EC, read in conjunction with Article 48 EC, the freedom of establishment for companies referred to in that latter article includes in particular the *formation* and *management* of those *companies* under the conditions defined by the legislation of the State of establishment for its own companies.'
79. See e.g., Opinion of AG La Pergola in *Centros*, pt. 15; Opinion of AG Tizzano in *Sevic*, pt. 38; Wouters, 191, and further (in particular about subsidiaries): 201–207; P. Troberg & J. Tiedje, 'Artikel 43 EG', in *Kommentar zum Vertrag über die Europäische Union und zur Gründung der Europäischen Gemeinschaft*, ed. H. von der Groeben & J. Schwarze (Baden-Baden: Nomos, 2003), 1490: 'Tochtergesellschaften sind durch ihre juristische Selbständigkeit charakterisiert (...). Die rechtlich unselbständigen sekundären Niederlassungen bezeichnet der Vertrag als "Agenturen" und "Zweigniederlassungen"'.
80. Wouters, 191, and further 191–201; Troberg & Tiedje, just cited, 1490.
81. Wouters, 208.
82. *Ibid.*, 21, and further 183 and 207.

The Court of Justice has given further guidance with respect to the methods of exercise of the freedom of establishment. Four particular methods are recognized in the Court's case-law: (taking part in the) incorporation of a company (*infra*, sub *b*); acquisition of shares (*infra*, sub *c*); cross-border merger operations (and 'other company transformation operations') (*infra*, sub *d*); and cross-border conversion (*infra*, sub *e*).[83]

b. Incorporation of a Company

The Court of Justice has explicitly acknowledged the (participation in the) incorporation of a company in another Member State as a method of exercise of the freedom of establishment. In *Daily Mail* the Court stated that:

> In the case of a company, the right of establishment is generally exercised by the *setting-up of agencies, branches or subsidiaries*, as is expressly provided for in the second sentence of the first paragraph of Article 52 [now, after amendment, Article 43 EC]. (...) A company may *also* exercise its right of establishment by *taking part in the incorporation of a company* in another Member State, and in that regard Article 221 of the Treaty [now, after amendment, Article 294 EC] ensures that it will receive the same treatment as nationals of that Member State as regards participation in the capital of the new company.[84] (emphasis added).

The quotation makes clear that this method of exercise of the freedom of establishment (i.e., taking part in the incorporation of a company) is recognized not as consequence of 'the right to set up agencies, branches or subsidiaries', but can be distinguished from it. Obviously, this method may be assumed to be included in '*the right to set up* and manage *undertakings*, in particular *companies*', of the second paragraph of Article 43 EC.[85]

---

83. Some argue that the list of 'forms of establishment' mentioned in Art. 43 EC is not exhaustive. See e.g., Opinion of AG Tizzano in *Sevic*, pt. 39 and Wouters, 183, both referring to Case 205/84 *Commission* v *Germany* [1986] ECR 3755, where the Court stated at para. 21 that: 'an insurance undertaking of another Member State which maintains a permanent presence in the Member State in question comes within the scope of the provisions of the Treaty on the right of establishment, even if that presence does not take the form of a branch or agency, but consists merely of an office managed by the undertaking's own staff or by a person who is independent but authorized to act on a permanent basis for the undertaking, as would be the case with an agency'. The problem with the argument just referred to, in my view, is that it does not take into account that the Court may have recognized this form or method of establishment as a consequence of 'the right to set up and manage undertakings', instead of 'the right to set up agencies, branches or subsidiaries'. This possibility is more plausible in my view than the conclusion that the Court of Justice has recognized (without any further explanation) a new form or method of establishment, in addition to those provided for in Art. 43 EC.
84. *Daily Mail*, para. 17. Art. 294 EC reads as follows: 'Member States shall accord nationals of the other Member States the same treatment as their own nationals as regards participation in the capital of companies or firms within the meaning of Article 48, without prejudice to the application of the other provisions of this Treaty.'
85. It should be realized, of course, that the delimitation of Art. 43, para. 2 EC ('the right to set up and manage undertakings, in particular companies') and Art. 43, para. 1 EC ('the right to

As regards the participation in the capital of the new company, referred to by the Court of Justice (at the end of the above quotation of *Daily Mail*),[86] let me note that it was already assumed in the doctrine that the shareholding should confer a certain influence over the company's decisions or activities in order for the (participation in the) incorporation to fall within the scope of the provisions on the freedom of establishment.[87] Along this line, in *Baars*, in 2000, the Court of Justice ruled as follows:

> Under Netherlands laws, a substantial holding, which is essentially a holding for the last five years of at least one third of the shares in a company and more than seven percent of paid-up nominal capital, *does not necessarily imply control or management of the company, which are factors connected with the exercise of the right of establishment*. Consequently, the fact that a Member State does not allow its taxpayers the undertaking exemption for a substantial holding, within the meaning of its domestic legislation, in companies established in other Member States does not necessarily affect freedom of establishment.
>
> However, the situation from which the main proceedings have arisen concerns a national of a Member State who resides in that Member State and who holds all the shares in a company established in another Member State. *A 100% holding in the capital of a company* having its seat in another Member State undoubtedly brings such a taxpayer within the scope of application of the Treaty provisions on the right of establishment.
>
> It is clear from the second paragraph of Article 52 of the Treaty [now, after amendment, Article 43 EC] that freedom of establishment includes the right to set up and manage undertakings, in particular companies or firms, in a Member State by a national of another Member State. So, a national of a Member State *who has a holding* in the capital of a company established in another Member State *which gives him definite influence over the company's decisions and allows him to determine its activities is exercising his right of establishment*.[88] (emphasis added).

Thus, the doctrinal view just referred to (that the shareholding at issue should confer a certain influence over the company's decisions or activities for the

---

set up agencies, branches or subsidiaries') is theoretical insomuch both 'rights' are within the scope of the Treaty provisions on freedom of establishment.

86. In the view of the Court, taking part in the incorporation of a company as a method of exercise of freedom of establishment goes together with participation in the capital.

87. See Wouters, 207–208 *jo.* 183–184, with further references, in particular to E. Steindorff, 'Konzentrationskontrolle und Niederlassungsfreiheit. Ein Beitrag zur Konsultationspflicht der Staaten nach Art. 5 EWGV', in *Festschrift zum 125jährigen Bestehen der Juristischen Gesellschaft zu Berlin*, ed. D. Wilke (Berlin/New York: De Gruyter, 1984), 791.

88. Case C-251/98 *Baars* [2000] ECR I-2787, paras 20–22.

In this connection, the AG referred to Annex I to Council Directive 88/361/EEC of 24 Jun. 1988 on the implementation of Art. 67 of the Treaty (OJ 1988 L 178, 5), which distinguishes between direct investments (Point I) and portfolio or financial investment (Point III et seq.). This Annex, of course, is given particular importance by the Court in its so-called golden shares judgments.

provisions on freedom of establishment to apply) seems to have been confirmed by the Court of Justice.

c. *Acquisition of Shares in an Existing Company*

The judgment of the Court of Justice in *Baars* is of importance for yet another reason. In particular, in view of the general wording of the last quoted paragraph (*supra*), the ruling seems to recognize (as a consequence of 'the right to set up and manage undertakings') another specific method of exercise of the freedom of establishment, namely the acquisition of shares in an *existing* company.[89] In any event, in *Überseering* the Court, referring to *Baars*, explicitly acknowledged that the acquisition of shares in an *existing* company may indeed constitute a(nother) method of exercise of the freedom of establishment.[90] The Court held:

> Furthermore, it must be borne in mind that as a general rule the acquisition by one or more natural persons residing in a Member State of shares in a company incorporated and established in another Member State is covered by the Treaty provisions on the free movement of capital, provided that the shareholding *does not confer on those natural persons definite influence over the company's decisions and does not allow them to determine its activities.*
>
> By contrast, where the acquisition involves all the shares in a company having its registered office in another Member State and *the shareholding confers a definite influence over the company's decisions and allows the shareholders to determine its activities*, it is the Treaty provisions on freedom of establishment which apply (see, to that effect, Case C-251/98 Baars [2000] ECR I-2787, paragraphs 21 and 22).[91] (emphasis added).

In conclusion, the acquisition of shares in an – existing – company of another Member State which shareholding confers a definite influence over the company's decisions and allows the shareholder to determine its activities, constitutes a method of exercise of the freedom of establishment.[92] Such an acquisition may be

89. To be precise, the paragraph last quoted in the main text does not explicitly mention the participation in the capital of an existing company. It just does not distinguish between participations in the capital of a new company or an existing one.
90. This ruling put Timmermans in the right. In view of *Daily Mail* he had already argued that the taking part in an *existing* company in another Member State (by means of an acquisition of shares) would have to be regarded as a form of establishment. See C.W.A. Timmermans (case note Daily Mail), *SEW* (1991): 70. Even before that, he had noted that a (successful) takeover bid for shares in a company of another Member State may be regarded as the exercise of the right of establishment. See C.W.A. Timmermans, 'Voorstel dertiende EEG-Richtlijn vennootschapsrecht betreffende het openbare bod', *TVVS* (1989): 150.
91. *Überseering*, para. 77.
92. Even though the Court refers to the acquisition of 'all the shares', the deciding factor seems to be, in particular, in view of the first part of para. 77, that the shareholding, in short, confers a definite influence. See also Case C-112/05 *Commission* v *Germany* ('Volkswagen') [2007] ECR I-8995, para. 13.

argued (in view of *Baars*) to be recognized as a consequence of 'the right to set up and manage undertakings, in particular companies'.[93]

d. Cross-Border Merger Operations (and 'Other Company Transformation Operations')

The Court of Justice's *Sevic* ruling of December 2005,[94] is another landmark judgment for companies' freedom of establishment. The Court of Justice decided, briefly, that the general refusal by a Member State to register a 'cross-border merger' in the commercial register, whereas such registration is possible for 'internal mergers', is contrary to Articles 43 EC and 48 EC. Within the context of this section, the Court's considerations on the scope of companies' freedom of establishment merit specific attention.[95] First, however, the facts and the dispute in the main proceedings will be dealt with briefly.

> A merger contract concluded in 2002 between Sevic AG, a company established in Germany, and Security Vision Concept SA, a company established in Luxembourg, provided for the dissolution without liquidation of the latter company and the transfer of the whole of its assets to Sevic AG. The German Amtsgericht Neuwied rejected the application for registration of the merger in the commercial register, arguing that the German law on the transformation of companies (*Umwandlungsgesetz*) provided only for mergers between legal entities established in Germany ('internal mergers') and that this law – therefore – did not apply to mergers between companies established in Germany and companies established in other Member States ('cross-border mergers').[96] In Germany, moreover, there were no general rules, analogous to those laid down by that law, which applied to cross-border mergers. Sevic AG brought an action against the decision by the Amtsgericht before the Landgericht Koblenz. That latter court asked the Court of Justice whether provisions such as the German provisions just referred to, are compatible with the Articles 43 EC and 48 EC.

The German Government and the Netherlands Government contended that Articles 43 EC and 48 EC do not apply to a (cross-border) merger such as that at issue in the main proceedings. In their view, that merger does not give rise to an 'establishment' within the meaning of the Treaty: the Luxembourg company is taken over by way of merger by a German company and consequently loses its

---

93. This conclusion gives rise to a complication in the delimitation of Art. 43, para. 2 EC ('the right to set up and manage undertakings, in particular companies') and Art. 43, para. 1 EC ('the right to set up agencies, branches or subsidiaries'). Since this complication is theoretical insomuch both the acquisition of shares as referred to in the main text and the 'acquisition' of a subsidiary, are within the scope of the Treaty provisions on freedom of establishment (Art. 43 EC, first and second paragraphs EC, resp.), it will not be elaborated upon.
94. Case C-411/03 *Sevic Systems* [2005] ECR I-10805.
95. Along established lines, (see e.g., *Überseering*) the Court, in *Sevic*, first examines whether the Treaty provisions on freedom of establishment *apply*, then, whether the national measure at issue constitutes a *restriction* (within the meaning of Art. 43, para. 1 EC) on this freedom and – finally – whether the restriction is *justified*. The first issue, to be clear, will be concentrated on here.
96. For the terms internal and cross-border merger, see *Sevic*, paras 12 and 9 resp.

legal personality. Since a dissolved company cannot, by definition, be 'established' in another Member State, so it was argued, the conditions for application of Articles 43 EC and 48 EC are not satisfied.[97]

The Court of Justice dismisses the arguments of the German and Netherlands Governments.[98] In this connection, the Court, however, does not go into the disputed establishment of the Luxembourg company in Germany (which would be the result of the merger). It regards the cross-border merger operation as such (which is concluded when both merging companies still exist) as a method of exercise of the freedom of establishment in respect of which Member States are required to comply with the freedom of establishment laid down by Article 43 EC.[99] The Court's approach brings with it, that the issue of whether the Luxembourg company (or German company for that matter) – as a result of the merger – will (actually) have an 'establishment', is not of relevance in this connection. The German – acquiring – company, incidentally, does seem to form an establishment in Luxembourg now that the Luxembourg company (which is being acquired) owned an undertaking in Luxembourg. The acquiring German company would thus have a branch (within the meaning of Article 43 EC) in Luxembourg.[100]

In its motivation of the decision that Articles 43 EC and 48 EC apply to a merger situation as that at issue in the main proceedings, the Court of Justice refers to the text of Article 43 EC read in conjunction with Article 48 EC. It emphasizes that freedom of establishment for companies 'includes in particular the formation and management' of companies within the meaning of Article 48 EC.[101] Although there is no 'formation' of a company in *Sevic*, apparently there seems to be a situation which qualifies as 'management'. In this respect, the following may have been of relevance. The merger between Sevic AG and Security Vision Concept SA is an intra-group merger. Sevic is the parent company; Security Vision Concept (the first letters of these words form the name SeViC) its subsidiary.[102]

Finally, three more specific aspects of the Court's ruling on the method of exercising freedom of establishment will now be entered into, which arguably show the broad reach of this ruling.

To begin with, the Court, discussing the applicability of Articles 43 EC and 48 EC to a merger such as that at issue in the main proceedings (a parent-subsidiary merger, more precisely an upstream merger), observes in broad terms that

97. For the observations submitted by Germany and the Netherlands, see the Opinion of AG Tizzano in *Sevic*, pts. 20–22.
98. *Sevic*, para. 16.
99. *Ibid.*, para. 19: 'Cross-border merger operations, like other company transformation operations, respond to the needs for cooperation and consolidation between companies established in different Member States. They constitute particular methods of exercise of the freedom of establishment.'
100. See, in this connection, the Opinion of AG Tizzano in *Sevic*, pts. 35–36.
101. *Sevic*, para. 17.
102. The fact that the case at issue concerns a parent-subsidiary merger (more precisely: an upstream merger), emerges from the report for the hearing ('*Sitzungsbericht*'), pt. 17. It is not reported in AG Tizzano's Opinion, nor in the Court's judgment.

'cross-border merger operations' constitute particular methods of exercise of the freedom of establishment.[103] In view of this, it may be assumed, in my opinion, that other types of (legal) merger, in particular merger by acquisition in general (i.e., not just the upstream merger) and merger by formation of a new company, are included as well and also must be regarded as 'particular methods of exercise of the freedom of establishment'.[104]

Secondly, even though the dispute before the national court concerned a merger between public limited-liability companies (a German AG and a Luxembourg SA), the preliminary question of the national court and the ruling of the Court of Justice in *Sevic* are not limited to these types of companies. With that, *Sevic* is also of relevance to cross-border mergers of other types of companies within the meaning of Article 48 EC, such as cooperatives, mutuals, foundations, and perhaps Community legal forms, too, such as the SE and SCE.[105]

Thirdly, in its considerations leading up to the conclusion just dealt with (that 'cross-border merger operations (. . .) constitute particular methods of exercise of the freedom of establishment') the Court puts cross-border mergers on a level with 'other company transformation operations'.[106] It could be inferred from this that these 'other (cross-border) transformation operations' as well, changes of legal form and demergers for instance, should also be considered as particular methods of exercise of the freedom of establishment. The fact is that the German law on the transformation of companies, which gave rise to the preliminary proceedings at issue, calls both examples – change of legal form and demerger – explicitly as forms of transformation.[107]

e. *Cross-Border Conversion*

The Court's *Cartesio* judgment of December 2008 is, as already indicated above, highly important to companies' freedom of establishment. First, the Court held that a Member State can prevent a company incorporated under its national law from transferring its seat to another Member State whilst retaining its status as a company governed by the law of the Member State of incorporation. This decision, together with the facts and the dispute in the main proceedings, were already discussed, to which discussion it is further referred.[108]

---

103. *Sevic*, para. 19, just quoted (in the fns).
104. The Third Directive distinguishes between: merger by acquisition (Ch. II of the Directive); merger by formation of a new company (Ch. III of the Directive) and merger by acquisition of one company by another which holds all of its shares (Ch. IV of the Directive).
105. The issue of companies within the meaning of Art. 48 EC, was dealt with above. See further G.-J. Vossestein, 'Companies' Freedom of Establishment after *Sevic*', *ECL* (2006): 177–182.
106. As stated, see *Sevic*, para. 19: 'Cross-border merger operations, *like other company transformation operations*, respond to the needs for cooperation and consolidation between companies established in different Member States. They constitute particular methods of exercise of the freedom of establishment.' (emphasis added).
107. See further: Vossestein, just cited; M.J.G.C. Raaijmakers, 'Sevic: grensoverschrijdende fusie binnen de EU', *AA* 55 (2006): 633–634.
108. See s. B.2.b, *supra*.

The second important decision in *Cartesio* is of particular relevance to the issue under discussion here, which is the methods of exercise of the freedom of establishment (for companies). This decision concerns the cross-border conversion of a company. In case of a cross-border conversion, a company governed by the law of one Member State moves to another Member State with an attendant change as regards the national law applicable; the company is converted into a form of company which is governed by the law of the Member State to which it has moved.[109] The essence of the operation is that the conversion of the company takes place without prior winding-up or liquidation.[110]

The Court decides that a Member State of incorporation may not prevent a company, by requiring its winding-up or liquidation, from converting into a company which is governed by the law of another Member State to the extent that it is permitted under that law to do so.[111] This would constitute a restriction on the freedom of establishment of the company concerned, which – unless it serves overriding requirements in the public interest – is prohibited under Article 43 EC.[112] This decision, including the underlying observations, covers only three paragraphs of the judgment.[113] The Court had not been asked to rule on cross-border conversion, but the ruling arguably also serves a better understanding of the issue that had in fact been brought before the Court (which concerned the cross-border transfer of seat, referred to at the beginning of this section).

Cartesio thus makes clear that cross-border conversion is within the substantive scope of freedom of establishment, even though the Court does not explicitly refer to it as a 'method of exercise of the freedom of establishment'[114] or an 'establishment operation'.[115] The standpoint that conversions are within the scope of freedom of establishment had, incidentally, already been taken (by some) in the literature.[116] It is noteworthy that in *Cartesio* the Court does not distinguish in this connection between cross-border conversion into a *comparable*

109. *Cartesio*, para. 111.
110. *Ibid.*, para. 113.
111. *Ibid.*, para. 112.
112. *Ibid.*, para. 113.
113. *Ibid.*, paras 111–113.
114. See for this term *Sevic*, para. 19. Moreover, in *Cartesio*, the Court neither refers to (one of) the methods of exercising freedom of establishment explicitly mentioned in Art. 43 EC.
115. See *Cartesio*, para. 122, where the Court stated that *Sevic* concerned an 'establishment operation' in another Member State by means of a cross-border merger. It could also be argued that cross-border conversion is to be considered as a 'cross-border transformation operation' (as discussed in the previous section) and, presumably, for that reason as a 'method of exercise of the freedom of establishment'. Cross-border conversion, finally, also may be argued to be included in the right to leave (which is discussed in the next section) and (also) for that reason to be within the substantive scope of freedom of establishment.
116. See e.g., Timmermans, who, discussing Art. 8 of the SE Regulation (which article concerns the transfer of the registered office of an SE), remarks at 10 that: 'the possible transfer of the seat [registered office] of a SE', '*is to be regarded as an exercise of the right of establishment*' (emphasis added).

type of company (e.g., of a private company into (again) a private company) or a *different* type of company (e.g., of a private company into a public company (or even a partnership)). It should not be excluded, therefore, that even this second, more drastic form of conversion is within the scope of the Treaty provisions on freedom of establishment.[117]

3. 'The Right to Leave'

The Court has stressed in *Daily Mail*, that even though the provisions of the Treaty guaranteeing freedom of establishment are directed mainly to ensuring that foreign nationals and companies are treated in the *host Member State* in the same way as nationals of that State, they also prohibit the *Member State of origin* from hindering the establishment in another Member State of one of its nationals or

---

117. Previous cases concerning conversion ('transfer of the registered office') were: Case C-86/00, *HSB-Wohnbau* [2001] ECR I-5353; and Case T-184/04 *Sulvida* v *Commission* [2005] ECR II-85. On procedural grounds the Community Courts did not rule substantively on such a transfer.

In *HSB-Wohnbau*, the Amtsgericht (Local Court) Heidelberg referred for a preliminary ruling two questions on the interpretation of Art. 43 EC and 48 EC. Those questions were raised in the context of an application by HSB-Wohnbau GmbH, a company incorporated under German law, for entry in the German commercial register of the transfer of its registered office to Spain, without changing the identity of the company. The Amtsgericht referred the following two questions for a preliminary ruling:

(1) does the transfer to Spain, with the company's identity being retained, of the registered office of a Gesellschaft mit beschränkter Haftung (GmbH, limited company) validly constituted under German law and registered in the German register, whose sole shareholder is a Spanish company, fall within the rights set out in Art. 43 EC and 48 EC?; and (2) do Art. 43 EC and 48 EC preclude a rule prohibiting the transfer to Spain, with the company's identity being retained, of the registered office of a Gesellschaft mit beschränkter Haftung (GmbH, limited company) validly constituted under German law and registered in the German register, whose sole shareholder is a Spanish company?

On procedural grounds, however, the Court held that it had no jurisdiction to rule on the questions put by the Amtsgericht.

In *Sulvida*, the Portuguese company Sulvida brought an action against the Commission for failure to act, seeking a declaration that the Commission would be required to adopt legislation authorizing and facilitating cross-border transfers of seats of companies and, in particular, to convert into a directive the 'proposal for a Fourteenth Company Law Directive of the European Parliament and of the Council on cross-border transfers of seats of companies with a change of the applicable law'.

Since the action had not been brought in conformity with, *inter al.*, the Statute of the Court of Justice, the application was dismissed as manifestly inadmissible.

The Court of First Instance considered, *obiter dictum*, that: 'a mere proposal for a directive, such as the applicant is demanding from the Commission, on cross-border transfers of seats of companies (. . .) would not be an act producing binding legal effects *vis-à-vis* third parties, but a purely intermediate preparatory measure. Such a measure is not a measure which may be the subject of an action for annulment under Article 230 EC, and the failure to adopt such a measure may likewise not be challenged by an action for failure to act under Article 232 EC'.

of a company incorporated under its legislation.[118] Following on this, the Court observed that:

> the rights guaranteed by Articles 52 et seq. [now Articles 43 et seq. EC] would be rendered meaningless if the Member State of origin could prohibit undertakings from *leaving* in order to establish themselves in another Member State. In regard to natural persons, *the right to leave* their territory for that purpose is expressly provided for in Directive 73/148.[119] (emphasis added).

The Court then elaborated upon this 'right to leave' in two ways. First, in case of an incorporation of a company in another Member State (a method of exercising freedom of establishment), the home Member State law (of the beneficiaries of the right of establishment) may not stand in the way of a (partial or total) transfer of activities to the new company. Such a transfer of activities is thus, in short, included in the right to leave.[120]

The Court's second elaboration in *Daily Mail* was, in short, that Articles 43 and 48 EC do not confer on companies incorporated under the law of a Member State a right to transfer their seat to another Member State. In other words, such a transfer of seat is *not* included in the right to leave. As was already dealt with above, in the section about the scope of freedom of establishment *ratione personae*,[121] the Court ruled in *Cartesio*, more specifically, that a Member State can prevent a company incorporated under its national law from transferring its seat to another Member State whilst retaining its status as a company governed by the law of the Member State of incorporation.[122] It was, incidentally, as stated,

118. *Daily Mail*, para. 16. See further G.-J. Vossestein, 'Exit restrictions on Freedom of Establishment after Marks & Spencer', *EBOR* 7 (2006): 863–878 (with further references to case-law on the right to leave in the field of taxation).

119. *Daily Mail*, para. 16. In this case the home Member State (United Kingdom) law required Treasury consent where a company sought to transfer its central management out of the United Kingdom while maintaining its legal personality and its status as a United Kingdom company. *Daily Mail*, para. 18. See also para. 17: 'In the case of a company, the right of establishment is generally exercised by the setting-up of agencies, branches or subsidiaries, as is expressly provided for in the second sentence of the first paragraph of Article 52. Indeed, that is the form of establishment in which the applicant engaged in this case by opening an investment management office in the Netherlands.'

120. See, to this effect, paras 16–18. The Court, to be precise, emphasized in this connection (with respect to the law of the home Member State in question, the United Kingdom), that 'it [does not] stand in the way of a partial or total transfer of the activities of a company incorporated in the United Kingdom to a company newly incorporated in another Member State, if necessary after winding-up and, consequently, the settlement of the tax position of the United Kingdom company'. See para. 18. Timmermans, incidentally, remarks that the Court obviously intended this: nor does it stand in the way of a transfer of the activities of a company incorporated in the United Kingdom to a company newly incorporated in another Member State, if necessary *followed by* (instead of *after*) winding-up of the United Kingdom company. See C.W.A. Timmermans (case note Daily Mail), *SEW* (1991): 70.

121. S. B, *supra*.

122. For a more elaborate discussion of the relationship in this respect between *Daily Mail*; *Überseering* and *Cartesio*, see G.-J. Vossestein, 'Cross-border transfer of seat and conversion

also explained in *Daily Mail*, that even so, directives on cross-border transfer of seat may be adopted on the basis of Article 54(3)(g) EEC (now Article 44(2)(g) EC).[123]

Let me finally make two remarks, particularly by way of illustration, on the Court's judgments in *Sevic* and (again) *Cartesio* (this time, however, on the Court's ruling in that case on 'conversion'). These judgments too may be said to involve the right to leave (or the Member State of origin's position). After the Court had explained in *Sevic*, that the cross-border merger operation is a particular method for exercising freedom of establishment – an issue extensively dealt with above – it considered:

> In so far as, under national rules, recourse to such a means of company transformation [merger] is not possible where one of the companies is established in a Member State other than the Federal Republic of Germany, German law establishes a difference in treatment between companies according to the internal or cross-border nature of the merger, which is likely to deter the exercise of the freedom of establishment [by foreign *and national companies*; GJV] laid down by the Treaty.
>
> Such a difference in treatment constitutes a restriction within the meaning of Articles 43 EC and 48 EC, which is contrary to the right of establishment.[124]

The Member State of origin too, so it may be inferred from *Sevic* in conclusion, may not hinder the exercise of freedom of establishment by means of a cross-border merger operation (where it allows, in short, internal mergers).[125] In *Cartesio*, as already explained, the Court held, in short, that a Member State of incorporation may not prevent a company from converting into a company which is governed by the law of another Member State (to the extent that it is permitted under that law to do so).[126] This would constitute a restriction on the freedom of establishment within the meaning of Article 43 EC. The Court explicitly referred to such a conversion as 'a situation where a company *moves* to another Member State',[127] the Member State of relocation.[128] In that case, the company, so it may be concluded, *leaves* its Member State of incorporation.

---

of companies under the EC Treaty provisions on freedom of establishment', *ECL* (2009) (forthcoming).

123. See, to that effect, *Daily Mail*, paras 21–23.
124. *Sevic*, paras 22–23.
125. For an analysis of *Sevic* from a Member State of origin perspective, see Vossestein, just cited, 863–878. Of course, *Sevic* can – and should – also be analyzed from the traditional ('host State') point of view, that is focusing on the question of whether legislation such as the German under consideration there, (also) restricts foreign (*in casu*: Luxembourg) companies' freedom of establishment. See, in that connection, G.-J. Vossestein, 'Companies' Freedom of Establishment after *Sevic*', *ECL* (2006): 177–182.
126. *Cartesio*, para. 112.
127. See *Cartesio*, para. 111.
128. *Ibid.*, para. 113.

4. Recognition of Companies

A final subject to be dealt with in the context of the substantive scope of freedom of establishment, is the long standing and much discussed[129] issue of recognition (by a host Member State) of companies from other Member States.

In *Überseering*, the Court made clear that a necessary *precondition* for the exercise of the freedom of establishment is the recognition of companies by any Member State in which they wish to establish themselves.[130] It subsequently elaborated on this, considering that where a company exercises its freedom of establishment in another Member State,[131] the question of recognition of its legal capacity and its capacity to be a party to legal proceedings in the Member State of establishment is within the scope of the Treaty provisions on freedom of establishment.[132]

Recognition of a company's legal capacity and its capacity to be a party to legal proceedings in the Member State of establishment (or host Member State), such as at issue in *Überseering*, is called recognition in a narrow sense.[133] There is also recognition in a broad sense, which encompasses both acknowledgement of a

---

129. See e.g., G. Beitzke, 'Anerkennung und Sitzverlegung von Gesellschaften und juristischen Personen im EWG-Bereich', *ZHR* (1965): 1–47; W.C.L. van der Grinten, 'Erkenning van vennootschappen en rechtspersonen in de Europese Economische Gemeenschap', *SEW* (1966): 201–210; B. Grossfeld, 'Die Anerkennung der Rechtsfähigkeit Juristischer Personen', *RabelsZ* 31 (1967): 1–50; B. Goldman, 'The Convention between the Member States of the European Economic Community on the Mutual Recognition of Companies and Legal Persons', *CML Rev.* 6 (1968–1969): 104–128; E. Stein, *Harmonization of European Company Laws*, The Bobbs-Merrill Company: Indianapolis (1971): 403–424; B. Grossfeld, 'Zur Geschichte der Anerkennungsproblematik bei Aktiengesellschaften', *RabelsZ* 38 (1974): 344–371; J.H. Diephuis & C.W.A. Timmermans, *Erkenning van vreemde vennootschappen en rechtspersonen* (Preadviezen [preliminary reports]), The Hague: Mededelingen van de Nederlandse Vereniging voor Internationaal Recht (no. 81), 1980; Edwards, 384–386; S. Rammeloo, *Corporations in Private International Law: A European Perspective* (Oxford: OUP, 2001); and more recently, as regards the Court's case-law, e.g., W.-H. Roth, 'Case-note on *Centros*', *CML Rev.* 37 (2000): 147–155; W.-H. Roth, 'From *Centros* to *Überseering*: Free Movement of Companies, Private International Law, and Community Law', *ICLQ* 52 (2003): 177–208.
130. *Überseering*, para. 59. Recognition, therefore, is not a specific *method of exercise of freedom* of establishment (it is a necessary *precondition for the exercise* of the freedom of establishment).
131. As to the form of establishment in the *Überseering* case, it is interesting to note that the Court explicitly left aside the matter whether there was a cross-border transfer of the central administration. See *Überseering*, para. 64. It could perhaps be argued that the Netherlands company Überseering had established itself in Germany through the acquisition of a piece of land in Germany which it used for business purposes (presumably the exploitation of a garage and motel; see *Überseering*, para. 6).
132. See *Überseering*, para. 73. The Court specified, that this is even the case when the company is found, under the law of the Member State of establishment (i.e., the host state), to have moved its actual centre of administration to that State.
133. For this term, see S. Rammeloo, 'The long and winding road towards freedom of establishment for legal persons in Europe', *MJ* (2003): 169–197.

company of another Member State as a 'legal being' *and* the acceptance of the home Member State law governing company matters.[134] As to the latter aspect (the acceptance of a company's home state law governing company matters), the Court's ruling in *Inspire Art* is of particular relevance.[135] The central considerations of the Court, in this respect, were that:

> The effect of the WFBV [Law on Formally Foreign Companies] is, in fact, that the Netherlands company-law rules on minimum capital and directors' liability are applied mandatorily to foreign companies such as Inspire Art when they carry on their activities exclusively, or almost exclusively, in the Netherlands.
>
> Creation of a branch in the Netherlands by companies of that kind is therefore subject to certain rules provided for by that State in respect of the formation of a limited-liability company. The legislation at issue in the case in the main proceedings, which requires the branch of such a company formed in accordance with the legislation of a Member State to comply with the rules of the State of establishment on share capital and directors' liability, has the effect of impeding the exercise by those companies of the freedom of establishment conferred by the Treaty.[136]

These considerations make it clear why the Treaty provisions on freedom of establishment apply (or why provisions such as the Netherlands rules under consideration are within the scope of these Treaty provisions). The Netherlands rules concern branches of companies incorporated under the law of another Member State and thus a particular method of exercise of the freedom of establishment (a method even explicitly mentioned in Article 43 EC).

After the Court has determined that the Treaty provisions on freedom of establishment apply, it examines whether the national measure under consideration constitutes a 'restriction' on freedom of establishment and whether such a restriction is 'justified'. The Court does not waste words in *Inspire Art* on the question whether the national law constitutes a 'restriction', as is clear from the last quoted paragraph.

The question, finally, whether the legislation at issue can be justified on one of the grounds set out in Article 46 EC or, failing that, by an overriding reason relating to the public interest (in particular protecting creditors, combating improper recourse to

134. *Ibid.*

135. See also *Überseering* in which the Court held at para. 72 that: 'despite the general terms in which paragraph 23 of *Daily Mail and General Trust* is cast, the Court did not intend to recognise a Member State as having the power, *vis-à-vis* companies validly incorporated in other Member States and found by it to have transferred their seat to its territory, to subject those companies' effective exercise in its territory of the freedom of establishment to compliance with its domestic company law'.

136. *Inspire Art*, paras 100–101. The Court states, in my view incorrectly, that Netherlands legislation requires 'the branch of such a company formed in accordance with the legislation of a Member State to comply with the rules of the State of establishment on share capital and directors' liability', where in fact it is the formally foreign company itself (or its directors) which has (have) to meet the requirements at issue. This becomes clear from paras 27 and 28 in particular where the relevant provisions of national law are discussed.

> freedom of establishment, and protecting both effective tax inspections and fairness in business dealings) is answered in the negative by the Court.[137]

The Court of Justice in *Inspire Art*, in conclusion, did not regard 'the acceptance of the home Member State law governing company matters' as a necessary precondition for the exercise of freedom of establishment as it did with respect to recognition in a narrow sense. Instead, the Court tied in with a specific form of establishment of Article 43 EC, the branch. It is in this 'indirect' way that the issue of 'the acceptance of the home Member State law governing company matters' is within the scope of the Treaty provisions on freedom of establishment.[138]

III. ARTICLE 44(1) EC: THE POWER TO ATTAIN FREEDOM OF ESTABLISHMENT

A. INTRODUCTION

To attain freedom of establishment, the Third Part of the EC Treaty contains in Title III, Chapter 2 ('Right of establishment') two instruments. First, there is the prohibition of Article 43 EC on restrictions on the freedom of establishment. Article 43 EC will especially be entered into in Chapter 5, where the issue of how this provision functions as a limit to EC company law is examined. The second instrument, provided by in particular Article 44 EC,[139] is the power of the Council and the European Parliament to attain freedom of establishment. As discussed previously, most of the Directives in the field of EC company law are based on Article 44 EC, more specifically, on Article 44(1) EC or Article 44(2)(g) EC.

Article 44 EC provides, in relevant part:

> 1. In order to attain freedom of establishment as regards a particular activity, the Council, acting in accordance with the procedure referred to in Article 251 and after consulting the Economic and Social Committee, shall act by means of directives.
> 2. The Council and the Commission shall carry out the duties devolving upon them under the preceding provisions, in particular:
>
> (...)
>
> (g) by coordinating to the necessary extent the safeguards which, for the protection of the interests of members and other, are required by Member States of companies or firms within the meaning of the second paragraph

137. See *Inspire Art*, para. 142.
138. The issue of mutual recognition is returned to in Ch. 5 (on the prohibition of Art. 43 EC as a limit to EC company law), where it is shown to be of particular importance for the question whether a *restriction* exists on (companies') freedom of establishment within the meaning of Art. 43 EC.
139. See also Art. 47 EC.

of Article 48 with a view to making such safeguards equivalent throughout the Community;

(h) (. . .).

The current section III will deal with Article 44(1) EC; the next section IV with Article 44(2)(g) EC. The structure of the current section III is as follows. First, the wording and function of Article 44(1) EC will be examined (s. B); this concerns, in short, the conditions for the use of Article 44(1) EC as a legal basis. Second, an analysis of EC company law modernization in view of these conditions will be presented (s. C); it will address the question whether these conditions are satisfied as regards the Directive on takeover bids, the Directive on cross-border mergers, the (now withdrawn) draft Directive on transfer of the registered office (conversion), and the Directive on shareholder rights, which are all (partly or also) based on Article 44(1) EC.

B. Wording and Function of Article 44(1) EC

1. 'In Order to Attain Freedom of Establishment . . . '

a. Function

It follows from the opening words of Article 44(1) EC ('In order to attain freedom of establishment . . . '), that this article confers on the Council and European Parliament the power to adopt directives in function of a specific objective, particularly to attain freedom of establishment.

This functional character brings with it, that the Community legislature is entrusted with a task under Article 44(1) EC to attain freedom of establishment. At the same time, however, this functional character brings with it a limit on the power to adopt directives: it is not a general power to regulate; directives based on Article 44(1) EC must be *instrumental* in attaining freedom of establishment. To construe this article as meaning that it vests in the Community legislature a general power to regulate, would not only be contrary to the express wording of the provision cited above, but it would also be incompatible with the principle embodied in Article 5 EC that the powers of the Community are limited to those specifically conferred on it.[140] For directives based on Article 44(2)(g) EC, which will be discussed below, the same applies.[141] What freedom of establishment – the

140. See, as regards Art. 95 EC and 47(2) EC, Case C-376/98 *Germany* v *Parliament and Council* ('Tobacco Advertizing') [2000] ECR I-8419, paras 83 and 87. On the principle of conferred powers: Ch. 1.

141. See e.g., Case C-122/96 *Saldanha and MTS Securities Corporation* v *Hiross* [1997] ECR I-5325, where the Court held that: 'Article 54(3)(g) [44(2)(g) EC] of the EC Treaty empowers the Council and the Commission, *for the purpose of giving effect to the freedom of establishment*, to coordinate to the necessary extent the safeguards (. . .) for the protection of the interests of members and others' (emphasis added). See also e.g., Edwards, 7; J. Wouters, 'European Company Law: Quo Vadis?', *CML Rev.* 37 (2000): 289–290.

objective of the functional power – encompasses, in particular for companies, was dealt with above.[142]

More can be said about this power to attain freedom of establishment. Historically, the Court has recognized two functions of the instruments provided in Article 54(1) and (2) EEC (now Article 44(1) EC):[143] first, the elimination during the transitional period of obstacles to freedom of establishment; and second, the introduction into the law of Member States of a set of provisions intended to facilitate the effective exercise of this freedom for the purpose of assisting economic and social interpenetration within the Community. More recently, in *Daihatsu*,[144] the Court referred to 'the objective of *abolishing restrictions* on freedom of establishment, which is assigned in very broad terms to the Council and the Commission by Article 54(1) and (2) of the Treaty',[145] and, as regards Article 54(3)(g) of the Treaty (now Article 44(2)(g) EC), pointed out that this article must also be read in the light of Article 3(1)(h) EC, which provides that the activities of the Community are to include the approximation of national laws to the extent required for the *functioning* of the common market.[146]

Within the framework of the Treaty provisions on freedom of establishment, directives based on Article 44(1) EC (and for that matter, Article 44(2)(g) EC) indeed do have two, closely-linked functions. First, in the words of *Daihatsu*, abolishing restrictions on the freedom of establishment. This instrument may be regarded as primarily concerned with the establishment of the internal market, as described by Article 3(1)(c) EC. Indeed, together with Article 43 EC, the power under Article 44(1) EC constitutes an elaboration of Article 3(1)(c) EC.[147] According to this last article, the activity of the Community shall include an internal market characterized by the abolition of obstacles, *inter alia*, to the free movement of persons (which includes freedom of establishment).[148]

Second, in the words of *Reyners*, the facilitation of the *effective* exercise of this freedom.[149] This instrument relates more to the functioning of the internal market. Although through the combined application of Articles 44(1) EC and 43 EC,

142. See s. II, *supra*.

143. See Case 2/74 *Reyners* v *Belgium* [1974] ECR 631, para. 21.

144. Case C-97/96 *Verband deutscher Daihatsu-Händler* v *Daihatsu Deutschland* [1997] ECR I-6843.

145. *Ibid.*, para. 21.

146. *Ibid.*, para. 18.

147. Similarly, in the area of free movement of goods, the Treaty provides for two instruments to abolish barriers to intra-State trade: the prohibitions of Art. 28 EC to 30 EC, and the power of the Community legislature under Art. 95 EC (see e.g., Opinion of AG Geelhoed in Case C-491/01 *British American Tobacco* [2002] ECR I-11453, pt. 146).

148. The phrase 'free movement of persons' is also used elsewhere in the Treaty. E.g., in the heading of Part Three, Title III of the EC Treaty, above Art. 39–48 EC and Art. 95(2) EC. For a discussion of these specific references to 'free movement of persons' (and their relationship to what is called 'free movement of companies'), see s. II.C.1, *supra*.

149. These terms give full meaning to the wording of Art. 44(1) EC (e.g., '*attain* freedom of establishment', '*verwezenlijken* van vrijheid van vestiging', '*Verwirklichung* der Niederlassungsfreiheit', '*réaliser* la liberté d'établissement', '*realizzare* la libertà di stabilimento').

barriers to inter-State trade may be removed and an internal market *established*, this does not guarantee that this market genuinely *functions* as a common market.[150] The use of Article 44(1) EC, to facilitate the effective exercise of freedom of establishment, may provide for this. The coordination of national safeguards, as expressly provided in Article 44(2)(g) EC, can also be read in this light.[151] As stated – and this must be emphasized – both functions are closely-related and some EC company law measures, as will be shown below, combine, in short, elements of elimination and facilitation.[152]

This double function – elimination and facilitation – now will be discussed in more detail.

b. *Elimination of Obstacles and Facilitation: Survey*

(1) Justified Restrictions: Creditors, Minority Shareholders, Employees

As stated, the first instrument for the Community legislature to attain freedom of establishment is the elimination of obstacles (to this freedom). Primarily, these obstacles will be 'restrictions' of freedom of establishment as referred to in Article 43 EC which are justified on one of the grounds set out in the Treaty itself, notably Article 46 EC, or by an overriding reason relating to the public interest.[153]

In its cases *Centros*, *Überseering*, and *Inspire Art*, the Court of Justice has recognized various overriding reasons relating to the public interest which are relevant in the area of company law: protection of creditors,[154] prevention of fraud,[155] protection of minority shareholders,[156] and protection of employees.[157]

Restrictions on the freedom of establishment justified by these reasons come within the reach of Article 44(1) EC. These obstacles (to freedom of establishment) will arguably not be eliminated by a directive which, in short, simply does away with the protection, but rather by a directive which substitutes Community-wide

150. Cf. Opinion of AG Geelhoed in *British American Tobacco*, just cited, pt. 147 and Ch. 1.
151. See *Daihatsu*, just cited, where the Court ruled at para. 18: 'It must be pointed out that Article 54(3)(g) must be read in the light not only of Articles 52 and 54 of the EC Treaty (. . .), but also of Article 3(h) of that Treaty, which provides that the activities of the Community are to include the approximation of national laws to the extent required for the *functioning* of the common market.' (emphasis added).
152. To the extent that they both attain freedom of establishment (the condition for the use of Art. 44 EC as a legal basis), it is not necessary to determine an exact dividing line between these two elements.
153. See, to this effect, Case C-168/98 *Luxemburg* v *Parliament and Council* [2000] ECR I-9131, para. 32. Cf. Opinion of AG Geelhoed in Case C-491/01 *British American Tobacco* [2002] ECR I-11453, pt. 103: 'National statutory measures to protect specific recognised public interests (. . .) constitute a prime example of measures which generate barriers.'
154. *Centros*, para. 35, *Überseering*, para. 92, *Inspire Art*, para. 132.
155. *Centros*, para. 38; see also Case 79/85 *Segers* v *Bedrijfsvereniging voor Bank- en Verzekeringswezen* [1986] ECR 2375, para. 17.
156. *Überseering*, para. 92.
157. *Ibid.*

protection of the public interest at issue, for the restrictive national measures.[158] An explanation of this method of elimination of obstacles has been provided by Advocate General Geelhoed (in the – in this respect comparable – context of free movement of goods). In his opinion in *British American Tobacco*, he noted:

> Proceeding on the assumption that a national measure (. . .) is justified by Article 30 EC, this will already mean that the barrier to trade exists. *In order to set aside this barrier to trade, the Community legislature is entitled to adopt measures by which it takes over from the national legislature the protection of the matter of public interest* (in casu, *public health). In other words, the realisation of the internal market may mean that a particular public interest – such as here public health – is dealt with at the level of the European Union.* In this the interest of the internal market is not yet the principal objective of a Community measure. The realisation of the internal market simply determines the level at which another public interest is safeguarded.[159] (emphasis added).

A directive, to conclude, may deal with these obstacles (i.e., justified restrictions on freedom of establishment) *ex post*, but, under circumstances, also *ex ante*, that is, to prevent the coming into being of such restrictions.[160]

(2) Non-justified Restrictions

The elimination of obstacles may, however, also concern other, non-justifiable restrictions. Even though these restrictions are prohibited by Article 43 EC and individuals may invoke this provision against national authorities (the so-called 'direct effect')[161] and the Commission may start an infringement procedure against a Member State which has failed to fulfil its obligations under Article 43 EC,[162] a directive under Article 44(1) EC may be a more effective means of eliminating the restrictions concerned. While, in short, 'direct effect' and the infringement procedure concern individual cases resulting from specific circumstances and measures in a particular Member State, a directive under Article 44(1) EC may on the other hand, by the introduction into the law of Member States of a set of similar provisions, be aimed at ensuring, in a general and systematic fashion, that all national

158. Cf. Case C-233/94 *Germany* v *Parliament and Council* ('Deposit Guarantees') [1997] ECR I-2405, in particular paras 17 and 41–44. See also J. Stuyck, 'European Consumer Law after the Treaty of Amsterdam: Consumer Policy In or Beyond the Internal Market?', *CML Rev.* 37 (2000): 392, who – in a similar connection – notes: 'If measures taken at the national level are legitimate, harmonization at the Community level becomes necessary'. Such directives, finally, may incidentally also contribute to the attainment of freedom of establishment by elimination of obstacles raised by the differences which exist between the Member States' laws.
159. Opinion of AG Geelhoed in *British American Tobacco*, just cited, pt. 106.
160. Cf. Case C-210/03 *Swedish Match* [2004] ECR I-11893, para. 30. For a discussion of, in brief, harmonization *ex ante*, see M. Seidel, 'Präventive Rechtsangleichung im Bereich des Gemeinsamen Marktes', *EuR* (2006): 26–45, 29 in particular.
161. Lenaerts & Van Nuffel, 702. On the question whether the Community institutions are bound by Art. 43 EC, see Ch. 5.
162. See Art. 226 EC.

legal systems correspond to the requirements of a genuine internal market in which the freedom of establishment is guaranteed.[163]

(3) Other Impediments: Transfer of the Seat and Conversion

May attainment of freedom of establishment also concern the elimination of 'obstacles' for which Article 43 EC does not provide a solution?[164]

From *Daily Mail* (as from *Überseering* and *Cartesio*), it seems to follow, as I will elaborate in a moment, that the answer to this question is affirmative as regards Article 44(2)(g) EC: the Community legislature arguably has the power under Article 44(2)(g) EC to take on such obstacles, at least insofar as it concerns the transfer of the seat. Now, if the Court of Justice indeed takes such a broad view of attainment of freedom of establishment *on the basis of Article 44(2)(g) EC*, it may not be excluded that the Court, as the case arises, will take a similar broad view as regards attainment of freedom of establishment *on the basis of Article 44(1) EC*.

I will now first address more closely the transfer of the seat as at issue in *Daily Mail*, *Überseering*, and *Cartesio* (*sub* a). Next, I will address the cross-border conversion as at issue in (again) *Cartesio* as a possible example of an impediment

---

163. Cf. Explanatory Memorandum to the Proposal for a Directive of the European Parliament and of the Council on services in the internal market, COM (2004) 2 final/3 of 5 Mar. 2004, 22–23, and Wouters, 246.

164. A somewhat similar question has arisen as regards Art. 95 EC vis-à-vis the free movement of goods (Art. 28 et seq. EC): Can the EC harmonize national rules falling outwith Art. 28 EC? The debate in the literature so far seems to be inconclusive. To some, the answer to this question is not clear (see e.g., S. Weatherill, 'European Private Law and the Constitutional Dimension', in *The Institutional Framework of European Private Law*, ed. F. Cafaggi (Oxford: OUP, 2006), 105 (discussing this in view of so-called confidence building measures in contract law, 103–106)). To others, one could read Case C-376/98 *Germany* v *Parliament and Council* ('Tobacco Advertizing') [2000] ECR I-8419, as meaning that harmonization would be limited to areas actually falling under Art. 28 EC (see K. Mortelmans, 'Verslag van de discussie', in *De EU: de interstatelijkheid voorbij?*, ed. E. Manunza & L. Senden (Nijmegen: Wolf Legal Publishers, 2006), 208–209). In a third view, Art. 95 EC may go beyond mere reaction to barriers of trade falling within the reach of Art. 28 EC (see J. Stuyck, 'Patterns of Justice in the European Constitutional Charter: Minimum Harmonisation in the Field of Consumer Law', in *Law and diffuse Interests in the European Legal Order: Liber Amicorum Norbert Reich*, ed. L. Krämer et al. (Baden-Baden: Nomos, 1997), 286 ('If (the application of) a particular national regulation of selling arrangements remains outside the ambit of Article 30 [of the EC Treaty], because it does not prevent market access, it may nevertheless be necessary for the achievement of the objectives of the internal market to harmonize the different national rules in the area concerned'); G. Davies, 'Can Selling Arrangements be Harmonized?', *EL Rev.* 30 (2005): 370; B.J. Drijber, 'De interstatelijkheid voorbij: een slotbeschouwing', in *De EU: de interstatelijkheid voorbij?*, just cited, 195). To make a *proviso* as to the similarity to which I referred at the beginning of this fn.: an important part of the above debate concerns the relation, if at all, between *Keck* (Joined Cases C-267/91 and C-268/91 [1993] ECR I-6097), which, as is well-known, limited the scope of Art. 28 EC, and Art. 95 EC (see further P.J. Slot & G. Straetmans, 'Harmonisatie van wetgeving in de EG', *TPR* (2003): 811–814). In the field of freedom of establishment, with which we are concerned, the Court of Justice has, so far, not made an express limitation like *Keck* to the scope of this freedom.

which, if the Court of Justice would follow the above broad view of Article 44(1) EC, may be addressed by this article (*sub* b).

a. First, with respect to transfer of the seat, it must be referred to the *Daily Mail, Überseering*, and *Cartesio* judgments discussed above.[165] It was established there, in short, that the Member States have far-reaching powers in respect of transfer of the seat. In particular, Articles 43 EC and 48 EC do not preclude legislation of a Member State under which a company incorporated under the law of that Member State may not transfer its seat to another Member State whilst retaining its status as a company governed by the law of the Member State of incorporation.

The EC Treaty regards the differences in the legislation of the various Member States as regards the question whether – and, if so, how – the seat may be transferred from one Member State to another (as just described, so with retention of the status as a company under the law of the Member State of incorporation) as *a problem which must be dealt with by future legislation or conventions.*[166] With regard to this 'future legislation or conventions', the Court, in *Daily Mail*, explicitly referred to not only the possibility of an agreement between the Member States on the basis of Article 220 EEC (now Article 293 EC), but also that of a directive on the basis of Article 54(3)(g) EEC (now Article 44(2)(g) EC).[167] So even though the differences in Member State legislation in the field of, in short, transfer of the seat are not resolved by Article 43 EC, the Community legislature does have the power under Article 44(2)(g) EC to take on these problems, ('obstacles') to freedom of establishment. (The Court in *Daily Mail*, incidentally, did not explain (or have to explain in view of the case before it), why the legal basis of a possible directive on transfer of the seat should be Article 44(2)(g) EC instead of Article 44(1) EC; nor did it enter into the question of how such a Directive would meet the terms of that (former) provision). A directive on cross-border transfer of the seat (*ex* Article 44(2)(g) EC) has not been adopted yet, an issue which came up in passing in *Cartesio*:

> following the judgments in *Daily Mail and General Trust* and *Überseering*, the developments in the field of company law envisaged in Articles 44(2)(g) EC and 293 EC, respectively, as pursued by means of legislation and agreements, have not as yet addressed the differences, referred to in those judgments, between the legislation of the various Member States and, accordingly, have not yet eradicated those differences.[168]

In any case, and this is of relevance here, such a (future) directive could be quoted as an example of attainment of freedom of establishment by means of elimination of problems, 'obstacles' for which Article 43 EC does not provide a solution.

165. See s. II.B.2.b, *supra*.
166. *Cartesio*, para. 108 with references to earlier case-law.
167. See, to that effect, *Daily Mail*, paras 21–23.
168. *Cartesio*, para. 114.

b. What now may be considered as a (further) impediment for which Article 43 EC provides no solution, but which may nonetheless, if the Court of Justice would follow the above broad view of Article 44(1) EC, be addressed by this Article 44(1) EC? The following example on cross-border conversions may be helpful. In *Cartesio*, which was discussed in more detail above, the Court held that a Member State of incorporation may not prevent a company, by requiring its winding-up or liquidation, from converting into a company which is governed by the law of another Member State *to the extent that it is permitted under that law to do so.*[169] This would constitute a restriction on the freedom of establishment of the company concerned, which – unless it serves overriding requirements in the public interest – is prohibited under Article 43 EC.[170] Now, where the Member State of relocation (and the Member State of incorporation) does (do) not permit such a conversion, there may be argued to exist an 'impediment' to freedom of establishment nevertheless (for which Article 43 EC does not provide a solution). The elimination of this type of obstacle may subsequently, in this view, be regarded as contributing to the attainment of freedom of establishment within the meaning of Article 44(1) EC. The fact is, cross-border conversion is within the substantive scope of freedom of establishment (and may constitute a method of exercise of the freedom of establishment).[171]

(4) Facilitating Effective Exercise of Freedom of Establishment

A further instrument to attain freedom of establishment is, as argued above, the introduction into the law of the Member States of a set of provisions intended to facilitate the effective exercise of this freedom for the purpose of assisting economic and social interpenetration within the Community.

This includes, first, the Community rules that try to resolve conflicts or disparities between national legal systems, by making the national rules 'compatible' with one another, in the sense of linking up the national arrangements.[172] This method of coordination has been followed in various, even nationally sensitive, sectors of law, such as direct taxation and social security legislation.[173] Examples

169. *Ibid.*, para. 112.
170. *Ibid.*, para. 113.
171. See s. II.C.2.e, *supra.*
172. See e.g., J. Rickford, 'Current developments in European law on the Restructuring of Companies: An introduction', *EBLR* (2004): 1232: 'some (. . .) legal relationships require (. . .) actual interlocking or coordination of two systems of laws – the result in one Member State has to be built on what is achieved in another. The laws need to be modified so that they work together, usually sequentially – something is done in Member State A (such as the dissolution of the "absorbed" company in a merger) which itself changes legal relations so as to enable a legal result to be achieved in Member State B (such as the registration of the new company, endowed with the combined undertaking of the merged companies)'. For this method of coordination, see further: Timmermans, 6; K. Mortelmans, 'The relationship between the Treaty rules and Community measures for the establishment and functioning of the internal market – towards a concordance rule', *CML Rev.* 39 (2002): 1310.
173. Timmermans, 6. With respect to direct taxation, Timmermans refers to Directive 90/434/EEC of 23 Jul. 1990 on the common system of taxation applicable to mergers, divisions, transfers of

in the field of company law include the Directive on cross-border mergers and the (now withdrawn) draft proposal for a Directive on transfer of the registered office (conversion).[174] What is at stake in these company law instruments is not so much a harmonization of substantive company law of the Member States, as a very topical harmonization limited to specifically cross-border situations.[175]

A second form of facilitation of the effective exercise of freedom of establishment is by means of coordination of a number of 'minimum requirements'. Or at least the coordination of the safeguards for the persons involved with the company, which is particularly addressed by Article 44(2)(g) EC, is argued to make it easier for companies to establish themselves in other Member States.[176] This will be taken up below.[177]

Related to the issue of 'other impediments' and 'facilitation', as just dealt with, I note that in my view, the Community legislature has the power under Article 44(1) EC (and, for that matter, Article 44(2)(g) EC) to enact measures promoting legal certainty and building confidence, provided it can be substantiated that lack of legal certainty or lack of trust (by companies, members, or others, in foreign, different legal regimes and foreign companies) genuinely hinders companies from exercising their right of establishment and the measures adopted actually lift these hindrances, and thus these grounds are not used as a mere pretence for a general power to regulate national company laws. This fits in with the above-discussed function of *giving effect* to the exercise of freedom of establishment.

In sum, attainment of freedom of establishment may, in short, encompass the elimination of restrictions and other impediments and the facilitation of the effective exercise of the right of establishment.

2. '...as Regards a Particular Activity'

Article 44(1) EC provides that 'In order to attain freedom of establishment as regards a particular activity', the Council shall act by means of directives. The previous section dealt with the component 'to attain freedom of establishment', this section will deal with the phrase 'as regards a particular activity'. This phrase may be regarded as a relic from the early years of the EEC, more precisely

---

assets, and exchanges of shares concerning companies of different Member States OJ 1990 L 225. With respect to social security legislation, he refers to Regulation (EEC) 1408/71 of the Council of 14 Jun. 1971 on the application of social security schemes to employed persons and their families moving within the Community, OJ 1971 L 149. This Regulation links up national arrangements, *inter al.*, by adding up insurance periods of time.

174. See s. II.C, *infra*.

175. See Timmermans, 6. See also: Rickford, just cited, 1232 and 1235; Lauwaars & Timmermans, 273.

176. Cf. Action Plan, 6 ('the harmonisation of a number of minimum requirements makes it easier for companies to establish themselves in other Member States where the regulatory framework is similar').

177. See s. IV, *infra*.

the so-called transitional period which ended 1969.[178] One of the objectives of the original chapter on the right of establishment in the EEC Treaty was to eliminate obstacles in the way of attaining freedom of establishment during the transitional period.[179] As is clear from the *Reyners* judgment,[180] it was for the purpose of this temporary objective that the Treaty had provided for a sectorial approach, in which directives 'intended to attain freedom of establishment in respect of the various activities in question' were central.[181] This relationship between the transitional period and the sectorial approach found expression through the General Programme for the abolition of restrictions on freedom of establishment,[182] adoption of which was required by Article 54(1), first paragraph EEC, before the end of the first stage of the transitional period. In accordance with Article 54(1), second paragraph EEC, the General Programme set out the conditions under which freedom of establishment was to be attained in the case of each type of activity per industry.[183]

Moreover, in *Daihatsu*, the Court of Justice ruled that Article 44(2) EC sets out a (non-exhaustive) list of measures to be taken in order to attain freedom of establishment within the meaning of Article 44(1) EC.[184] The measure of Article 44(2)(g) EC in particular, is formulated in such broad terms (coordination

---

178. Art. 8(1) EEC provided that:

> The common market shall be progressively established during a transitional period of twelve years. This transitional period shall be divided into three stages of four years each; the length of each stage may be altered in accordance with the provisions set out below.

The EEC Treaty entered into force on 1 Jan. 1958. The first stage ended on 31 Dec. 1961; the second on 31 Dec. 1965, and the third on 31 Dec. 1969. See further Lenaerts & Van Nuffel, 141.

179. See Art. 54(1) EEC and 52 EEC. The latter article provided that:

> Within the framework of the provisions set out below, restrictions on the freedom of establishment of nationals of a Member State in the territory of another Member State shall be abolished by progressive stages in the course of the transitional period. Such progressive abolition shall also apply to restrictions on the setting up of agencies, branches or subsidiaries by nationals of any Member State established in the territory of any Member State.
>
> Freedom of establishment shall include the right to take up and pursue activities as self-employed persons and to set up and manage undertakings, in particular companies or firms within the meaning of the second paragraph of Art. 58, under the conditions laid down for its own nationals by the law of the country where such establishment is effected, subject to the provisions of the Chapter relating to capital.

180. Case 2/74 *Reyners* v *Belgium* [1974] ECR 631.
181. *Reyners*, para. 19, and further paras 20–22.
182. General Programme for the abolition of restrictions on freedom of establishment of 18 Dec. 1961, OJ Special Edition, Second Series, Jan. 1974 (IX Resolutions of the Council and of the Representatives of the Member States), 7–15.
183. The categorization of these activities was based on the 'International Standard Industrial Classification of All Economic Activities (ISIC)' drawn up by the United Nations. See General Programme, Annex I to V (fn. 1).
184. Case C-97/96 *Verband deutscher Daihatsu-Händler* v *Daihatsu Deutschland* [1997] ECR I-6843, para. 21.

of safeguards for the protection of members and other) that it goes beyond the attainment of freedom of establishment just 'as regards a particular activity'.

In view of the above, it must be concluded that the phrase 'as regards a particular activity' may not be interpreted as limiting the Community legislature's power under Article 44(1) EC to adopt directives relating to 'a particular activity'. This conclusion may seem self-evident, which would explain that the issue of the meaning of the phrase 'as regards a particular activity' is rarely, if at all, dealt with in the literature. As to the significance of this conclusion, it must be noted that on the basis of the interpretation rejected here, the Directive on cross-border mergers for example, which is not confined to a specific sector, would be outside the scope of Article 44 EC.

3. Harmonization

Finally, Article 44(1) EC does not state as a condition that directives based on it must be aimed at the approximation or harmonization of the laws of the Member States. This, as opposed to Article 44(2)(g) EC (or Article 95 EC for that matter), which will be discussed hereafter.[185] Nevertheless, such a harmonization requirement is often – in my view mistakenly – read into Article 44 EC (i.e., in its entirety, including Article 44(1) EC).[186] The (practical) relevance of the absence of the said harmonization requirement will be returned to below, where the question whether Article 308 EC may be regarded as the proper legal basis for adoption of the Regulations concerning the European Economic Interest Grouping (EEIG), the SE and the SCE will be discussed.[187]

C. Analysis of EC Company Law Modernization in View of the Conditions of Article 44(1) EC

1. Introduction

The previous section dealt with the wording and function of Article 44(1) EC; it concerned, in short, the conditions for the use of Article 44(1) EC as a legal basis. The present section will address the question whether these conditions are

185. In this chapter's s. IV and the next chapter respectively.

186. See e.g., the Opinion of AG Stix-Hackl in Case C-436/03 *Parliament* v *Council* ('SCE Regulation') [2006] ECR I-3733 pts. 41–42: '[41] Recourse may be had to that provision [Art. 44 EC] *to approximate national company laws* (. . .). [42] However, *the coordination requirement* also creates a restriction as regards the creation of new forms under company law. Such legal measures could not therefore be based on Article 44 EC'. (emphasis added). In a fn. under pt. 42 of her Opinion the AG refers to, *inter al.*, 'Troberg/Tiedje, paragraph 27 on Article 44'; in this connection, it should, however, be noted that Troberg/Tiedje only discuss the coordination requirement within the context of Art. 44(2)(g) EC, not Art. 44 EC in its entirety.

187. See Ch. 4.

satisfied as regards the Directive on takeover bids, the Directive on cross-border mergers, the (now withdrawn) draft Directive on transfer of the registered office, and the Directive on shareholder rights, which are all (partly) based on Article 44(1) EC.[188]

As stated, Article 44(1) EC confers on the Council and European Parliament the power to adopt directives *to attain freedom of establishment*. Before discussing the question whether the Directives at issue satisfy the conditions for the use of Article 44(1) EC, or more generally Article 44 EC, first some words on the general background of these measures: in particular, the view of the Commission on EC company law modernization as expressed in its Action Plan on *Modernising Company Law and Enhancing Corporate Governance*.

As indicated above,[189] in its 2002 *Report on a modern regulatory framework for company law in Europe*, the High Level Group of Company Law Experts made its recommendations to modernize European Company Law. It noted that the harmonization exercise based on Article 44(2)(g) EC thus far had focused on the protection of members and third parties, in order to prevent a race to the bottom by Member States.[190] It then added that:

> In doing so, we may have lost sight of what the Group believes to be the primary purpose of company law: to provide a legal framework for those who wish to undertake business efficiently, in a way they consider to be best suited to attain success. Company law should first of all facilitate the running of efficient and competitive business enterprises.[191]

---

188. To be precise, the Directive on takeover bids is based on Art. 44(1) EC and 44(2)(g) EC, the Directive on cross-border mergers on Art. 44 EC, and the (now withdrawn) proposed Directive on cross-border transfer of the registered office on Art. 44(1) EC and 44(2)(g) EC. The Directive on shareholders' rights, to be analyzed last, is the only Directive (of the Directives mentioned in the main text) which is based also (namely in addition to Art. 44 EC) on Art. 95 EC.

    In implementation of the ACTION PLAN, there is also Directive 2006/68/EC of 6 Sep. 2006 (which amends the Second Directive) and Directive 2006/46/EC of 14 Jun. 2006 (which amends the Fourth and Seventh Directive). Both 2006 Directives are based on Art. 44(1) EC. Let me say that the choice of this specific legal basis is remarkable in view of the fact that the original (amended) Directives themselves have been based on Art. 54(3)(g) EEC (now Art. 44(2)(g) EC). The Community legislature does not provide an explanation for this. A factor (as far as the Second Directive is concerned) which may play role here is that Directive 2006/68/EC does away with certain procedures that were originally designed to protect the persons involved with the company and helps to (or is argued to help) improve companies' competitiveness and to cut their costs. In this connection, the European Economic and Social Committee distinguishes between 'genuine simplification', which does not alter the meaning or scope of existing provisions, and 'modifying simplification', which brings about a change to the protective nature of previous directives. See Opinion of the European Economic and Social Committee on the Proposal for the amending Directive, OJ 2005 C 294, 1. The 2006 Directive, in its view, may then concern 'genuine simplification'.

189. See Ch. 2.
190. HIGH LEVEL GROUP REPORT II, 29.
191. *Ibid.*

While it did 'not ignore (...) that protection of shareholders and creditors is an integral part of any company law',[192] the *High Level Group of Company Law Experts* saw this protection in function of the efficiency of company law: 'proper mechanisms for the protection of shareholders and creditors add to the efficiency of company law regulation, as they reduce the risks and costs involved for those who participate in and do business with companies'.[193]

The influence of the High Level Group's 2002 Report can be seen in the Commission's 2003 Action Plan, where the Commission identified two policy objectives that future actions at the European level in the area of company law seek as much as possible to meet: (i) strengthening shareholders rights and third party protection, and (ii) fostering efficiency and competitiveness of business. Although the Commission, in contrast to the High Level Group, first mentions the 'protection' objective, it, just like the High Level Group, saw the 'protection' objective as in function of business efficiency and competitiveness:

> A sound framework for protection of members and third parties, which properly achieves a high degree of confidence in business relationships, *is a fundamental condition for business efficiency and competitiveness*. In particular, an effective regime for the protection of shareholders and their rights, protecting the savings and pensions of millions of people and strengthening the foundations of capital markets for the long term in a context of diversified shareholding within the EU, is essential if companies are to raise capital at the lowest cost.[194] (emphasis added).

The Commission thus has expressed its view as to the preferred shaping of content of future action at a European level: action should foster business efficiency and competitiveness. The Commission at this point not only follows the *High Level Group of Company Law Experts*, but also company law literature which argues that enhancing efficiency should be the goal of company law, particularly by reducing so-called transaction and agency costs.[195]

While the Commission here focuses on what the Community legislature from a company law policy perspective *should* do, it does not reveal any close attention being paid to the prior question whether the Community legislature is *competent* to do so in the first place – that is, does the objective of fostering efficiency and

192. *Ibid.*
193. *Ibid.*, 30. Timmermans commented on the Report, mentioning that: 'What is perhaps missing in the Report is an analysis of what harmonisation is really needed for the purposes of the internal market.' See C.W.A. Timmermans, *Neue Rechtsprechung des Gerichtshofs der EG zum Europäischen Gesellschaftsrecht* (Zentrum für Europäisches Wirtschaftsrecht. Vorträge und Berichte, no. 132) (Bonn: The members of the Zentrum, 2003), 25.
194. Action Plan, 8.
195. H. Hansmann & R. Kraakman, 'What is Corporate Law?', in *The Anatomy of Corporate Law, A Comparative and Functional approach*, ed. R. Kraakman et al. (Oxford: OUP, 2004), 18 and fn. 32: 'The appropriate goal of corporate law is to advance aggregate welfare, (...) in the language of welfare economics as pursuing Kaldor-Hicks efficiency within acceptable patterns of distribution.'

competitiveness of business provide a ground at all for Community action?[196] If we analyze this objective in the light of Article 44(1) EC, and more generally Article 44 EC, I observe the following. The Community's power here is linked to integration: in order for the Community legislature to be competent on the basis of the above provisions to deal with national company law, it is required that its acts *attain freedom of establishment*. The above provisions thus do not confer on the Council and European Parliament the power to enact directives on the ground of fostering efficiency or competitiveness of business *per se*, without a contribution to attainment of freedom of establishment. Nor do these provisions, more generally, provide the Community legislature with a *general power* to deal with national company law as it sees fit, just based on its own technical perspective on company law, or based on its mere legislative policy preferences on the proper scope and objectives of company law in the Member States. (This is not to say that legislative policy views as to the proper purpose of company law (in this case fostering efficiency and competitiveness of business) may not inform the shaping of the content of a Community measure. In fact, they may, *provided* the Community legislature's competence to act has been established, that is, once it has been established that such a measure attains freedom of establishment[197]). In its Action

196. Observe that also in the area of contract law the Commission has shown a somewhat similar reticence in addressing its (or the Community legislature's) competence to act: see, particularly, S. Weatherill, 'Constitutional Issues – How Much is Best Left Unsaid?', in *The Harmonisation of European Contract Law: Implications for European Private Laws, Business and Legal Practice*, ed. S. Vogenauer & S. Weatherill (Oxford: Hart Publishing, 2006), 89–103 (giving three reasons why the Commission has preferred to set aside detailed inquiry into matters of competence in its various Communications on action to be taken in the field of contract law: (i) a tactical reason of preventing protest that it was revealing a predilection for a certain option (for future EC action in the field of contract law) aired in its Communications (this reason arguably does not apply to the Commission's Action Plan on Modernising Company Law which lacks a similar line of options to be debated); (ii) a now redundant reason: the possibility, at the time, of a Treaty revision, in view of the Laeken Declaration of 2001 inviting reconsideration of the role of Art. 95 EC and 308 EC (this might perhaps have been a consideration as regards the Commission's Action Plan on Modernising Company Law, which was published 21 May 2003. Shortly after this publication, however, in Jun. 2003, the Draft Constitutional Treaty retained both provisions. In fact, also the Lisbon Treaty retained these provisions unchanged); (iii) the major reason, that the answers as to when it is competent are very far from clear, particularly in view of the Court's *Tobacco Advertizing* judgment (Case C-376/98 *Germany* v *Parliament and Council* [2000] ECR I-8419). This also may have informed the Commission as regards its Action Plan on Modernising Company Law, even though in the field of company law Art. 95 EC is not the only (or even primary) legal basis for action, rather Art. 44(2)(g) EC has mostly been used. In my view, what (in addition) may explain the Commission's lack of detailed inquiry into matters of competence in its Action Plan on Modernising Company Law, is in fact perhaps less its uncertainty as to its competence, but rather its long-standing conviction that it has a broad competence under Art. 44(2)(g) EC to act in the field of company law (see *Rapport fait au nom de la Commission du marché intérieur, par M. Berkhouwer*, European Parliament Session 1966–1967 of 9 May 1966, Document 53, about which Ch. 2)).

197. Cf., in respect of Art. 95 EC, S. Weatherill, just cited, 93 and S. Weatherill, 'The Constitutional Competence of the EU to Deliver Social Justice', *ERCL* (2006): 143 (noting resp. that the

Plan, however, the Commission does not specifically address these competence issues. Its focus is (largely) on legislative policy goals without establishing its competence, if any, to pursue these goals.[198] Now, this means that if actual action, based on Article 44 EC, or Article 44(1) EC, would follow-up the Commission's Action Plan legislative policy goals without establishing a proper link with the attainment of freedom of establishment, such action would not satisfy the conditions for the use of the above articles and could be declared void or invalid. The next sections explore the question whether the measures following-up on the Action Plan which have been adopted on the basis of Article 44(1) EC or Article 44 EC satisfy the conditions for the use of these articles, and particularly whether these measures show a proper link with the attainment of freedom of establishment.

2. Directive on Takeover Bids: Breakthrough Rule

In April 2004, the Directive on takeover bids was adopted.[199] The legal basis for the Directive is formed by Article 44(1) EC *juncto* Article 44(2)(g) EC.[200] Article 44 EC, as was explained, requires that a directive based on it contributes to the attainment of freedom of establishment.

The preamble to the Directive explains as an objective that Member States must take the necessary measures to afford any 'offeror'[201] the possibility of acquiring *majority interests* in other companies and of *fully exercising control* of them.[202] This objective is within the substantive scope of freedom of

public health and social justice values may inform the shaping of the harmonization programme once it has been established before that a Community measure passes the threshold of contributing to improving the conditions for the establishment and functioning of the internal market). Competitiveness of the industry is explicitly mentioned in Art. 3(1)(m) EC and Art. 157 EC and can be taken into account by the Community legislature.

198. Where the ACTION PLAN does deal with a legal basis (Art. 44(2)(g) EC), 6, 1.1, it does not address the question whether it provides a base for its objective of fostering efficiency and competitiveness of business.

199. Directive 2004/25/EC of the European Parliament and of the Council of 21 Apr. 2004 on takeover bids, OJ 2004 L 142, 12.

200. See the first consideration of the Directive: 'Having regard to the Treaty establishing the European Community, and in particular Article 44(1) thereof.' The first recital in the preamble to the Directive subsequently refers to Art. 44(2)(g) of the Treaty, which is about the coordination of safeguards for the persons involved with the company. This aspect of the Directive will be returned to below. See s. IV.C.2.

201. 'Offeror' is defined in Art. 1(c) of the Directive as 'any natural or legal person governed by public or private law making a bid'.

202. See recital 19 in the preamble to the Directive. See also G. Kemperink & J. Stuyck, 'The Thirteenth Company Law Directive and Competing Bids', *CML Rev.* 45 (2008): 96, who observe that: 'When looking at the preamble of the Directive, it is difficult to perceive the objectives that are exactly pursued', but noting (at 98) that the objective seems to be 'the creation of a level playing field within the Community that enables EU companies and investors to freely *establish* themselves in a Member State through the *acquisition of control* of a listed company that is based in that particular Member State.' (emphasis added).

establishment. In this connection, it is important to recall the Court's case-law, according to which the acquisition of shares in an – existing – company of another Member State which shareholding confers a definite influence over the company's decisions and allows the shareholder to determine its activities, constitutes a method of exercise of the freedom of establishment.[203] How does the Directive, then, contribute to the 'attainment' of freedom of establishment?

Of particular relevance in this connection is Article 11 of the Directive, which contains the so-called breakthrough rule. The breakthrough rule may be considered as a key provision of the Directive.[204] This rule prescribes, in short, that restrictions on the transfer of securities, restrictions on voting rights, extraordinary appointment rights, and multiple voting rights are suspended at various moments during the takeover process.[205]

Assuming that such restrictions and rights constitute 'restrictions on the freedom of establishment' within the meaning of Article 43, paragraph 1 EC (whether justified or not),[206] they fall within the reach of Article 44 EC.[207]

On the other hand, assuming that these restrictions and rights do not fall within the scope of the prohibition of Article 43 EC[208] (the general opinion indeed seems

---

203. See s. II.C.2.c, *supra*.
204. See 'Report on the implementation of the Directive on Takeover Bids' (Commission Staff Working Document), SEC (2007) 268 of 21 Feb. 2007, 3.
205. See also recital nineteen in the preamble to the Directive. The Directive on takeover bids allows Member States *not to require* companies established within their territories *to apply* the provisions of the Directive rendering ineffective barriers, provided for in the articles of association or in specific agreements (the breakthrough rule of Art. 11). See Art. 12(1) Directive on takeover bids. The Member States must nevertheless allow companies established within their territories to make the choice, which must be reversible, to apply the breakthrough rule. In other words, companies must be allowed an opt-in. See Art. 12(2) Directive on takeover bids. In this light, G. Kemperink & J. Stuyck, 'The Thirteenth Company Law Directive and Competing Bids', *CML Rev.* 45 (2008): 112, observe that: 'The Directive is a further step in the EU company law harmonization process, but [that] it is clearly a compromise.' The Member State opt-out (and its effects) is returned to in Ch. 5.
206. In this context, it is interesting to take note of the Opinion of AG Poiares Maduro in Joined Cases C-282/04 and C-283/04 *Commission* v *Netherlands* ('KPN/TPG') [2006] ECR I-9141. In his Opinion, the AG raises the question whether legislation which enables some shareholders to obtain certain special rights in order to shield them from the market process, may itself constitute a restriction on the free movement of capital. He observes (pt. 23): 'Legislation of this type may restrict access to capital in the national market by protecting the position of certain operators who have acquired a stronghold in that market. Such operators, moreover, are likely to be domestic shareholders. Legislation of this kind may therefore hinder access to the national market for investors established in other Member States.' (fn. omitted). The question raised and the response of the AG, admittedly, concern free movement of capital, but a similar reasoning, it seems to me, could be followed with respect to freedom of establishment. For a recent discussion of the applicability of Art. 43 EC to barriers to takeovers, see Kemperink & Stuyck, just cited, 113–119.
207. See, to this effect, s. B.1.b, *supra*.
208. For a recent discussion of the applicability of Art. 43 EC to barriers to takeovers, see Kemperink & Stuyck, just cited, 113–119.

to be that (many) barriers to takeover bids do not fall within this scope[209] (on the basis that they are not created by the Member States, but by private persons on the basis of regular national company or contract law)), the question arises whether the Directive insofar 'attains freedom of establishment'. As I have argued above, attainment of freedom of establishment encompasses more than abolishing (justified) restrictions within the meaning of Article 43, paragraph 1 EC.[210] So, even if barriers to takeover bids would not constitute restrictions in the above sense, this does not automatically mean that they are outside the scope of the competence of Article 44(1) EC. The fact is, attainment of freedom of establishment may then be contributed to, by reason of the fact that the breakthrough rule may eliminate *impediments* to, in brief, 'the acquisition of shares of an existing company (which shareholding confers a definite influence)', a method of exercise of the freedom of establishment explicitly recognized by the Court of Justice. In view of all this, on this point, the Community legislature – so it can be argued – has correctly chosen Article 44(1) EC as the legal basis for this Directive.[211]

3. Directive on Cross-Border Mergers

In October 2005, the Directive on cross-border mergers of limited liability companies was adopted.[212] The legal basis for the Directive is Article 44 EC.[213]

---

209. See e.g., C.W.A. Timmermans, 'Chapter Ten (Takeovers-Discussion)', in *European Business Law. Legal and Economic Analyses on Integration and Harmonization*, ed. R.M. Buxbaum, G. Hertig, A. Hirsch & K.J. Hopt (Berlin/New York: Walter de Gruyter, 1991), 388–389; C.W.A. Timmermans, 'De joint venture naar komend EG-recht', in *Grensoverschrijdende samenwerking van ondernemingen*, ed. H.J.M.N. Honée et al. (Deventer: Kluwer, 1992), 69–70; J. Wouters, 'Het wetsvoorstel beschermingsconstructies in Europees perspectief', in *Het wetsvoorstel beschermingsconstructies* (preliminary report Vereeniging 'Handelsrecht' 1998) (Deventer: W.E.J. Tjeenk Willink, 1998), 99–103. Cf. also H. Fleischer, 'Case note Case C-367/98, *Commission of the European Communities v. Portuguese Republic* (Golden shares); C-483/99, *Commission of the European Communities v. French Republic* (Golden shares); and C-503/99, *Commission of the European Communities v. Kingdom of Belgium* (Golden shares), Judgments of the Full Court of 4 Jun. 2002', *CML Rev.* 40 (2003): 500, who remarks that fundamental freedoms are not primarily concerned with permissive rules between private market participants.

    As regards the issue in general of whether the so-called basic prohibitions for Member States of restrictions to free movement must be regarded as applying to private persons as well, it can be referred to, *inter al.*, Case C-281/98 *Angonese* [2000] ECR I-4139, para. 36, and, recently, Case C-438/05 *The International Transport Workers' Federation and the Finnish Seamen's Union* ('Viking') [2007] ECR I-10779; and, Case C-341/05 *Laval un Partneri* [2007] ECR I-11767, about which cases: Kemperink & Stuyck, just cited, 113–119.

210. See s. B.1.b, *supra*.
211. The fact that the Directive has been based also on Art. 44(2)(g) EC will be returned to in s. IV, *infra*, in which connection the mandatory bid rule of Art. 5 of the Directive in particular will be discussed.
212. Directive 2005/56/EC of the European Parliament and of the Council of 26 Oct. 2005 on cross-border mergers of limited liability companies, OJ 2005 L 310, 1.
213. See the opening consideration in the preamble to the Directive.

Article 44 EC, as was explained, requires that a directive based on it contributes to the attainment of freedom of establishment.

In its *Sevic* ruling of December 2005, the Court of Justice made clear that cross-border merger is a method of exercise of the freedom of establishment and that, as such, it falls within the scope *ratione materiae* of freedom of establishment.[214]

How does the Directive, then, contribute to the 'attainment' of freedom of establishment? The motivation of the Community legislature in this respect is rather curt and not very specific:

> There is a need for cooperation and consolidation between limited liability companies from different Member States. However, as regards cross-border mergers of limited liability companies, they encounter many legislative and administrative difficulties in the Community. It is therefore necessary, with a view to the completion and functioning of the single market, to lay down Community provisions to facilitate the carrying-out of cross-border mergers between various types of limited liability company governed by the laws of different Member States.[215]

I would emphasize, to begin with, that the Directive could be regarded as eliminating obstacles to freedom of establishment, more precisely, certain 'non-justified restrictions on freedom of establishment'.[216] Let me elaborate on this.

Cross-border mergers are within the scope of the Treaty provisions on freedom of establishment as a consequence of which restrictions of this method of exercise of the freedom of establishment are prohibited by Article 43 EC.[217] Even though these restrictions – such as the German Law on transforming companies in *Sevic* – are prohibited by Article 43 EC and individuals may invoke this provision both against Community and national authorities (the so-called direct effect) and the Commission may start an infringement procedure against a Member State which has failed to fulfil its obligations under Article 43 EC, the Directive may be seen as a more effective means of eliminating (many of) the restrictions concerned.[218]

---

214. See *Sevic*, paras 16–19 ('Applicability of Articles 43 EC and 48 EC'), para. 19 in particular. *Sevic* was discussed in s. II.C.2.d, *supra*.
215. Recital 1 in the preamble to the Directive.
216. May the Directive also be considered as eliminating restrictions of freedom of establishment as referred to in Art. 43 EC which are justified, in short, by an overriding reason relating to the public interest? (see s. B.1.b.(1), *supra*). I think this question must be answered in the affirmative. I have in mind particularly, the protection of employees under Art. 16 of the Directive. The Directive, incidentally, could have achieved perhaps a more far-reaching harmonization (as far as these justified restrictions are concerned), as is implied in the third recital in the preamble to the Directive: 'None of the provisions and formalities of national law, to which reference is made in this Directive, should introduce restrictions on freedom of establishment (. . .) save where these can be justified in accordance with the case-law of the Court of Justice and in particular by requirements of the general interest and are both necessary for, and proportionate to, the attainment of such overriding requirements.'
217. See *Sevic*, which was dealt with in s. II.C.2.d, *supra*.
218. It is referred here to '(many of) the restrictions' for the reason that the 'personal' scope of the Courts' *Sevic* ruling is wider than that of the Directive. Even though in *Sevic* the dispute before

While, in short, as was mentioned above, 'direct effect' and the infringement procedure concern individual cases resulting from specific circumstances and measures in a particular Member State, the Directive on the other hand, by the introduction into the law of Member States of a set of similar provisions, may be aimed at ensuring, in a general and systematic fashion, that all national legal systems correspond to the requirements of a genuine internal market in which the freedom of establishment is guaranteed.

The Directive should also, and I think especially, be seen as contributing to the attainment of freedom of establishment by means of introduction into the law of the Member States of a set of provisions 'facilitating the effective exercise of freedom of establishment', as discussed above.[219] In particular, the Directive aims to resolve conflicts or disparities between national legal systems, by making the national rules 'compatible' with one another, in the sense of linking up the national arrangements.[220] The Directive thus provides for 'coordination' relating to the specific problems cross-border mergers (which involve the application of several national legal systems in a single legal operation) pose.[221] Article 11 of the Directive (scrutiny of the legality of the cross-border merger) is a case in point:

> Focusing on another method of exercise of the freedom of establishment (than cross-border merger itself), the Directive may also facilitate the setting up of a branch. An acquiring company from Member State A may obtain through a merger with a disappearing company from Member State B an undertaking (a branch) in Member State B.[222] Therefore, also from this perspective, the Directive on cross-border mergers contributes to the facilitation of freedom of establishment.[223]

---

the national court concerned a merger between public limited-liability companies (a German AG and a Luxembourg SA), the preliminary question of the national court and the ruling of the Court of Justice are not limited to these types of companies. With that, *Sevic* is also of relevance to cross-border mergers of other types of companies within the meaning of Art. 48 EC, such as cooperatives, mutuals, foundations, and perhaps Community legal forms too, such as the SE and SCE. See s. II.C.2.d, *supra*.

219. See s. B.1.b.(4), *supra*. In this connection it is also referred to para. 26 of *Sevic*, where the Court held that: 'It should be noted in that respect [the Commission's proposal for a Directive on cross-border mergers] that, whilst Community harmonisation rules are useful *for facilitating cross-border mergers*, the existence of such harmonisation rules cannot be made a precondition for the implementation of the freedom of establishment laid down by Articles 43 EC and 48 EC.' (emphasis added).
220. Cf. Recital 15 in the preamble to the Directive, where, in the context of the principle of subsidiarity, 'the objective of the proposed action' – the Directive – is described as 'laying down rules with common features applicable at transnational level'.
221. Cf. *Sevic*, paras 24 and 27. For an extensive list of conflicts or disparities between national legal systems in this context, see H. Bungert, 'Grenzüberschreitende Verschmelzungsmobilität – Anmerkung zur Sevic-Entscheidung des EuGH', *BB* (2006): 55.
222. See in particular Opinion of AG Tizzano in *Sevic*, pts. 35–37.
223. It could further be argued that the cross-border merger by formation of a new company (see Art. 2(2)(b)) is to be regarded as an important means of incorporation of a company in another Member State, which the Court has explicitly acknowledged as a method of exercise of the freedom of establishment. Formation of a new company, as was explained above, is recognized by the Court as a consequence of 'the right to set up and manage undertakings, in

In view of the above, it must be concluded that Article 44 EC may indeed serve as a legal basis for the Directive on cross-border mergers.

4. Directive on Cross-Border Transfer of the Registered Office (Conversion)

Adoption of a Directive on cross-border transfer of the registered office of limited companies (the 'Fourteenth Company Law Directive') is part of the 2003 Commission Action Plan.[224] The Commission published an outline of the planned proposal (hereinafter also: draft proposal) in 2004.[225] The legal basis proposed for the Directive would be Article 44(1) EC and 44(2)(g) EC.[226]

---

particular companies'. See s. II.C.2.b, *supra*. From this perspective too, the Directive contributes to the facilitation of freedom of establishment.

Finally, there is the so-called upstream merger. This is the operation whereby a company, on being dissolved without going into liquidation, transfers all its assets and liabilities to the company holding all (or most of) the shares in its capital (see Art. 2(2)(c)). This type of cross-border merger could be said to contribute to the facilitation of freedom of establishment for the reason that it is conducive to a free choice between methods of exercise of the freedom of establishment. It is sometimes argued that such a free choice between the various methods of establishment must be possible. See, to this effect, Case 270/83 *Commission* v *France* ('Avoir Fiscal') [1986] ECR 273, para. 22. See also Case C-330/91 *Commerzbank* [1993] ECR I-4017, para. 13. Wouters, 210 refers in this connection even to a principle of free choice with respect to forms of establishment. For a similar view, see: W. Schön, 'The Free Choice Between the Right to Establish a Branch and to Set-up a Subsidiary – a Principle of European Business Law', *EBOR* 2 (2001): 339–364; Lauwaars & Timmermans, 222–223. This free choice is furthered, in that in case of an upstream merger, a subsidiary (a form of establishment) is converted into a branch (another form of establishment, provided, of course, that the subsidiary was not just an 'empty' company but ran an undertaking). This was in fact the case in *Sevic*.

224. See Ch. 2. The literature on (aspects of) cross-border transfer of the registered office includes, *inter al.*: J. Bisacre, 'The Migration of Companies within the European Union and the Proposed Fourteenth Company Law Directive', *ICCLJ* (2001): 251–270; F.M. Mucciarelli, 'The Transfer of the Registered Office and Forum-Shopping in International Insolvency Cases: an Important Decision from Italy – Case Note on the Decision "B & C" of the Italian Corte di Cassazione', *ECFR* (2005): 512–533; E. Vaccaro, 'Transfer of Seat and Freedom of Establishment in European Company Law', *EBLR* (2005): 1348–1365; S.M. van den Braak, 'Grensoverschrijdende omzetting van rechtspersonen', *WPNR* (2007): 688–693; M. Ventoruzzo, 'Cross-border Mergers, Change of Applicable Corporate Laws and Protection of Dissenting Shareholders: Withdrawal Rights under Italian Law', *ECFR* (2007): 47–75; E. Wymeersch, 'Is a Directive on Corporate Mobility Needed?', *EBOR* (2007): 161–169.

225. In Feb. 2004 the Commission launched an open consultation (that is to say, a consultation on the basis of an on-line, largely multiple choice questionnaire) on an outline of the planned proposal for a 'Directive on the right of limited companies to transfer their registered office from one Member State to another.' See IP/04/270 of 26 Feb. 2004 (Company law: Commission consults on the cross border transfer of companies' registered offices). The outline was not laid down in a separate consultation document. The outline was only published as an integrated part of the Commission's Internal Market website: <http://ec.europa.eu/internal_market>.

226. For the proposed legal basis, see outline, just cited, under 'Current framework', *sub* 3; and under 'Coordination Directive relating to transfers of registered offices', *sub* 1.

The Commission, however, decided not to proceed with the Directive in 2007.[227] This decision is rather remarkable[228] in view of the fact that adoption of the Directive was a short-term priority of the 2003 Action Plan; three consultations by the Commission (2003–2006) showed broad support for a Directive,[229] and the fact that the Directive still featured in the Commission Legislative and Work Programme 2007.[230] The Advisory Group on Corporate Governance and Company Law[231] – finally – also supported the initiative of a Directive on cross-border transfer.[232]

However, it cannot be ruled out, not even for the near future, that a proposal will after all be submitted and a Directive on cross-border transfer will be adopted. The last few years the European Parliament has repeatedly urged the Commission to submit a proposal[233] and the competent European Parliament Committees have continued their work on a Directive.[234] Moreover, the Court's recent *Cartesio* judgment, as will be shown below, may make adoption of a Directive an urgent matter.

---

227. SPEECH/07/592 of 3 Oct. 2007 (Speech by Commissioner McCreevy at the European Parliament's Legal Affairs Committee, Brussels).
228. I have examined the Commission's change in policy elsewhere and argued there that the reasons the Commission provided for not submitting a proposal for a Directive do not seem convincing. See G.-J. Vossestein, 'Transfer of the Registered Office. The European Commission's Decision not to Submit a Proposal for a Directive', *UL Rev.* (2008): 53–65.
229. Consultation on the Action Plan (2003), in which connection it can be referred to: Synthesis of the responses to the Communication of the Commission to the Council and the European Parliament 'Modernising Company Law and Enhancing Corporate Governance in the European Union – A Plan to Move Forward' – COM (2003) 284 final of 21 May 2003. A Working Document of DG Internal Market, 15 Nov. 2003, <http://ec.europa.eu/internal_market/>.

    Consultation on an outline for a Directive on transfer of the registered office (2004), IP/04/270, just cited.

    Consultation on future priorities for the Action Plan (Dec. 2005–Mar. 2006), in which connection it can be referred to: Directorate General for Internal Market and Services, Consultation and hearing on future priorities for the Action Plan on modernising company law and enhancing corporate governance in the European Union (summary report) of Jul. 2006, <http://ec.europa.eu/internal_market/>.
230. Commission Legislative and Work Programme 2007, COM (2006) 629 final of 24 Oct. 2006.
231. See Ch. 1.
232. See Advisory Group on Corporate Governance and Company Law, Minutes of the meeting of 27 Jan. 2006, 4, <http.//ec.europa.eu/internal_market/company/advisory/index_en.htm>.
233. European Parliament Resolution on restructuring and employment (P6_TA(2006)0088) of 15 Mar. 2006, pt. 13; European Parliament Resolution on recent developments and prospects in relation to company law, P6_TA(2006)0295 of 4 Jul. 2006 (OJ 2006 C 303 E/114), pts. 32–33; European Parliament Resolution on the European Private Company and the Fourteenth Company Law Directive on the transfer of the company seat, P6_TA-PROV(2007)0491 of 25 Oct. 2007, pts. 5 and 6. About these resolutions, of which the last postdates the Commission's decision not to submit a proposal, see Vossestein, just cited, 55–57.
234. See Committee on Legal Affairs, 'Draft Report with recommendations to the Commission on cross-border transfers of company seats', of 17 Oct. 2008, 2008/2196 (INI); Opinion of the Committee on Economic and Monetary Affairs for the Committee on Legal Affairs on Cross-border transfers of company seats of 7 Nov. 2008, also 2008/2196 (INI).

Before dealing with the question central to this section, namely whether a Directive on cross-border transfer of the registered office (conversion) may be adopted on the basis of Article 44(1) EC, let me first address the issue of what exactly constitutes such a transfer (or conversion). According to the 2004 draft proposal just mentioned, a company transferring its registered office would be registered in the host Member State and would 'acquire a legal identity or legal personality' there, while at the same time being removed from the register in its home Member State and giving up its legal identity (personality) there. If necessary, companies would have to adapt their structures and assets in order to meet the substantive and formal conditions required for registration in the host Member State. However, they would not be obliged to go through liquidation proceedings in their home Member State or to create a new company in the host Member State.[235] The essence of the transfer of a company's registered office would be that the applicable company law changes.[236] It should be noted, that the Commission, in describing transfer of the registered office, regularly refers to the 'acquisition of a legal identity or legal personality' in the host Member State. In my view, this expression is not entirely accurate for the operation the Commission has in mind. In case of a transfer of the registered office – as envisaged by the Commission – the company in question ceases to be a company under the law of the home Member State and becomes a company under the law of the host Member State. During this operation, legal personality is retained: the assets and liabilities of the legal person are not transferred in any way but remain belonging to it.[237] In other words, there is a change in nationality (of the legal form), not in the (identity of the) person as such.

To return now to the central question of this section: If the Commission would indeed submit a proposal and a Directive would be adopted (again, on the basis of Article 44(1) EC and 44(2)(g) EC), would such a Directive satisfy the requirement of Article 44(1) EC that it contributes to the attainment of freedom of establishment? Of particular relevance here is the Court's recent *Cartesio* judgment, which (also) concerns transfer of the registered office or in the wording of the Court 'conversion'. In *Cartesio*, the Court ruled, as explained,[238] that a Member State of incorporation may not prevent a company, by requiring its winding-up or liquidation, from converting into a company which is governed by the law of another Member State (so with an attendant change as regards the national law applicable) to the extent that it is permitted under that law to do so.[239] This would constitute a

235. See IP/04/270 of 26 Feb. 2004 (Company law: Commission consults on the cross border transfer of companies' registered offices), 1 and 2.
236. See outline, just cited, under 'A need felt by the market', *sub* 1 and 3; 'Current framework', *sub* 2.
237. As the Commission itself observed in the outline, just cited, under 'Coordination Directive relating to transfers of registered offices', *sub* 1(7): 'Transfer of the registered office (...) should not affect the company's legal relationships, whether active or passive, with third parties.'
238. See s. II.C.2.e, *supra*.
239. *Cartesio*, para. 112.

restriction on the freedom of establishment of the company concerned, which – unless it serves overriding requirements in the public interest – is prohibited under Article 43 EC.[240]

It is first of all clear, from *Cartesio* that cross-border transfer of the registered office or conversion is within the substantive scope of freedom of establishment.[241]

How would the Directive, next, contribute to the 'attainment' of freedom of establishment? The answer to this question is, to a certain extent, similar to that given above where the Directive on cross-border mergers was discussed. The future Directive, to begin with, could be regarded as eliminating obstacles to freedom of establishment, more precisely, certain 'non-justified restrictions on freedom of establishment'. In *Cartesio*, the Court in fact has made clear that a company may request, on certain conditions, a cross-border conversion relying directly on Articles 43 EC and 48 EC.

> As stated earlier, although restrictions on freedom of establishment are prohibited by Article 43 EC (*juncto* Article 48 EC) and individuals (companies) may invoke this provision both against Community and national authorities (the so-called direct effect) and the Commission may start an infringement procedure against a Member State which has failed to fulfil its obligations under Article 43 EC,[242] a Directive may be a more effective means of eliminating the restrictions concerned. While, in short, 'direct effect' and the infringement procedure concern individual cases resulting from specific circumstances and measures in a particular Member State, a Directive may be aimed, on the other hand, by the introduction into the law of Member States of a set of similar provisions, at ensuring, in a general and systematic fashion, that all national legal systems correspond to the requirements of a genuine internal market in which the freedom of establishment is guaranteed.

Furthermore, the attainment of freedom of establishment may also concern, in short, the elimination of 'obstacles' for which Article 43 EC does not provide a solution (as opposed to, in principle, the restrictions just dealt with). Since this issue was already discussed above (both in general and in respect of conversion), I can be brief. Where both the Member State of incorporation and that of relocation do not permit a conversion, there may be argued to exist an 'impediment' to freedom of establishment (nevertheless) for which Article 43 EC does not provide a solution. The elimination of this type of obstacle (by means of a provision in the Directive requiring all Member States to provide for a conversion) could subsequently be regarded as contributing to the attainment of freedom of establishment within the meaning of Article 44(1) EC.

Moreover, a future Directive may also be viewed as an example of introduction into the law of the Member States of a set of provisions 'facilitating the effective exercise of freedom of establishment', as discussed above.[243] In particular, the

240. *Ibid.*, para. 113.
241. For a more detailed discussion of the substantive scope of freedom of establishment and in particular conversions, see s. II.C.2.e, *supra*.
242. See Art. 226 EC et seq.
243. See s. B.1.b.(4).

Directive would resolve conflicts or disparities between national legal systems, by making the national rules 'compatible' with one another, in the sense of linking up the national arrangements.[244]

In conclusion, Article 44(1) EC may indeed serve as a legal basis for the Directive on cross-border transfer of the registered office (conversion). (The draft Directive submitted by the Commission also referred to Article 44(2)(g) EC. Where an EC company law instrument refers to Article 44(2)(g) EC as its legal basis, it should obviously meet the terms of that provision. These terms will be dealt with below, in s. IV).

5. Directive on Shareholder Rights

In July 2007, the Directive on the exercise of certain rights of shareholders in listed companies ('Directive on shareholder rights') was adopted.[245] The legal basis for the Directive is Article 44 EC and Article 95 EC.[246] Article 44 EC, as was explained, requires that a directive based on it contributes to the attainment of freedom of establishment. (The requirements of Article 95 EC will be dealt with below[247]). How does this Directive, then, contribute to the 'attainment of freedom of establishment'?

The motivation of the Community legislature in this respect is as follows. According to recital 14 in the preamble to this Directive, the objective of this Directive is 'to allow shareholders effectively to make use of their rights throughout the Community'. In the preamble, it is further argued that:

> *effective shareholder control is a prerequisite to sound corporate governance and should, therefore, be facilitated and encouraged.* It is therefore necessary to adopt measures to approximate the laws of the Member States to this end. Obstacles which deter shareholders from voting, such as making the exercise of voting rights subject to the blocking of shares during a certain period before the general meeting, should be removed.[248] (emphasis added).

The reference to sound corporate governance seems to follow the view of the *High Level Group of Company Law Experts* that: 'In a proper system of corporate

244. Focusing on another method of exercise of the freedom of establishment, a Directive on cross-border transfer of the registered office (conversion) also may facilitate the setting up of a branch. The setting up of a branch as method of exercise of the freedom of establishment, incidentally, was discussed above. See s. II.C. The fact is that in case of a cross-border transfer within the meaning of the draft proposal, the company in question becomes a company of another Member State, whereas the company's undertaking remains where it was (this may very well be the Member State where the company was originally incorporated). As a result of this, the undertaking is transformed into or qualifies as a branch (with a location in another Member State than that of the company itself).
245. Directive 2007/36/EC of the European Parliament and of the Council of 11 Jul. 2007 on the exercise of certain rights of shareholders in listed companies, OJ 2007 L184, 17–24.
246. See the opening consideration in the preamble to the Directive.
247. See Ch. 4.
248. Recital 3 in the preamble to the Directive.

governance, shareholders should have effective means to actively exercise influence over the company.'[249] And while the Directive, or its proposal, does not reiterate the additional statement of the *High Level Group of Company Law Experts* that 'shareholders need to be able to ensure that management pursues – and remains accountable to – their interests',[250] this may nonetheless have been the idea of the Commission's proposal: on occasion of the presentation of this proposal, *Internal Market and Services Commissioner* Charlie McCreevy indeed confirmed the need that management acts in the interests of shareholders:

> Shareholders need to be able to get relevant information on time and vote without encountering unnecessary obstacles, wherever they are in the EU. Otherwise they can't exercise their influence properly and make sure *that management is acting in their best interests.* Our proposals will introduce a range of key minimum standards to make this happen – using modern, reliable technology. All this will help to strengthen the role of shareholders and spread EU investing.[251] (emphasis added).

Returning to the above question, how does this Directive, then, contribute to the 'attainment of freedom of establishment'? In my view, it is not evident that the Community legislature has sufficiently established a link between the Directive and the freedom of establishment. The stated objective of the Directive – to allow shareholders effectively to make use of their rights throughout the Community – is not necessarily linked to the freedom of establishment. In effect, it should be noted that, as I have discussed above,[252] the Court of Justice has held that the acquisition (and use) of shares as a general rule is covered by the Treaty provisions on the free movement of capital (provided that the shareholding does not confer definite influence over the company's decisions and does not allow the shareholder to determine its activities).

Apart from the issue of insufficient explanation by the Community legislature (of how the Directive contributes – specifically – to freedom of establishment), it must be noted that, even if it is (otherwise) established that the Directive (also) seeks to enhance shareholdings allowing to exert a definite influence on the company's decisions and to determine its activities (which falls within the ambit *ratione materiae* of the provisions of the EC Treaty on freedom of

249. High Level Group Report II, 47. In the next sentence, the Report explained this as follows: 'As we emphasized in our Consultative Document, shareholders are the residual claimholders (they only receive payment once all creditors have been satisfied) and they are entitled to reap the benefits if the company prospers and are the first to suffer if it does not. *Shareholders need to be able to ensure that management pursues – and remains accountable to – their interests*. Shareholders focus on wealth creation and are therefore, in the Group's view, very suited to act as "watchdog" not only on their own behalf, but also, in normal circumstances, on behalf of other stakeholders.' (emphasis added).
250. See previous fn.
251. IP/06/10 of 10 Jan. 2006 (Corporate governance: Commission proposals to make it easier for shareholders to exercise their rights within the EU), 1.
252. See s. II.C.2.c.

establishment[253]),[254] it must still be concluded, as will be explained in Chapter 4 (where Article 95 EC – on which the Directive is also founded – is discussed), that contribution to free movement of capital seems to be the main or predominant purpose or component of the Directive. If it is assumed that this is the main or predominant purpose or component indeed, the Directive as a consequence (as will be explained there in Chapter 4 too), would, in short, have been based incorrectly also on Article 44 EC (instead of just Article 95 EC).

6. Conclusion

The previous section B concerned, in short, the conditions for the use of Article 44(1) EC as a legal basis. In the current section C, EC Company Law Modernization has been analyzed in view of these conditions.

First, the Commission's 2003 Action Plan has been examined. It was established that the Commission, in its Action Plan, does not specifically address these conditions or, more generally, competence issues. Its focus is (largely) on legislative policy goals without establishing its competence, if any, to pursue these goals.

Subsequently, the question was dealt with whether the measures following-up on the Action Plan which have been adopted on the basis of Article 44(1) EC (or Article 44 EC), satisfy the conditions for the use of these articles, and particularly whether these measures show a proper link with the attainment of freedom of establishment. It was found that most of the measures under consideration do contribute to freedom of establishment. Article 44(1) EC (or Article 44 EC) may thus indeed serve as a legal basis for the Directive on takeover bids and the Directive on cross-border mergers, as well as the Directive on cross-border transfer of the registered office (conversion). Regarding the Directive on shareholder rights, however, it was concluded (even apart from a lack of explanation by the Community legislature of how the Directive contributes – specifically – to freedom of establishment) that it may have been based incorrectly also on Article 44 EC (instead of just Article 95 EC).

---

253. See, to that effect, in particular: Case C-251/98 *Baars* [2000] ECR I-2787, para. 22, and Case C-112/05 *Commission* v *Germany* ('Volkswagen') [2007] ECR I-8995, para. 13; and s. II.C.2.c, *supra*.

254. It is questionable (indeed) whether the Directive seeks to enhance such shareholdings, in short, giving *control* of a company. This, in any case, as just explained, is not the stated objective of the Directive. Neither does its previous history make clear that the Directive pursues this purpose. The Directive, by contrast, does seem to be (predominantly) designed to protect *minority* (non-controlling) shareholders; this objective of the Directive (as will be explained in Ch. 4) is related to free movement of capital.

IV. ARTICLE 44(2)(G) EC: COORDINATION OF THE SAFEGUARDS FOR THE PERSONS INVOLVED WITH THE COMPANY

A. INTRODUCTION

Article 44(2)(g) EC is of specific relevance to EC company law: all the numbered company law Directives are based on this provision.[255] Article 44(2)(g) EC or, to be precise, Article 44(2), opening words and (g) EC provides:

> [2] The Council and the Commission shall carry out the duties devolving upon them under the preceding provisions, in particular:
>
> [(g)] by coordinating to the necessary extent the safeguards which, for the protection of the interests of members and other, are required by Member States of companies or firms within the meaning of the second paragraph of Article 48 with a view to making such safeguards equivalent throughout the Community;

The structure of the current section IV is as follows. First, it will deal with the wording and function of Article 44(2)(g) EC (s. B); this concerns, in short, the conditions for the use of Article 44(2)(g) EC as a legal basis. Second, it will address the question whether these conditions are satisfied as regards various Directives modernizing company law which are based on this article, particularly as regards the Directive on takeover bids and the Directive amending the Third and Sixth Directive (s. C).

B. WORDING AND FUNCTION OF ARTICLE 44(2)(G) EC

1. Wording of Article 44(2)(g) EC

a. *Introductory Remarks*

Before discussing the specific terms of Article 44(2)(g) EC, I shall make three more general remarks on this provision. First, it must be reiterated that Article 44(2)(g) EC is part of a non-exhaustive list of measures to be taken in order to attain freedom of establishment.[256] Even though – in consideration of this – it must be assumed that Article 44(2)(g) EC does not restrict the scope of

255. It should be added that the legal basis for the Eleventh Directive is Art. 54 EEC in general and Art. 54(3)(g) EEC in particular (now Art. 44 EC and Art. 44(2)(g) EC). See the opening consideration and the first recital in the preamble to this Directive. The legal basis for the Twelfth Directive, however, is Art. 54 EEC in general (now Art. 44 EC). See the opening consideration in the preamble to this Directive. For a list containing all numbered Directives, see Annex I.
256. See s. III.B.2.

Article 44(1) EC,[257] the provision can hardly be denied to have some indicative value for the purposes of determining whether a directive may contribute to the attainment of freedom of establishment. It indicates the kind of measures the authors of the Treaty primarily envisaged which the Council (and, later, Parliament) was competent to take. Of particular relevance in this connection is the fact that Article 44(2)(g) EC does not refer in general to the coordination of company law or even to the coordination of safeguards for the persons involved with a company, but the article refers specifically to 'the safeguards which, for the protection of the interests of members and other, are required by Member States of companies or firms within the meaning of the second paragraph of Article 48'.[258] Apparently, the issue of coordination of safeguards other than those mentioned in Article 44(2)(g) EC is not the first instrument to be considered to attain freedom of establishment.

My second more general remark is that where an EC company law instrument refers to Article 44(2)(g) EC as its legal basis, it should obviously meet the terms of that provision. If it does not, but nevertheless contributes to the attainment of freedom of establishment, it should refer to Article 44(1) EC.

As a final, more technical remark, before discussing the specific terms of Article 44(2)(g) EC, it should be noted that 44(2)(g) EC, in and of itself, does not seem to provide for a complete or perfect legal basis. It does not designate the competent institution, the decision making procedure to be followed, nor the type of instrument that may be used.[259] These elements are all included in Article 44(1) EC. In my view, the more correct reference to 'Article 44(2), opening words and (g) EC' (which opening words refer to the first paragraph of the article) would meet this objection. For ease of reference, however, I will refer to Article 44(2)(g) EC, instead of 'Article 44(2), opening words and (g) EC'.

b. Coordination

Article 44(2)(g) EC provides for the power to *coordinate* safeguards which are *required by Member States* of companies. Does the 'coordination'

---

257. In Case C-97/96 *Verband deutscher Daihatsu-Händler* v *Daihatsu Deutschland* [1997] ECR I-6843, the Court held at para. 21: 'Moreover, the objective of *abolishing restrictions* on freedom of establishment, which is assigned in very broad terms to the Council and the Commission by Article 54(1) and (2) of the Treaty, cannot be circumscribed by the provisions of Article 54(3). Article 54(3) merely sets out a non-exhaustive list of measures to be taken in order to attain that objective, as is borne out by the use in that provision of the words "in particular".' (emphasis added). It must be noted that Art. 54(3) not: 'merely sets out a non-exhaustive list of measures to be taken in order to attain that objective' (i.e., the objective of *abolishing restrictions*). This article is also intended to *facilitate the effective exercise* of freedom of establishment. See, to this effect, *Daihatsu*, para. 18.

258. For a discussion of the more limited scope of this coordination as against the coordination of 'safeguards for the persons involved with a company', see in particular s. e, *infra*.

259. See Ch. 1, and s. I, *supra*.

Article 44(2)(g) EC provides for also include 'complete harmonization'? In *Centros*, the Court of Justice ruled in this respect that:

> it is always open to the Council, on the basis of the powers conferred upon it by Article 54(3)(g) of the EC Treaty, to achieve complete harmonisation.[260]

Complete harmonization entails exhaustive regulation of a given field, the corollary being the pre-emption of national action in that area.[261] A case in point is the Eleventh Directive, which concerns disclosure requirements imposed in a Member State in respect of branches of companies from other Member States. In *Inspire Art*, the Court held at paragraph 69 that:

> It follows that (. . .) harmonisation of the disclosure to be made by branches, as brought about by the Eleventh Directive, is exhaustive, for only in that case can it attain the objective it pursues.

In view of this, the Court concluded that it is contrary to Article 2 of the Eleventh Directive for national legislation to impose on the branch of a company formed in accordance with the laws of another Member State disclosure obligations not provided for by that Directive.[262]

Now, according to *Centros*, Article 44(2)(g) EC allows for complete harmonization. Does Article 44(2)(g) EC also allow for unification? Complete harmonization may not be equated with unification.[263] Contrary to unification, with complete harmonization, differences between Member State laws remain possible, for instance because the directive concerned contains minimum solutions[264] or it leaves Member States the choice between alternative solutions.[265]

It is generally recognized that even though unification is not the purpose of the Treaty provision at issue here (this ensues both from the end result formulated: 'with a view to making such safeguards "equivalent"' as the instrument prescribed: the directive, which is binding as to the result to be achieved, leaves to the national authorities the choice of form and methods),[266] it is not excluded,

260. *Centros*, para. 28.

261. Craig & de Búrca, 626. See also Kapteyn & VerLoren van Themaat, 317. For a more elaborate discussion of complete harmonization, see P.J. Slot & G. Straetmans, 'Harmonisatie van wetgeving in de EG', *TPR* (2003): 722–726.

262. *Inspire Art*, para. 72.

263. For a discussion of the relationship between (complete) harmonization and unification, beyond the specific context of Art. 44 EC, see Slot & Straetmans, just cited, 712–714.

264. See e.g., Art. 2(2) Eleventh Directive, which contains a list of optional measures imposing disclosure requirements on branches. In this connection, it may be referred to *Inspire Art*, where the Court held at para. 70: 'It must likewise be pointed out that Article 2(1) of the Eleventh Directive is exhaustive in formulation. Moreover, Article 2(2) contains a list of optional measures imposing disclosure requirements on branches, a measure which can have no *raison d'être* unless the Member States are unable to provide for disclosure measures for branches other than those laid down in the text of that directive.' (emphasis added).

265. Lauwaars & Timmermans, 272.

266. For this definition of directives, see Art. 249, para. 3 EC.

either.[267] There are areas where in practice only unification will bring about the 'equivalence' just referred to. If it is sought, for instance, to protect shareholders and third parties by mandatory disclosure of the company's constitution then, since either a document requires disclosure or it does not, harmonization in this area will amount to the imposition of a uniform rule.[268]

c. '. . . to the Necessary Extent'

The second specific term of Article 44(2)(g) EC to be dealt with is that coordination within the meaning of this provision is only required 'to the necessary extent'. I shall make three remarks.

First of all, as will be elaborated upon below,[269] coordination of safeguards (let alone company law in general) is not an end in itself. The fact is, that in, for example, *Saldanha* the Court of Justice held, at paragraph 23, that Article 54(3)(g) EC Treaty (now Article 44(2)(g) EC):

> empowers the Council and the Commission, *for the purpose of giving effect to the freedom of establishment*, to coordinate to the necessary extent the safeguards.[270] (emphasis added).

Community legislation adopted under Article 44(2)(g) EC must therefore, as will further be elaborated below (s. 2 'Function of Article 44(2)(g) EC'), pursue the objective of attainment of freedom of establishment. The condition 'to the necessary extent', in my view has to be read in view of this objective. In order for this condition to be satisfied, it has to be clear that coordination is required for the genuine realization of the freedom of establishment.[271] Mere coordination of safeguards which does not contribute to the genuine realization of the freedom of establishment does not satisfy this condition.

Second, in connection with the specific term at issue, it must be stressed, that Article 44 EC only allows for the elimination of obstacles to freedom of establishment, not (also) freedom to provide services. This is the view held by Advocate General Stix-Hackl in the case of *European Parliament* v *Council*:

> A further restriction on the application of Article 44 EC lies in the fact that it enables only restrictions on freedom of establishment to be abolished, but not restrictions on freedom to provide services.[272]

---

267. See: P. Van Ommeslaghe, 'La première directive du conseil du 9 mars 1968 en matière de sociétés', *CDE* (1969): 517; C.W.A. Timmermans, 'De Harmonisatie van nationale voorschriften op het gebied van het vennootschapsrecht' (preliminary report Netherlands Association for European Law 1971), *SEW* 19 (1971): 620; R.H. Lauwaars & J.M. Maarleveld, *Harmonisatie van wetgeving in Europese organisaties* (Deventer: Kluwer, 1987), 241–242.
268. Edwards, 8. This was, incidentally, also noted in 1971 by Timmermans, just cited, 620.
269. See s. 2, *infra*.
270. Case C-122/96 *Saldanha and MTS Securities Corporation* v *Hiross* [1997] ECR I-5325.
271. Cf. Lauwaars & Maarleveld, just cited, 241.
272. Opinion of AG Stix-Hackl in Case C-436/03 *Parliament* v *Council* ('SCE Regulation') [2006] ECR I-3733, pt. 43. This view seems to be supported by Art. 55 EC. According to this

Even though it is only referred to the elimination of obstacles, it may be assumed that the same applies with respect to the facilitation of the effective exercise of this freedom.[273]

Third, it must be noted that the adoption of the SE Regulation in 2001 may have a bearing on the issue of 'necessity'. In this connection, I refer to Timmermans, who aptly remarks, that:

> the Statute [for a European company (SE)], for various important issues of company law (minority protection, liability of directors, for instance), simply refers to the national company law of the Member State of incorporation of the SE. This could be interpreted as establishing at least a *presumption of equivalence* between the national regimes on those issues. At any rate, existing differences have apparently not been considered so serious as to necessitate more harmonised results. If that is so, the need for harmonisation of national legislation on these issues for national companies *would not seem to be obvious*.[274] (emphasis added).

In short, the acceptance by the SE Regulation to such a large extent of existing divergences between national company laws, may plead against the necessity for any further harmonization in this field.

d. *Safeguards*

The next element to be discussed concerns the object of coordination: the 'safeguards' for the protection of persons involved with the company. EC company law instruments providing clear illustrations of coordination of 'safeguards' are – *inter alia* – the First Directive (disclosure, power of representation, validity of transactions entered into by companies), Second Directive (maintenance and alteration of capital) and Fourth Directive (presentation and content of annual accounts, valuation rules, and publication).

---

provision, Art. 45 EC to 48 EC are also applicable to the freedom of services; Art. 55 EC thus does not declare Art. 44 EC applicable to the freedom of services.

273. *Parliament* v *Council*, just cited, concerns the lawfulness of the SCE Regulation, in particular the question of whether the correct legal basis had been used. It is in this context that AG Stix-Hackl examines (briefly) whether the SCE Regulation could have been adopted on the basis of Art. 44 EC. In this connection, she notes explicitly, at pt. 44 of her Opinion, that the issue of transfer of seat (registered office) of the SCE concerns freedom of establishment (whereas other provisions in the SCE Regulation concern the other freedoms). The issue of transfer of seat of the SCE seems more concerned with facilitation of freedom of establishment, than with elimination of obstacles. It must be reiterated here that it is not necessary, in my view, to determine the exact dividing line between the two instruments. Both may be used to attain freedom of establishment. Moreover, some EC company law measures combine, in short, elimination and facilitation.

274. Timmermans, 8. See also: C.W.A. Timmermans, 'Europees vennootschapsrecht', *SEW* (2002): 250; C.W.A. Timmermans, *Neue Rechtsprechung des Gerichtshofs der EG zum Europäischen Gesellschaftsrecht* (Zentrum für Europäisches Wirtschaftsrecht. Vorträge und Berichte, no. 132) (Bonn: The members of the Zentrum, 2003), 22–23.

It is often contended that since all provisions in company law are aimed at protecting the persons involved with the company, the whole of company law is covered by the term 'safeguards' as included in Article 44(2)(g) EC.[275] This contention must be dismissed in my view. Admittedly, a large part of company law is about the protection of the interests of the persons involved with the company. At the same time, however, I should stress that company law is also about providing undertakings with restructuring facilities. The Directive on cross-border mergers and the (now withdrawn) draft proposal for a Directive on cross-border transfer of the registered office (conversion) are good examples.[276] One might argue that these (future) Directives would also coordinate 'safeguards', provisions for the protection of persons involved with the company.[277] Those safeguards, however, are – in principle – merely incidental upon the introduction of the corporate restructuring facility, which introduction is the main or predominant rationale of the Directives involved.

e. '...Required of Companies or Firms'

Article 44(2)(g) EC could have generally referred to the coordination of the safeguards for the protection of persons involved with the company (or firm), without further specifying the persons of whom those safeguards were required, the addressees of the safeguards. That, however, was not the choice of the Treaty drafters. Article 44(2)(g) EC carefully defines the addressee of the safeguards: companies (or firms).[278]

Therefore, in my view, safeguards required of others, for example, shareholders, are outside the scope. This is of practical relevance with respect to the mandatory bid rule, included in the Directive on takeover bids. This rule, which

---

275. See e.g., R.H. Lauwaars & J.M. Maarleveld, *Harmonisatie van wetgeving in Europese organisaties* (Deventer: Kluwer, 1987), 241; Edwards, 7. See also C.W.A. Timmermans, 'De Harmonisatie van nationale voorschriften op het gebied van het vennootschapsrecht' (preliminary report Netherlands Association for European Law 1971), *SEW* 19 (1971), 619. In 2002, however, Timmermans explicitly reconsidered his view and remarked that he is no longer confident (as he was thirty years ago) that the whole of company law qualifies for harmonization. See C.W.A. Timmermans, 'Europees vennootschapsrecht', *SEW* (2002): 248. Timmermans referred in this 1971 article, at 618 (fn. 25), to several authors who are of the opinion that company law is not entirely about safeguards within the meaning of Art. 44(2)(g) EC; he added, however, that they do not specify which issues of company would be outside the scope of the 'safeguards'. The view presented in the main text, finally, has traditionally also been that of the Commission, see *Rapport fait au nom de la Commission du marché intérieur, par M. Berkhouwer*, European Parliament Session 1966–1967 of 9 May 1966, Document 53 (the 'Berkhouwer report'), 7, no. 13.
276. I addressed the issue of facilitation of freedom of establishment brought about both by the Directive on cross-border mergers and the (draft proposal for a) Directive on cross-border transfer of the registered office (conversion), in s. III.C, *supra*.
277. See e.g., Art. 5 Directive on cross-border mergers (publication of the draft terms of cross-border merger and the information that must be furnished).
278. Below, for convenience, it will be referred to as 'company' or 'companies'.

will be discussed below,[279] is addressed to (controlling) shareholders *qualitate qua*, not companies *qualitate qua*.[280]

Does the notion of safeguards of companies in Article 44(2)(g) EC extend to companies formed in accordance with the law of third countries? Article 44(2)(g) EC refers to safeguards required of companies 'within the meaning of the second paragraph of Article 48'. 'Companies' are defined there as 'companies (. . .) constituted under civil or commercial law, including cooperative societies, and other legal persons governed by public or private law, save for those which are non-profit-making.' In itself, this second paragraph may cover companies from third countries. Having regard to the main function of the second paragraph of Article 48 EC (it is intended to indicate the various *types* of companies which may benefit from freedom of establishment, as was explained above[281]), as well as its place in the Treaty (it specifies the notion of 'companies' in the first paragraph of Article 48 EC, which only relates to *Member State* companies), the view that this second paragraph of Article 48 EC would include third country companies, and Article 44(2)(g) EC would include the coordination of safeguards required of third country companies, in my view, must be rejected.[282]

f. Members and Other

The final element of Article 44(2)(g) EC to be discussed is that of 'members and other'. Article 44(2)(g) EC allows for a harmonization of safeguards for these persons. In *Daihatsu*, the Court of Justice held:

> Furthermore, the very wording of Article 54(3)(g) of the Treaty refers to the need to protect the interests of 'others' generally, without distinguishing or excluding any categories falling within the ambit of that term.
>
> Consequently, the term 'others', as contemplated in Article 54(3)(g) of the Treaty, cannot be limited merely to creditors of the company.[283]

The term 'other' may therefore, in principle, even be read as including employees. It should, however, be realized that *Daihatsu* concerned the First Directive and in particular the obligation included therein to disclose accounting documents. This

---

279. See s. C.2.
280. The aim of the mandatory bid rule is to ensure that every time a natural or legal person or entity acquires control of a listed company as a result of an acquisition of securities, minority shareholders are protected. See further s. C.2, *infra*.
281. See s. II.B.3, *supra*.
282. See in this connection also Art. 43, para. 2 EC which just like Art. 44(2)(g) EC refers to the second para. of Art. 48 EC. This reference (of Art. 43, para. 2 EC) as well, relates to *Member State* companies. For the, more general, issue of whether the Community legislature has the authority to include in directives based on Art. 44 EC provisions relating to the treatment of companies of non-member countries, see s. V, *infra*.
283. Case C-97/96 *Verband deutscher Daihatsu-Händler* v *Daihatsu Deutschland* [1997] ECR I-6843, paras 19–20.

disclosure is designed to enable any interested persons, not specifically employees, to inform themselves.[284] Moreover, the information to be disclosed concerns the company's accounting and financial situation. So, neither with regard to its addressees nor with regard to its content, does the provision under consideration in *Daihatsu* specifically concern employees.[285]

2. Function of Article 44(2)(g) EC

As briefly indicated above, Article 44(2)(g) EC does not invest the Community legislature with a general power to regulate. Its wording circumscribes its scope *ratione materiae*: 'to coordinate to the necessary extent the safeguards (. . .) for the protection of the interests of members and other'. This is not all. Article 44(2)(g) EC, placed within the chapter entitled 'Freedom of establishment', is part of Article 44 EC. Within the system of Article 44 EC, Article 44(2)(g) EC is one of the means by which the Community legislature shall carry out its duties devolving upon it under Article 44(1) EC.[286] The objective assigned under Article 44(1) EC is to 'attain freedom of establishment'. It follows then, from its place in the Treaty and in particular the system of Article 44 EC, that the power conferred by Article 44(2)(g) EC is in function of a specific objective, particularly to attain freedom of establishment.

Case-law of the Community Courts arguably supports this conclusion. In three cases, the Court of Justice has expressly dealt with the function of Article 44(2)(g) EC: *Saldanha*[287] and *Daihatsu*[288] (both of 1997), as well as *Springer*[289] (2004). In 2006, also the Court of First Instance, in its *Danzer* case,[290] dealt with the function of this article. In *Saldanha*, the Court held, at paragraph 23, that:

> Article 54(3)(g) [44(2)(g) EC] of the EC Treaty empowers the Council and the Commission, *for the purpose of giving effect to the freedom of establishment*, to coordinate to the necessary extent the safeguards (. . .) for the protection of the interests of members and others. (emphasis added).

284. See also *Daihatsu*, just cited, para. 22.
285. The Court ruled, incidentally, at para. 23 of *Daihatsu*, that: 'the answer to this part of the question must be that Article 6 of the First Directive is to be interpreted as precluding the legislation of a Member State from restricting to members or creditors of the company, the central works council or the company's works council the right to apply for imposition of the penalty provided for by the law of that Member State in the event of failure by a company to fulfil the obligations regarding disclosure of annual accounts laid down by the First Directive'.
286. See the opening words of Art. 44(2)(g) EC: 'The Council and the Commission shall carry out the duties devolving upon them under the preceding provisions, in particular (. . .).'
287. Case C-122/96 *Saldanha and MTS Securities Corporation* v *Hiross* [1997] ECR I-5325.
288. Case C-97/96 *Verband deutscher Daihatsu-Händler* v *Daihatsu Deutschland* [1997] ECR I-6843.
289. Joined Cases C-435/02 and C-103/03 *Springer* [2004] ECR I-8663.
290. Case T-47/02 *Danzer* v *Council* [2006] ECR II-1779.

Next, in *Daihatsu*, the Court of Justice held, at paragraph 21:

> The *objective of abolishing restrictions on freedom of establishment*, which is assigned in very broad terms to the Council and the Commission by Article 54(1) and (2) of the Treaty, cannot be circumscribed by the provisions of Article 54(3). Article 54(3) merely sets out a non-exhaustive list of *measures to be taken in order to attain that objective*, as is borne out by the use of in that provision of the words 'in particular'. (emphasis added).

In *Springer*, the Court held, at paragraph 3:

> Under Article 54(3)(g) of the Treaty (now, after amendment, Article 44(2)(g) EC), the Council of the European Union and the Commission of the European Communities *are to work to abolish restrictions on the freedom of establishment* by coordinating to the necessary extent the safeguards which, for the protection of the interests of members and others, are required by Member States of companies or firms within the meaning of the second paragraph of Article 58 (now the second paragraph of Article 48 EC) with a view to making such safeguards equivalent throughout the Community. (emphasis added).

Finally, the Court of First Instance noted in *Danzer*, at paragraph 46:

> In respect of directives based on Article 44 EC, the objective of coordinating the different sets of legislation consists in *removing impediments to the freedom of establishment* arising from the legislative differences in the various Member States by establishing in the Community, particularly with respect to the objective provided for by Article 44(2)(g) EC, equivalent minimum legal conditions in terms of the scope of financial information which competing companies must make available to the public. (emphasis added).

To summarize the above: Article 44(2)(g) EC, as part of the Treaty chapter on freedom of establishment and read in conjunction with Article 44(1) EC and Article 44(2), opening words EC, forms a means by which the objective of Article 44(1) EC (i.e., freedom of establishment) must be obtained. Directives based on it must be *instrumental* in attaining freedom of establishment.[291] To construe this article otherwise would be incompatible with the principle embodied in Article 5 EC that the powers of the Community are limited to those specifically conferred on it.

As to the question of what constitutes attainment of establishment – that is, the objective of the functional power assigned by Article 44(2)(g) EC – I refer to my elaborations above concerning Article 44(1) EC, for which the same objective applies.

---

291. See also e.g., Edwards, 7; J. Wouters, 'European Company Law: Quo Vadis?', *CML Rev.* 37 (2000): 289–290.

C. ANALYSIS OF EC COMPANY LAW MODERNIZATION IN VIEW OF THE CONDITIONS OF ARTICLE 44(2)(G) EC

1. Introduction

The previous section B dealt with, in short, the conditions for the use of Article 44(2)(g) EC as a legal base. The present section addresses the question whether various modernization initiatives in the field of EC company law, based on Article 44(2)(g) EC, satisfy the above conditions. It thus addresses the Directive on takeover bids[292] and the Directive amending the Third and Sixth Directive.[293] As was shown in the previous section, Article 44(2)(g) EC does not provide a general power to adopt EC company law instruments. Rather, it provides a functional power, a power conferred for the purpose of attaining freedom of establishment.

Before addressing this question, first some words on the Commission's *Action Plan on Modernising Company Law and Enhancing Corporate Governance*. As will be recalled, the Commission in its Action Plan identified as one of the policy objectives that future actions at the European level in the area of company law seek as much as possible to meet strengthening shareholder rights and third party protection (in function of the other objective, 'fostering efficiency', which has been discussed above). 'Protection' has been a long-standing objective of the Commission. In fact, already in 1965, in its remarks to the European Parliament, the Commission identified this as one of the objectives of Article 54(3)(g) EEC (now Article 44(2)(g) EC).[294] Looking at this objective in the light of Article 44(2)(g) EC, I note that this article does not confer on the Council and European Parliament the power to coordinate on the ground of 'protection' (in function of business efficiency and competitiveness) *per se*, without a contribution to attainment of freedom of establishment. In order for the Community legislature

292. The Directive on takeover bids is, *stricto sensu*, not an initiative of the ACTION PLAN; it may, however, be considered as part of the company law modernization operation the Commission started in 2001; furthermore, the Directive was adopted in 2004, one year after the ACTION PLAN had been launched. See further Ch. 2.

293. Also based on Art. 44(2)(g) EC is Directive 2006/43 on statutory audits. It will not be dealt with. Observe that the (now withdrawn) draft Directive on transfer of the registered office (conversion), besides Art. 44(1) EC, also referred to Art. 44(2)(g) EC as its legal base. The Community legislature's competence to deal with the transfer on the registered office (conversion), in light of Art. 44(1) EC has been dealt with above, in s. III.C.4. Note further that the Directive on shareholder rights does not refer to Art. 44(2)(g) EC as its legal base. Rather, it refers to Art. 44 EC and Art. 95 EC. The shareholder rights at issue seem to qualify as 'safeguards for the protection of the interests of members' within the meaning of Art. 44(2)(g) EC. (However, any analysis by the Community legislature of how this particular harmonization (of shareholder rights) would contribute to freedom of establishment is failing).

294. *Rapport fait au nom de la Commission du marché intérieur, par M. Berkhouwer*, European Parliament Session 1966–1967 of 9 May 1966, Document 53 (the 'Berkhouwer report'; *Rev.trim.dr.eur.* 1966, at 441: 'la protection des associés et des tiers doit être, le cas échéant, renforcée'. (protection of members and third parties needs, as the occasion arises, to be reinforced; own translation). See already Ch. 2 (s. III).

to be competent on the basis of the above provision to deal with national company law, it is required that its acts *attain freedom of establishment*. In its Action Plan, however, the Commission (at 2.1) phrases its objective of 'protection', as 'a fundamental condition for business efficiency and competitiveness' without specifically addressing the above competence issues. And where it does expressly link coordination under Article 44(2)(g) EC with facilitating establishment, it notes:

> the harmonisation of a number of minimum requirements makes it easier for companies to establish themselves in other Member States where the regulatory framework is similar;[295]

This hardly is a (sufficient) explanation. It is not explained why differences among national rules genuinely hamper establishment and coordination then *actually* adds to establishment. Differences *in se* do not justify action (otherwise the EC would have a general power to act). This lack of specific explanation is structural.

> This seems for instance to be the case with the *Second Directive*[296] and the *Fourth Directive*,[297] both based on Article 54(3)(g) EEC (now Article 44(2)(g) EC). They are, however, only 'justified' in terms of equivalent protection for shareholders and creditors,[298] but fail to explain what their contribution to freedom of establishment is. The same seems to hold true for the *Third*,[299] *Sixth*[300] and *Seventh*

295. ACTION PLAN, 6 (1.1. *sub* a) and similarly in very broad terms e.g., 6 (1.1 *sub* b) and 9 (2.1, fourth indent).
296. See the preamble to this Directive, second recital ('Whereas *in order to ensure minimum equivalent protection for both shareholders and creditors of public limited liability companies*, the coordination of national provisions relating to their formation and to the maintenance, increase or reduction of their capital is particularly important'; emphasis added). See also e.g., Joined Cases C-19/90 and C-20/90 *Karella a.O.* v *Ypourgio a.O.* [1991] ECR I-2691, paras 25–26: '*the aim of the Second Directive is to provide a minimum level of protection for shareholders in all the Member States*'. (emphasis added).
297. See the first recital in the preamble to this Directive ('Whereas the *coordination* of national provisions concerning the presentation and content of annual accounts and annual reports, the valuation methods used therein and their publication in respect of certain companies with limited liability *is of special importance for the protection of members and third parties*'; emphasis added). See also e.g., Case C-306/99 *Banque internationale pour l'Afrique Occidentale SA* ('BiAO') [2003] ECR I-1, para. 69: 'the Fourth Directive is intended in particular to ensure the coordination of national provisions on the structure and content of annual accounts and reports and methods of valuation, *for the purposes of protecting members and third parties*'. (emphasis added).
298. J. Wouters, 'European Company Law: Quo Vadis?', *CML Rev.* 37 (2000): 270 even remarks, that: 'Any link [these Directives] have with the realization of freedom of establishment for companies is at best indirect; the emphasis is entirely on legislative policy aims of equivalent protection for shareholders and creditors in the common market.'
299. See the preamble to this Directive, third recital ('Whereas *the protection of the interests of members and third parties requires* that the laws of the Member States relating to mergers of public limited liability companies be coordinated and that provision for mergers should be made in the laws of all the Member States'; emphasis added).
300. See the preamble to this Directive, fifth recital ('Whereas *the protection of the interests of members and third parties requires* that the laws of the Member States relating to divisions of

Directive,[301] which are also based on Article 54(3)(g) EEC (now Article 44(2)(g) EC). This lack of explanation, finally, also shows itself in respect of the Eleventh Directive. Here, the use of Article 44((2)(g)) EC as a legal basis for disclosure requirements for *third* country companies seems to me to be inadequately explained. This specific issue is elaborated on in section V, *infra* (on freedom of establishment and external provisions), to which I refer.

To support its claim that harmonization of minimum requirements makes it easier for companies to establish themselves in other Member States, an aspect to which the Commission in general could pay attention, is that obstacles for companies to establish themselves will primarily be restrictions justified by an overriding reason relating to the public interest: for example, protection of creditors, prevention of fraud, protection of minority shareholders, and protection of employees. Harmonizing such restrictive national requirements may contribute to companies' freedom of establishment.[302]

The problem I have tried to bring to the attention here is that of lacking explanation in the Commission's Action Plan on Modernisation, as well as in older Directives in the field of EC company law. It was suggested that the Commission (or Community legislature) structurally fails to explain how Directives based on Article 44(2)(g) EC contribute to the attainment of freedom of establishment. In the remainder of this section, the focus will be on modernization initiatives adopted since the Action Plan, on the base of Article 44(2)(g) EC: the Directive on takeover bids and the Directive amending the Third and Sixth Directive.[303]

2. Directive on Takeover Bids: Mandatory Bid Rule

The legal basis for the Directive on takeover bids is formed by Article 44(1) EC *juncto* Article 44(2)(g) EC.[304] Article 44(1) EC aspects were dealt with above.[305]

The Directive contains the so-called mandatory bid rule, which rule is laid down in Article 5 of the Directive. Article 5(1) and (2) read as follows:

> 1. Where a natural or legal person, as a result of his/her own acquisition or the acquisition by persons acting in concert with him/her, holds securities of

---

public limited liability companies be coordinated where the Member States permit such operations'; emphasis added).

301. See the preamble to this Directive, first recital ('Whereas consolidated accounts must be drawn up so that financial information concerning such bodies of undertakings may be conveyed to members and third parties') and third recital ('Whereas the *aim of coordinating* the legislation governing consolidated accounts *is to protect* the interests subsisting in companies with share capital'; emphasis added).
302. See s. III.B.1.b, *supra*.
303. Also based on Art. 44(2)(g) EC is Directive 2006/43 on statutory audits. It will not be dealt with.
304. See the opening consideration and the first recital in the preamble to the Directive.
305. See s. III ('Article 44(1) EC: the power to attain freedom of establishment'). The analysis of EC Company Law Modernization in view of Art. 44(1) EC, then, concerned, *inter al.*, the so-called *breakthrough rule* of the Directive on takeover bids. A brief analysis of the *mandatory bid rule* in view of Art. 44(1) EC, after that in view of Art. 44(2)(g) EC (which is the subject of this section indeed), is included in the final fn. of this section.

> a company as referred to in Article 1(1) which, added to any existing holdings of those securities of his/hers and the holdings of those securities of persons acting in concert with him/her, directly or indirectly give him/her a specified percentage of voting rights in that company, giving him/her control of that company, Member States shall ensure that such a person is required to make a bid *as a means of protecting the minority shareholders of that company*. Such a bid shall be addressed at the earliest opportunity to all the holders of those securities for all their holdings at the equitable price as defined in paragraph 4.
>
> 2. Where control has been acquired following a voluntary bid made in accordance with this Directive to all the holders of securities for all their holdings, the obligation laid down in paragraph 1 to launch a bid shall no longer apply. (emphasis added).

The aim of Article 5 in general, and the paragraphs just quoted in particular, is to ensure that, every time a person or entity acquires control of a listed company as a result of an acquisition of securities, minority shareholders are protected.[306] To that end – according to the Explanatory Memorandum to the Directive proposal – 'the Directive requires that national rules afford proper safeguards to minority shareholders by obliging that acquiring person or entity to address a bid to all holders of securities, for all their holdings, at an equitable price'.[307]

It must be reiterated here that Article 44(2)(g) EC carefully defines the 'addressee' of the safeguards which may be harmonized on the basis of that provision: companies (or firms). Therefore, outside the scope are safeguards required of others, for example, shareholders. It will be recalled that the mandatory bid rule, under consideration here, is a case in point. It is addressed to ('controlling') shareholders (of companies), not to companies themselves.[308] In view of this, it must be concluded that Article 44(2)(g) EC may not be used to harmonize rules with respect to the mandatory bid. This is, however, what may have happened. The legal basis for the Directive on takeover bids is formed by Article 44(1) EC *juncto Article 44(2)(g) EC*.[309]

306. Commission Proposal for a Directive of the European Parliament and of the Council on takeover bids (COM (2002) 534 final), OJ 2003 C 45 E, 1 (Explanatory Memorandum, *sub* 2, Art. 5).

307. *Ibid.*

308. The aim of the mandatory bid rule, as was explained, is to ensure that every time a natural or legal person or entity acquires control of a listed company as a result of an acquisition of securities, minority shareholders are protected.

309. See the opening consideration and the first recital in the preamble to the Directive.

As to the question whether Art. 44(1) EC may provide a legal basis for adoption of a *mandatory bid rule* (for comparable analyses in view of Art. 44(1) EC, see s. III.C, *supra*), one may advance that Member State mandatory bid rules form an obstacle for companies to establish themselves in another Member State. More particularly, a mandatory bid rule may be contended to constitute a restriction of freedom of establishment within the meaning of Art. 43 EC. However, one that is presumably justified by an overriding reason relating to the

3. Directive Amending Third and Sixth Directive

The legal basis for the Directive amending the Third and Sixth Directive[310] is Article 44(2)(g) EC. This amendment seeks to abolish certain requirements in the case of a merger or division. Prior to their amendment, the Third and Sixth Directive provided for the obligation, in the event of a merger or division, to have the draft terms of the merger or division examined by an independent expert and to have a written report established by that expert.[311] The above provisions of the Third and Sixth Directive are now amended: no longer is an independent examination and report required if all the shareholders have so agreed.[312]

As to its contribution to the attainment of freedom of establishment, the (preamble to this) Directive remains, however, silent:

> The first recital of the preamble, referring to the Lisbon Strategy and the Better Regulation policy, emphasizes 'the importance of reducing the administrative burdens imposed on enterprises by existing legislation as a crucial element for improving the competitiveness of such enterprises and for achieving the objectives of the Lisbon agenda'.[313] The second and third recitals refer to the Directive on cross-border

---

public interest (the protection of minority shareholders). Harmonizing such restrictive requirements may contribute to companies' freedom of establishment. See further s. III.B.1.b, *supra*. This argues in favour of the answer that the mandatory bid rule could be based on Art. 44(1) EC. A specific issue, however, remains, and that is whether the Community legislature has the authority under Art. 44(1) EC to include *third* country companies into the scope of the mandatory bid rule (as does Art. 5 of the Directive on takeover bids). This issue will be dealt with below, in a separate section on freedom of establishment and so-called external provisions (see s. V).

For protection of minority shareholders on the (more general) legal basis of Art. 95 EC (as in the case of the Directive on shareholder rights), see Ch. 4. Whereas the mandatory bid rule, as explained, is directly related to freedom of establishment (in rather general terms it could be added: it is in the case of a takeover, which is a method for exercising freedom of establishment, that this group of shareholders is protected; cf. recital 2 in the preamble to the Directive on takeover bids which notes the need to 'protect the interests of holders of the securities of companies governed by the law of a Member State when those companies are the subject of takeover bids or of changes of control'), the protection the Directive on shareholder rights offers minority shareholders is, in short and as will be explained in Ch. 4, related to free movement of capital (rather than to freedom of establishment).

310. Directive 2007/63/EC of the European Parliament and of the Council of 13 Nov. 2007 amending Council Directives 78/855/EEC and 82/891/EEC as regards the requirement of an independent expert's report on the occasion of merger or division of public limited liability companies, OJ 2007 L 300, 47.

311. See Art. 10(1) Third Directive and Art. 8(1) Sixth Directive. The Sixth Directive determines that Member States may permit the non-application of these provisions, if all the shareholders have so agreed. See Art. 10 Sixth Directive.

312. See Art. 1–3 Directive.

313. According to the Impact Assessment (Commission Staff Working Document) accompanying the proposal amending the *Third* and *Sixth Directive*, SEC (2007) 298, at 3, estimates suggest that the annual administrative cost of producing these reports may be substantial. The Impact Assessment further notes that efficiency gains can be realized: 'The nature of the current requirement means that financial and other resources are misallocated if a report is produced

> mergers for an exemption from the obligation to have the draft terms of merger examined by independent experts and a report drawn up by such experts for the shareholders, thus in fact arguing for consistency with the Directive on cross-border mergers. The fourth recital then notes that 'There is no reason to require (...) an examination by an independent expert for the shareholders if all the shareholders agree that it may be dispensed with'.

The Community legislature, so it may be concluded, thus fails to explain adequately how this Directive based on Article 44(2)(g) EC meets the terms of this provision.

Apart from the issue of insufficient explanation, it is, moreover, debatable whether the Directive contributes to freedom of establishment (as required under Article 44(2)(g) EC). The Directive, it is recalled, concerns *internal* mergers and *internal* divisions (not such *cross-border* restructuring operations),[314] and Wouters' criticism against the Third and Sixth Directive themselves,[315] that 'any link they [these Directives] have with the realization of freedom of establishment for companies is at best indirect',[316] would seem to apply to the amending Directive as well. In any case, it is definitely so that the Community legislature has not provided an explanation of how the Directive, in its view, would (aim to) contribute to freedom of establishment.

4. Conclusion

The previous section B dealt with, in short, the conditions for the use of Article 44(2)(g) EC as a legal base. In the present section C, EC Company Law Modernization has been analyzed in view of these conditions.

First, it was argued that before the Action Plan was adopted the Community legislature structurally failed to explain how Directives based on Article 44(2)(g) EC contribute to the attainment of freedom of establishment. It turns out that this also seems to be the case in the Action Plan itself – it, too, arguably, shows such lack of explanation.

Subsequently, the question has been dealt with whether the modernization initiatives which have been adopted on the basis of Article 44(2)(g) EC satisfy the conditions for the use of this article. It thus addressed the Directive on takeover bids and the Directive amending the Third and Sixth Directive. The analysis of

---

although there is no need or demand for it. Those resources could be employed more purposefully elsewhere. Thus, the problem may be defined as the current requirements under the existing Directives preventing a better use of resources, be they financial or otherwise, in some instances. This means that efficiency gains can be realised by changing the mandatory nature of the existing obligation.' Observe, however, that the relation between efficiency gains and the freedom of establishment remains unexplored in the Impact Assessment, just as in the (preamble to the) Directive amending the *Third* and *Sixth Directive*.

314. I.e., mergers between and divisions involving (public limited liability) companies from the same Member State. Cf. also *Sevic*, paras 22 and 27.
315. The Third and the Sixth Directive too are based on Art. 54(3)(g) EEC (now Art. 44(2)(g) EC).
316. J. Wouters, 'European Company Law: Quo Vadis?', *CML Rev.* 37 (2000): 270.

this latter amending Directive, in view of Article 44(2)(g) EC, showed, in any case, again, a lack of (comprehensive) explanation (as to whether the terms of this article have been satisfied). As regards the Directive on takeover bids, it was even concluded that the Community legislature had no authority under Article 44(2)(g) EC to adopt the mandatory bid rule (laid down in Article 5 of the Directive on takeover bids).

V. FREEDOM OF ESTABLISHMENT AND EXTERNAL PROVISIONS

A. Introduction

It is of regular occurrence that the Community includes in its directives adopted on the basis of Article 44 EC provisions relating to the treatment of nationals (or companies) of non-member countries.[317] In the field of EC company law it can be referred to the Eleventh Directive and the Directive on takeover bids. The Eleventh Directive concerns disclosure requirements imposed in a Member State in respect of branches of companies. Apart from such disclosure requirements for companies from (other) Member States, the Directive also contains these requirements for companies from third countries. The Directive on takeover bids lays down a so-called mandatory bid rule, which, in short, requires also third country companies acquiring control of a listed company to address a bid to all holders of securities.

Does the Community legislature have the authority under Article 44 EC to include provisions relating to the treatment of nationals (companies) of non-member countries? These third country nationals (companies), it is recalled, are – after all – not beneficiaries of the freedom of establishment[318] (and the provisions at issue, therefore, cannot contribute to *these* companies' freedom of establishment).

I shall first enter briefly into Opinion 1/94 of the Court, which will be shown to be of particular relevance to the question just raised (s. B). Against the background of this Opinion, the requirements for companies from third countries included in the Eleventh Directive and the Directive on takeover bids will then be analyzed in view of Article 44 EC (s. C).

B. Court of Justice Opinion 1/94

In November 1994, the Court of Justice issued its Opinion *Competence of the Community to conclude international agreements concerning services and the*

317. See Opinion 1/94 (to be discussed in s. B), para. 90.
318. See s. II.B, *supra*.

protection of intellectual property.[319] In this Opinion, the Court also discussed the subject of Community legislative acts containing provisions relating to the treatment of nationals of non-member countries. Of particular relevance is paragraph 90 of the Opinion where the Court observed:

> Although the only objective expressly mentioned in the chapters on the right of establishment and on freedom to provide services is the attainment of those freedoms for nationals of the Member States of the Community, it does not follow that the Community institutions are prohibited from using the powers conferred on them in that field in order to specify the treatment which is to be accorded to nationals of non-member countries.

In brief, the Community legislature may use the powers conferred on it for the attainment of freedom of establishment for nationals (and companies) of the Member States,[320] in order to specify the treatment of nationals (and companies) of third countries.[321] Whether that is the case where the Eleventh Directive and the Directive on takeover bids are concerned, is analyzed in sections B and C.

Before that, however, three further aspects of the Court's Opinion, merit attention. First, there is a terminological issue. The Court refers to provisions relating to the treatment of nationals of non-member countries (included in its ('internal'[322]) legislative acts on the basis of the Treaty provisions on freedom of establishment) as 'external provisions'.[323] That term will be used here as well, for the provisions just described (in general) and for the provisions of the Eleventh Directive and Directive on takeover bids under consideration here (in particular).

Secondly, the Court emphasizes that 'very different objectives may be pursued by incorporation of external provisions'.[324] In this connection, the Court enters at

319. Opinion 1/94 'Competence of the Community to conclude international agreements concerning services and the protection of intellectual property' ('GATS and TRIPS') [1994] ECR I-5267.
320. The (explicit) objective of the Treaty provisions on freedom of establishment is indeed the attainment of freedom of establishment for *nationals of the Member States*. See also Opinion 1/94, just cited, para. 81: 'As has rightly been observed by the Council and most of the Member States which have submitted observations, the sole objective of those chapters [i.e., the chapters on the right of establishment and on freedom to provide services] is to secure the right of establishment and freedom to provide services for *nationals of Member States*.' (emphasis added).
321. Timmermans (already) paid attention to this issue of the personal scope of the Treaty provisions on freedom of establishment on the one hand and the subject of Community legislative acts containing provisions relating to the treatment of nationals of non-member countries on the other, in 1991 – so before Opinion 1/94. He advanced that: 'Article 54(3)(g) is so closely linked to the right of establishment, which is exclusively granted to companies from the Community, that, so it seems to me, Council and Commission have no authority under this Article to take action with regard to third country companies.' See C.W.A. Timmermans, 'Methods and Tools for Integration', in *European Business Law. Legal and Economic Analyses on Integration and Harmonization*, ed. R.M. Buxbaum et al. (Berlin/New York: Walter de Gruyter, 1991), 144.
322. See Opinion 1/94, just cited, para. 95.
323. *Ibid.*, para. 91.
324. *Ibid.*

some length into, *inter alia*, the (objective of the external provisions of the) Eleventh Directive:

> The directives on coordination of disclosure requirements and company accounts applied only to companies as such and not to their branches. That gave rise to some disparity, as regards the protection of members and third parties, between companies operating in other Member States by setting up branches and companies operating there by setting up subsidiaries. Consequently, Council Directive 89/666/EEC of 21 December 1989 concerning disclosure requirements in respect of branches opened in a Member State by certain types of company governed by the law of another State (OJ 1989 L 395, p. 36) ['the Eleventh Directive'], which is based on Article 54 of the Treaty, was introduced to regulate the disclosure requirements applying to such branches. In order to avoid any discrimination based on a company's country of origin, that directive also had to cover branches established by companies governed by the laws of non-member countries.[325]

Thirdly, the Court, after having ruled that the Community legislature is not prohibited from using Article 44 EC to specify the treatment which is to be accorded to nationals (companies) of non-member countries, cites various Community acts which 'contain provisions in that regard', including the Eleventh Directive. In advance of the (substantive) analysis of the external provisions included in the Eleventh Directive (s. C, *infra*), it may be concluded from this that, apparently, in the Court's view, these external provisions can actually be based on Article 44 EC.[326]

C. Analysis of External Provisions Included in EC Company Law Instruments in View of the Conditions of Article 44 EC

1. Eleventh Directive

The Eleventh Directive concerns disclosure requirements imposed in a Member State in respect of branches of companies; apart from such disclosure requirements for companies from (other) Member States,[327] the Directive also contains these requirements for companies from third countries.[328] The Eleventh Directive is based on Article 44(1) EC and Article 44(2)(g) EC.[329] Does the Community

325. *Ibid.*, para. 92.
326. *Ibid.*, para. 90.
327. Article 1-6 Eleventh Directive.
328. Article 7-10 Eleventh Directive.
329. The legal basis for the Eleventh Directive, to be precise, is Art. 54 EEC in general and Art. 54(3)(g) EEC in particular (now Art. 44 EC and Art. 44(2)(g) EC). See the opening consideration and the first recital in the preamble to the Directive.

legislature have the authority under Article 44 EC to include these requirements for third country companies, these external provisions?[330]

The Court has made clear, as was explained in the previous section, that the Community legislature may use the powers conferred on it for the attainment of freedom of establishment for nationals (and companies) of the Member States, in order to specify the treatment of nationals (and companies) of third countries. Is that the case where the Eleventh Directive is concerned?

The disclosure requirements for companies from (other) *Member States* (the 'internal' provisions) laid down in the Eleventh Directive, can, in my view, be based on Article 44(1) EC and Article 44(2)(g) EC. In brief, the opening of a branch in another Member State, it is reiterated, is a method for exercising freedom of establishment,[331] and the disclosure requirements at issue, subsequently, may be argued to both eliminate obstacles to freedom of establishment and facilitate the effective exercise of this freedom.[332] These powers, of Article 44(1) EC and Article 44(2)(g) EC, may (then) also be used to *specify* the treatment of companies of third countries (as in the case at hand by the extension of the disclosure requirements to third country companies as well).

With regard to the use of specifically Article 44(2)(g) EC, there may, however, be a complication. This provision confers a power to coordinate safeguards for the persons involved with the company. The provision was discussed in more detail above, in section IV. It was pointed out there that the persons of whom those safeguards are required are 'companies' and, it was further explained, why the notion of safeguards of 'companies' (presumably) does not extend to companies of third countries.[333] In view of this, the conclusion would seem justified that the disclosure requirements for third country companies included in the Eleventh Directive (presumably) cannot be based on Article 44(2)(g) EC. In any event, Article 44(1) EC would (still) provide a legal basis for the adoption of the disclosure requirements for third country companies. Moreover, the view that the present external provisions may indeed be based on Article 44 EC (or, more particularly, Article 44(1) EC) is also (otherwise, in more concrete terms) supported by Opinion 1/94. As was mentioned in the previous section, the fact is, in this Opinion, the Court, after having ruled that the Community legislature is not prohibited from using Article 44 EC to specify the treatment which is to be accorded to nationals (companies) of non-member countries,[334] cites various Community acts which

330. The preamble to the Eleventh Directive does not specifically address this issue. It merely refers to the objective pursued by incorporation of the disclosure requirements for third country companies: '(. . .) to avoid any discrimination on the basis of a company's country of origin, this Directive must also cover branches opened by companies governed by the law of non-member countries (. . .)'.

331. See s. II.C, *supra*.

332. See further s. III.B.1.b, *supra* and s. IV.B.1, *supra*.

333. See s. IV.B.1.e, *supra*.

334. See already s. B, *supra*.

'contain provisions in that regard', including precisely the disclosure requirements of the Eleventh Directive.[335]

2. Directive on Takeover Bids

The Directive on takeover bids contains the so-called mandatory bid rule. This rule is laid down in Article 5 of the Directive. It prescribes, in short, that when a person acquires control of a listed, EC company as a result of an acquisition of securities, that person must address a bid to all holders of securities, for all their holdings, at an equitable price.[336] The mandatory bid rule, it must be emphasized here, not only applies to EC companies, but also to third country companies acquiring control. Does this (in this respect external) provision meet the terms of Article 44(1) EC *juncto* Article 44(2)(g) EC (which constitute the legal basis for the Directive[337])?[338]

With regard to, first, Article 44(2)(g) EC, it must be reiterated[339] that that provision carefully defines the 'addressee' of the safeguards which may be harmonized on the basis of that provision: companies (or firms). Outside the scope are therefore, safeguards required of others, for example shareholders. The mandatory bid rule provides an example; it is addressed to ('controlling') shareholders (of companies), not to companies (themselves). In view of this, it must be concluded that Article 44(2)(g) EC may not be used to harmonize rules with respect to the mandatory bid, whether the 'controlling' shareholder is an EC company or not.[340]

Does the Community legislature, then, have the authority under Article 44(1) EC to adopt a mandatory bid rule which also applies to third country companies acquiring control? The Court has made clear in Opinion 1/94, as was explained above, that the Community legislature may use the powers conferred on it for the attainment of freedom of establishment for nationals (and companies) of the Member States, in

335. It could perhaps further be noted that third country companies subject to a national rule which imposes lower disclosure standards are (or would be) at an advantage in terms of compliance costs vis-à-vis companies subject to higher standards. This may hinder or make less attractive the exercise of freedom of establishment (for, in short, EC companies) by means of setting-up a branch.
336. See further s. IV.C.2, *supra*.
337. See the opening consideration and the first recital in the preamble to the Directive.
338. The (preamble to the) Directive keeps silent about this question.
339. See s. IV.B.1.e.
340. Moreover, even if, contrary to the interpretation here, the term company is to be understood as also encompassing, in short ('controlling') shareholders, and the mandatory bid rule as such could be based on Art. 44(2)(g) EC, it is questionable whether it could be addressed (on that specific basis) to *third country* acquirers. It was explained above, and emphasized again in the previous section on the Eleventh Directive, that Art. 44(2)(g) EC (presumably) does not allow for harmonization of safeguards required of *third country* companies. See s. IV.B.1.e and s. 1, *supra*.

order to specify the treatment of nationals (and companies) of third countries. Is that the case here, where the Directive on takeover bids is concerned?

The question whether the 'internal' aspects of the mandatory bid rule meet the terms of Article 44(1) EC was dealt with above.[341] It was concluded there that the mandatory bid rule to the extent that it, in short, requires *EC* acquiring shareholders to make a bid, could be based on Article 44(1) EC. This power of Article 44(1) EC may (then) also be used to *specify* the treatment of companies of third countries (as in the case at hand by the extension of the requirement to make a bid to acquiring third country companies as well). Article 44(1) EC, therefore, does seem to provide a legal basis for adoption of the mandatory bid rule, both as regards the requirement it entails for EC companies (as shareholders) to make a bid as well as for third country companies (as shareholders).[342]

---

341. See s. IV.C.2.
342. As noted in the fns above, Timmermans had advanced, however before Opinion 1/94, that: 'Article 54(3)(g) is so closely linked to the right of establishment, which is exclusively granted to companies from the Community, that, so it seems to me, Council and Commission have no authority under this Article to take action with regard to third country companies.' Timmermans then furthermore argued that Art. 95(1) EC could be used for the inclusion of third country companies into the scope of a harmonization directive provided that 'this Article is applied only where divergences between national laws distort competition'. Starting from these assumptions (and in advance of Ch. 4, where Art. 95 EC is discussed in more detail), it could be brought forward, I think, that differences between national rules as to a requirement for companies (including third country companies) to make a bid, may (indeed) give rise to appreciable distortions of competition. Let me explain this briefly. (Offeree) Companies with controlling shareholders may have an incentive to opt for a jurisdiction that does not impose a mandatory bid. See L. Enriques, 'The Mandatory Bid Rule in the Proposed EC Takeover Directive: Harmonization as Rent-Seeking?', in *Reforming Company and Takeover Law in Europe*, ed. G. Ferrarini et al. (Oxford: OUP, 2004), 789. A mandatory bid rule may be thus formulated (by a Member State) that it applies in respect of offeree companies which have a stock exchange listing in that Member State. It is also possible, however, that it applies in respect of offeree companies which have their registered office in the Member State in question (if, obviously, the mandatory bid rule is phrased in these terms). For a comparison between the various types of mandatory bid rules, see M.P. Nieuwe Weme, *Het verplicht bod op effecten* (Deventer: Kluwer, 2004), 106-112). For them (companies with controlling shareholders), the mandatory bid could impede their (shareholders') freedom to sell (it could reduce the likely gains from a sale of control, which is to say their private benefits of control). See further L.A. Bebchuk, 'Efficient and Inefficient Sales of Corporate Control', *QJE* 109 (1994): 957-993. The differences in national rules and the resulting 'relocation' of companies as just described, may then have considerable repercussions on the conditions of competition for undertakings associated with these companies, in particular the financial and professional services industries. Cf. Case C-376/98 *Germany* v *Parliament and Council* ('Tobacco Advertizing') [2000] ECR I-8419, para. 110. It is also said that, because companies, who are not subject to a mandatory bid rule, may be able to pay higher control premiums financed by the profits from exploiting the remaining shareholders, competition for resources (corporate control) is distorted (Grundmann, no. 1014, p. 600). The removal of these distortions could then (in this view, that Art. 44 EC would not constitute a proper legal basis) be dealt with under Art. 95 EC.

VI. FREEDOM OF ESTABLISHMENT AND REGULATORY COMPETITION

In this final section on Article 44 EC, I will briefly examine the topic of regulatory competition, which, in short, is competition between legislators to attract investment or business activity or to promote the competitiveness of indigenous industries by providing a more favourable regulatory environment.[343] It is sometimes argued or hinted at in academic literature that the freedom of establishment should be interpreted as guaranteeing regulatory competition in the field of company law, and thus limiting the Community legislature from adopting harmonization measures at the expense of regulatory competition.[344] This section will briefly examine this claim, in advance of Chapter 5, where regulatory competition is dealt with more extensively.

The interpretation of freedom of establishment as a guarantee for competition among rules is based in particular on the *Centros* and *Inspire Art* cases, where indeed it was referred to, notably by the Advocates General in their Opinions, 'competition among rules' or 'concurrence entre les différents régimes des États membres'.[345] In *Centros*, Advocate General La Pergola argued, as regards the situation where a company is incorporated in the United Kingdom because the founders wish to avail themselves of the opportunity to operate with paid-up capital

343. For this definition, see S. Woolcock, 'Competition among rules in the single European Market', in *International Regulatory Competition and Coordination. Perspectives on Economic Regulation in Europe and the United States,* ed. W. Bratton, J. McCahery et al. (Oxford: Clarendon Press, 1996), 297–298. See further: G. Hertig & J.A. McCahery, 'Company and Takeover Law Reforms in Europe: Misguided Harmonization Efforts or Regulatory Competition', *EBOR* 4 (2003): 179–211; L. Timmerman, 'Van digitaal naar analoog vennootschapsrecht en de gevolgen daarvan voor de concurrentie tussen vennootschapssystemen', *Ondernemingsrecht* (2003): 41–42; C. Teichmann, 'Law as a Product – Regulatory Competition in the Common Market and the European Private Company', in *European Company Law in Accelerated Progress*, ed. S. Bartman (Alphen aan den Rijn: Kluwer Law International, 2006), 145–157; W.W. Bratton, J.A. McCahery & E.P.M. Vermeulen, 'How Does Corporate Mobility Affect Lawmaking? A Comparative Analysis', Amsterdam Center for Law & Economics Working Paper no. 2008-01, <http://ssrn.acle.nl>.

344. For a discussion of this view ('Niederlassungsfreiheit als Garantie des institutionellen Wettbewerbs'), see E.-M. Kieninger, *Wettbewerb der Privatrechtsordnungen im Europäischen Binnenmarkt* (Tübingen: Mohr Siebeck, 2002), 356–357. Kieninger herself incidentally, rejects the view in question: 'M.E. ginge eine solche Deutung zu weit'. See further J. Rickford, 'Foreword', in Rickford, 6–7. Rickford seems to be favourable to the interpretation referred to in the main text, where he remarks – in general terms – that: 'the case for avoiding "restraining competition between different regimes" of national law is now explicitly recognised by the Court's Advocate General'. In this connection, Rickford refers to the Opinion of AG Alber in *Inspire Art*, pt. 138. See also T. Körber, *Grundfreiheiten und Privatrecht* (Tübingen: Mohr Siebeck, 2004), 297–298, who takes the view that Art. 43 EC is of great importance to regulatory competition, but does not explicitly address the issue whether freedom of establishment should be considered as guaranteeing regulatory competition.

345. See: Opinion of AG La Pergola in *Centros*, pt. 20; Opinion of AG Alber in *Inspire Art*, pt. 138.

commensurate with the resources at their disposal and less than is required under Danish law:

> That situation, whether one likes it or not, is the *logical consequence of the rights guaranteed under the Treaty*. Moreover, it is consistent with the objective behind the inclusion of the freedom of establishment in the Treaty, namely the need to promote the free movement of persons (and capital) and, by the same token, the achievement of a common market. In that respect, the fact that a national of a Member State may take advantage of the flexibility of United Kingdom company law (. . .) must be viewed in that context [that is, in the context of the Community system]. In short, in the absence of harmonisation, competition among rules must be allowed free play in corporate matters.[346] (emphasis added; quotation marks and footnotes omitted).

It is clear from this quotation, however, that regulatory competition is only accepted conditionally, namely in the absence of harmonization. The Court confirmed this in *Centros*. In connection with its statement that 'a national of a Member State who wishes to set up a company [and] chooses to form it in the Member State whose rules of company law seem to him the least restrictive',[347] it added that:

> it is always open to the Council, on the basis of the powers conferred upon it by Article 54(3)(g) of the EC Treaty, to achieve complete harmonisation.[348]

So, the freedom of establishment does not limit the Community legislature from adopting harmonizing measures at the expense of regulatory competition. Quite the opposite, the Court emphasizes that the Community legislature is allowed to adopt such measures under Article 44 EC (where it attains freedom of establishment). Moreover, as is also evident from the quotations, harmonization (by virtue of Article 44 EC) is conceived by the Advocates General and the Court as (principally) restricting regulatory competition, not the development or facilitation thereof. Historically, prevention of regulatory competition was even the most important motive for including Article 44(2)(g) EC in the EC Treaty.[349]

---

346. Opinion of AG La Pergola in *Centros*, pt. 20, referring to AG Darmon's Opinion in Case 79/85 *Segers* v *Bestuur van de Bedrijfsvereniging voor Bank- en Verzekeringswezen, Groothandel en Vrije Beroepen* [1986] ECR 2375.

    With respect to the remark that 'in the absence of harmonisation, competition among rules must be allowed free play in corporate matters', La Pergola refers in fn. 48 of his Opinion to C.D. Ehlermann, 'Compétition entre systèmes réglementaires', *RMCUE* (1995): 220–227, according to whom there is no possibility of 'free competition' between the company laws of the Member States degenerating into a kind of 'Delaware effect', since Member States can have recourse to the mechanism for the harmonization of company laws within the meaning of Art. 54(3)(g) of the EC Treaty (now Art. 44(2)(g) EC).

347. *Centros*, para. 27.

348. *Ibid.*, para. 28.

349. See J. Wouters, 'European Company Law: Quo Vadis?', *CML Rev.* 37 (2000): 269. Wouters mentions as an aim of Art. 44(2)(g) EC avoiding a situation whereby the freedom of establishment in effect entails movements of capital and activities on the basis of the more stringent

From this, it follows that a view according to which the freedom of establishment as provided for by Articles 43–48 EC must be considered as a guarantee for competition among rules, must be rejected.[350]

This first chapter on EC competence in the field of company law dealt with Article 44 EC as a legal basis for EC company law instruments. The next chapter is closely linked to this chapter. It is about other legal bases which also play a role in the field of EC company law, Articles 95 EC and 308 EC in particular. In Chapter 4, also some 'combined' concluding remarks that relate to both this chapter and to Chapter 4 are made.

---

or more lax character of national legislation. He refers to this aim as the prevention of a Delaware effect in the EC, and observes: 'Historically, this seems in fact to be the most important motive for including Article 44(2)(g) in the EC Treaty chapter on right of establishment: a number of delegations (in particular, the French) insisted on harmonization at the time the Treaty was being negotiated, as a *quid pro quo* for the liberal grant of a right of establishment to companies. They were determined that the Netherlands, which was famous at the time for the flexibility of its company law, should not become a European "Delaware", with companies being established there because of the low burden of legal rules.'

350. In Ch. 5, the issue whether Community law requires the Community legislature to use its powers to – actively – stimulate regulatory competition is dealt with. In advance of this, it can – on the basis of this section – be observed that at least under Art. 44 EC there is no requirement for the Community legislature to boost regulatory competition.

Chapter 4

EC Competence in the Field of Company Law (II): Other Legal Bases

I. INTRODUCTION

The previous chapter dealt with Article 44 EC, concerning freedom of establishment. As stated, most of the Directives in the field of EC company law are based upon it. There are, however, other legal bases which are of relevance, too, for EC company law. These other legal bases will be dealt with now, in the current chapter. First, Article 95 EC will be discussed (s. II). This article provides a competence to approximate national laws for – in short – the completion of an integrated market for Europe. Then, Article 308 EC will be taken up (s. III). This provision gives the Community a supplementary competence to achieve the Community objectives. Of the 'other legal bases', which form the subject of this Chapter 4, it are these provisions (i.e., Articles 95 EC and 308 EC) which may be considered the most relevant to EC company law. After these Treaty Articles have been dealt with, the remaining legal bases, which (may) also play a certain, more limited role in the field of EC company law, will be briefly entered into: Article 61(c) EC *juncto* Article 67 EC; Article 137 EC; Article 211 EC, and, finally, Article 293 EC (s. IV). Finally, some 'combined' concluding remarks, that is, relating to both Chapters 4 and 5, are made (s. V).

II. ARTICLE 95 EC: APPROXIMATION OF LAWS FOR THE COMPLETION OF AN INTEGRATED MARKET FOR EUROPE

A. INTRODUCTION

Traditionally, EC company law Directives have been based on Article 44 EC. The Directive on shareholder rights, however, could mark a new era in this respect; in addition to Article 44 EC, it also has Article 95 EC as its legal basis. Another important reason to discuss Article 95 EC is the Court's judgment of May 2006 on the legality of the SCE Regulation.[1] In this case, the European Parliament presented the Court with the question whether the Regulation at issue should have been adopted on the basis of Article 95 EC (instead of Article 308 EC on which the Regulation had actually been based).

The structure of this section II is as follows. First the relationship between the – closely connected – general legal bases of Article 94 EC and 95 EC (on the one hand) and other, specific legal bases (on the other hand), such as Article 44 EC, will be examined (s. B). Then, the relationship between Article 94 EC and 95 EC themselves will be focused on (s. C). The limits on the use of Article 95(1) EC will be dealt with thereafter (s. D). Finally, specific EC company law modernization measures will be analyzed in view of the conditions of Article 95 EC (s. E). This analysis includes the already mentioned SCE Regulation and the Directive on shareholder rights.

B. RELATIONSHIP BETWEEN THE GENERAL LEGAL BASES OF ARTICLE 94 EC AND 95 EC AND OTHER, SPECIFIC LEGAL BASES

Most legal bases which the Treaty offers, such as Article 44 EC which was just dealt with, relate to a specific subject-matter area.[2] The competence attributed to the Community by Articles 94 and 95 EC, by contrast, is horizontal in character and is not limited in advance to a specific subject-matter area;[3] both articles

1. Case C-436/03 *Parliament* v *Council* ('SCE Regulation') [2006] ECR I-3733.
2. For these specific provisions, see: Lauwaars & Timmermans, 275; Craig & de Búrca, 93 and 615.
3. Cf. Opinion of AG Fennelly in Case C-376/98 *Germany* v *Parliament and Council* ('Tobacco Advertizing') [2000] ECR I-8419, pt. 62 ('The competence attributed to the Community by Article 100A(1) of the Treaty is horizontal in character. It is not limited in advance by reference to a particular subject-matter defined *ratione materiae*. Instead, the Community is authorised to adopt approximation measures which have as their object the establishment and functioning of the internal market. Thus, the scope of Community competence is defined by reference to a criterion of a *functional* nature, extending laterally to all measures designed to ensure the attainment of the single market. It leads to Community legislation touching the most diverse areas of national law, provided this is relevant to the establishment and functioning of the internal market. In this way, the scope of competence under Article 100A is defined exclusively by reference to its stated objective, rather than its material subject-matter'). (fn. omitted).

provide a competence to approximate national laws for – in short – the completion of an integrated market for Europe. Article 94 EC provides:

> The Council shall, acting unanimously on a proposal from the Commission and after consulting the European Parliament and the Economic and Social Committee, issue directives for the approximation of such laws, regulations or administrative provisions of the Member States as directly affect the establishment or functioning of the common market.

Article 95 EC provides, in relevant part:

> 1. By way of derogation from Article 94 and save where otherwise provided in this Treaty, the following provisions shall apply for the achievement of the objectives set out in Article 14. The Council shall, acting in accordance with the procedure referred to in Article 251 and after consulting the Economic and Social Committee, adopt the measures for the approximation of the provisions laid down by law, regulation or administrative action in Member States which have as their object the establishment and functioning of the internal market.
> 2. Paragraph 1 shall not apply to fiscal provisions, to those relating to the free movement of persons nor to those relating to the rights and interests of employed persons.
> 3. The Commission, in its proposals envisaged in paragraph 1 concerning health, safety, environmental protection and consumer protection, will take as a base a high level of protection, taking account in particular of any new development based on scientific facts. Within their respective powers, the European Parliament and the Council will also seek to achieve this objective.

It has long been established that general powers, such as those laid down in the Articles 94 EC and 95 EC, cannot be used to regulate a matter falling clearly within the ambit of a more specific provision.[4] In this connection, let me also refer to *Commission* v *Council* of 2004, in which the Court considered that:

> So far as concerns the scope of Article 95 EC, which the Commission and Parliament argue ought to have been used as the legal basis (. . .), it must be pointed out that it is clear from the very wording of Article 95(1) EC that that article applies only if the Treaty does not provide otherwise.
>
> It follows that, if the Treaty contains a more specific provision that is capable of constituting the legal basis for the measure in question, that measure must be founded on such provision. (. . .).[5]

4. J.A. Usher, 'Annotation, Case C-376/98, *Germany v. European Parliament and Council* (tobacco advertising). Judgment of the Full Court of 5 October 2000, [2000] ECR I-8419', *CML Rev.* 38 (2001): 1540–1541; see also Lauwaars & Timmermans, 276.
5. Case C-338/01 *Commission* v *Council* ('Directive on mutual assistance between Member States in the recovery of public-law claims') [2004] ECR I-4829, paras 59–60. See also Case C-533/03 *Commission* v *Council* [2006] ECR I-1025, paras 43–48.

The complementary or residual character of the Articles 94 EC and 95 EC thus entails that where other, more specific Treaty provisions, such as Article 44 EC, can provide a legal basis for a particular measure, these specific provisions should be used.[6] Conversely, to the extent that more specific Treaty provisions like Article 44 EC are not capable of constituting the legal basis for the measure in question, Articles 94 EC and 95 EC may become relevant. (The conditions for the use of Article 44 EC were of course dealt with in the previous chapter).

C. Relationship between Article 94 EC and 95 EC

Article 94 EC dates from the 'primordial' EEC Treaty. Originally, it was Article 100 of that Treaty and subsequently it became Article 100 of the EC Treaty. Article 95 EC is of a later date. It was introduced in 1987 as Article 100a of the EEC Treaty, when the Single European Act entered into force,[7] and became Article 100a of the EC Treaty later on.

Article 95 EC was adopted to facilitate the passage of harmonizing measures; it allows the Council to act by a qualified majority, whereas Article 94 EC requires unanimity. Other 'formal' differences between these two articles are that: (1) Article 94 EC envisages directives, whereas Article 95 EC concerns the adoption of 'measures', which not only includes directives but also regulations; and (2) Article 94 EC merely requires the European Parliament to be consulted, whereas Article 95 EC provides the Parliament with more far-reaching powers by subjecting the proposed 'measures' to the co-decision procedure of Article 251 EC.

As to the respective subject-matter area of the Articles 94 and 95 EC, it is to be noted that in relation to Article 94 EC, Article 95 EC may be considered as a *lex specialis*.[8] Article 95 EC provides that it applies 'by way of derogation from Article 94'. This derogation, however, is of such a broad nature that (the introduction of) Article 95 EC has limited the scope of application of Article 94 EC considerably.

A final remark on the wording of both articles: Whereas Article 94 EC allows for the approximation of national measures directly affecting the establishment or functioning of the *common market*, Article 95 EC allows for the approximation of national measures to achieve the establishment and functioning of the *internal market*. Article 14 EC defines the internal market as an area without internal frontiers in which the free movement of goods, persons, services, and capital is ensured in accordance with the provisions of the Treaty; the common market

6. See Craig & de Búrca, 615.
7. See the Introduction of this book.
8. See Case C-350/92 *Spain* v *Council* [1995] ECR I-1985, para. 29 et seq.; Lauwaars & Timmermans, 276.

concept by contrast is undefined in the EC Treaty.[9] Now, even though in the legal doctrine the common market is considered to be broader to the extent that it – the common market – also includes a system of undistorted competition,[10] as to Article 95 EC the Court of Justice seems to see no distinction between the two market concepts and appears to treat the internal market and the common market as if they were interchangeable concepts:[11] according to the Court, Article 95 EC provides also a basis for measures contributing to removing distortions of competition.[12] I will elaborate on this further below.

D. Limits on the Use of Article 95(1) EC

1. Introduction

Article 95 EC, as said, allows for the approximation of national measures to achieve the establishment and functioning of the internal market. In this section, I will address three important, what may somewhat loosely be termed, limits on the use of Article 95(1) EC. The first two to be dealt with, are laid down *expressis verbis* in the Treaty itself (s. 2 and 3, *infra*), a third limit results from the case-law of the Court of Justice, particularly the so-called *Tobacco Advertizing* judgment (s. 4, *infra*).

2. The Exception of Article 95(2) EC

Article 95(2) EC contains an exception to the power granted by Article 95(1) EC to harmonize national law, by providing that this latter paragraph shall not apply to

9. L.W. Gormley, 'Competition and Free Movement: Is the Internal Market the Same as a Common Market?', *EBLR* (2002): 517.
10. See also Gormley, just cited, 518. See further Lenaerts & Van Nuffel, 143–144, with extensive references.
11. Gormley, just cited, 519 and 520.
12. See e.g., Case C-300/89, *Commission* v *Council* ('Titanium Dioxide') [1991] ECR I-2867, paras 14–15 ('According to the second paragraph of Article 8a of the EEC Treaty, that market [the internal market] is to comprise "an area without internal frontiers in which the free movement of goods, persons, services and capital is ensured". By virtue of Articles 2 and 3 of the Treaty, a precondition for such a market is the existence of *conditions of competition which are not distorted*. (. . .) In order to give effect to the fundamental freedoms mentioned in Article 8a, harmonizing measures are necessary to deal with disparities between the laws of the Member States in areas where such disparities are liable to create or maintain *distorted conditions of competition*. For that reason, Article 100a empowers the Community to adopt measures for the approximation of the provisions laid down by law (. . .) in Member States.' See also: Case C-376/98 *Germany* v *Parliament and Council* ('Tobacco Advertizing') [2000] ECR I-8419, paras 84, 94 and 106; Case C-301/06 *Ireland* v *Parliament and Council* ('Data retention'), judgment of 10 Feb. 2009, n.y.r., para. 63 ('The Community legislature may have recourse to Article 95 EC in particular where disparities exist between national rules which are such as to obstruct the fundamental freedoms or to create *distortions of competition* and thus have a direct effect on the functioning of the internal market'; emphasis added).

fiscal provisions, to those relating to the free movement of persons or to those relating to the rights and interests of employed persons. Legislation for these areas will therefore have to be passed by using either Article 94 EC or – as was explained above – a more specific provision of the Treaty (where one exists).[13]

The exclusion, by virtue of Article 95(2) EC, of the use of Article 95(1) EC in the field of free movement of persons, may – at first – be regarded as thoroughly limiting the latter's relevance to company law. Indeed, the term 'free movement of persons' of Article 95(2) EC, would seem to include, besides free movement of workers, also the right of establishment.[14] The right of establishment – the vital importance thereof to issues of company law was dealt with above[15] – would in that view be excluded from the scope of Article 95(1) EC.[16]

Of interest, however, is the Court's 2006 ruling in *European Parliament* v *Council* (which ruling, incidentally, concerned the lawfulness of the SCE Regulation).[17] In it, the Court considered *expressis verbis* that Article 95(1) EC is of importance for the attainment of freedom of establishment:

> Article 95 EC empowers the Community legislature to adopt measures to improve the conditions for the establishment and functioning of the internal market and they must genuinely have that object, contributing to the elimination of obstacles to the economic freedoms guaranteed by the Treaty, which include the *freedom of establishment* (see, in particular, Case C-376/98 *Germany* v *Parliament and Council* [2000] ECR I-8419, paragraphs 83, 84 and 95, and Case C-491/01 *British American Tobacco (Investments) and Imperial Tobacco* [2002] ECR I-11453, paragraph 60).[18] (emphasis added).

From this, it may be concluded that Article 95(1) EC does empower the Community legislature, in short, to adopt measures for the approximation of Member State provisions relating to freedom of establishment.[19] Those measures – and this is of

13. See also Craig & de Búrca, 617.
14. See e.g., the heading of Part Three, Title III of the EC Treaty ('Free movement of persons, services and capital'), in which connection 'free movement of persons' relates to the Arts 39–48 EC, which include both free movement of workers as well as the right of establishment. See further Lauwaars & Timmermans, 276–277.
15. See Ch. 3.
16. See in this connection also C.W.A. Timmermans, 'Methods and Tools for Integration', in *European Business Law. Legal and Economic Analyses on Integration and Harmonization*, ed. R.M. Buxbaum et al. (Berlin/New York: Walter de Gruyter, 1991), 143: 'I doubt, moreover, that this provision [Art. 100A, now Art. 95 EC] can be applied at all for the purposes of company and capital market harmonization. Article 100A(2) [now, Art. 95(2) EC] explicitly excludes the use of this article in the field of free movement of persons. Admittedly, the application of this article would be more acceptable for capital market harmonization, due to its links with the free movement of capital and with the realization of a European capital market.'
17. Case C-436/03 *Parliament* v *Council* ('SCE Regulation') [2006] ECR I-3733. See further s. E.2, *infra*. For a discussion of this judgment, see also my case-note in *JOR* 2006/149.
18. *Parliament* v *Council*, just cited, para. 38.
19. It is remarkable that the case-law the Court refers to in this connection, Case C-491/01 *British American Tobacco* [2002] ECR I-11453, para. 60 in particular, concerns the free movement of goods and the freedom to provide services, not, however, the right of establishment.

relevance – include regulations, whereas Article 44 EC only provides for the adoption of directives.[20]

To sum up, the exception of Article 95(2) EC should – notably in view of the 2006 *European Parliament* v *Council* ruling – be read as meaning that: Article 95(1) EC shall not apply to fiscal provisions, to those relating to the freedom of movement for workers nor to those relating to the rights and interests of employed persons. Since these issues (with a possible exception for the 'rights and interests of employed persons') are unlikely to concern the subject matter of company law, the exception of Article 95(2) EC will be of limited relevance to (future) EC company law instruments.

3. 'Approximation' of Laws 'in Member States'

The wording of Article 95(1) EC, by mentioning the 'approximation' of laws, regulations, and administrative action 'in Member States', calls for a reference by the Community measures to national law. Such a reference to (or link with) national law exists – as has been explained by Advocate General Kokott[21] – if, by means of provisions of Community law that are to be transposed, approximated national provisions come into being in all the Member States, or if Community law (such as a regulation) displaces or prevents national law that diverges from it.

> As regards the method of approximation, the Court has noted that by using the words 'measures for the approximation' in Article 95 EC, the authors of the Treaty intended to confer on the Community legislature a discretion, depending on the general context and the specific circumstances of the matter to be harmonized, as regards the method of approximation most appropriate for achieving the desired result, in particular in fields with complex technical features.[22] Those measures for the approximation may, depending on the circumstances, consist of requiring all the Member States to authorize the entry on the market (of a product, or for that matter, a service, capital or companies), subjecting such an obligation of authorization to certain conditions, or even provisionally or definitely prohibiting the entry on the market.[23]

Purely Community measures which take effect *alongside* the law of a Member State without altering its normative content, on the other hand, do not in fact effect

20. As stated in the main text, Art. 95 EC has a complementary or residual character, meaning that if the Treaty contains a more specific provision that is capable of constituting the legal basis for the measure in question, that measure must be based on that provision. As Art. 44 EC, the more specific provision for attaining freedom of establishment, is not capable of constituting the legal base for a Regulation, Art. 95(1) EC may provide such a base (Art. 95(2) EC does not preclude this).
21. Opinion of AG Kokott in Case C-66/04 *United Kingdom* v *Parliament and Council* ('Regulation on smoke flavourings') [2005] ECR I-10553.
22. Case C-380/03 *Germany* v *Parliament and Council* ('Tobacco Advertizing II') [2006] ECR I-11573, para. 42 and case-law cited therein.
23. *Ibid.*, para. 43 and case-law cited therein.

any approximation of the laws of the Member States.[24] This was decided by the Court with respect, for instance, to new intellectual property rights which took effect alongside the existing national rights.[25] The 'limit' on the use of Article 95(1) EC under consideration here, will be shown to be of practical importance to EC instruments of company law as well.[26]

4. The *Tobacco Advertizing* Judgment of the Court of Justice

The third 'limit' on the use of Article 95(1) EC emerges from the Court of Justice's *Tobacco Advertizing* judgment of October 2000, which I enter into at some length as the Court discussed the conditions for taking recourse to Article 95(1) EC as a legal basis.[27]

The facts of this case may be summarized as follows. In 1998, Germany brought an action for annulment[28] of the so-called Tobacco Advertizing Directive.[29] The Directive was adopted on the basis of, *inter alia*, Article 100a of the EC Treaty (now, after amendment, Article 95 EC) which according to Germany did not constitute a proper legal basis for the Directive.[30]

---

24. Opinion of AG Kokott in Case C-66/04, just cited, pt. 31. See also the Opinion of AG Kokott in Case C-217/04 *United Kingdom and Northern Ireland* v *Parliament and Council* ('Regulation establishing ENISA') [2006] ECR I-3771, pt. 22.
25. See Opinion 1/94 'Competence of the Community to conclude international agreements concerning services and the protection of intellectual property' [1994] ECR I-5267, para. 59; Case C-377/98 *Netherlands* v *Parliament and Council* ('Biotechnology Directive') [2001] ECR I-7079, para. 24, where it is referred, in this connection, to the Regulation on the Community trade mark.
26. See s. E, *infra*.
27. Case C-376/98 *Germany* v *Parliament and Council* ('Tobacco Advertizing') [2000] ECR I-8419. For an extensive discussion of this judgment, see D. Wyatt, 'Community Competence to Regulate the Internal Market', *Working Paper No. 9/2007* (Jul. 2007, University of Oxford Faculty of Law Legal Studies Research Paper Series). This paper is available at <http://ssrn.com>.
28. For the action for annulment, provided for by Art. 230 EC, see Ch. 1.
29. Directive 98/43/EC of the European Parliament and of the Council of 6 Jul. 1998 on the approximation of the laws, regulations, and administrative provisions of the Member States relating to the advertising and sponsorship of tobacco products, OJ 1998 L 213, 9. (This Directive prohibited all forms of advertizing and sponsorship of tobacco products as well as any free distribution having the purpose or the effect of promoting such products. Its scope did not extend, however, to communications between professionals in the tobacco trade, advertizing in sale outlets, or in publications published and printed in third countries which are not principally intended for the Community market. Furthermore, pursuant to its Art. 5, the Directive did not preclude Member States from laying down, in accordance with the Treaty, such stricter requirements concerning the advertizing or sponsorship of tobacco products as they deemed necessary to guarantee the health protection of individuals).
30. Germany argued (*Tobacco Advertizing*, just cited, paras 23–35), e.g., that a mere reference to Art. 100a of the EC Treaty in the preamble to the Directive is not sufficient for taking recourse to that article: the measure must actually contribute to the improvement of the internal market, which is not the case here, as the Directive constituted in practice a total prohibition on tobacco advertizing (*ibid.*, para. 24), and it argued that public health policy was the centre of gravity of the Directive, yet harmonizing measures in that field were expressly prohibited by Art. 129(4), first indent of the EC Treaty (*ibid.*, para. 35).

In its analysis of the question whether the legal basis was incorrect, the Court considered with respect to the scope of Article 100a of the EC Treaty that:

> [83] (...) the measures referred to in Article 100a(1) of the Treaty are intended to improve the conditions for the establishment and functioning of the internal market. To construe that article as meaning that it vests in the Community legislature a general power to regulate the internal market would not only be contrary to the express wording of the provisions cited above [Articles 3c and 7a, now, after amendment, 3(1)(c) and 14 EC, resp.] but would also be incompatible with the principle embodied in Article 3b of the EC Treaty (now Article 5 EC) that the powers of the Community are limited to those specifically conferred on it.
> [84] Moreover, a measure adopted on the basis of Article 100a of the Treaty must genuinely have as its object the improvement of the conditions for the establishment and functioning of the internal market. If a mere finding of disparities between national rules and of the abstract risk of obstacles to the exercise of fundamental freedoms or of distortions of competition liable to result there from were sufficient to justify the choice of Article 100a as a legal basis, judicial review of compliance with the proper legal basis might be rendered nugatory. (...).
> [95] It [is] therefore necessary to verify whether the Directive actually contributes to eliminating obstacles to the free movement of goods and to the freedom to provide services, and to removing distortions of competition.

As to the actual contribution to 'the elimination of obstacles to the free movement of goods and the freedom to provide services' the Court concluded that the Community legislature could not rely on the need to eliminate obstacles to the free movement of advertizing media and the freedom to provide services in order to adopt the Directive on the basis of Article 100a of the EC Treaty.[31]

> The Court started by noting that, as a result of disparities between national laws on the advertizing of tobacco products, obstacles to the free movement of goods or the freedom to provide services exist or may arise, referring particularly to periodicals, magazines, and newspapers which contain advertizing for tobacco products. In principle, the Court continued, a Directive prohibiting the advertizing of tobacco products in such press products could be adopted on the basis of Article 100a of the EC Treaty with a view to ensuring the free movement of press products.[32] The prohibition of the Directive at issue, however, was more broadly drawn, covering numerous types of advertizing of tobacco products (advertizing on posters, parasols, ashtrays, and other articles used in hotels, restaurants, and cafés and advertizing spots in cinemas) for which the prohibition could not be justified by the need to eliminate obstacles to the free movement of advertizing media or the freedom to provide

31. *Tobacco Advertizing*, just cited, para. 99.
32. *Ibid.*, paras 96–98.

services in the field of advertizing.[33] Prohibitions of these types of advertizing, the Court found, in no way helped to facilitate trade in the products concerned.[34] Moreover, the Court added that – and this is a further important reason why the Directive failed – the Directive did not ensure free movement of products which are in conformity with its provisions, rather Member States retained the right to lay down such stricter requirements concerning advertizing as they deemed necessary.[35]

From the above aspects of the judgment it follows, that recourse to Article 95 EC is justified where differences between the national rules of the Member States are such as to obstruct the fundamental freedoms and thus have a direct effect on the functioning of the internal market.[36] A measure based on Article 95 EC must genuinely have as its object the improvement of the conditions for the establishment and functioning of the internal market.[37] A mere finding of disparities between national rules and the abstract risk of obstacles to the exercise of fundamental freedoms do not suffice for the choice of Article 95 EC as a legal basis.[38] (Otherwise, the Community legislature would have a general power to regulate the internal market, which is incompatible with the principle that the powers of the Community are those specifically conferred on it.[39])

More generally, the above obstruction to the fundamental freedoms may, in my view, concern obstacles which remain – or which are created – by virtue of the fact that the national legislature applies, in brief, one of the derogations from the prohibitions in the field of the relevant free movement.[40] This may further

33. *Ibid.*, para. 99. Observe that the objective of the Directive was to eliminate obstacles to the movement of the products which serve as the media for advertizing and sponsorship for tobacco products (*ibid.*, para. 90).
34. *Ibid.*, para. 99. What may have played a role in the Court's findings is that in these cases the advertizing element of the product and the product itself are inextricably linked, since the products will be produced to order, bearing relevant advertizing material, and it could thus not be assumed that banning tobacco advertizing would lead to increased cross frontier trade in posters, parasols, ashtrays, and so forth. See D. Wyatt, just cited, 17.
35. More particularly, the Directive contained no provision holding that where the conditions laid down in the Directive are fulfilled, products of that kind in which trade is allowed in one Member State may move freely in the other Member States, including those where such products are prohibited. Rather, Member States retained the right to lay down such stricter requirements concerning advertizing as they deemed necessary to guarantee the health protection of individuals, and in contrast to other Directives allowing Member States to adopt stricter measures for the protection of the general interest, the Directive at issue contained no provision ensuring the free movement of products which conform to its provisions (*ibid.*, paras 102–104).
36. See to this effect, *Tobacco Advertizing*, just cited, paras 84 and 95. See also Case C-380/03 *Germany* v *Parliament and Council* ('Tobacco Advertizing II') [2006] ECR I-11573, para. 37 with further references.
37. *Tobacco Advertizing*, just cited, paras 83 and 95.
38. *Ibid.*, para. 84.
39. *Ibid.*, paras 83–84.
40. See, to this effect, Case C-168/98 *Luxemburg* v *Parliament and Council* [2000] ECR I-9131, para. 32; cf. Opinion of AG Geelhoed in Case C-491/01 *British American Tobacco* [2002] ECR I-11453, pt. 103.

> concern restrictions on these fundamental freedoms, which are not justified.[41] This may also concern obstacles for which the above prohibitions do not provide a solution.[42]

On the issue whether the Directive was justified as a method of 'removing distortions of competition', the Court stated first, in the abstract, that the distortion of competition which the Community legislature purports to eliminate needs to be appreciable:

> In examining the lawfulness of a directive adopted on the basis of Article 100a of the Treaty, the Court is required to verify whether the distortion of competition which the measure purports to eliminate is appreciable (*Titanium Dioxide*, cited above, [Case C-300/89 *Commission* v *Council* [1991] ECR I-2867] paragraph 23).
>
> In the absence of such a requirement, the powers of the Community legislature would be practically unlimited. National laws often differ regarding the conditions under which the activities they regulate may be carried on, and this impacts directly or indirectly on the conditions of competition for the undertakings concerned. It follows that to interpret Articles 100a, 57(2) and 66 of the Treaty as meaning that the Community legislature may rely on those articles with a view to eliminating the smallest distortions of competition would be incompatible with the principle, already referred to in paragraph 83 of this judgment, that the powers of the Community are those specifically conferred on it.[43]

---

41. Having recourse for the Community legislature to Art. 95 EC is thus in my view not excluded, even though these restrictions are prohibited by the respective provisions of these fundamental freedoms (and individuals may invoke these provisions against national authorities and the Commission may start an infringement procedure against Member States *ex* Art. 226 EC). See also Ch. 3 (s. III.B.1.b.(2)).
42. Above I have dealt with the question of whether Art. 44 EC (attainment of freedom of establishment) provides the Community legislature also with a power to eliminate 'obstacles' for which Art. 43 EC does not provide a solution. See Ch. 3. In that connection it was already briefly noted that a somewhat similar question has arisen as regards Art. 95 EC, *vis-à-vis* the free movement of goods (Art. 28 et seq. EC): Can the EC harmonize national rules falling outwith Art. 28 EC? The debate in the literature so far was found to be inconclusive. As to *Tobacco Advertizing* it must be noted that the Court, as was mentioned in the main text, refers in broad terms to the elimination of 'obstacles', not just 'restrictions' on fundamental freedoms or 'obstacles *stricto sensu*'). See for this latter term (and the relevance of such obstacles to Art. 95 EC), Wyatt, just cited, 41–46. In my view, the Community legislature has the power under Art. 95 EC (similar to its power under Art. 44 EC, as mentioned) to enact measures promoting legal certainty and building confidence, provided it can be substantiated that lack of legal certainty or lack of trust (e.g., by companies, members or others, in foreign, different legal regimes and foreign companies) genuinely hinders, in short, the establishment or functioning of the internal market and the measures adopted actually lift these hindrances, and thus these grounds are not used as a mere pretence for a general power to regulate (national company laws). This in my view fits in with a reading of Art. 95(1) EC in light of Art. 3(1)(h) EC, which latter provision provides for 'the approximation of the laws of Member States to the extent required for the *functioning* of the common market'. (emphasis added).
43. *Tobacco Advertizing*, just cited, paras 106–107.

The Court then examined whether the Directive actually contributed to eliminating appreciable distortions of competition. It came to the conclusion that the Community legislature could not rely on the need to eliminate distortions of competition, either in the advertizing sector or in the tobacco products sector, in order to adopt the Directive on the basis of Article 100a of the EC Treaty.

While the Court did not generally define what constitute 'appreciable distortions of competition', its ruling nonetheless provides some indications on what constitute such distortions. The Court held that some effects of the differences between national advertizing regulations did *not constitute* distortions which could be described as appreciable. In this connection, it referred to effects of advantages on competition which were remote and indirect, notably, as regards advertizing agencies and producers of advertizing media, to the advantage in terms of economies of scale and increase in profits of undertakings established in Member States which impose fewer restrictions on tobacco advertizing. The Court added that they are not comparable to the distortions of competition caused by differences in production costs, such as those which prompted the Community legislature to adopt the Directive on titanium dioxide.[44] As differences between regulations on tobacco advertizing which may give rise to *appreciable distortions* of competition, the Court referred to the fact that sponsorship is prohibited in some Member States and authorized in others, giving rise, in particular, to certain sports events being relocated, with considerable repercussions on the conditions of competition for undertakings associated with such events.[45]

It would thus seem that the Court's view as to distortions of competition is as follows. Mere differences between national regulations regarding the conditions under which the activities they regulate may be carried on and the ensuing impact on the conditions of competition for the undertakings concerned (advantages in terms of economies of scale and increase in profits) in themselves are insufficient for the Community legislature to rely on the need to eliminate distortions of competition. In view of the fact that national laws often differ regarding such conditions, more is required in order for the Community legislature to be able to rely on Article 95 EC with a view to eliminating distortions of competition. (Otherwise, the Community legislature would have a general power to regulate the internal market, which is incompatible with the principle that the powers of the Community are those specifically conferred on it.[46]). What is required is that the distortion of competition which the Community legislature purports to eliminate is *appreciable*. This seems to be case where national rules differ substantially, particularly in respect to rules having significant economic implications for the undertakings concerned, in so far as they involve substantial

44. *Ibid.*, para. 109.
45. Even though, according to the Court, such distortions could be a basis for recourse to Art. 100a of the EC Treaty in order to prohibit *certain* forms of sponsorship, they are not such as to justify the use of that legal basis for an *outright* prohibition of advertizing of the kind imposed by the Directive (*ibid.*, paras 110–111).
46. *Tobacco Advertizing*, just cited, para. 107 *jo.* 83.

investment, operating[47] and production costs.[48] Similarly, differences giving rise to the relocation of economic activity may have considerable repercussions on conditions of competition.[49]

As the Community legislature thus could not rely on the need to eliminate obstacles to the exercise of fundamental freedoms or on the need to eliminate distortions of competition, the Court held that Article 100a of the EC Treaty did not constitute an appropriate legal basis for the Directive and annulled the Directive in its entirety.[50]

To sum up, two key conditions for the use of Article 95(1) EC can be extracted from the judgment: (1) a mere finding of disparities between national rules and of the abstract risk of obstacles to the exercise of fundamental freedoms or of distortions of competition liable to result there from does not suffice for recourse to Article 95 EC: a measure adopted on the basis of Article 95 EC must genuinely have as its object the improvement of the conditions for the establishment and functioning of the internal market.[51] It must actually contribute to eliminating

47. See Opinion of AG Bot in Case C-301/06 *Ireland* v *Parliament and Council* ('Data retention'), judgment of 10 Feb. 2009, n.y.r., pts. 84–85 (retention of data by the providers of electronic communications services represents a significant financial burden on them, and that burden is proportionate to the amount of data to be retained and the retention period. Differences between national regulations on the amount of data to be retained and the retention period may give rise to distortions in competition between undertakings operating on the electronic communications market). Similarly, the views of the European Parliament (*Data retention*, just cited, para. 36) and of the Commission (*ibid.,* para. 50: 'The obligations relating to data retention have significant economic implications for service providers. Divergences between those obligations could lead to distortions in the internal market'). The Court seems to have followed these views (*ibid.*, paras 66–72, referring to substantial differences between national measures in respect of the nature of the data retained and the periods of data retention and the fact that the obligations relating to data retention have significant economic implications for service providers insofar as they may involve substantial investment and operating costs), albeit without expressly phrasing its conclusion as to the national regulations in terms of 'distortion of competition' but in more general terms as 'liable to have a direct impact on the functioning of the internal market' (*ibid.*, para. 71).
48. *Tobacco Advertizing*, cited above, para. 109; Case C-300/89 *Commission* v *Council* ('Titanium Dioxide') [1991] ECR I-2867, para. 23.
49. *Tobacco Advertizing*, cited above, para. 110. See also Opinion of AG Geelhoed in Case C-491/01 *British American Tobacco* [2002] ECR I-11453, pt. 162 (observing that the divergent national provisions at issue could result in the transfer of investments within the European Union and for that reason lead to an appreciable distortion of the common market, after having noted that national regulations applying to the composition of cigarettes exercise a significant influence on the investment decisions of tobacco product manufacturers, and that manufacturers will prefer to invest in countries which have the most flexible legislation).
50. *Tobacco Advertizing*, cited above, paras 115–118. The Court noted that even though a Directive prohibiting certain forms of advertizing and sponsorship of tobacco could have been adopted on the basis of Art. 100a of the Treaty, given the general nature of the prohibition laid down by the Directive at issue, partial annulment of the Directive would entail amendment by the Court of provisions of the Directive. As such amendments are a matter for the Community legislature, the Court could not annul the Directive partially (*ibid.*, para. 117).
51. *Ibid.*, para. 84.

obstacles[52] to the economic freedoms guaranteed by the Treaty[53] and to removing distortions of competition;[54] (2) distortions of competition caused by differences in national legislation must be appreciable in order to justify the use of Article 95(1) EC.[55] In subsequent case-law, the Court has confirmed these principles.[56]

I add that in the doctrine, the first condition has been interpreted as meaning that legislation adopted under Article 95 EC must *in any case* contribute to the

52. *Ibid.*, paras 84 and 95.
53. The case before the Court related to free movement of goods and to the freedom to provide services. (See, in this connection, para. 95, just cited in the main text). See, however, also Case C-436/03 *Parliament* v *Council* ('SCE Regulation') [2006] ECR I-3733, para. 38: 'Article 95 EC *empowers the Community legislature to adopt measures* to improve the conditions for the establishment and functioning of the internal market and they must genuinely have that object, *contributing to the elimination of obstacles to the economic freedoms* guaranteed by the Treaty, which include the *freedom of establishment* (see, in particular, Case C-376/98 *Germany* v *Parliament and Council* [2000] ECR I-8419, paragraphs 83, 84 and 95, and Case C-491/01 *British American Tobacco (Investments) and Imperial Tobacco* [2002] ECR I-11453, paragraph 60).' (emphasis added). For this observation of *Parliament* v *Council* ('SCE Regulation'), see already s. 2, *supra*. For a further discussion of this judgment, see s. E.2, *infra*.
54. *Tobacco Advertizing*, cited above, para. 95.
55. *Ibid.*, para. 106. Monitoring compliance with the Court's conclusion that distortion of competition must be 'appreciable' to justify harmonization is, obviously, not without difficulty. See further Wyatt, just cited, 20 and 22. In the main text of the present section, *supra*, I have, however, provided some indications as to what may constitute 'appreciable distortion of competition'. It is furthermore worth noting, that the question has been put forward whether the view expressed in *Tobacco Advertizing* that a distortion of competition should be appreciable before it can justify Community legislation under Art. 95 EC also extends to legislation adopted under Art. 94 EC. This issue will not be dealt with further here. I just refer to: J.A. Usher, 'Annotation, Case C-376/98, *Germany v. European Parliament and Council* (tobacco advertising). Judgment of the Full Court of 5 Oct. 2000, [2000] ECR I-8419', *CML Rev.* 38 (2001): 1528.
56. Case C-491/01 *British American Tobacco* [2002] ECR I-11453, para. 60; Case C-434/02 *Arnold André* [2004] ECR I-11825, para. 30; Case C-210/03 *Swedish Match* [2004] ECR I-11893, para. 29; Joined Cases C-154/04 and C-155/04 *Alliance for Natural Health a.O.* [2005] ECR I-6451, para. 28; Case C-380/03 *Germany* v *Parliament and Council* ('Tobacco Advertizing II') [2006] ECR I-11573, para. 37. Observe that from this case-law it seems to follow that one should be cautious to have a too restrictive view on the required link between, in short, the Community measure and the functioning of the internal market: (i) recourse to Art. 95 EC as a legal base is (also) possible if the aim is to prevent *future* obstacles to trade resulting from the heterogeneous development of national rules, provided the emergence of such obstacles is likely and the measure in question is designed to prevent them (see e.g., Case C-376/98 *Germany* v *Parliament and Council* ('Tobacco Advertizing') [2000] ECR I-8419, para. 97; *Swedish Match*, just cited, para. 30) and (ii) recourse to Art. 95 EC as a legal base does not presuppose the existence of an actual link with free movement between the Member States in *every* situation covered by the measure founded on that basis where the measure adopted is actually intended to improve the conditions for the establishment and functioning of the internal market (*Tobacco Advertizing II*, just cited, para. 80); Wyatt, just cited, explains the correctness of the latter aspect as follows: 'Where disparities between national rules lead to harmonisation to remove obstacles to trade, it is self-evident that not all products to which the internal market rules relate will actually be traded across national frontiers!' See extensively on the above cases, Wyatt, just cited, 24–40.

elimination of obstacles to free movement within the internal market.[57] The interpretation, however, that fulfilment of either condition will suffice has also been advocated.[58] The Court itself has clarified this issue in *British American Tobacco* of December 2002.[59] It held:

> First of all, it is clear from paragraphs 83, 84 and 95 of the tobacco advertising judgment that the measures referred to in that provision are intended to improve the conditions for the establishment and functioning of the internal market and must genuinely have that object, actually contributing to the elimination of obstacles to the free movement of goods or to the freedom to provide services, *or* to the removal of distortions of competition.[60] (emphasis added).

The emphasized 'or' in the quoted passage makes clear that fulfilment of either condition will suffice.[61]

Finally, two more general remarks on the significance of *Tobacco Advertizing* should be made. To begin with, *Tobacco Advertizing* has been argued to be the first time the Court struck down a legislative act because the Community legislature had exceeded its legislative powers.[62] The ruling is assumed to reveal 'a judicial determination to establish firmer limits on what may be validly achieved by the Community legislator in the name of harmonisation'.[63]

The second general remark relates to the phenomenon, that since the introduction of qualified majority voting within the Council in 1987 and the extension of this decision-making principle on subsequent Treaty revisions, the issue of precisely what competences are attributed to the Community by the Treaty has risen in importance.[64] It is stressed in this connection that under unanimity voting within the Council, Member States which feel that the legal basis for proposed

57. Usher, just cited, 1536.
58. S. Weatherill, 'The Commission's Options for Developing EC Consumer Protection and Contract Law: Assessing the Constitutional Basis', *EBLR* (2002): 506.
59. Case C-491/01 *British American Tobacco* [2002] ECR I-11453. See also Case C-380/03 *Germany* v *Parliament and Council* ('Tobacco Advertizing II') [2006] ECR I-11573, para. 67.
60. *British American Tobacco*, just cited, para. 60.
61. See also S. Weatherill, *Cases and Materials on EU Law* (Oxford: OUP, 2003), 66.
62. See P.J. Slot, 'A Contribution to the Constitutional Debate in the EU in the Light of the Tobacco Judgment', *EBLR* (2002): 3. Slot remarks in this connection that, occasionally, 'lack of competence' as ground for review of Community legislation has been invoked successfully to challenge legislative acts. Those disputes, however, still according to Slot, related to the division of powers between the different EC institutions: 'In the Tobacco judgment the dispute concerns the question whether the Community has the required powers or whether these rest with the Member States. Thus it is a more principled, constitutional issue.' See further G. de Búrca, 'The Tobacco Advertizing Saga: Political Aspirations and Constitutional Constraints', *CELS Occasional Paper* no. 5 (Jul. 2001, Cambridge), <www.cels.law.cam.ac.uk/>, p. 7 (noting on the significance of *Tobacco Advertizing* that until *Tobacco Advertizing* the Court had never actually annulled an entire legislative measure of the Community for 'lack of competence' under Art. 230 EC (ex Art. 173 of the EC Treaty).
63. S. Weatherill, 'The European Commission's Green Paper on European Contract Law: Context, Content and Constitutionality', *JCP* 24 (2001): 364.
64. See Weatherill, in *JCP*, just cited, 366; Weatherill, in *EBLR*, just cited, 502–503.

Community action is inadequate or open to contestation, can simply use their veto. An objective determination of the exact scope of the EC's competence does not come into play. Under qualified majority voting by contrast, an outvoted Member State's only – legal – option[65] in this respect is to turn to the Court of Justice which is to decide subsequently on the precise contours of the (disputed) competence. *Tobacco Advertizing* now brings this phenomenon into the open. Germany, of the opinion that Article 100a of the EC Treaty (now, after amendment, Article 95 EC) was not the proper legal basis for the Directive, could simply have used its veto if unanimity would have been required. However, decision-making under Article 95 EC merely requires a qualified majority, as mentioned earlier, and Germany had been outvoted. Germany thus had an interest in bringing the case before the Court of Justice (through an action for annulment of the Tobacco Advertizing Directive); as a consequence of which the precise competence attributed to the Community by Article 95(1) EC became an issue (to be decided upon, as mentioned, by the Court).

E. Analysis of EC Company Law Modernization in View of the Conditions of Article 95 EC

1. Introduction

At issue in this paragraph is the relevance of Article 95 EC to specific EC company law measures. I will deal with the Court's judgment in *European Parliament* v *Council*,[66] already referred to at the beginning of this section II (s. 2, *infra*). In this case, it may be reiterated, the European Parliament sought annulment of the SCE Regulation on the basis that Article 95 EC should have been used (instead of Article 308 EC). Secondly, the Directive on shareholder rights (s. 3, *infra*) will be entered into.

Before dealing with these issues, first some words on the Commission's view as expressed in its Action Plan on *Modernising Company Law and Enhancing Corporate Governance*.

As stated earlier, the Commission identified two policy objectives that future action at the European level in the area of company law seek as much as possible to meet: (i) strengthening shareholders rights and third party protection, and (ii) fostering efficiency and competitiveness of business. As I have also noted, the Commission focuses here on what the Community *should* do, but it does not reveal any close attention being paid to the prior question whether the Community legislature is *competent* to do so in the first place: do the above objectives provide a

65. Member States may invoke Art. 95(4) EC to maintain national provisions in spite of harmonization measures *ex* Art. 95(1) EC. However, the Member States' concerns which can legitimately trigger Art. 95(4) EC do not include 'constitutionality' objections. For a general discussion of Art. 95(4) EC, see N. De Sadeleer, 'Procedures for derogations from the principle of approximation of laws under Article 95 EC', *CML Rev.* 40 (2003): 889–915.
66. Case C-436/03 *Parliament* v *Council* ('SCE Regulation') [2006] ECR I-3733.

ground at all for Community action? Analyzing these objectives in light of Article 44 EC, I concluded that this article does not provide a ground for attaining these objectives *per se*, without a contribution to the freedom of establishment. A similar conclusion holds true in my view as to Article 95 EC. This article requires that a measure actually contributes to the improvement of the establishment and functioning of the internal market by eliminating obstacles to the fundamental freedoms. Fostering efficiency and competitiveness of business (and strengthening shareholder rights and third party protection) *per se*, without eliminating obstacles to the fundamental freedoms does not provide a ground for action under Article 95 EC. (As with Article 44 EC, this is not to say that legislative policy views as to the proper purpose of company law (e.g., in this case fostering efficiency and competitiveness of business) may not inform the shaping of the content of a Community measure. In fact, they may, *provided* the Community legislature's competence to act has been established). Not only the above objectives, but also various arguments advanced in the Action Plan in favour of Community harmonization, may in themselves, if they were acted upon by the Community legislature on the basis of Article 95 EC, be insufficient for valid action. It would seem in fact that the idea underlying various arguments advanced is that 'a mere finding of disparities and an abstract risk of obstacles' suffices for harmonization,[67] an idea rejected by the Court in *Tobacco Advertizing* and its progeny.

2. *European Parliament* v *Council*: Lawfulness of the SCE Regulation

On 22 July 2003, the SCE Regulation was adopted which provided for the creation of a new form of cooperative society.[68] The Council adopted the Regulation on the basis of Article 308 EC, which provides for a unanimous decision of the Council

67. In the ACTION PLAN the Commission notes e.g.: 'The new member countries will *increase the diversity* of the national regulatory frameworks in the EU, underlying further the importance of a principle-based approach to maintain a high level of legal certainty in intra-Community operations' (at 7); 'A certain degree of harmonization of defined national issues *reduces uncertainties* and can thereby significantly enhance business efficiency and competitiveness' (at 9); '*Differences* in national corporate governance regimes *may create uncertainty* and costs for both issuers and investors, which need to be addressed to promote an efficient integration of EU capital markets' (at 11). I observe that an abstract risk of uncertainties and costs may always be present in case of differences between national laws, regulations and administrative provisions. This in itself does not suffice as a ground for action on the basis of Art. 95 EC, otherwise this article would amount to a general power to regulate the internal market. The differences (and accompanying uncertainties and lack of confidence) need to be such as to obstruct the fundamental freedoms and thus have a direct effect on the functioning of the internal market (see, to that effect, Case C-376/98 *Germany* v *Parliament and Council* ('Tobacco Advertizing') [2000] ECR I-8419, para. 60; Case C-434/02 *Arnold André* [2004] ECR I-11825, para. 30; Case C-210/03 *Swedish Match* [2004] ECR I-11893, para. 29; Joined Cases C-154/04 and C-155/04 *Alliance for Natural Health a.O.* [2005] ECR I-6451, para. 28; Case C-380/03 *Germany* v *Parliament and Council* ('Tobacco Advertizing II') [2006] ECR I-11573, para. 37).
68. Council Regulation (EC) No. 1435/2003 of 22 Jul. 2003 on the Statute for a European Cooperative Society (SCE), OJ 2003 L 207, 1–24.

after (merely) *consulting* the European Parliament. Article 308 EC may be used as the legal basis for a measure only where no other provision of the Treaty gives the Community institutions the necessary power to adopt it.[69] In the view of the European Parliament, however, such a provision existed, namely Article 95 EC. The use of this article had incidentally also been suggested by the Commission in its initial proposal of 6 March 1992 and in its amended proposal of 6 July 1993.[70] Article 95 EC, as was explained above, empowers the European Parliament and the Council to *adopt* acts together (the so-called 'co-decision' procedure), which obviously gives the European Parliament a greater say than the compulsory consultation Article 308 EC provides for. In October 2003, the European Parliament brought the issue before the Court. It claimed, under Article 230 EC, that the Court should annul the SCE Regulation in view of an improper legal basis.

How does the Court rule on the (material) scope of Article 95 EC? Does this article offer an appropriate legal basis for adoption of the SCE Regulation? Of crucial importance is that Community measures based on Article 95 EC must, as was dealt with above, in section D, be aimed at approximating the laws of the Member States. Article 95 EC explicitly refers to the adoption of:

> measures for the *approximation* of the provisions laid down by law, regulation or administrative action *in Member States*. (emphasis added).

This (harmonization) objective, however, is absent in the case of the SCE Regulation. The Court observes that:

> the contested regulation, which leaves unchanged the different national laws already in existence, cannot be regarded as aiming *to approximate the laws of the Member States* applicable to cooperative societies, but has as its purpose the creation of a new form of cooperative society in addition to the national forms.[71] (emphasis added).

For this reason, said the Court, Article 95 EC could not constitute an appropriate legal basis for the adoption of the SCE Regulation.[72]

---

69. Case C-436/03 *Parliament* v *Council* ('SCE Regulation') [2006] ECR I-3733, para. 36.
70. See: Proposal for a Council Regulation on the Statute for a European Cooperative Society, OJ 1992 C 99, 17–36; Amended proposal for a Council Regulation on the Statute for a European Cooperative Society, OJ 1993 C 236, 17–36. For an early criticism against the choice of this particular legal basis (for the SE): W.C.L. van der Grinten, 'Europese n.v.?', in *Grensoverschrijdend privaatrecht* (liber amicorum Van Rijn van Alkemade) (Deventer: Kluwer, 1993), 110.
71. *Parliament* v *Council*, just cited, para. 44.
72. *Ibid.*, para. 46. See also the Opinion of AG Stix-Hackl in the case at issue. The AG observed, in short, that with the SCE a new legal form is created, alongside national forms of cooperatives. The connection to national law required by Art. 95 ('approximation', 'in Member States') is absent ('le règlement est sans incidence sur le droit national applicable aux coopératives'; 'national law on cooperative societies is not affected by the regulation'; pt. 90). On the basis of this observation, the AG subsequently rejected the creation of the SCE on the basis of Art. 95(1) EC. The view of AG Stix-Hackl has been concurred with by the Opinion of AG Kokott in Case C-217/04 *United Kingdom and Northern Ireland* v *Parliament and Council*

It should be noted, that in support of its action, the European Parliament put forward the *single* plea in law, that Article 308 EC could not be used as a legal basis, as Article 95 EC would be the appropriate legal basis for the Regulation. On the above quoted ground, the Court rejected this plea and held: 'As the sole plea is unfounded, the action must be dismissed.'[73] Could the Parliament have put forward another plea? Is there perhaps another Treaty provision (instead of the rejected Article 95 EC) which may be argued to form an appropriate legal basis, preventing the use of Article 308 EC? This issue will be taken up in section III, *infra*, where Article 308 EC will be discussed.

Finally, even though the inter-institutional conflict between the European Parliament and the Council concerned the *SCE*, the Court's judgment under consideration here, is – in my opinion – also of relevance to the other Community legal forms based on Article 235 EEC (now Article 308 EC) and Article 308 EC: the European Economic Interest Grouping (EEIG) and the European company (SE). The Court's considerations[74] may be applied *mutatis mutandis* to these legal forms. The Regulations on the EEIG and the SE therefore, following the line of reasoning of the Court, which related only to the above single plea, have correctly been adopted on the basis of Article 235 EEC (now Article 308 EC) and Article 308 EC respectively, and not on the basis of Article 95 EC.

3. Directive on Shareholder Rights

On 11 July 2007, the Directive on the exercise of certain rights of shareholders in listed companies ('Directive on shareholder rights') was adopted.[75] The legal basis for the Directive is Article 44 EC and Article 95 EC.[76] Does Article 95 EC provide an appropriate legal basis for adoption of the Directive? (The appropriateness of Article 44 EC was dealt with above[77]).

Article 95 EC, as was shown above,[78] empowers the Community legislature to adopt measures contributing to the elimination of obstacles to the economic freedoms guaranteed by the Treaty.[79]

('Regulation establishing ENISA') [2006] ECR I-3771. AG Kokott concluded at pt. 24 of that Opinion that: 'Advocate General Stix-Hackl's view [in *Parliament* v *Council* on the SCE Regulation; GJV] must be accepted in the case of the creation of new kinds of companies, if they take their place *alongside* the kinds of companies in the individual States' legal systems. In that case the necessary (approximating) reference to those legal systems is absent.'

73. *Parliament* v *Council*, just cited, para. 47.
74. *Ibid.*, in particular, paras 40–46.
75. Directive 2007/36/EC of the European Parliament and of the Council of 11 Jul. 2007 on the exercise of certain rights of shareholders in listed companies, OJ 2007 L 184, 17–24.
76. See the opening consideration in the preamble to the Directive.
77. See Ch. 3.
78. See in particular s. D.
79. Case C-376/98 *Germany* v *Parliament and Council* ('Tobacco Advertizing') [2000] ECR I-8419, para. 95; Case C-491/01 *British American Tobacco* [2002] ECR I-11453, para. 60; Case C-436/03 *Parliament* v *Council* ('SCE Regulation') [2006] ECR I-3733, para. 38.

As regards, first, the element that the adopted measure, in short, contributes to the *economic freedoms* guaranteed by the Treaty, it is reiterated here that these freedoms include the free movement of goods, the right of establishment, the freedom to provide services, and the free movement of capital.[80]

Now, according to its preamble, the objective of the Directive is: 'to allow shareholders effectively to make use of their rights throughout the Community'.[81] The underlying objective is that of 'good or sound corporate governance'.[82] I already argued above that I think that it is not evident that the Community legislature has thus sufficiently established a link between the Directive and the freedom of establishment.[83] In my view, the same applies in respect of the other economic freedoms guaranteed by the Treaty. The contribution to economic freedoms (required under Article 95 EC) is in fact not specifically addressed in the preamble to the Directive. The Community legislature's focus is (largely) on legislative policy goals (enhancing shareholders' rights and good corporate governance) without establishing (or explaining) its competence to pursue these goals.

It may, however, not automatically be concluded from this lack of explanation that the Directive would not contribute to the economic freedoms guaranteed by the Treaty, in particular free movement of capital. Let me explain this.

The EC Treaty does not define the term 'movement of capital' in Article 56 EC, but it is settled case-law that Directive 88/361, together with the nomenclature annexed to it,[84] may be used for the purposes of defining what constitutes a capital movement.[85] 'Movement of capital' thus includes in particular *direct investments* in the form of participation in an undertaking through the holding of shares which confers the possibility of effectively participating in its

80. *Ibid.* See, especially, Case C-436/03 *Parliament* v *Council* ('SCE Regulation') [2006] ECR I-3733, para. 38 (also dealt with above in s. D), and e.g., also Lauwaars & Timmermans, 276–277 (regarding free movement of capital).
81. See recital 14 in the preamble to the Directive.
82. In recital 3 in the preamble to the Directive it is argued that 'effective shareholder control is a prerequisite to *sound corporate governance* and should, therefore, be facilitated and encouraged'. (emphasis added). Recital 10 states, in this connection, that: '*Good corporate governance* requires a smooth and effective process of proxy voting. Existing limitations and constraints which make proxy voting cumbersome and costly should therefore be removed. But *good corporate governance* also requires adequate safeguards against a possible abuse of proxy voting.' (emphasis added).
83. See Ch. 3.
84. Council Directive 88/361/EEC of 24 Jun. 1988 for the implementation of Art. 67 of the Treaty, OJ 1988 L 178, 5–18.
85. See: Case C-222/97 *Trummer and Mayer* [1999] ECR I-1661, paras 20 and 21, and, more recently, Case C-174/04 *Commission* v *Italy* [2005] ECR I-4933, about which latter judgment G.-J. Vossestein, 'case note', *JOR* 2005/204.

management and control,[86] and, further, *the acquisition of shares on the capital market.*[87]

The Directive may then be argued to contribute to the elimination of obstacles to *free movement of capital* by removing various hindrances for shareholders to effectively make use of their rights, thus enhancing investor protection leading to more liquidity in financial markets, particularly more willingness to buy shares. I refer in this regard first to the 'Impact Assessment' of the proposal (for the Directive).[88] In it is stated that:

> Investor protection leads to broader and more liquid financial markets. Corporate governance and investment decisions are linked insofar as outside investors – facing the risk of expropriations by management or larger shareholders – will be more willing to buy shares in corporations where management strategies and actions are properly supervised and where minority investors enjoy a high level of protection.[89]

Liquidity in financial markets is then enhanced by removing various obstacles for shareholders. It may be referred to the Directive's preamble, which states in this respect, *inter alia*, that:

> *Obstacles* which deter shareholders from voting, such as making the exercise of voting rights subject to the blocking of shares during a certain period before the general meeting, *should be removed.*[90] (emphasis added);
>
> Non-resident shareholders should be able to exercise their rights in relation to the general meeting as easily as shareholders who reside in the Member State in which the company has its registered office. This requires that existing *obstacles* which hinder the access of non-resident shareholders to the information relevant to the general meeting and the exercise of voting rights

86. In *Volkswagen*, direct investments are defined more extensively: 'investments of any kind undertaken by natural or legal persons and which serve to establish or maintain lasting and direct links between the persons providing the capital and the undertakings to which that capital is made available in order to carry out an economic activity (. . .). As regards shareholdings in new or existing undertakings (. . .) the objective of establishing or maintaining lasting economic links presupposes that the shares held by the shareholder enable him (. . .) to participate effectively in the management of that company or in its control (. . .)'. See Case C-112/05 *Commission* v *Germany* ('Volkswagen') [2007] ECR I-8995, para. 18.
87. See: Case C-367/98 *Commission* v *Portugal* [2002] ECR I-4731, para. 38; Case C-483/99 *Commission* v *France* [2002] ECR I-4781, para. 37; Case C-503/99 *Commission* v *Belgium* [2002] ECR I-4809, para. 38; Case C-98/01 *Commission* v *United Kingdom* [2003] ECR I-4641, para. 40, and, to that effect, Joined Cases C-282/04 and C-283/04 *Commission* v *Netherlands* ('KPN/TPG') [2006] ECR I-9141, para. 19.
88. Commission staff working document. Annex to the Proposal for a Directive of the European Parliament and of the Council on the exercise of voting rights by shareholders of companies having their registered office in a Member State and whose shares are admitted to trading on a regulated market and amending Directive 2004/109/EC. Impact assessment, SEC (2006) 181 of 17 Feb. 2006.
89. Impact assessment, just cited, 7.
90. Recital 3.

> without physically attending the general meeting *be removed*.[91] (emphasis added);
>
> Companies *should face no legal obstacles* in offering to their shareholders any means of electronic participation in the general meeting. Voting without attending the general meeting in person, whether by correspondence or by electronic means, should not be subject to constraints other than those necessary for the verification of identity and the security of electronic communications.[92] (emphasis added).

The above recitals (and the elimination of obstacles) are given effect in the Directive by, in particular, Articles 5, 7, and 8. In view of the fact that the Directive thus actually contributes to eliminating obstacles to the free movement of capital,[93] it may be concluded that Article 95 EC provides an appropriate legal basis for adoption of the Directive.

> The Directive could perhaps also be argued, to fulfil the alternative condition of Article 95 EC, that it contributes to the removal of (appreciable) distortions of competition.[94] Let me explain. The Directive's stated objective is to enhance shareholder rights (which concerns the *supply* of capital). The Directive, however, also may be looked at from the perspective of companies (which typically concerns the *demand* for capital).[95] As mentioned above, one of the ideas underlying this Directive is that investors – facing the risk of expropriations by management or larger shareholders – may be more willing to buy shares in corporations where management strategies and actions are properly supervised and where minority investors enjoy a high level of protection. Now, in this line of thinking, companies established in Member States offering a higher level of protection for shareholders may be at an advantage in terms of obtaining capital *vis-à-vis* companies established in Member States with a lower level of protection. The cost of capital for the latter group of companies may be assumed to be higher. These higher costs, in turn, may perhaps affect their competitiveness. The effect of the above advantages on competition may constitute a distortion of competition which could be described as appreciably where such diverging

---

91. Recital 5.
92. Recital 9. See also the Impact Assessment accompanying the proposal of this Directive as to the various legal obstacles and differences between Member States regarding e.g., proxy voting (p. 10), methods to appoint proxies (p. 10), share blocking (p. 11) and access to information relating to the General Meeting (p. 12–13).
93. Let me note further in this connection that in its case-law on 'golden shares' the Court has identified as a restriction within the meaning of Art. 56 EC, (national) measures liable to dissuade or deter investors from other Member States from investing in the company at issue. A, in short, low level of protection for (minority) shareholders could have this deterrent effect on investments; it may be capable of depressing the (stock market) value of the shares and thus reduce the attractiveness of an investment in the shares of the companies concerned. Cf. Joined Cases C-282/04 and C-283/04 *Commission* v *Netherlands* ('KPN/TPG') [2006] ECR I-9141, paras 27–28.
94. About this condition, s. D.4, *supra*.
95. A good example of this perspective offers recital 9 in the preamble to the Directive, just cited in the main text ('Companies should face no legal obstacles in offering to their shareholders any means of electronic participation in the general meeting'). See, in this connection, Art. 8 Directive.

rules have significant economic implications for the undertakings concerned, in so far as they involve substantial investment costs (cost of capital) for companies established in Member States with lower shareholder protection, or would give rise to certain economic activities (establishment of companies) being relocated to Member States offering higher levels of shareholder protection. If this indeed were the case, the Directive might in this sense be argued to (also) contribute to the removal of appreciable distortions of competition. This would provide an extra ground for the above conclusion that Article 95 EC empowers the Community legislature to adopt the Directive on shareholder rights.

Finally, even if it is established that the Directive (also) seeks to contribute to the attainment of freedom of establishment within the meaning of Article 44 EC (which is questionable, as is explained in Chapter 3), it seems that it must (still) be concluded that Article 95 EC constitutes the (only) appropriate legal basis for the Directive, as contribution to the elimination of obstacles to *free movement of capital* is the main or predominant purpose or component of the Directive.

Some remarks are here in order as to the Court's case law relating to the choice of legal basis.

Community competences are conferred by specific provisions of the EC Treaty, known as legal bases. The legal bases of relevance to EC company law are discussed in Chapter 3 and the current chapter. The choice of the correct legal basis is of considerable practical and institutional, indeed 'constitutional importance'.[96] It determines not only the legislative procedure applicable (rights of the Parliament to participate, unanimity, or qualified majority in the Council),[97] but it may also prescribe the type of instrument that may be used – for example, only directives.[98]

The case-law relating to the choice of the legal basis may be summarized as follows. Firstly, it must be observed that in the context of the organization of the powers of the Community, the choice of the legal basis for a measure may not depend simply on an institution's conviction as to the objective pursued, but it must be based on objective factors which are amenable to judicial review. Those factors include in particular the aim and content of the measure.[99]

Secondly, it has long been established, as shown above, that general or complementary powers, such as those laid down in the Articles 94 EC, 95 EC,

---

96. Opinion of AG Kokott in Case C-94/03 *Commission* v *Council* [2006] ECR I-1, pt. 24. The AG refers in this connection to Opinion 2/00 'Cartagena Protocol on Biosafety' [2001] ECR I-9713, para. 5. See also the Opinion of AG Kokott in Case C-178/03 *Commission* v *Parliament and Council* [2006] ECR I-107, pt. 29.
97. See the Opinion of AG Kokott cited first in the previous fn., pt. 24. The AG refers in this connection to Case C-211/01 *Commission* v *Council* ('Carriage of Goods') [2003] ECR I-8913, para. 52. See also the Opinion of AG Kokott cited last in the previous fn., pt. 29.
98. A. Dashwood, 'The relationship between the Member States and the European Union/European Community', *CML Rev.* 41 (2004): 358. See also Weatherill & Beaumont, 155, who remark that it can be of major significance to the legislative procedure to be followed which legal basis is chosen. It may mean the difference between the European Parliament being consulted and being involved in the cooperation procedure or between the Council acting by unanimity and some form of majority voting.
99. Case C-300/89 *Commission* v *Council* ('Titanium dioxide') [1991] ECR I-2867, para. 10.

and 308 EC, cannot be used to regulate a matter falling clearly within the ambit of a more specific provision.

Thirdly, the Court has developed a set of rules (concerning the choice of the legal basis) with respect to 'Community measures which pursue a twofold purpose'.[100] In a recent judgment the Court of Justice summarized its case-law on this particular issue. After having reiterated that:

> [34] According to settled case-law, the choice of the legal basis for a Community measure must rest on objective factors amenable to judicial review, which include the aim and content of that measure (see, to that effect, inter alia, Case C-300/89 *Commission* v *Council* ('Titanium dioxide') [1991] ECR I-2867, paragraph 10, and Case C-338/01 *Commission* v *Council* [2004] ECR I-4829, paragraph 54) (. . .),

the Court ruled as follows:

> [35] If examination of a measure reveals that it pursues two aims or that it has two components and if one of those aims or components is identifiable as the main one, whereas the other is merely incidental, the measure must be founded on a single legal basis, namely that required by the main or predominant aim or component (see, to that effect, inter alia, Case C-155/91 *Commission* v *Council* [1993] ECR I-939, paragraphs 19 and 21; Case C-36/98 *Spain* v *Council* [2001] ECR I-779, paragraph 59; Case C-338/01 *Commission* v *Council*, paragraph 55; and Case C-91/05 *Commission* v *Council*, paragraph 73).
> [36] With regard to a measure that simultaneously pursues a number of objectives, or that has several components, which are inseparably linked without one being incidental to the other, the Court has held that, where various provisions of the Treaty are therefore applicable, such a measure will have to be founded, exceptionally, on the various corresponding legal bases (see, to that effect, Case C-211/01 *Commission* v *Council* [2003] ECR I-8913, paragraph 40, and Case C-91/05 *Commission* v *Council*, paragraph 75).
> [37] None the less, the Court has previously held, in particular in paragraphs 17 to 21 of the judgment in Titanium dioxide, that recourse to a dual legal basis is not possible where the procedures laid down for each legal basis are incompatible with each other (see also, to that effect, Joined Cases C-164/97 and C-165/97 *Parliament* v *Council* [1999] ECR I-1139, paragraph 14; Case C-338/01 *Commission* v *Council*, paragraph 57; Case C-94/03 *Commission* v *Council* [2006] ECR I-1, paragraph 52; and Case C-178/03 *Commission* v *Parliament and Council* [2006] ECR I-107, paragraph 57).[101]

100. Cf. Case C-338/01 *Commission* v *Council* ('Directive on mutual assistance between Member States in the recovery of public-law claims') [2004] ECR I-4829, paras 54–58.
101. Case C-155/07 *Parliament* v *Council* ('Decision 2006/1016/EC – Community guarantee to the European Investment Bank'), judgment of 6 Nov. 2008, n.y.r. Regarding para. 35 of this judgment, just cited in the main text, the following must be noted. It is settled case-law, that an incorrect reference to a Treaty Article as a second legal basis for a directive does not of itself mean that the directive is invalid. Such an error in the citations of a Community act is no more than a purely formal defect, unless it gave rise to irregularity in the procedure

It has already been mentioned[102] that if the Treaty provision which is stated as being the legal basis for the act is substantively insufficient to support its content, the institution which adopted the act in question will have exceeded its powers. This is even the case if the institution could have adopted the same measure on the basis of some other Treaty provision.[103] If indeed a Community institution exceeds its powers like this, the act concerned can be declared void or invalid.[104]

Protection of non-controlling or minority shareholders, as explained in the main text, may contribute to free movement of capital. In light of its aim and content, this seems to be the main or predominant purpose or component of the Directive on shareholder rights indeed (whereas any contribution to freedom of establishment would be merely incidental). I shall make some brief remarks in this regard.

The objective of protection of non-controlling (minority) shareholders is frequently and explicitly referred to in the legislative history of the Directive (as opposed to that of controlling shareholders, which protection may be related to freedom of establishment as explained in Chapter 3). The quotation above from the 'Impact Assessment' of the proposal for the Directive, which emphasizes the need to protect investors against the risk of expropriation by management and *larger shareholders*, may serve as an example. Article 6 of the Directive may also serve as an example. It provides that Member States shall ensure that shareholders, acting individually or collectively, have the right to put items on the agenda of the general meeting and to table draft resolutions, and that any threshold required for the exercise of those rights should not exceed 5% of the company's share capital. The Commission insisted on adoption of this provision in view of 'the (. . .) difficulty (. . .) that *minority shareholders* are usually prevented from any access to these rights'.[105] (emphasis added).

---

applicable to the adoption of that act. See Case C-210/03 *Swedish Match* [2004] ECR I-11893, para. 44 (with further references). See, in this connection, Case C-491/01 *British American Tobacco* [2002] ECR I-11453, where the Court held, at para. 111 that: 'recourse to the twofold legal basis of Articles 95 EC and 133 EC did not give rise to irregularity in the procedure for adopting the directive and that the directive was not invalid on that account'. Similarly, the Opinion of AG Kokott delivered on 26 Mar. 2009 in Case C-13/07 *Commission* v *Council* ('Accession of Vietnam to WTO'), pt. 51: 'It is true that the citation of an incorrect legal basis or a reference to an incorrect legal basis in addition to the legal basis that is actually applicable means that the disputed act will be annulled only if the error is more than purely formal, that is to say, an error that could affect the applicable procedure and, thereby, ultimately the content of the legal measure.' (fn. omitted). (Both Art. 44 EC and Art. 95 EC provide for the Council to act in accordance with the procedure referred to in Art. 251 EC after consulting the Economic and Social Committee).

For the complicated issue, finally, of compatibility of procedures (of para. 37, just cited in the main text) it is further referred to the Opinion of AG Kokott (in the present case), pts. 81–91, and paras 73–82 of the Court's judgment.

102. See Ch. 1.
103. Lenaerts, Arts & Maselis, 291–292.
104. See further Ch. 1.
105. See 'Fostering an appropriate regime for shareholders' rights. Second consultation document of the Services of the Internal Market Directorate General' of 13 May 2005, p. 13–14. The text of this consultation document is available at the Commission's Internal Market website: <http://ec.europa.eu/internal_market/>.

It is, moreover, in the legislative history of the Directive recognized that controlling (foreign) shareholders do manage to be present at general meetings and to vote there.[106]

Let me, finally, note that the Directive is aimed at protecting the rights not only of shareholders in the EU but *outside the EU too.*[107] Indeed, its scope *ratione personae* is not limited to shareholders only in the EU (see Articles 1 and 2 of the Directive). Free movement of capital, as opposed to freedom of establishment, may (in principle) *also* be relied on by companies and nationals of third countries.[108]

If, in view of the above observations, it is assumed that free movement of capital is the main or predominant purpose or component indeed, the Community legislature has, in short, incorrectly based the Directive on shareholder rights also on Article 44 EC instead of just Article 95 EC.[109] (That incorrect reference to Article 44 EC as a (second) legal basis for the Directive, incidentally, is a 'purely formal defect', which does not render the Directive invalid[110]).

106. See 'Commission staff working document. Annex to the Proposal for a Directive of the European Parliament and of the Council on the exercise of voting rights by shareholders of companies having their registered office in a Member State and whose shares are admitted to trading on a regulated market and amending Directive 2004/109/EC. Impact assessment,' SEC (2006) 181 of 17 Feb. 2006, p. 9.
107. Cf. Opinion of the European Economic and Social Committee on the Proposal for a directive of the European Parliament and of the Council on the exercise of voting rights by shareholders of companies having their registered office in a Member State and whose shares are admitted to trading on a regulated market and amending Directive 2004/109/EC, *sub* 2.1, OJ 2006 C 318, 42.
108. See, to that effect, Case C-452/04 *Fidium Finanz AG* [2006] ECR I-9521, para. 25.
109. See already in this connection: G.-J. Vossestein, 'Capital and Companies: On the Move!', *ECL* 2006, p. 124; G.-J. Vossestein, 'Annotation of Case C-436/03 *Parliament* v *Council* [2006] ECR I-3733', *JOR* 2006/149.

     The Commission proposal for the Directive, incidentally, indeed referred to (just) Art. 95 EC as the legal basis for the Directive (see Proposal for a Directive on the exercise of voting rights (. . .), COM (2005) 685 final of 5 Jan. 2006); it was the European Parliament that added Art. 44 EC (see European Parliament legislative resolution on the proposal for a directive on the exercise of voting rights (. . .), OJ 2007 C 287 E, 486–497. Neither the European Parliament Report on the Proposal, A6-0024/2007 of 2 Feb. 2007, nor the debates in Parliament (of 15 Feb. 2007) explain the Parliament amendment under consideration.
110. For the Court's (settled) case-law on this type of 'purely formal defects', see the observations above, and in particular: Case C-491/01 *British American Tobacco* [2002] ECR I-11453, paras 98, 103–111; Case C-210/03 *Swedish Match* [2004] ECR I-11893, para. 44 (with further references), and, recently, the Opinion of AG Kokott delivered on 26 Mar. 2009 in Case C-13/07 *Commission* v *Council* ('Accession of Vietnam to WTO'), pt. 51. See further Ch. 1 (on judicial review) in which connection it is reiterated that an action for annulment must be instituted within two months of the publication of the measure (and that no such action has been instituted against the Directive on shareholder rights).

III. ARTICLE 308 EC: FILLING IN THE LACUNAE IN THE SYSTEM OF POWERS

A. INTRODUCTION

The relevance of Article 308 EC to EC company law is shown in particular in the area of Community legal forms. It is on the basis of this article that all Community legal forms have been created: the European Economic Interest Grouping (EEIG); the *Societas Europaea* (SE), and the *Societas Cooperativa Europaea* (SCE). Article 308 EC reads as follows:

> If action by the Community should prove necessary to attain, in the course of the operation of the common market, one of the objectives of the Community, and this Treaty has not provided the necessary powers, the Council shall, acting unanimously on a proposal from the Commission and after consulting the European Parliament, take the appropriate measures.

Article 308 EC's function is, as the Court held in its Opinion 2/94, to fill the gap where no specific provisions of the Treaty confer on the Community institutions powers to act, if such powers appear nonetheless to be necessary to enable the Community to carry out its functions with a view to attaining one of the objectives laid down by the Treaty.[111] The Court of Justice has consistently held that the use of Article 308 EC as the legal basis for a measure is justified only where no other provision of the Treaty gives the Community institutions the necessary power to adopt the measure in question.[112] This condition – that the Treaty has not provided the necessary power – does not require that no powers exist at all. It may be that powers do exist, but that they do not provide for a satisfactory and effective solution, for instance where harmonization by means of directives is provided for, but in actual fact uniform rules by means of regulations are needed.[113]

---

111. Opinion 2/94 'Accession by the Communities to the Convention for the Protection of Human Rights and Fundamental Freedoms' [1996] ECR I-1759, para. 29. See also: Case C-436/03 *Parliament* v *Council* ('SCE Regulation') [2006] ECR I-3733, para. 36; Joined Cases C-402/05 P and C-405/05 P, *Kadi a.O.* v *Council and Commission*, judgment of 3 Sep. 2008, n.y.r., para. 211.
112. Case C-271/94 *Parliament* v *Council* [1996] ECR I-1689, para. 13; The Court refers in particular to Case 45/86 *Commission* v *Council* [1987] ECR 1493, para. 13, and Case C-350/92 *Spain* v *Council* [1995] ECR I-1985, para. 26. See also Case C-436/03 *Parliament* v *Council* ('SCE Regulation') [2006] ECR I-3733.
113. Kapteyn & VerLoren van Themaat, 221. See also Lauwaars & Timmermans, 74. A good example provides Case 8/73 *Hauptzollamt Bremerhaven* v *Massey Ferguson* [1973] ECR 897. See further *Kadi a.O.*, just cited, para. 216 (noting that lack of power, attributable to the limited ambit *ratione personae* of the provisions at hand, could be made good by having recourse to Art. 308 EC as a legal basis for the regulation at issue).

B. Analysis of the SCE Regulation in View of Article 308 EC

Does the Regulation concerning the SCE, which was adopted after publication of the Action Plan, meet the above condition for the use of Article 308 EC that the 'Treaty has not provided the necessary powers'?[114] Here, the Court's judgment of May 2006 in *European Parliament* v *Council* is of relevance.[115] In this case, it will be recalled, the European Parliament sought annulment of the SCE Regulation. In support of its action, the Parliament put forward a *single* plea in law, according to which Article 95 EC would be the appropriate legal basis for the Regulation. The Court, in this connection, after examining this plea in light of Article 95 EC, concluded that this article could not constitute an appropriate legal basis:[116] 'As the sole plea is unfounded, the action must be dismissed', said the Court.[117]

Could the Parliament have put forward another plea? Is there perhaps another Treaty provision (instead of the rejected Article 95 EC) which may be argued to form an appropriate legal basis, preventing the use of Article 308 EC? I am thinking of Article 44 EC. This article too, as Article 95 EC (which the European Parliament had suggested) prescribes co-decision, giving the European Parliament a greater say than the compulsory consultation Article 308 EC provides for. The plus-point of Article 44(1) EC (*not*: Article 44(2)(g) EC) *vis-à-vis* Article 95 EC, however, is that it does not require Community measures based on it to be aimed at harmonization;[118] (It will be remembered that as the SCE Regulation did not satisfy this 'harmonization' requirement of Article 95 EC, it could not be based on this article and the European Parliament's plea (that Article 95 EC would be the appropriate legal basis) was dismissed).

Article 44 EC, in this respect (i.e., as a legal basis for the SCE Statute), does not seem to encounter any fundamental difficulties from the point of view of substantive law. It empowers the Community legislature (Parliament and Council) to adopt directives 'in order to attain freedom of establishment'. The Statute for an SCE is intended, particularly, to remove barriers to cross-border cooperation of companies and to contribute to the possibilities for reorganization (in the sense of

114. Note that other conditions of Art. 308 EC seem to be satisfied, i.e. that action, on the one hand, relates to the 'operation of the common market' (it lifts obstacles to freedom of establishment (cross-border cooperation and restructuring (*cf.* its preamble)) and, on the other, intends to attain 'one of the objectives of the Community' (it, briefly, develops economic activities (Art. 2 EC) by lifting obstacles (Art. 3(1)(c) EC)). More generally, as to the modernization objectives of the Action Plan (strengthening 'protection' and 'efficiency') in view of Art. 308 EC, I recall that for its use various conditions (discussed above and in the main text) need to be satisfied. Art. 308 EC thus does not grant a general power to act for the modernization objectives *per se*. (In its Action Plan, incidentally, the Commission states these objectives, without specifically addressing these competence issues (2.1 and 2.2)).

115. Case C-436/03 *Parliament* v *Council* ('SCE Regulation') [2006] ECR I-3733.

116. This aspect of the Court's judgment was entered into above, see s. II.E.

117. *Parliament* v *Council*, just cited, para. 47.

118. See Ch. 3.

adaptation of the structures of production to the Community dimension).[119] With this, the Statute may subsequently be argued to be a subject which is within the scope *ratione materiae* of freedom of establishment.[120]

The issue that remains to be dealt with then, and this, however, is more troublesome, is that Article 44 EC only empowers the Community legislature to adopt directives. Now, directives are primarily a measure for harmonization and leave Member States the choice of form and methods as to the result to be achieved. The Statute for an SCE, on the other hand, does not seek harmonization, and contains, or is asserted to contain detailed provisions. Observe that Article 249, third indent EC, defines the directive as follows:

> A directive shall be binding, as to the result to be achieved, upon each Member State to which it is addressed, but shall leave to the national authorities the choice of form and methods.

I will make two remarks in this regard. First, even though most directives are (or will be) aimed at harmonization, Article 249 EC does not seem to preclude the use of directives for other purposes (here: the creation of a Community legal form). In this connection, it may also be referred to Prechal, who observes that in recent years the EC has started to use directives as instruments for liberalization, particularly in the field of public utilities, such as communication, electricity, and gas. The objective of these directives is not primarily harmonization, but the (re)-regulation of the markets.[121]

Second, according to Article 249 EC, Member States have the choice of form and methods for the realization of the result prescribed by a directive. The prevailing view in respect of the relationship between 'result' and 'form and methods' is that a directive may contain detailed and uniform provisions, provided that this is necessary in view of the regulatory objectives pursued.[122] It is similarly accepted, however, that a directive *as a whole* must leave some latitude to the Member States as the form and methods of implementation are concerned.[123] Where the Statute for an SCE contains, or is asserted to contain, detailed provisions, one may argue that this is necessary in view of the objective pursued, namely the creation of a *Community* legal form. Moreover, in respect of many issues (drawing up the statutes of the SCE – Article 5(2); law applicable – Article 8(1) *sub* c(ii); law applicable during formation – Article 17(1); organization and conduct of general meetings – Article 53), the Statute does not provide for uniform rules, but it refers to the law applicable to cooperatives in the Member State in which the SCE has its registered office. Member States are in a position to

119. See recital 2 in the preamble to the SCE Regulation and *Parliament* v *Council*, just cited, para. 2.
120. See Ch. 3, and in particular *Sevic*, paras 16–19, in which cooperation and reorganization are considered by the Court as central elements of freedom of establishment.
121. S. Prechal, *Directives in EC Law* (Oxford: OUP, 2005), 3–5.
122. See: C.W.A. Timmermans, 'Community Directives Revisited', *YEL* (1997): 2; Prechal, just cited, 14.
123. Lauwaars & Timmermans, 109; Prechal, just cited, 15.

amend *that law* (the 'latitude' required). From this perspective, adoption of the Statute for an SCE by means of a directive would – perhaps – not be excluded. (The Court itself, incidentally, recognizes in *Parliament* v *Council* that the SCE Regulation does not lay down exhaustively all of the rules applicable to European cooperative societies and that, for certain matters, it refers to the law of the Member State in the territory of which the European cooperative society has its registered office[124]). However, the difficulty still remains – and this is, as Advocate General Stix-Hackl has noted,[125] the reason for choosing the form of a regulation in this case – that a directive would first have had to be transposed into national law. This would have led in turn to a large number of implementing provisions which would each have applied only in the territory of the particular Member State concerned.[126] Hence, the advantages that a regulation offers would not nearly have been achieved because a regulation can create uniform law of direct application.[127] A regulation that creates an additional legal form thus enables the Community legislature to resolve such territoriality problems.[128]

In conclusion, it would seem that Article 44 EC does not stand in the way of the adoption of the SCE regulation based on Article 308. In fact, in light of its prescribed use of directives, Article 44 EC may not provide for the necessary powers for a satisfactory and effective solution for cross-border cooperation and restructuring of cooperatives. As the above observations apply similarly to the EEIG and SE, this conclusion holds true for these Community legal forms as well.

IV. FURTHER LEGAL BASES

A. Introduction

This section briefly discusses the remaining legal bases which (may) also play a certain, more limited role in the field of EC company law: Article 61(c) EC *juncto* Article 67 EC on judicial cooperation in civil matters (s. B); Article 137 EC, which confers a power to adopt directives in the field of information and consultation of workers and co-determination (s. C); Article 211 EC, which concerns the general power of the Commission to make recommendations (s. D); and finally, Article 293 EC concerning conventions concluded between Member States (s. E).

124. See *Parliament* v *Council*, just cited, para. 45.
125. Opinion of AG Stix-Hackl in *Parliament* v *Council*, just cited, pt. 54.
126. *Ibid.*
127. *Ibid.*
128. *Ibid.*

B. Article 61(c) EC *juncto* Article 67 EC: Judicial Cooperation in Civil Matters

This section concerns the legal basis consisting of Article 61(c) EC *juncto* Article 67 EC. These articles are generally bracketed together with Article 65 EC.[129] It is argued in legal literature that 'Articles 61 and 65 would appear to be the proper basis for the conflict rules pertaining to the law of persons including legal persons and companies.'[130] The articles provide, in relevant part:

> [Article 61]
> In order to establish progressively an area of freedom, security and justice, the Council shall adopt:
>
> (...)
> (c) measures in the field of judicial cooperation in civil matters as provided for in Article 65;
> (...)
>
> [Article 65]
> Measures in the field of judicial cooperation in civil matters having cross-border implications, to be taken in accordance with Article 67[131] and in so far as necessary for the proper functioning of the internal market, shall include:
>
> (a) improving and simplifying:
> – the system for cross-border service of judicial and extrajudicial documents,
> – cooperation in the taking of evidence,
> – the recognition and enforcement of decisions in civil and commercial cases, including decisions in extrajudicial cases;
> (b) promoting the compatibility of the rules applicable in the Member States concerning the conflict of laws and of jurisdiction;
> (c) eliminating obstacles to the good functioning of civil proceedings, if necessary by promoting the compatibility of the rules on civil procedure applicable in the Member States.

The provisions just quoted are of a relatively recent date. They are part of (a new) Title IV of the EC Treaty on 'Visas, asylum, immigration and other policies related to free movement of persons' (Articles 61–69 EC) which was introduced by the

129. See e.g., J. Basedow, 'Codification of private law in the European Union: The making of a hybrid', *ERPL* 1 (2001): 44.
130. J. Basedow, 'The Communitarization of the conflict of laws under the Treaty of Amsterdam', *CML Rev.* 37 (2000): 697–698. See also, in this connection, J. Rickford, 'Current Developments in European Law on the Restructuring of Companies: An Introduction', *EBLR* (2004): 1232; M.K. Bulterman & P.J. Slot, 'Harmonisatie van wetgeving betreffende migrerende EU-burgers en derdelanders: op weg naar een uniform toetsingskader?', *SEW* (2005): 346–347.
131. This article provides for the decision-making procedure (very short: the Council acts unanimously). For an in-depth discussion of the specific procedural rules laid down in Art. 67 EC, see Lenaerts & Van Nuffel, 625–626.

Treaty of Amsterdam.[132] The main objective of this Title IV is the progressive establishment of an area of freedom, security, and justice.[133]

So far, no EC company law instruments have been adopted on the basis of these articles and, at present, there exist no plans for that, either.[134] As regards the modernization Directives, in particular the Directive on takeover bids, the Directive on cross-border mergers, and the Directive on shareholder rights, it may be noted that they have as their main or predominant purpose the attainment of freedom of establishment or free movement of capital;[135] any conflict rules in this context are (or would be) merely incidental. The modernization Directives at issue here, have (therefore) been correctly adopted on the basis of Article 44 EC or Article 95 EC,[136] and not (also) on Article 61(c) EC *juncto* Article 67 EC.[137]

C. Article 137 EC: Information and Consultation of Workers and Co-determination

Article 137 EC deals with information and consultation of workers and co-determination. On the basis of this article, for instance, Directive 2002/14/EC, establishing a general framework for informing and consulting employees in the European Community, has been adopted.[138] Article 137 EC provides, *inter alia*, that:

> 1. With a view to achieving the objectives of Article 136, the Community shall support and complement the activities of the Member States in the following fields:
>
> (...)
> (e) the information and consultation of workers;
> (f) representation and collective defence of the interests of workers and employers, including co-determination, subject to paragraph 5;
> (...)
>
> 2. To this end, the Council:
>
> (...)

132. Treaty of Amsterdam amending the Treaty on European Union, the Treaties establishing the European Communities and certain related acts, signed in Amsterdam, 2 Oct. 1997, OJ 1997 C 340, 1. The Treaty entered into force on 1 May 1999. On this Treaty: Craig & de Búrca, 20.
133. See Art. 61(1) EC.
134. For an overview of Community measures that have been adopted in the field of judicial cooperation in civil matters, see Directory of Community legislation in force, no. 19, Area of Freedom, Security and Justice, *sub* no. 19.20, <http://eur-lex.europa.eu>.
135. See Ch. 3 and s. II.E, *supra*.
136. For a critical discussion of the choice of the double legal basis of the Directive on shareholder rights (namely, Art. 44 EC and Art. 95 EC), however, see Ch. 3 and s. II.E, *supra*.
137. See also, in this connection, s. II.E, *supra* (on the issue of choice of the legal basis).
138. Directive 2002/14/EC of the European Parliament and of the Council of 11 Mar. 2002 establishing a general framework for informing and consulting employees in the European Community, OJ 2002 L 80, 29–33.

(b) may adopt, in the fields referred to in paragraph 1(a) to (i), by means of directives, minimum requirements for gradual implementation, having regard to the conditions and technical rules obtaining in each of the Member States. Such directives shall avoid imposing administrative, financial and legal constraints in a way which would hold back the creation and development of small and medium-sized undertakings.[139]

As regards the issue of *information and consultation* of workers (Article 137, paragraph 1(e) EC), the Council must act in accordance with the *co-decision* procedure referred to in Article 251 EC. As regards the issue of *co-determination* (Article 137, paragraph 1(f) EC), the Council must act unanimously on a proposal from the Commission, after (merely) *consulting* the European Parliament.[140] What is the relevance of the legal basis of Article 137 EC for EC company law modernization? (Directive 2002/14/EC, just mentioned, is generally considered *not* to belong to the EC company law *acquis*).

The Directive on cross-border mergers, and in particular its Article 16, merits in my opinion specific attention here.[141] The Directive was already discussed above, in the previous chapter about Article 44 EC, on which article the Directive is based.[142] Article 16 of the Directive deals with 'employee participation',[143] more particularly with the participation of employees in the decision-making bodies of the acquiring (existing) company or of the new company created by the

139. Art. 137(1) EC refers to Art. 136 EC, which latter article provides that: 'The Community and the Member States, having in mind fundamental social rights such as those set out in the European Social Charter signed at Turin on 18 October 1961 and in the 1989 Community Charter of the Fundamental Social Rights of Workers, shall have as their objectives the promotion of employment, improved living and working conditions, so as to make possible their harmonisation while the improvement is being maintained, proper social protection, dialogue between management and labour, the development of human resources with a view to lasting high employment and the combating of exclusion. To this end the Community and the Member States shall implement measures which take account of the diverse forms of national practices, in particular in the field of contractual relations, and the need to maintain the competitiveness of the Community economy.'

Art. 137(1)(f) EC refers to Art. 137(5) EC, which latter paragraph provides that: 'The provisions of this article shall not apply to pay, the right of association, the right to strike or the right to impose lock-outs.'

140. See Art. 137(2), *in fine* EC. In Art. 137(2)(b) EC it is further provided that: 'The Council, acting unanimously on a proposal from the Commission, after consulting the European Parliament, may decide to render the procedure referred to in Article 251 applicable to paragraph 1(d), (f) and (g) of this article.'

141. Directive 2005/56/EC of the European Parliament and of the Council of 26 Oct. 2005 on cross-border mergers of limited liability companies, OJ 2005 L 310, 1.

142. See the opening consideration in the preamble to the Directive.

143. See also the heading above Art. 16: 'Employee participation'. It takes account in that respect of the principles and solutions incorporated in the SE Regulation and the accompanying Directive on worker involvement (which are based both on Art. 308 EC).

cross-border merger.[144] Now, since this 'employee participation' of Article 16 of the Directive apparently corresponds with the *co-determination* of Article 137 EC, the question presents itself whether Article 137 EC (which provides a legal basis specifically for co-determination/employee participation issues) should have (also) been used as a base for the Directive. The Community legislature, incidentally, has not examined this matter, at least not explicitly explained it.[145]

This is where the Court's above-mentioned case-law concerning the choice of the legal basis is of relevance.[146]

If freedom of establishment would be identified as the 'main or predominant purpose or component' of the Directive, whereas co-determination/employee participation would be identified as 'merely incidental', the act should be based on a single legal basis, namely that required by the main or predominant purpose or component, here Article 44 EC. If it is established, on the other hand, that the measure simultaneously pursues objectives which are inseparably linked without one being secondary and indirect in relation to the other, the measure must, in

144. For the definition of 'employee participation', see Art. 2(k) SE Directive, to which it is referred in Art. 16(2) Directive on cross-border merger.

The reference in Art. 16(1) to 'the company *resulting* from the cross-border merger' conveys the impression that Art. 16 would only apply to mergers by formation of a new company (and not to mergers by acquisition, which involves only existing companies). The reference may not be understood in this limited sense, however. This may be inferred, in my view, from recital 8 in the preamble to the Directive, where 'the company resulting from the cross border merger' is referred to as encompassing an acquiring company or a new company. So, to be clear, where the Directive refers to the company resulting from the cross-border merger, both the new company (formed by the merging companies) and the existing acquiring company are included.

145. It can, however, be referred to the European Economic and Social Committee's Opinion on the proposal for a Directive on cross-border mergers. In it, the Committee stated with respect to the legal basis of this EC company law instrument, that: 'The legal basis used, which concerns company law (Article 44 EC), should be broadened to include Article 308 EC, since it is not only the survival of the merged companies which is at stake, but also that of their employees' jobs. Article 308 also becomes a legal basis for Directive 2001/86 supplementing the Statute for a European company as regards employee participation, which is referred to in Article 14 of the present proposal [Art. 14 of the proposal has become Art. 16 in the final text of the Directive; GJV].' See Opinion of the European Economic and Social Committee on the 'Proposal for a Directive of the European Parliament and of the Council on cross-border mergers of companies with share capital', OJ 2004 C 117, 43–48. As was shown above (see s. III), it is standard case-law that the use of Art. 308 EC as the legal basis for a measure is justified only where no other provision of the Treaty gives the Community institutions the necessary power to adopt the measure in question. Presumably, the European Economic and Social Committee holds the opinion that Art. 44 EC (or any other Treaty provision) does not provide a sufficient legal basis, and that for that reason, Art. 308 EC should be used. I think it is questionable that such a view is tenable. See main text, *infra*.

146. See s. II.E.3.

principle, be founded on the corresponding legal bases, here Article 44 EC and Article 137 EC.[147]

Now, does establishment form the main component and is co-determination/ employee participation 'merely incidental'? An explanation by the Community legislature of why it (apparently) considered, in short, establishment to be the main component of the Directive (the Directive is, it is reiterated, based only on Article 44 EC), would have been helpful here. Nevertheless, it may be argued, I think, that indeed establishment is the main component of the Directive (and co-determination incidental). The Directive's objective is to facilitate the cross-border merger (freedom of establishment),[148] which by way of consequence (as an accessory of the whole operation), may affect co-determination/employee participation. The scope of application of the Directive, incidentally, is by no means limited to cross-border mergers which affect co-determination/employee participation. Let me finally note this. Article 44(2)(g) EC provides for the power to coordinate safeguards for the protection of 'members and other'. As explained,[149] the term 'other' may be read as including employees. It could even be argued then that Article 44(2)(g) EC constitutes the proper (more specific than Article 137 EC) legal basis for coordination of co-determination/employee participation when such coordination is related to freedom of establishment (as here for example, in the event of cross-border merger).[150] Departing from this view (too), the relevance of Article 137 EC to EC company law modernization (which is largely concerned with freedom of establishment) would, in conclusion, be rather limited.

D. Article 211 EC: General Power of the Commission to Make Recommendations

Article 211 EC, which sets out the powers of the Commission, provides:

> In order to ensure the proper functioning and development of the common market, the Commission shall:
>
> – (...)
> – formulate recommendations or deliver opinions on matters dealt with in this Treaty, if it expressly so provides or if the Commission considers it necessary,
> – (...)
> – (...).

147. However, no dual legal basis is possible where the procedures laid down for each legal basis are incompatible with each other. For the complicated issue of compatibility of procedures, see in particular Case C-155/07 *Parliament* v *Council* ('Decision 2006/1016/EC – Community guarantee to the European Investment Bank'), judgment of 6 Nov. 2008, n.y.r., paras 73–82, and the Opinion of AG Kokott in that case, pts. 81–91.
148. See Ch. 3.
149. *Ibid.*
150. It was explained that the power conferred by Art. 44(2)(g) EC is in function of the specific objective to attain freedom of establishment. See Ch. 3.

Article 249 EC, in which the instruments of Community lawmaking are laid down, provides:

> (...) Recommendations and opinions shall have no binding force.

Article 211, second indent EC fulfils a double function. It confirms that the Treaty contains express provisions on the basis of which the Commission may formulate recommendations.[151] In addition to this confirmation, Article 211 EC forms itself a legal basis which allows the Commission to make recommendations (for the functioning and development of the common market on matters dealt with in the Treaty) if it considers this necessary. First, the recommendations which may be regarded as EC company law instruments will be discussed. Then, the competence question will be briefly dealt with.

The Action Plan recommended the adoption of a Commission recommendation which should promote the swift application of an appropriate regulatory regime for directors' remuneration.[152] In its Action Plan, the Commission furthermore made public its intention to adopt a recommendation on the role of (independent), non-executive, or supervisory directors.[153]

In October 2004, it was acted upon the Action Plan, when the Commission reached agreement on both Recommendations. The Commission formally adopted the Recommendation on directors' remuneration in December 2004.[154] It formally adopted the Recommendation on the role of non-executive and supervisory directors in February 2005.[155] The substantive provisions of the Recommendations under consideration are dealt with in Annex II.

Both Recommendations are addressed to the Member States.[156] The Member States were invited to take the necessary measures to promote the application of the (principles set out in the) Recommendations by 30 June 2006.[157]

The question of why the Commission has decided to adopt non-binding Recommendations and not proposed directives, is dealt with in a Commission FAQ's memo, which was published together with the Recommendations under

---

151. See for express legal bases for Commission recommendations to Member States: Art. 53 EC (services); Art. 77 EC (transport); Art. 97(1) EC (distortions of competition); Art. 119(1) EC (transitional provisions – economic and monetary policy); Art. 134 EC (common commercial policy).
152. ACTION PLAN, 16 and 24.
153. *Ibid.*, 15 and 24.
154. Commission Recommendation 2004/913/EC of 14 Dec. 2004 fostering an appropriate regime for the remuneration of directors of listed companies, OJ 2004 L 385, 55.
155. Commission Recommendation 2005/162/EC of 15 Feb. 2005 on the role of non-executive or supervisory directors of listed companies and on the committees of the (supervisory) board, OJ 2005 L 52, 51.
156. Recommendation on directors' remuneration, pt. 8.2; Recommendation on the role of non-executive and supervisory directors, pt. 15.
157. Recommendation on directors' remuneration, pt. 8.1; Recommendation on the role of non-executive and supervisory directors, pt. 14.

consideration.[158] The Commission considered recommendations to be more suitable than directives, so as to allow Member States to take due account of national corporate governance traditions and practices.[159]

As to the issue of competence, it must be noted that the Commission has adopted both Recommendations on the basis of Article 211, second indent EC.[160] Was the Commission correct in using this Treaty provision? It must be remarked first, that it is clear that other, more specific legal bases providing for a power of the Commission to adopt recommendations could not have been used to adopt the Recommendations at issue, as these legal bases have a different scope *ratione materiae* (they are concerned with services, transport etc.).[161] As to Article 211 EC itself then, it is of importance that it requires that recommendations, 'in order to ensure the proper functioning and development of the common market', concern 'matters dealt with in this Treaty'.

The Commission does not explicitly address this requirement. In my view, the Recommendations may in particular be regarded as concerned with free movement of capital, just as the Directive on the shareholder rights, which was dealt with above.[162] For a more elaborate treatment, I refer to my views presented there. In short, however, it can be pointed out that the Recommendations as well (just as the Directive referred to) are concerned with both direct investments and portfolio investments (two types of capital movements).[163]

The Recommendations thus seek to ensure the proper functioning and development of the common market and concern 'matters dealt with in this Treaty'.

158. MEMO/04/231 of 6 Oct. 2004 (European Commission Recommendations on directors' remuneration and the role of nonexecutive and supervisory directors – frequently asked questions), 1.

159. The text of the Recommendations on this point is formulated rather stringently, however. The Recommendation on directors' remuneration stipulates – in general terms – that Member States should take all appropriate measures to ensure that companies comply with the Recommendation (pt. 1.1); the Recommendation on the role of non-executive and supervisory directors invites Member States to adopt the Recommendation either through legislation or through a 'comply or explain' approach (pt. 1.1). In addition, Member States are invited to notify the Commission of the measures taken in compliance with the Recommendations, in order to allow the Commission to monitor closely the situation and, on this basis, to assess the need for further measures (Recommendation on directors' remunerationpt, pt. 8.1; Recommendation on the role of non-executive and supervisory directors, pt. 14).

160. See the first consideration in the preambles to both Recommendations.

161. For these legal bases, see the first fn. of this section.

162. See s. II.E.

163. The preambles to the Recommendations, incidentally, indicate the intention: 'to strengthen shareholders' rights' (the first recital in the preamble to the Recommendation on directors' remuneration); to protect 'the interests of shareholders' (the second recital in the preamble to the Recommendation on directors' remuneration); to 'strengthen a company's accountability to shareholders' (the fifth recital in the preamble to the Recommendation on directors' remuneration); and to protect 'the interests of shareholders' (the seventh recital in the preamble to the Recommendation on the role of non-executive and supervisory directors).

As regards the acquisition of shares on the capital market (which is also recognized as a form of capital movement), it is noted, finally, that the Recommendations, to be clear, concern listed companies (indeed).

Accordingly, the Commission may be assumed to have acted correctly in adopting the Recommendations on the – general – legal basis of Article 211 EC.

Finally, it should be mentioned that recommendations – notwithstanding their non-binding character – are susceptible to judicial review. However, only in the so-called preliminary ruling procedure may the Court of Justice decide on the validity of recommendations.[164] This preliminary ruling procedure was discussed in Chapter 1.

E. ARTICLE 293 EC: CONVENTIONS CONCLUDED BETWEEN MEMBER STATES

In some areas, the EC Treaty requires the Member States, so far as necessary, to enter into negotiations so as to lay down rules by mutual agreement.[165] Article 293 EC sets out a number of objectives which the Member States may achieve by mutual agreement.[166] Article 293 EC provides:

> Member States shall, so far as is necessary, enter into negotiations with each other with a view to securing for the benefit of their nationals:
>
> – (. . .)
> – (. . .),
> – the mutual recognition of companies or firms within the meaning of the second paragraph of Article 48, the retention of legal personality in the event of transfer of their seat from one country to another, and the possibility of mergers between companies or firms governed by the laws of different countries,
> – (. . .)

This article has had only limited relevance in the area of company law. As regards, first, mutual recognition, it can be noted that pursuant to Article 220 of the EC Treaty (now Article 293 EC) the Convention on the mutual recognition of companies was entered into in 1968.[167] The Convention, however, was not ratified by the Netherlands as a consequence of which it never came into force.[168]

---

164. Schermers & Waelbroeck, 316, see also 331–332 and 548.
165. Lenaerts & Van Nuffel, 647, who refer, in this connection, to Art. 20 EC and Art. 293 EC.
166. Lenaerts & Van Nuffel, 799.
167. Convention on the mutual recognition of companies and bodies corporate (signed on 29 Feb. 1968), Bull. EG, Suppl. 2/69. For a discussion of the Convention, see, *inter al.*: B. Goldman, 'The Convention between the Member States of the European Economic Community on the Mutual Recognition of Companies and Legal Persons', *CML Rev.* 6 (1968–1969): 104–128; J.H. Diephuis & C.W.A. Timmermans, *Erkenning van vreemde vennootschappen en rechtspersonen* (Preadviezen [Preliminary reports]) (The Hague: Mededelingen van de Nederlandse Vereniging voor Internationaal Recht (no. 81), 1980); Lutter, 695–701; Edwards, 384–386; S. Rammeloo, *Corporations in Private International Law. A European Perspective* (Oxford: OUP, 2001), 34–37.
168. See: Lutter, 696; Edwards, 384. In *Überseering*, the Court referred at para. 60 to: 'the fact that no convention on the mutual recognition of companies has as yet been adopted on the basis of Article 293 EC'.

With respect to, secondly, the issue of mergers between companies from different countries, it can be referred to – merely – a draft Convention on the cross-border mergers of public companies which came into being in December 1972.[169]

As regards, thirdly and finally, the transfer of seat, results (within the context of Article 293 EC) have been even more modest. There is just a report by Beitzke to be referred to. It was produced at the Commission's request in 1962.[170]

Conventions concluded pursuant to Article 293 EC are, incidentally and on a more technical note, not part of Community law.[171] They are agreements governed by international law, to which Article 234 EC (preliminary rulings) does not apply.[172] The Conventions just referred to, may therefore not be regarded as instruments of *EC* company law.[173]

Let us have a closer look at Article 293 EC itself. According to this article, Member States shall, *so far as is necessary*, enter into negotiations with each other with a view to, in short, concluding specific international agreements. May conventions on the basis of Article 293 EC be regarded as *necessary* now that other Treaty provisions offer a legal basis? This question was raised and answered in the negative by Timmermans, for over twenty-five years ago. There is no mistaking, he said, that a legal basis for the issues dealt with in Article 220, third indent EEC, can be found in Article 54(3)(g) EEC *juncto* Article 100 EEC.[174] Indeed, and

---

169. Bull. EG, suppl. 13/73. For a discussion of the draft Convention, see: C.W.A. Timmermans, 'Het Verdrag van 29 februari 1968 inzake de onderlinge erkenning van vennootschappen en rechtspersonen. Enkele Europeesrechtelijke kanttekeningen', in Diephuis & Timmermans, just cited, 73–78; G. van Solinge, *Grensoverschrijdende juridische fusie* (Deventer: Kluwer, 1994), 24–31.
170. For a summary of this report, see G. Beitzke, 'Anerkennung und Sitzverlegung von Gesellschaften und juristischen Personen im EWG-Bereich', *ZHR* (1965): 1–47. There is also a KPMG report from 1993 (Commission of the European Communities, *Study on transfer of the head office of a company from one Member State to another, carried out by K.P.M.G. Business Centre*, Luxembourg: Office for Official Publications of the European Communities 1993). About this 1993 report, *inter al.*, J.W. Bellingwout, *Zetelverplaatsing van rechtspersonen* (Deventer: Kluwer, 1996), 429. It must be noted, however, that, whereas Art. 220 EEC (now Art. 293 EC) was the point of departure of Beitzke's report, the KPMG report stated with regard to the terms of reference, at 1: 'Within the framework of the harmonization of company law, *based on Article 54 of the Treaty of Rome*, the Commission plans to examine which measures would be appropriate in order to facilitate the transfer of the head office of a company from one Member State to another Member State without dissolution of the company in question.' (emphasis added).
171. See e.g., Lauwaars & Timmermans, 103; Lenaerts & Van Nuffel, 647 and 799.
172. In the case of the 1968 Convention on recognition of companies, however, a Protocol conferring jurisdiction on the Court of Justice to give preliminary rulings on the interpretation of the Convention was signed on 3 Jun. 1971. As the Convention itself, however, it never came into force. On this Protocol: Lutter, 695; Edwards, 384.
173. It is therefore correct, that the Commission did not mention the (draft) Conventions at issue here, in Annex 2 ('List of Existing and Proposed European Company Law Instruments') of its Action Plan.
174. See, to this effect, C.W.A. Timmermans, in Diephuis & Timmermans, just cited, 55; C.W.A. Timmermans, 'Ontwerp EEG-Richtlijn over internationale fusies', *TVVS* (1985): 98 and 99, in which the author concentrates on cross-border mergers and Art. 220 EEC.

confirming Timmermans' view, from the Court's case-law it follows that the company law issues dealt with in Article 220 EC (mutual recognition, cross-border mergers, transfer of the seat) fall within the scope of the freedom of establishment,[175] and come thus within the ambit of the Community's specific power to realize the freedom of establishment under Article 44 EC (or at least its residual, more general power under Article 95 EC).[176] Where the issue of mutual recognition of companies is concerned, it may further be noted that after introduction in 1999 of Article 61(c) EC *juncto* Article 65 EC and Article 67 EC, these articles may perchance be argued to (also) form a proper legal basis, making adoption of a convention unnecessary.

What is the function then of Article 293, third indent EC? Here it must be recalled that the article was inserted in the original EEC Treaty at the final moment, fourteen days before the Treaty was signed. This was done to be absolutely safe in case the Treaty should not provide for a legal basis for Community action[177] (which it does, as just explained). In *Überseering*, the Court of Justice may be argued to have confirmed this in that it held there, following Advocate General Ruiz-Jarabo Colomer, that 'Article 293 EC does not constitute a reserve of legislative competence vested in the Member States.'[178] Moreover, Article 293 EC is characterized in *Überseering* – by the Advocate General – as 'only an invitation to Member States' and 'an admonition to Member States' to enter into negotiations[179] and – by the Court – as giving 'Member States the opportunity to enter into negotiations'.[180]

V. CONCLUDING REMARKS

This and the previous chapter were about the *competence* or *powers* of the EC in the field of company law. The following conclusions can be drawn.

Article 44(1) EC and Article 44(2)(g) EC do not provide a general power to adopt EC company law instruments. The power conferred is of a functional nature; it is conferred for the purpose of attaining freedom of establishment.

Both the Commission (in its 2003 *Action Plan on Modernising Company Law and Enhancing Corporate Governance*) and the Community legislature, however, arguably fail to explain (frequently how Company Law Directives based on Article 44 EC (or 44(1) EC and 44(2)(g) EC) contribute to the attainment of

175. As to mutual recognition, see: *Überseering*, *Inspire Art* and *Cartesio*; as to cross-border mergers, see *Sevic*; and as to transfer of the seat, see *Daily Mail Cartesio*.
176. As indicated repeatedly, the prohibition of Art. 43 EC may not suffice to eliminate all obstacles to freedom of establishment, particularly in view of justified derogations from Art. 43 EC, which may still hinder the freedom of establishment. Community action may then be in order, for which a legal base can be found in Art. 44 EC (or in the residual base of Art. 95 EC).
177. For the previous history and function of Art. 293, see C.W.A. Timmermans, in Diephuis & Timmermans, just cited, 55–56.
178. *Überseering*, para. 54.
179. Opinion of AG Ruiz-Jarabo Colomer in *Überseering*, pt. 43.
180. *Überseering*, para. 54.

freedom of establishment. (It may, however, not automatically be concluded from this lack of explanation that the Community measures would in fact not contribute to the attainment of freedom of establishment as required by Article 44 EC).

The legal basis for the *Directive on takeover bids* is formed by Article 44(1) EC *juncto* Article 44(2)(g) EC. This Directive contains a mandatory bid rule, which is laid down in Article 5: when a person or entity acquires control of a listed company as a result of an acquisition of securities, minority shareholders are protected, for the mandatory bid rule requires that person or entity to address a bid to all holders of securities, for all their holdings, at an equitable price.

Article 44(2)(g) EC carefully defines the addressee of the safeguards which may be harmonized on the basis of that provision: companies (or firms). Outside the scope are, therefore, safeguards required of others – for example, shareholders. The mandatory bid rule, under consideration here, is a case in point. It is addressed to (controlling) shareholders. In view of this, Article 44(2)(g) EC may not be used to harmonize rules with respect to the mandatory bid. This is, however, what may have happened. The legal basis for the Directive on takeover bids is formed by Article 44(1) EC *juncto Article 44(2)(g) EC. Article 44(1) EC*, however, does seem to provide a legal basis for adoption of a mandatory bid rule, both as regards the requirement it entails for EC companies (as shareholders) to make a bid as well as for third country companies (as shareholders) to make a bid.

The legal basis for the *Directive on shareholder rights* is formed by Article 44 EC and Article 95 EC. Article 44 EC requires, as just mentioned, that a directive based on it, contributes to the attainment of freedom of establishment. Article 95 EC, in short, empowers the Community legislature (also) to adopt measures contributing to the elimination of obstacles to the economic freedoms guaranteed by the Treaty. These freedoms include, *inter alia*, the free movement of capital.

It is not evident that the Community legislature has sufficiently established a link between the Directive and the freedom of establishment. The stated objective of the Directive – to allow shareholders effectively to make use of their rights throughout the Community – is not necessarily linked to the freedom of establishment. Apart from the issue of insufficient explanation by the Community legislature (of the Directive's contribution to, specifically, freedom of establishment), even if it is (otherwise) established that the Directive (also) seeks to enhance shareholdings allowing to exert a definite influence on the company's decisions and to determine its activities (which falls within the ambit *ratione materiae* of the provisions of the EC Treaty on freedom of establishment), there are various indications that contribution to free movement of capital seems to be the main or predominant purpose or component of the Directive. If this is the main or predominant purpose or component indeed, the Community legislature has, in short, incorrectly based the Directive on shareholder rights also on Article 44 EC (instead of just Article 95 EC). It is settled case-law that if examination of a measure reveals that it pursues two aims or that it has two components and if one of those aims or components is identifiable as the main one (here, free movement of capital), whereas the other is merely incidental (here, freedom of establishment), the measure must be founded on a single legal basis, namely that required by the main or predominant aim or component, *in casu* Article 95 EC. (That incorrect reference to Article 44 EC as a (second) legal basis for the Directive, incidentally, is a 'purely formal defect', which does not render the Directive invalid).[181]

181. Incidentally, in Ch. 3 and 4, I have discussed in particular *modernization* goals (and action) in light of the Community legislature's competences. To return briefly to the older, 'traditional' goals (Ch. 2.III) which are not (any longer) mentioned as such in the Community's Action Plan as an objective EC action should seek to attain (in particular, 'facilitating freedom of establishment', 'ensuring certainty in the law' and 'preventing establishment on account of the severity of national company laws and preventing a race to the bottom'), I note that, as follows from the main text, these aims may (under circumstances) still warrant future action by the Community legislature. This holds, in short, as to 'facilitating freedom of establishment', see, e.g., Ch. 3.III.B.1.b. Also as to 'ensuring legal certainty', see, e.g., Ch. 3.III.B.1.b.(4). And as to 'preventing establishment on account of severity of laws and preventing a race to the bottom', see, e.g., Ch. 3.VI (recall briefly (as to Art. 44 EC) *Centros*, para. 27 and the history of Art. 44 (2)(g) EC; cf. also (as to Art. 95 EC) Case C-376/98 *Germany* v *Parliament and Council* ('Tobacco Advertizing'), para. 110 and Opinion AG Geelhoed in Case C-491/01 *British American Tobacco* [2002] ECR I-11453, pt. 161–162, and (as to Art. 308 EC) Joined Cases C-402/05 P and C-415/05 P *Kadi a.O.* v *Council and Commission*, judgment of 3 Sept. 2008, n.y.r., para. 230). (As to 'reinforcing protection' and 'making companies more competitive', incidentally, the other two 'older' goals, I refer to the analyses of the modernization goals, to which they are closely linked, see Ch. 3 and 4).

Chapter 5

Requirements for the Exercise of Community Powers: Subsidiarity and Article 43 EC

I. INTRODUCTION

The previous two chapters were about the competence or powers of the EC in the field of company law. This chapter is about the requirements for the lawful exercise of these powers.[1] More specifically, it is about the principle of subsidiarity and the observance of Article 43 EC. These two requirements especially, are of relevance (or are argued to be of particular relevance in the literature) to EC company law.[2]

---

1. For the distinction between competence and the exercise thereof, see e.g., Opinion of AG Geelhoed in Case C-434/02 *Arnold André* [2004] ECR I-11825 and Case C-210/03 *Swedish Match* [2004] ECR I-11893. After the AG has noted (pt. 84) that: 'The Community legislature has a broad discretion' under Art. 95 EC, he notes that 'this discretion is not unlimited'. He then goes on to 'assess the limits on the Community legislature when it *exercises* this competence'. (emphasis added). In this connection, AG Geelhoed examines, *inter al.*, the proportionality principle and various general principles of law.

   See further Craig & de Búrca, 82, who distinguish between 'the existence and scope of Community powers' on the one hand and 'the basic requirements for their lawful exercise' on the other. These authors also note (82) in this connection: 'Closely related to the question of the *existence* of Community competence and the adequacy of the legal basis for action is the question of when such competence is properly *exercised*.'
2. Other requirements for the lawful exercise of Community powers do not (specifically) relate to the content of EC company law or, alternatively, their impact (in the breadth) on EC company law may be assumed to be relatively limited. Procedural requirements in particular, such as the requirement to consult (e.g., the European Parliament or the EESC) and the requirement to state

First, section II examines the principle of subsidiarity. Next, section III is about the prohibition of Article 43 EC (of restrictions on freedom of establishment) and how it functions as a limit to EC company law. Section IV, finally, contains some concluding remarks.

II. THE PRINCIPLE OF SUBSIDIARITY (ARTICLE 5, PARAGRAPH 2 EC)

This section deals with the principle of subsidiarity. First, Article 5, paragraph 2 EC, in which the principle is laid down, will be discussed (s. A). Next, the issue of regulatory competition, which some identify with the principle of subsidiarity, will be dealt with (s. B). Both issues have been debated extensively in academic literature,[3] debates which I will not reiterate. I will only focus on some aspects which may be relevant for the compatibility with the EC Treaty of the Community's action in the field of company law.

---

reasons under Art. 253 EC, may be quoted as examples, but it may also be referred to other requirements, such as rules of international law and general principles of law (which general principles include, *inter al.*, respect for fundamental rights). For the (relative) importance of these fundamental rights to EC company law, see G.-J. Vossestein, case note on ECHR *Sovtransavto Holding v. Ukraine,* no. 48553/99, judgment of 25 Jul. 2002 (Reports of Judgments and Decisions ECHR 2002-VII) and ECHR *Olczak v. Poland*, no. 30417/96, decision of 7 Nov. 2002 (Reports of Judgments and Decisions ECHR 2002-X), *JOR* 2003/111 and 112; and G.-J. Vossestein, case note on ECHR *Cēsnieks v. Latvia*, no. 56400/00, decision of 12 Dec. 2002, *JOR* 2003/224; for the relevance of fundamental rights to national (Netherlands) company law, see: L. Timmerman, 'Some Thoughts on the Impact of Fundamental Rights on Dutch company law', in *Constitutionalisation of Private Law*, ed. T. Barkhuysen & S. Lindenbergh (Leiden/Boston: Martinus Nijhoff, 2006), 23–32; L. Timmerman, 'Mensenrechten van minderheidsaandeelhouders: voice, exit of gelijke behandeling', in *De nieuwe macht van de kapitaalverschaffer*, ed. H. Beckman et al. (Deventer: Kluwer, 2007), 31–42. For in-depth discussions, finally, of the other requirements for the lawful exercise of Community powers, it is referred to textbooks on EU (procedural) law. See e.g., Schermers & Waelbroeck, 359–404; Lenaerts, Arts & Maselis, 287–310.

3. See, regarding the issue of subsidiarity, e.g., L.A. Geelhoed, 'Het subsidiariteitsbeginsel: een communautair principe?', *SEW* 39 (1991): 422–435; K. Lenaerts & P. van Ypersele, 'Le principe de subsidiarité et son contexte: étude de l'article 3b du Traité CE', *CDE* (1994): 3–85; P. Demaret, 'A Short Walk in the Realm of Subsidiarity', in *European Economic and Business Law*, ed. R.M. Buxbaum et al. (Berlin: Walter de Gruyter, 1996), 13–31; C. Timmermans, 'Subsidiarity and Transparency', *Fordham Int'l L.J.* 22 (1999): 106–127; M. Diez de Velasco Vallego & J.M. Sobrino Heredia, 'El control jurisdiccional del principio de subsidiaridad en la Unión Europea', in *Une communauté de droit – Festschrift für Gil Carlos Rodríguez Iglesias*, ed. N. Colneric et al. (Berlin: BWV, 2003), 581–589; G. Davies, 'Subsidiarity: The wrong idea, in the wrong place, at the wrong time', *CML Rev.* 43 (2006): 63–84; C.W.A. Timmermans, 'La justiciabilité de la subsidiarité', in *Festskrift til Claus Gulmann. Liber Amicorum*, ed. B. Vesterdorf et al. (Copenhagen: Forlaget Thomson, 2006), 450–459.

   See, regarding the issue of regulatory competition, s. B, *infra*.

A. ARTICLE 5, PARAGRAPH 2 EC

1. Introduction

The principle of subsidiarity is set out in the second paragraph of Article 5 EC, according to which, in areas which do not fall within its exclusive competence, the Community is to take action only if and in so far as the objectives of the proposed action cannot be sufficiently achieved by the Member States and can therefore, by reason of the scale or effects of the proposed action, be better achieved at Community level.[4]

As a preliminary remark, it should be emphasized that the principle of subsidiarity does not concern the question of the *existence* of Community competence; it is intended to regulate the *exercise* of Community competence.[5] The subsidiarity question thus can only arise if the Community is competent to act under the Treaty in the first place: if there is no adequate legal basis for a proposed legislative initiative, there can be no legislation and the question of subsidiarity does not even arise.[6] This aspect is not given proper attention in the Commission's Action Plan on Modernising Company Law: the Action Plan's objective of fostering efficiency and competitiveness of business is particularly discussed in relation to subsidiarity (and proportionality), without – as discussed in Chapter 3 – explicitly dealing with the prior question, whether the Community is competent at all to foster efficiency and competitiveness of business:

> 2. The Commission considers that future actions at EU level in the area of company law should seek as much as possible to meet the following (. . .) policy objectives (. . .)
> 2.1. (. . .)
> 2.2. Fostering efficiency and competitiveness of business
> Business efficiency and competitiveness, which are crucial components of economic growth and job creation, depend on many factors, one of which is a sound framework of company law. Key to the achievement of this objective is the setting up of a proper balance between actions at EU level and actions at national level. Some

---

4. See also Case C-491/01 *British American Tobacco* [2002] ECR I-11453, para. 177.
5. This already ensues from the wording of Art. 5, para. 2 EC, but it is more clearly expressed in Art. 3 of the *Protocol on the application of the principles of subsidiarity and proportionality*, OJ 1997 C 340, 5. (This Protocol is annexed to the EC Treaty and has Treaty status itself. See Art. 311 EC: 'The protocols annexed to this Treaty by common accord of the Member States shall form an integral part thereof'). In Art. 3 of the Protocol it is stated, *inter al.*, that: 'The principle of subsidiarity *does not call into question the powers* conferred on the European Community by the Treaty, as interpreted by the Court of Justice', and further that 'The principle of subsidiarity provides a guide *as to how those powers are to be exercised* at the Community level.' (emphasis added). See also S. Weatherill, 'The European Commission's Green Paper on European Contract Law: Context, Content and Constitutionality', *JCP* 24 (2001): 363; Craig & de Búrca, 100.
6. Weatherill, just cited, 363.

company law rules are likely to be best dealt with, and updated, more efficiently at national level, and some competition between national rules may actually be healthy for the efficiency of the single market. With due respect of the subsidiarity and proportionality principles, business efficiency and competitiveness should be promoted along the following lines:

- EU initiatives in the area of company law should certainly address a number of specific cross-border issues (e.g. cross-border merger or transfer of seat, cross[-]border impediments to the exercise of shareholders rights . . .), where Community action may be the only way to achieve the pursued objectives.
- In addition to these specific cross-border issues, the necessary attention should be paid to the other initiatives which the promotion of business efficiency and competitiveness requires. As stated above, a certain degree of harmonisation of defined national issues reduces legal uncertainties and can thereby significantly enhance business efficiency and competitiveness.
- Flexibility should be available to companies as much as possible: where systems are deemed to be equivalent, maximum room should be left open to the freedom of the parties involved.[7]

As discussed in Chapter 1, Article 5, paragraph 2 EC makes it clear that subsidiarity must be considered only in relation to areas which do not fall within the exclusive competence of the Community. If an area does fall within the exclusive competence of the Community, EC action is not subject to the requirements of the principle of subsidiarity of Article 5, paragraph 2 EC.

What does this mean for the powers of the Community legislature under Article 44 EC, Article 95 EC and Article 308 EC, the legal bases most frequently used for EC action in the field of company law? Is the exercise of these powers subject to the requirements of the principle of subsidiarity?

Advocate General Léger, in *Deposit Guarantees*,[8] and Advocate General Fennelly, in *Tobacco Advertizing*,[9] have argued that the exercise of Community competence under Article 95 EC (and Article 47(2) EC) is exclusive in character and that the principle of subsidiarity therefore is not applicable.[10] The Court of Justice, however, ruled otherwise in *British American Tobacco*. It held that:

> the principle of subsidiarity applies where the Community legislature makes use of Article 95 EC, inasmuch that provision does not give it exclusive

7. See Action Plan, 7–8. As stated in Ch. 3, where the Action Plan does deal with a legal basis (Art. 44(2)(g) EC, at 6, *sub* 1.1), it does not address the question whether it provides a base for its objective of fostering efficiency and competitiveness of business.
8. Case C-233/94 *Germany* v *Parliament and Council* ('Deposit Guarantees') [1997] ECR I-2405.
9. Case C-376/98 *Germany* v *Parliament and Council* ('Tobacco Advertizing') [2000] ECR I-8419.
10. AG Léger in his Opinion in *Deposit Guarantees*, just cited, pts. 86 and 82; AG Fennelly in his Opinion in *Tobacco Advertizing*, just cited, pt. 142.

> competence to regulate economic activity on the internal market, but only a certain competence for the purpose of improving the conditions for its establishment and functioning, by eliminating barriers to the free movement of goods and the freedom to provide services or by removing distortions of competition.[11]

The Court has confirmed this statement in *Alliance for Natural Health.*[12] Exercise of Community competence under Article 95 EC therefore must comply with the requirements of the principle of subsidiarity.

As regards exercise of Community competence under Article 44 EC, in my view, arguably the same applies.[13] Also this provision does not give exclusive competence to regulate economic activity on the internal market, but gives a certain competence for the purpose of improving the conditions for the establishment and functioning of the internal market, particularly the freedom of establishment, by abolishing restrictions on the freedom of establishment[14] and by giving effect to it.[15]

Similarly, Article 308 EC does not give exclusive competence to regulate economic activity on the internal market but gives a certain competence for, as its wording shows, the purpose of attaining, in the course of the operation of the common market, one of the objectives of the Community.[16] Indeed, and as is stated

---

AG Léger in his Opinion in *Deposit Guarantees*, pt. 82 observed that Art. 57 of the Treaty (now, after amendment, Art. 47 EC) refers at no point to the competence of the Member States and that that provision entrusts the Community alone with the responsibility for the coordination of national legislation in this field which shows that, from the very outset, the authors of the Treaty considered that, as regards the taking-up and pursuit of activities as self-employed persons, coordination was better achieved by action at Community level rather than national level.

AG Fennelly in his Opinion in *Tobacco Advertizing*, pt. 139 noted (as to whether harmonizing action pursuant to Art. 57(2) and 100A of the EC Treaty (now, after amendment, Art. 47(2) and 95 EC) falls within the exclusive competence of the Community): 'Where disparate national rules give rise either to obstacles to trade in goods or the provision of services or to distortions of competition, the Community has an interest in achieving uniformity of trading conditions which is quite distinct from its interest in the substantive content of the uniform rules adopted. The coordination or approximation of national rules which affect economic activity is the very essence of these competences, provided it serves the purposes of the internal market, and is not merely an instrument for achieving some separate, materially defined objective. *It is clear that only the Community can adopt measures which satisfy these requirements.*' (emphasis added).

11. *British American Tobacco*, just cited, para. 179.
12. Joined Cases C-154/04 and C-155/04 *Alliance for Natural Health a.O.* [2005] ECR I-6451.
13. Cf. C.W.A. Timmermans, 'La justiciabilité de la subsidiarité', in *Festskrift til Claus Gulmann. Liber Amicorum*, ed. B. Vesterdorf et al. (Copenhagen: Forlaget Thomson, 2006), 454, noting that the Court's reasoning in *British American Tobacco* on subsidiarity may also apply to other legal bases in the EC Treaty serving the realization of the internal market.
14. Case C-97/96 *Verband deutscher Daihatsu-Händler* v *Daihatsu Deutschland* [1997] ECR I-6843, para. 21; Joined Cases C-435/02 and C-103/03 *Springer* [2004] ECR I-8663, para. 3.
15. Case C-122/96 *Saldanha and MTS Securities Corporation* v *Hiross* [1997] ECR I-5325, para. 23.
16. Cf. Case T-306/01 *Yusuf* v *Council and Commission* [2005] ECR II-3533, para. 147 (where the Court held: 'if a mere finding that there was a danger of disparities between the various national

in Chapter 1, most Community competences, including those in the field of company law, are non-exclusive. Accordingly, the exercise of these competences must comply with the principle of subsidiarity.[17]

2. The Requirements of the Principle of Subsidiarity

Now to turn to the requirements of the principle of subsidiarity, this principle, set out in Article 5, paragraph 2 EC, consists of two parts.[18] The Community is to take action only if and in so far, first, the objectives of that action cannot be sufficiently achieved by the Member States (sometimes called 'requirement of necessity'[19]), and second, the objectives can, because of their scale or effects, better be achieved at Community level (sometimes called 'requirement of added value of Community action'[20]). It is important to note that the Community is to

---

rules and an abstract risk of obstacles to the free movement of capital or payments or of distortions of competition liable to result there from were sufficient to justify the choice of Article 308 EC as a legal basis for a regulation together with Article 3(1)(c) and (g) EC, not only would the provisions of Chapter 3 of Title VI of the EC Treaty be rendered ineffective, but also review by the court of compliance with the proper legal basis might be rendered quite nugatory (. . .) (see, to that effect, with regard to Article 100a of the EC Treaty, now, after amendment, Article 95 EC, Case C-376/98 *Germany* v *Parliament and Council* ["Tobacco Advertizing"] [2000] ECR I-8419, paragraphs 84, 85 and 106 to 108, and the case-law cited therein)'). An appeal against this judgment of the Court of First Instance was brought before the Court of Justice. See Joined Cases C-402/05 P and C-415/05 P *Kadi a.O.* v *Council and Commission*, judgment of 3 Sep. 2008, n.y.r. The observation just cited, however, was not reconsidered by the Court of Justice. (See, further, in support of the main text, para. 200 (of the, final, Court of Justice's judgment): 'Recourse to that provision [Art. 308 EC] demands that the action envisaged should, on the one hand, relate to the "operation of the common market" and, on the other, be intended to attain "one of the objectives of the Community"'; and in respect of this first condition, paras 229–231, and in respect of this second condition para. 220). Cf. also Timmermans, 'La justiciabilité de la subsidiarité', just cited.

17. See also C.W.A. Timmermans, 'Is het subsidiariteitsbeginsel vatbaar voor rechterlijke controle?', *SEW* (2007): 226, who, after having remarked that *British American Tobacco* makes clear that the principle of subsidiarity applies to Art. 95 EC, concludes that it seems probable that this would apply as well to the other legal bases for the establishment of the internal market.
18. See the wording of Art. 5, para. 2 EC, and particularly the *Protocol on the application of the principles of subsidiarity and proportionality*, which speaks of two aspects of the principle of subsidiarity which have to be met (followed by the two requirements addressed here in the main text). As stated above, in s. 1, this *Protocol* has Treaty status itself.
19. C.W.A. Timmermans, 'La justiciabilité de la subsidiarité', in *Festskrift til Claus Gulmann. Liber Amicorum*, ed. B. Vesterdorf et al. (Copenhagen: Forlaget Thomson, 2006), 456, referring to this requirement as 'condition de la necessité de l'action' (requirement of necessity). Lenaerts & Van Nuffel, 104, note in this connection that: 'Community action will conflict with the principle of subsidiarity only where it can be shown that the objective sought can be achieved just as much in all Member States either by individual action or by co-operation between the Member States concerned.'
20. Timmermans, just cited, 456, referring to this requirement as 'condition de la valeur ajoutée d'une action communautaire' (requirement of added value of Community action). On the two tests mentioned in the main text and how they relate to each other, see also Timmermans, just cited.

take action only 'in so far as' the objectives of the proposed action cannot be sufficiently achieved by the Member States and the objectives can better be achieved at Community level. This seems to imply that scrutiny whether the requirements of the subsidiarity principle are met also comprises the intensity of the action undertaken by the Community.[21] The Court of Justice indeed scrutinizes whether the intensity of the action is in keeping with the requirements of the principle of subsidiarity,[22] that is, the Court of Justice examines whether the action undertaken by the Community did not go beyond what was necessary to achieve the objective pursued. (The strictness of the Court's review I shall address below).

Now, the *Protocol on the application of the principles of subsidiarity and proportionality*[23] offers the following set of guidelines for making the assessment of whether the subsidiarity principle is complied with:

- the issue under consideration has transnational aspects which cannot be satisfactorily regulated by action by Member States;
- actions by Member States alone or lack of Community action would conflict with the requirements of the Treaty (such as the need to correct distortion of competition or avoid disguised restrictions on trade or strengthen economic and social cohesion) or would otherwise significantly damage Member States' interests;
- action at Community level would produce clear benefits by reason of its scale or effects compared with action at the level of the Member States.[24]

Still according to this Protocol, subsidiarity is a dynamic concept and should be applied in the light of the objectives set out in the Treaty. It allows Community action within the limits of its powers to be expanded where circumstances so require, and conversely, to be restricted or discontinued where it is no longer justified.[25] In Advocate General Geelhoed's view, this dynamic concept 'leaves the necessary scope to the appraisal of the Community legislature'.[26] In the doctrine, it has also been noted that the criteria laid down in Article 5, paragraph 2 EC appear to leave a considerable freedom of discretion to the politically responsible Community institutions; subsidiarity then can be invoked as a justification for Community action, but also in opposition to it.[27]

---

21. Timmermans, just cited, 458–459, remarks in this connection that: 'La définition de la subsidiarité, figurant à l'article 5 CE, semble impliquer un élément de proportionnalité. L'action de la Communauté n'est justifiée que "dans la mesure où" une action d'un État membre ne serait pas suffisante et les objectifs de l'action peuvent être mieux réalisés par une action au niveau communautaire. L'examen de la subsidiarité ne peut donc pas se limiter à la question de la nécessité de l'action dans sa globalité. Il doit aller au-delà et cerner aussi l'intensité de l'action et la nécessité de celle ci'.
22. See e.g., Case C-491/01 *British American Tobacco* [2002] ECR I-11453, para. 184.
23. Cited above, in s. 1.
24. Article 5 Protocol. See further Weatherill & Beaumont, 28–29.
25. Article 3 Protocol.
26. Opinion of AG Geelhoed in *British American Tobacco*, just cited, pt. 285.
27. See Kapteyn & VerLoren van Themaat, 141 and 143.

The Court of Justice seems, in the limited number of cases on which it so far has ruled on the subsidiarity principle,[28] to leave the Community legislature considerable scope of appraisal by taking a somewhat deferential approach in reviewing Community action in light of the subsidiarity principle.[29] As regards the abovementioned 'requirement of necessity' and 'requirement of added value' Timmermans has noted that: 'L'examen de ces deux conditions nécessitant des appréciations souvant complexes et impliquant des évaluations de nature politique, un contrôle jurisdictionnel à cet égard ne peut être que de nature limitée. La jurisprudence confirme amplement ce dernier constat.'[30] The case-law so far, which particularly concerns Article 95 EC, indeed seems to confirm limited subsidiarity review by the Court.

Recall that in Chapter 1, where the issue of judicial review was discussed in general (i.e., not specifically in light of the subsidiarity principle), it is already established that in areas of complex policy choices, where the Community legislature enjoys a broad discretionary power, substantive judicial review of legislative acts is limited.[31]

> On the issue of limited subsidiarity review, it follows from the Court's case-law, in fact, that where the objective of a Community measure is to eliminate the barriers raised by the differences which exist between the Member States' laws, the Court readily accepts that such an objective cannot be sufficiently achieved by the Member States individually and calls for action at Community level, at least where insufficiency of individual Member State action is demonstrated by the multifarious development of national laws.[32]
>
> As regards the Court's control on the intensity of the action undertaken (i.e., did the action not go beyond what was necessary to achieve the objective pursued?), the

28. See particularly the cases referred to in the fns *infra*.
29. S. Weatherill, 'The Constitutional Competence of the EU to Deliver Social Justice', *ERCL* (2006): 140.
30. Timmermans, just cited, 456.
31. See also the Opinion of AG Geelhoed in Case C-244/03 *France* v *Parliament and Council* [2005] ECR I-4021, pt. 90.
32. *British American Tobacco*, just cited, para. 182; the Court came to similar conclusions in e.g., Joined Cases C-154/04 and C-155/04 *Alliance for Natural Health a.O.* [2005] ECR I-6451, paras 105–106 (noting that the objective of EC action was to remove barriers resulting from differences between national rules and that leaving Member States with the task of regulating trade would perpetuate the uncoordinated development of national rules and of obstacles to trade between Member States and distortions of competition, concluding that objective could be best achieved at Community level); Case C-377/98 *Netherlands* v *Parliament and Council* ('Biotechnology Directive') [2001] ECR I-7079, para. 32 (noting that the objective of EC action to ensure smooth operation of the internal market by preventing or eliminating differences between the legislation and practice of the various Member States could not be achieved by action taken by the Member States alone and that, as the scope of the objective had immediate effects on intra-Community trade, the objective in question could be better achieved by the Community).

    It should be emphasized, finally, that all three cases dealt with here concern the principle of subsidiarity where the Community legislature makes use of *Art. 95 EC*. Moreover, the Directives in question themselves refer to, in short, the objective of the elimination of barriers raised by the differences which exist between the Member States' laws.

Court has expressly referred to its case-law on the proportionality principle (a general principle of Community law), that:

> the Community legislature must be allowed a *broad discretion* in an area (. . .) which entails political, economic and social choices on its part, in which it is called to undertake complex assessments. Consequently, the legality of a measure adopted in that sphere can be affected only if the measure is manifestly inappropriate having regard to the objective which the competent institution is seeking to pursue.[33] (emphasis added).

The Court here thus only exercises 'marginal control' and will not easily accept that action at Community level went beyond what was necessary. (I note, incidentally, that the above does not absolve the Community legislature from a duty to state reasons in its measures in light of the principle of subsidiarity. In fact, the Court, while not requiring an *express* reference to that principle, does hold that the obligation under Article 253 EC to give reasons also relates to the principle of subsidiarity[34]).

From the above case-law of the Court of Justice, it follows that where the objectives of a Community measure seek to eliminate the barriers raised by the differences which exist between the Member States' laws, the requirements of the subsidiarity principle will be readily met.

3. Analysis of EC Company Law Modernization in View of the Principle of Subsidiarity

In light of the above (the two requirements dealt with in the previous section in particular), looking at the Commission's Action Plan on Modernising Company Law and other recent EC action in the field of company law, I note the following. By defining the two objectives of the Commission's Action Plan as 'strengthening shareholders rights and third parties protection' and 'fostering efficiency and competitiveness' – and not in the terms of the Court's case-law as eliminating the barriers raised by the differences which exist between the Member States'

33. *British American Tobacco*, just cited, para. 184, referring, *inter al.*, to para. 123, where the Court makes the cited statement.
    Where the proportionality principle, referred to in the main text, is concerned, it is settled case-law that in areas which entail political, economic and social choices on its part, in which it is called to undertake complex assessments, the Community legislature must be allowed a broad discretion; and, that only if a measure is manifestly inappropriate in relation to the objective which the competent institutions are seeking to pursue the lawfulness of such a measure can be affected. See e.g., Case C-380/03 *Germany* v *Parliament and Council* ('Tobacco Advertizing II') [2006] ECR I-11573, para. 145; and also: Case C-434/02 *Arnold André* [2004] ECR I-11825, para. 46; Case C-210/03 *Swedish Match* [2004] ECR I-11893, para. 48.
34. Case C-233/94 *Germany* v *Parliament and Council* ('Deposit Guarantees') [1997] ECR I-2405, para. 28 (holding that the Community legislature did explain why it considered that its action was in conformity with the principle of subsidiarity and, accordingly, that it complied with the obligation to give reasons as required under Art. 190 of the Treaty (now Art. 253 EC), but noting that an express reference to that principle cannot be required). See also the judgment in *Biotechnology Directive*, just cited, para. 33.

laws – it is not apparent that such objectives cannot be sufficiently achieved by the Member States individually and call for action at Community level.[35] It is therefore not evident that action at Community level which would seek to achieve such objectives meets the requirements of the subsidiarity principle.[36]

On the other hand, looking to various individual measures adopted since the Action Plan on Modernising Company Law, it seems at first sight evident that they comply with the subsidiarity principle if one looks at their stated objectives. Thus the *Directive on takeover bids* notes as an objective providing 'minimum guidelines (. . .) throughout the Community (. . .) in the case of cross-border takeovers and acquisitions of control',[37] the *Cross-border merger Directive* notes as objective 'laying down rules with common features applicable at transnational level'[38] and the *proposal for a Statute of a European Private Company* notes as objective 'the creation of a company form with common features throughout the Community'.[39] In fact, by their nature, these objectives could not be achieved by action taken by the Member States alone and can be better achieved by the Community. In this view, by thus defining the objectives the Community legislature could easily satisfy the requirements of the subsidiarity principle. The above quoted objectives in my view, however, do not suffice to hold that the measures in question satisfy the subsidiarity principle. If one looks more closely at these

35. See also P.L. Davies, *Gower and Davies' Principles of Modern Company Law* (London: Sweet & Maxwell, 2003), 114 ('It is not obvious that the Community, in principle, is better equipped to identify an efficient system of company law than the Member States').
36. Assuming the Community is *competent* to seek these objectives in the first place (otherwise the subsidiarity question is even not at issue). On the Community's competence as regards these objectives, see Chs 3 and 4.
37. See recital 25 in the preamble to this Directive ('Since the objectives of the action envisaged, namely to establish minimum guidelines for the conduct of takeover bids and ensure an adequate level of protection for holders of securities throughout the Community, cannot be sufficiently achieved by the Member States because of the need for transparency and legal certainty in the case of cross-border takeovers and acquisitions of control, and can therefore, by reason of the scale and effects of the action, be better achieved at Community level, the Community may adopt measures, in accordance with the principle of subsidiarity as set out in Article 5 of the Treaty'). For the objectives of this Directive, see also Ch. 3 (in particular the discussion there of the Directive's breakthrough rule).
38. See recital 15 in the preamble to this Directive ('Since the objective of the proposed action, namely laying down rules with common features applicable at transnational level, cannot be sufficiently achieved by the Member States and can therefore, by reason of the scale and impact of the proposed action, be better achieved at Community level, the Community may adopt measures in accordance with the principle of subsidiarity as set out in Article 5 of the Treaty').
39. See recital 19 in the preamble to the proposal for this Regulation ('Since the objectives of the proposed action cannot be sufficiently achieved by the Member States in so far as they involve the creation of a company form with common features throughout the Community and can therefore, by reason of the scale of the action, be better achieved at Community level, the Community may adopt measures, in accordance with the principle of subsidiarity laid down in Article 5 of the Treaty'). See also recital 2 of this preamble ('it is appropriate to provide for a European company form specifically designed for small businesses, which it is possible to create throughout the Community').

measures, the objective of the Community legislature seems to be to ease various problems for the establishment and functioning of the internal market, in the field of takeover bids,[40] cross-border mergers,[41] and small businesses.[42] Providing for 'minimum guidelines', 'rules with common features' and 'a company form with common features' are the intended *means* – the 'proposed action' in the terms of Article 5, paragraph 2 EC – by which the Community legislature seeks to achieve its (ultimate) *objective* of resolution of underlying internal market problems. In light of the subsidiarity principle, the proper question then is whether *resolution of these problems* – 'the *objectives* of the proposed action' in the terms of Article 5, paragraph 2 EC – could not be achieved by action taken by the Member States alone and can be better achieved by the Community. In my view, this is the question which the Community legislature should have answered here.

Whereas achieving 'minimum guidelines', 'rules with common features' and 'a company form with common features' at Community level in fact by its nature complies with the requirements of the subsidiarity principle, the above proposed analysis requires an examination of the various substantive problems the Community measures seek to redress and asks whether the resolution of these substantive problems could not be achieved by action taken by the Member States alone and can be better achieved by the Community. To be clear, my point is not that such an analysis

40. See recital 19 in the preamble to the *Directive on takeover bids* ('To that end, restrictions on the transfer of securities, restrictions on voting rights, extraordinary appointment rights and multiple voting rights should be removed or suspended during the time allowed for the acceptance of a bid and when the general meeting of shareholders decides on defensive measures, on amendments to the articles of association or on the removal or appointment of board members at the first general meeting of shareholders following closure of the bid') and recital 3 ('It is necessary to create Community-wide clarity and transparency in respect of legal issues to be settled in the event of takeover bids and to prevent patterns of corporate restructuring within the Community from being distorted by arbitrary differences in governance and management cultures'). Recital 2 further notes the need to 'protect the interests of holders of the securities of companies governed by the law of a Member State when those companies are the subject of takeover bids or of changes of control'.
41. See recital 1 in the preamble to the *Cross-border merger Directive* ('as regards cross-border mergers of limited liability companies, they encounter many legislative and administrative difficulties in the Community. It is therefore necessary, with a view to the completion and functioning of the single market, to lay down Community provisions to facilitate the carrying out of cross-border mergers between various types of limited liability company governed by the laws of different Member States').
42. See recital 1 in the preamble to the *proposal for a Statute of a European Private Company* ('The legal framework in which business is carried out in the Community remains largely national. This exposes companies to a wide diversity of national laws, company forms and company regimes. The approximation of national laws by means of directives based on Article 44 of the Treaty can overcome some of these difficulties. Such approximation, however, does not release persons seeking to create companies from the obligation to adopt in each Member State a company form governed by the national law of that Member State') and recital 2 ('In view of the problems faced by such businesses as a result of the diversity of company law regimes and the unsuitability of the SE for small businesses, it is appropriate to provide for a European company form specifically designed for small businesses, which it is possible to create throughout the Community').

> will lead to the conclusion that the subsidiarity principle is not complied with (in fact, this may well be the case[43]), rather that the Community legislature's proffered explanation as to why the requirements of the principle of subsidiarity are met does not suffice to hold that the above measures satisfy these requirements.

Various other measures adopted since the Action Plan on Modernising Company Law *adapt* Directives by simplifying or lifting burdens imposed by them.[44] In these cases, the requirements of the subsidiarity principle are easily met, as Member State action would not suffice to reduce burdens in this area, as the various burdens were imposed by way of EC Directives.[45]

As a final, more general observation on the objectives of Community measures in the field of company law *vis-à-vis* subsidiarity, I note the following. Subsidiarity concerns, in short, the *level* where action should be taken to achieve

---

43. As follows from the Court's case-law dealt with in the main text, where the objective of a Community measure is to eliminate the barriers raised by the differences which exist between the Member States' laws, the Court readily accepts that such an objective cannot be sufficiently achieved by the Member States individually and calls for action at Community level. Such may be the case with the above measures: cf. *Directive on takeover bids* (seeking to lift restrictions on the transfer of securities, restrictions on voting rights and, in particular, 'the prevention of distorted patterns of restructuring due to differences in governance and management cultures'); the *Cross-border merger Directive* (albeit rather curt, noting: lifting of legislative and administrative difficulties for companies governed by the laws of different Member States in the Community); and, *Proposal for a Statute of a European Private Company* (lifting of problems faced by such businesses as a result of the diversity of company law regimes). See also the Explanatory Memorandum to the *Proposal for a Statute of a European Private Company*, 5: 'The difficulties which businesses face *as a result of the diversity of company forms* essentially consist of compliance costs on the formation of a company (e.g., mandatory minimum capital requirement, registration and notary fees, cost of expert legal advice) and of difficulties and compliance costs associated with the operation of a company, which make the day-to-day operation of foreign subsidiaries more expensive compared with domestic subsidiaries.' (emphasis added).
44. See, particularly, Directive 2006/68/EC of the European Parliament and of the Council of 6 Sep. 2006 amending Council Directive 77/91/EEC as regards the formation of public limited liability companies and the maintenance and alteration of their capital, OJ 2006 L 264, 32; and Directive 2007/63/EC of the European Parliament and of the Council of 13 Nov. 2007 amending Council Directives 78/855/EEC and 82/891/EEC as regards the requirement of an independent expert's report on the occasion of merger or division of public limited liability companies, OJ 2007 L 300, 47.
45. See Explanatory memorandum to the Proposal for Directive 2006/68/EC, just cited, COM (2004) 730 final, pt. 3.2 ('The proposed simplifications for public limited liability companies necessitate Community action in that they touch on a series of provisions of Community law which up until now exclude or limit the use of these proposed simplifications by public limited liability companies. The proposal is therefore in compliance with the principle of subsidiarity as laid down in Article 5 of the Treaty'); Explanatory memorandum to the Proposal for Directive 2007/63/EC, just cited, COM (2007) 91, 4 ('Action by the Member States would not suffice to reduce administrative burdens in this area as the information requirements were imposed for mergers and divisions of public limited liability companies by way of EC Directives. EU action will ensure that all future mergers and divisions of public limited liability companies taking place in Europe can benefit from this administrative burdens reduction').

the objectives of the proposed action (*who* should do the work of achieving these objectives, i.e., the Community level or Member States?).[46] It does not concern or limit the logically prior decision *whether* and for *what purpose action should be taken* (this lies with the Community institutions).[47]

> Various cases of the Court of Justice are in Line with this reading of Article 5, paragraph 2 EC.[48] In these cases, the Court, in answering whether a Directive is in keeping with the principle of subsidiarity, (only) analyzes whether the objectives of the proposed action could be better achieved at Community level (and did not go beyond what was necessary to achieve the objective pursued). Under its subsidiarity analysis, the Court then does not control *whether* and *for what purpose action should be taken*.[49]

One should therefore not overestimate the limits subsidiarity places on the Community legislature.[50] Where the Community legislature proposes action for the purpose of eliminating barriers for takeovers, cross-border mergers, or small business, these purposes are not controlled by the Court under the subsidiarity principle. Under this principle, the Court merely controls the level where action should be taken to achieve these objectives.

> The notion that the Court does not control *whether* and *for what purpose action should be taken* sometimes, however, seems to be taken too far. It has, for example, been suggested that where the Community legislature decides that a European form of company should be introduced, legal harmonization in the area of takeover law is necessary or more generally, 'safeguards for the protection of members and others' in a particular area of company law are to be coordinated, these objectives cannot be

---

46. G. Davies, 'Subsidiarity: The wrong idea, in the wrong place, at the wrong time', *CML Rev.* (43) 2006, p 67–68 (and further noting, at 69, that the subsidiarity question is whether Member States can achieve *the Community goal* sufficiently, and also noting that subsidiarity 'assumes the Community goals, privileges their achievement absolutely, and simply asks who should be the one to do the implementing work'; emphasis added), and next fn.
47. The wording of Art. 5, para. 2 EC is (argued to be) unambiguous in this respect. E.-M. Kieninger, *Wettbewerb der Privatrechtsordnungen im Europäischen Binnenmarkt*, Tübingen: Mohr Siebeck 2002, 359 observes in this connection: 'Nach dem eindeutigen Wortlaut von Art. 5 Abs. 2 EGV kommt das Subsidiaritätsprinzip nur innerhalb des Rahmens zur Anwendung, der durch die Festlegung des Ziels der Angleichungsmaßnahmen abgegrenzt ist. Die Zielbestimmung selbst unterliegt nicht dem Subsidiaritätsprinzip. Da sich Ziele nicht von alleine ergeben, obliegt es den Gemeinschaftsorganen, die maßgeblichen Ziel zu bestimmen.' See further: W. Schön, 'Gesellschaftsrecht nach Maastricht – Art. 3b EGV und das europäische Gesellschaftsrecht', *ZGR* (1995): 22–23; K.J. Hopt, *Company Law in the European Union: Harmonization or Subsidiarity* (Saggi, conferenze e seminari, No. 31), Rome: Centro di studi e ricerche di diritto comparato e straniero 1998, 10 ('one must not overestimate the limits which (. . .) [the principle of subsidiarity] places upon harmonization. It is the European organs which determine the objects of legal harmonization'); Davies, just cited, 67–68.
48. See: Case C-377/98 *Netherlands* v *Parliament and Council* ('Biotechnology Directive') [2001] ECR I-7079, para. 32; Case C-491/01 *British American Tobacco* [2002] ECR I-11453, paras 180–183; Case C-103/01 *Commission* v *Germany* [2003] ECR I-5369, para. 47.
49. *Ibid.*
50. Hopt, just cited, 10.

called into question.[51] Now in my view, if these were the sole goals of these measures (without resolving problems with the establishment and functioning in the internal market), it is doubtful that the Community's legislature is competent in the first place, subsidiarity then does not arise. If these measures do seek to resolve problems with the internal market, this objective is not controlled under subsidiarity, but the level of the action to achieve this objective (and the intensity: did it go beyond what was necessary?) is: action at Community level (harmonization, coordination) or action at Member State level?

To conclude: it is clear from the above that, certainly where company law is concerned, one must not overestimate the limits which the principle of subsidiarity places upon the Community legislature.[52]

B. Regulatory Competition in Company Law

Apart from 'constitutional' objections, other objections to the adoption of EC company law may be distinguished, such as cultural, political, and economic.[53] Important as they may be, these other objections are outside the scope of this book. One of these alternative objections, a principally politico-economic argument against harmonization, will be examined nevertheless, for its alleged relatedness to the principle of subsidiarity.

The argument turns on regulatory competition, which, as already mentioned, is competition between legislators to attract investment or business activity or to promote the competitiveness of indigenous industries by providing a more favourable regulatory environment.[54] The notion of regulatory competition, derived from economic literature,[55] is very widely debated both in the United States and in

---

51. Only the level where action should be taken to achieve these objectives, so the argument goes, can be debated and as regards these objectives it is difficult to see that Member States alone could achieve these objectives. See Schön, just cited, 22–23 ('Ob eine europäische Gesellschaftsform eingeführt werden soll (. . .) oder Schutzmaβnahmen für Gesellschafter oder Dritte ergriffen werden müssen, all' dies ist bereits Bestandteil der "Zielsetzung" einer Maβnahme und damit nicht mehr von der Ausübungskontrolle des Art. 3b Abs. 2 EGV erfaβt'). See further Hopt, just cited, 10 ('It is the European organs which determine the objects of legal harmonization. These objects may only be called into question by member states in relation to their realization; they might argue that these objects can be achieved nationally, without any action taken by the European Union', adding that 'If (. . .) legal harmonization in the area of takeover law is considered by the European organs to be a necessary step, then it is difficult to imagine how member states can possibly achieve this without the help of Community-wide measures').
52. For a similar conclusion: Schön, just cited, 23; Hopt, just cited, 10. See also, beyond the context of company law, Lauwaars & Timmermans, 41.
53. In the more general context of private law, Weatherill identifies and examines three types of objection that confront the EC's harmonization programme: the constitutional, the cultural, and the economic. See S. Weatherill, 'Why Object to the Harmonization of Private Law by the EC?', *ERPL* (2004): 633–660.
54. See Ch. 3 (on the subject of regulatory competition).
55. Cf. particularly C. Tiebout, 'A Pure Theory of Local Expenditures', *J. of Pol. Econ.* (64) 1956, 416–424 and the literature cited in Ch. 3 (on the subject of regulatory competition).

Europe,[56] and covers various fields of law.[57] The issues focused on range from, *inter alia*, the benefits (or disadvantages) of regulatory competition, the preconditions which have to be satisfied for regulatory competition to work, to the question whether in a given field of law these conditions are satisfied and whether specific legislative measures contribute to regulatory competition.

My focus, however, is different. I will examine the question whether the principle of subsidiarity holds, as sometimes is claimed, a commitment to regulatory competition,[58] in the sense that *as a rule regulatory competition* between Member States is the means to achieve the goals of the proposed action.[59] I have a number of observations on this view, which have to do both with certain economic aspects of this issue (a, *infra*) as well as with various legal aspects (b-d, *infra*).

---

56. See, apart from the contributions cited in Ch. 3 (on the subject of regulatory competition), e.g., W.L. Cary, 'Federalism and Corporate Law: Reflections upon Delaware', *Yale L.J.* 83 (1974): 672 and 705; L.A. Bebchuk, 'Federalism and the Corporation: The Desirable Limits on State Competition in Corporate Law', *Harv. L. Rev.* 105 (1992): 1458; N. Reich, 'Competition between legal orders: a new paradigm?', *CML Rev.* 29 (1992): 861–896; S. Lombardo, *Regulatory Competition in Company Law in the European Community*, Frankfurt am Main: Peter Lang 2002, about which: G.-J. Vossestein, 'Book reviews', *CML Rev.* 40 (2003): 1304–1306; K. Heine & W. Kerber, 'European Corporate Laws, Regulatory Competition and Path Dependence', *Eur. J. of L. and Econ.* 13 (2002): 47–71; K. Heine, *Regulierungswettbewerb im Gesellschaftsrecht* (Berlin: Duncker & Humblot, 2003); J.A. McCahery & E.P.M. Vermeulen, 'Does the European Company Prevent the "Delaware Effect"?', TILEC Discussion Paper, Mar. 2005; M.J. Roe, 'Regulatory Competition in Making Corporate Law in the United States – and its Limits', *Oxf. Rev. Econ. Policy* 21 (2005): 232–242; L. Enriques & M. Gelter, 'How the Old World Encountered the New One: Regulatory Competition and Cooperation in European Corporate and Bankruptcy Law', ECGI-Law Working Paper no. 63/2006, Feb. 2006, <www.ecgi.org/wp/>.
57. See as regards company law the previous fn., and further e.g., (in the field of private law) E.-M. Kieninger, *Wettbewerb der Privatrechtsordnungen im Europäischen Binnenmarkt* (Tübingen: Mohr Siebeck, 2002); (in the field of tax law) W. W. Bratton & J. McCahery, 'Fiscal Federalism, Jurisdictional Competition, and Tax Coordination: Translating Theory to Policy in the European Union', in *Regulatory Competition and Economic Integration*, ed. D.C. Esty & D. Geradin (Oxford: OUP, 2001), 157–189; W. Schön, 'Playing Different Games? Regulatory Competition in Tax and Company Law Compared', *CML Rev.* 42 (2005): 331–365.
58. See on this view W. Schön, 'Mindestharmonisierung im europäischen Gesellschaftsrecht', *ZHR* 160 (1996): 228–229 (noting: 'Das Prinzip der Subsidiarität (. . .) wird im Schrifttum (. . .) häufig als europarechtlichter Auftrag zu einem 'Wettbewerb der Systeme' verstanden' referring in this connection to a substantial number of scholarly articles, but rejecting the view himself). See further S. Grundmann, 'Wettbewerb der Regelgeber im Europäischen Gesellschaftsrecht – jedes Marktsegment hat seine Struktur', *ZGR* (2001): 801–802 and the next fn.
59. R. Van den Bergh, 'Towards an Institutional Legal Framework for Regulatory Competition in Europe', *Kyklos* 53 (2000): 435 (observing that the principle of subsidiarity 'makes competition between legislators the rule and centralized governance (unification, harmonization) the exception'). Cf. S. Grundmann, *Europäisches Gesellschaftsrecht* (Heidelberg: C.F. Müller Verlag, 2004), 75 (noting that regulatory competition, in light of the principle of subsidiarity and the goals of integration (Art. 2, 3(1)(c) and 4 EC), 'EG-verfassungsrechtlich geboten' is (is required by the EC constitution) (with further references). Competition among rules would, in this view, have 'constitutional status'; see M. Rohe, 'Binnenmarkt oder Interessenverband?', *RabelsZ* 61 (1997): 40.

a. To begin with, the idea that *as a rule* regulatory competition between Member States is the means to achieve the goals of the proposed action, may from an economic viewpoint not necessarily be wise policy. Such a general rule loses sight of the fact that regulatory competition may not only provide benefits but also disadvantages, and that for regulatory competition to work, certain conditions have to be met.

I will elaborate at some length on this point, particularly the benefits and disadvantages of regulatory competition and the conditions which have to be met in order for regulatory competition to work, not only to question the economic wisdom of a general rule in favour of regulatory competition, but also to show that an assessment whether regulatory competition between Member States may work, requires a complex economic and politico-legislative assessment. (As I have argued,[60] such assessments are typically the domain of the (Community) legislature and only 'marginally' scrutinized by the Court of Justice).

As is well-known, regulatory competition is associated with a number of advantages over other approaches to dealing with diverse national rules under conditions of international economic interdependence, including harmonization.

The advantages, *inter alia*, include:

(1) Choice or diversity in national regulatory systems. This enables national regulation to be tailored to the specific needs of the national economy, rather than being obliged to adopt an EC norm which may not be appropriate to local conditions;[61]

(2) Simplification of procedures. Competition among rules obviates the need for a significant amount of *ex ante* harmonization and thus simplifies the task for EC and national regulators and politicians;[62]

(3) Reducing the danger of regulatory failure. The competition between national rules reduces the risk of political compromises resulting in 'bad' central harmonization, that means regulation which is determined more by political expediency and the need to reach a compromise than by good regulatory practice.[63] The 2004 Directive on takeover bids may be considered a case in point. After the Council had reached an agreement on a general approach on the – then proposed – Directive,[64] Internal Market Commissioner Bolkestein said:

> I am not going to pretend that I am pleased with this agreement. Nor am I going to be hypocritical by pretending that the version of the Directive agreed today represents a step forward for EU competitiveness or for the integration of EU capital markets. The Competitiveness Council says that it wants to be seen to be taking decisions. In all sincerity, I have to say that if the Council continues to take decisions like this one, the European Union

60. See s. A.2, *supra*.
61. See: Woolcock, just cited, 298; Van den Bergh, just cited, 437.
62. Woolcock, just cited, 299.
63. *Ibid.*
64. For the text on the basis of which the Council on 27 Nov. 2003 reached agreement, see Council document No. 15476/03 (DRS 106 CODEC 1702 of 28 Nov. 2003).

> will never reach its target of becoming the most competitive economy in the world by 2010. On this issue, we have actually gone a long way in reverse gear since the Council endorsed the previous takeovers Directive in June 2001 (. . .). A particular source of disappointment is the way in which the takeovers Directive has fallen victim to horsetrading and unholy alliances of convenience related to totally extraneous issues.[65]

Competition between national legislatures may also check the danger of bureaucratic capture in which the regulators protect their own interests at the expense of consumers;[66]

(4) Regulatory competition enables experimentation, flexibility, and innovation in regulatory policy. Just as monopolistic markets tend to be inflexible and unresponsive to consumer demands, so a single set of harmonized rules is less responsive than competition among rules and a 'market for regulation'.[67] This advantage of regulatory competition is quite relevant. Presently, the so-called petrification of EC-company law is considered to be a major concern. The High Level Group of Company Law Experts noted in this respect, that once Member States have agreed to a certain approach in an area of company law and have implemented a directive accordingly, it becomes very difficult to change the directive and the underlying approach. In addition, the Group observed, that there is a growing need to continuously adapt existing rules in view of rapidly changing circumstances and views.[68]

On the other hand, regulatory competition is also associated with various potential disadvantages.

The disadvantages, *inter alia*, include:

(1) The flexibility of competition among rules may have a down side in the shape of higher transaction costs and uncertainty for business.[69]
(2) Furthermore, there is the risk that competition among rules will result in competitive deregulation and ultimately in a 'race to the bottom' and zero or sub-optimal regulation.[70] The race to the bottom theory claims that competition between (state) legislatures in company law harms shareholders by driving states to adopt company law rules that are too lax with respect to managers and controlling shareholders.[71]
(3) Finally, if there is a market for regulation, there is no reason to assume that this will be a perfect market. Indeed, with only a limited number of strong national legislatures within the EC, one could envisage an oligopolistic form

65. MEMO/03/245 of 28 Nov. 2003 (Results of the Competitiveness Council of Ministers, Brussels, 27 Nov. 2003), 1.
66. Woolcock, just cited, 299.
67. *Ibid.*, 299; Van den Bergh, just cited, 438.
68. See High Level Group Report II, 31. For this Report, see Ch. 2. The Group recommended in this respect, that: 'The EU should consider a broader use of alternatives to primary legislation (secondary regulation, standard setting and monitoring, model laws).' See Recommendation II.2, 5.
69. Woolcock, just cited, 300.
70. *Ibid.*, 300–301.
71. Cf. Cary, just cited, 672 and 705 and other literature just cited on regulatory competition.

> of competition among rules. Regulators also may find it more comfortable to retain the status quo and thus avoid the uncertainties and risks of regulatory competition.[72]

In addition, certain preconditions have to be met in order for regulatory competition to work.[73] If these preconditions are not met, competition among rules may in fact not be an alternative to harmonization to begin with. Focussing on company law, free choice of law in case of *initial* incorporations and free choice of law for *existing* companies through reincorporation abroad are essential requirements.[74] (This issue will be elaborated upon presently). However, even when there would be enough free choice as a matter of (company) law, tax issues and various economic, cultural, and political factors can make reincorporations (and possibly cross-border incorporations as well) *de facto* unlikely.[75]

To return now to the issue of free choice of company law, it is of importance to establish first that the case-law of the EC Court of Justice has contributed to a great extent to a – *de iure* – free choice of law for initial incorporations.[76] Moreover, a – *de iure* – free choice of law for existing companies through reincorporation abroad is – ever more – within the bounds of the possible.

In the United States, it is typically the so-called 'downstream merger' which is used to reincorporate.[77]

> A merger between a parent company and its subsidiary is called an 'upstream' merger if the surviving company is the parent company; it is a 'downstream' merger if the surviving company is the subsidiary.[78] As mentioned, downstream mergers are used to change the state of incorporation of companies. The procedure is as follows. A company creates a wholly-owned subsidiary in the new state of incorporation and then merges itself into its subsidiary in a downstream merger with all shares and financial interest of the parent being mirrored in the shares and financial structure

72. Woolcock, just cited, 301.
73. For a general – i.e., not specifically geared to company law – discussion of these preconditions, see: Woolcock, just cited, 301–305; Van den Bergh, just cited, 442 and 438 ('The achievement of the advantages of regulatory competition presupposes a sufficient number of rule-makers, information about the alternatives that are available and mobility of citizens or production factors').
74. See: J. Wouters, 'European Company Law: *Quo Vadis*?', *CML Rev.* 37 (2000): 283; L. Enriques, 'EC Company Law and the Fears of a European Delaware', *EBLR* (2004): 1260.
75. For in-depth discussions of these factors: Enriques, just cited, 1266; J.A. McCahery & E.P.M. Vermeulen, 'The Changing Landscape of EU Company Law', TILEC discussion paper, DP 2004-023 (Tilburg University, 2004), 4–5, available at <http://ssrn.com>.
76. See in particular the Court's rulings in: *Centros*, *Überseering* and *Inspire Art*. For a further discussion of this free choice, see G.-J. Vossestein 'De invloed van de EG op het vennootschapsrecht. Concurrentie tussen lidstaten: het Nederlandse beleid', in *De invloed van het Europese recht op het Nederlandse privaatrecht* (vol. II), ed. A.S. Hartkamp, C.H. Sieburgh & L.A.D. Keus (Deventer: Kluwer, 2007), 397–428.
77. See e.g., P. Dodd & R. Leftwich, 'The Market for Corporate Charters: "Unhealthy Competition" versus Federal Regulation', *J. Bus.* 53 (1980): 263; Bebchuk, just cited, 1458; F.A. Gevurtz, *Corporation Law* (St. Paul (Minnesota): West Group, 2000), 41.
78. R.W. Hamilton, *The Law of Corporations* (St. Paul (Minnesota): West Group, 2000), 622.

of the subsidiary.[79] When the merger occurs, each shareholder and creditor of the old company incorporated in State A automatically becomes a shareholder and creditor in a company incorporated in State B.[80]

This reincorporation technique is also available to companies formed under the law of a Member State. This became certain in 2005, with the Court's *Sevic* ruling (which showed, in brief, that cross-border mergers may be enforced under Article 43 EC) and the adoption of the *Directive on cross-border mergers*. Before that, the *SE Regulation*, of course, made the reincorporation technique at issue[81] already available, even though rather inefficiently.

The fact is, that an SE may be formed by merging[82] an operating company in State A into a shell company subsidiary in Member State B. The subsidiary takes the form of an SE when the merger takes place.[83] The law applicable to the SE subsequently is dealt with in Article 9 of the SE Regulation.[84] This provision entails that the great majority of the law applicable to the newly formed SE will be the national company law of the Member State where the SE has its registered office, in the example just given, the company law of Member State B. Furthermore, commencing two years after its formation, an SE may convert into a domestic company of the reincorporation State,[85] in which case – evidently – the national company law of that State will apply fully. Even though the SE Regulation thus offers the possibility to reincorporate and to change applicable company law, formation of an SE has important disadvantages, in particular that the cumbersome procedures for the protection of employees' interests have to be followed,[86] and that the SE has to have its 'head

79. *Ibid.*, 622–623.
80. *Ibid.*, 623. For these cross-border mergers see in particular § 11.02(a) of the Model Business Corporation Act (1984) (printed in: J.D. Bauman, *Corporations and Other Business Associations: Statutes, Rules and Forms. 2001 edition* (St. Paul (Minnesota): West Group, 2001), 1–245): 'One or more domestic corporations may merge with a domestic or foreign corporation or other entity pursuant to a plan of merger.' 'Foreign corporation' is defined in § 1.40(10) MBCA as: 'a corporation for profit incorporated under a law other than the law of this state'.
81. The SE provides also for another reincorporation technique. An SE may be formed by transformation or conversion of an existing public limited-liability company (formed under the law of a Member State) into an SE 'if for at least two years it has had a subsidiary company governed by the law of another Member State'. See Art. 2(4) and Art. 37 SE Regulation. This two-year period makes transformation less attractive – from the viewpoint of choice of company law – than the downstream merger.
82. For the formation of an SE by merger, see Art. 2(1) and 17–31 SE Regulation. See also on this formation method P.J. Dortmond, 'De Europese vennootschap en juridische fusie', *Ondernemingsrecht* (2001): 190–193.
83. Article 17(2), para. 2 SE Regulation.
84. For a discussion of Art. 9 SE Regulation, see J. Winter, 'Thalassa! Thalassa! – The SE as a glimpse of the future?', in Rickford, 113–122.
85. For this conversion, see Art. 66 SE Regulation.
86. According to Art. 1(4) SE Regulation, employee involvement in the SE is governed by the provisions of the SE Directive. See further: P. Davies, 'Employee Involvement in the European Company', in Rickford, 67–82; L.L. Hansen, 'Employee Involvement and the Formation of a European Company', *ECL* (2004): 126–130.

office' in State B.[87] In case of conversion of an SE into a domestic company, an additional problem is the two-year requirement just mentioned.[88]

Finally yet importantly, recall, in this connection, the Court's recent *Cartesio* judgment, which is dealt with extensively in Chapter 3. The Court decided, as explained, that a Member State of incorporation may not prevent a company, by requiring its winding-up or liquidation, from converting into a company which is governed by the law of another Member State to the extent that it is permitted under that law to do so. This would constitute a restriction on the freedom of establishment of the company concerned (which – unless it serves overriding requirements in the public interest – is prohibited under Article 43 EC). Thus (by means of conversion), so it can be concluded, reincorporation may be possible without even having to use a shell company in the reincorporation state (the Member State of relocation).

While the Court's case-law and various actions of the Community legislature thus have enlarged the – *de iure* – free choice of company law, it should be reiterated, however, that tax issues and various economic, cultural, and political factors may make reincorporations (or cross-border incorporations) *in practice* unlikely.

b. Secondly, if indeed regulatory competition would be as significant to the principle of subsidiarity as it (sometimes) is argued to be (i.e., that *as a rule regulatory competition* between Member States is the means to achieve the goals of the proposed action), one would expect it to occupy a prominent place in the 'Protocol on the application of the principles of subsidiarity and proportionality',[89] which provides, as will be recalled,[90] a set of guidelines for making the assessment of whether the subsidiarity principle is complied with. This, however, is not the case. In fact, regulatory competition is not mentioned or referred to at all in the Protocol (or for that matter in Article 5, paragraph 2 EC itself). Moreover, I recall that according to the Protocol, subsidiarity is a dynamic concept and should be applied in the light of the objectives set out in the Treaty; it expressly allows Community action within the limits of its powers to be *expanded* where *circumstances so require*, and conversely, to be *restricted* or discontinued where it is no longer justified.[91] Subsidiarity then can be invoked as a justification for Community action, but also in opposition to it.[92] Contrary then to what (sometimes) is argued,[93] it does not contain a presumption in favour of Member State action in the sense that *regulatory competition* between the Member States is the rule and Community action (read: harmonization) the exception.

c. Thirdly, the view that *as a rule regulatory competition* between Member States is the means to achieve the goals of the proposed action does not seem to fit

87. Article 7 SE Regulation.
88. These disadvantages were already drawn attention to by Enriques, just cited, 1261.
89. For this Protocol, see s. A.1, *supra*.
90. See s. A.2, *supra*.
91. Article 3 Protocol.
92. See Kapteyn & VerLoren van Themaat, 141.
93. See Van den Bergh, just cited.

well with the analysis by the Court of Justice and its Advocate General in *Centros* and *Inspire Art*. While these cases do not deal with subsidiarity *in se*, in part they *do* concern the issue of regulatory competition *vis-à-vis* harmonization. Recall,[94] from *Centros* and *Inspire Art*, it flows, in short, that under the freedom of establishment a national of a Member State who wishes to set up a company may choose to form it in the Member State whose rules of company law seem to him the least restrictive and then set up branches in other Member States. While these cases, on the basis of the prohibition of Article 43 EC, *may* incite regulatory competition between Member States (I have dealt with the conditions for regulatory competition above), this competition seems, however, as I further recall, only to be accepted by the Court and its Advocate General conditionally, namely in the absence of harmonization.[95]

Harmonization by the Community legislature may therefore set aside this competition between Member States. Indeed, the Treaty has established a system in which the internal market is attained not only by the basic prohibitions on the free movement ('negative integration') but also by action of the Community legislature ('positive integration'). Within the Treaty system, the Community legislature has the express competence and duty to coordinate or harmonize differences between Member States laws for the purpose of the establishment and functioning of the internal market. (As stated earlier, historically, prevention of regulatory competition was arguably even the most important motive for including Article 44(2)(g) EC in the EC Treaty[96]).

94. See Ch. 3.
95. See Opinion of AG La Pergola in *Centros*, pt. 20: 'In short, *in the absence of harmonisation*, competition among rules must be allowed free play in corporate matters' and the Court of Justice in *Centros*, which, after noting that a national of a Member State who wishes to set up a company may choose to form it in the Member State whose rules of company law seem to him the least restrictive, observed (at para. 28) that 'it is *always* open to the Council, on the basis of the powers conferred upon it by Article 54(3)(g) of the EC Treaty, to achieve *complete harmonisation*'. (emphasis added). See further Ch. 3.
96. See also Ch. 3. Incidentally, also in the United States – the jurisdiction familiarly associated with the issue of regulatory competition between individual States – prevention of regulatory competition by the central (federal) legislature has been held constitutional. It has thus been argued by Easterbrook that: 'National courts tend to scorn competition among jurisdictions; the Supreme Court has used the potential power of this competition as a justification for national legislation [in *United States vs. Darby*, 312 US 100, 119-23 (1941)], disregarding the benefits competition brings' (F.H. Easterbrook, 'Federalism and European Business Law', in *European Economic and Business Law*, ed. R.M. Buxbaum, G. Hertig, A. Hirsch & K. J. Hopt (Berlin: Walter de Gruyter, 1996), 1–11). In *Darby*, the Supreme Court held that Congress had constitutional power to prohibit the shipment in interstate commerce of lumber manufactured by employees whose wages are less than a prescribed minimum or whose weekly hours of labor at that wage are greater than a prescribed maximum. It ruled, at 122: 'As we have said the evils aimed at by the Act are the spread of substandard labor conditions through the use of the facilities of interstate commerce for competition by the goods so produced with those produced under the prescribed or better labor conditions; and the consequent dislocation of the commerce itself caused by the impairment or destruction of local businesses by competition made effective through interstate commerce. The Act is thus directed at the suppression of a method or kind of competition in interstate commerce which it has in effect condemned as "unfair"'.

d. Finally, the view that *as a rule regulatory competition* between Member States is the means to achieve the goals of the proposed action does not seem to fit well with the case-law of the Court of Justice on subsidiarity.[97] It must be reiterated in this regard that 'the objectives of the proposed action', mentioned in Article 5, paragraph 2 EC, are – within the limits of the powers conferred on them[98] – determined by the Community institutions, which determination itself is not subject to the principle of subsidiarity. Where the objective of the proposed action is to strike down barriers between Member States and bring about uniform rules or common standards, the Court of Justice readily accepts that the conditions of the subsidiarity principle are complied with. Indeed, it is questionable at least, that such an objective could be achieved at national level through competition among rules.[99] In fact, regulatory competition theorists themselves argue (or, in this context, would have to admit) that competition among rules leads or may lead to the adoption of varying standards.[100]

In sum, the view that the principle of subsidiarity holds a commitment to regulatory competition in the sense that *as a rule regulatory competition* between Member States is the means to achieve the goals of the proposed action: (i) may from an economic viewpoint not necessarily be wise policy; (ii) does not find support in the *Protocol on the application of the principles of subsidiarity and proportionality*, which expressly allows Community action within the limits of its powers to be *expanded* where *circumstances so require* and conversely, to be *restricted* or discontinued where it is no longer justified; (iii) does not seem to fit well with the case-law of the Court of Justice in *Centros* and *Inspire Art* and in its case-law on subsidiarity.

An important development in the academic debate on regulatory competition has taken shape in the past few years. This development and its 'constitutional' dimension will now briefly be addressed.

---

97. See s. A.2, *supra*.
98. For these powers, see Chs 3 and 4.
99. See Kieninger, just cited, 357–358 and 360. See further K.J. Hopt, *Company Law in the European Union: Harmonization or Subsidiarity* (Saggi, conferenze e seminari, No. 31) (Rome: Centro di studi e ricerche di diritto comparato e straniero, 1998), 15–16 ('European legal harmonization is particularly appropriate where individual Member States use their legal system to erect or maintain barriers to market access. In the area of takeover bids it was this very problem, namely the absence of a level playing field, which led to efforts to achieve legal harmonization. This is true for barriers to takeover bids generally, and specifically for the numerous and far-reaching defence mechanisms which are permissible in many Member States. The American example shows that individual states may have interests – income from taxes, jobs, structural policy etc. – which are quite contrary to the interests of shareholders, and which may lead them to use restrictive legal norms in order to protect their own enterprises from takeovers').
100. See e.g., D.C. Esty & D. Geradin, 'Regulatory Co-Opetition', in *Regulatory Competition and Economic Integration*, ed. D.C. Esty & D. Geradin (Oxford: OUP, 2001), 30. See also S. Deakin, 'Regulatory Competition versus Harmonization in European Company Law', in Esty & Geradin, just cited, 191, who notes that it is difficult to answer the question whether regulatory competition leads to – in short – diversity or convergence.

Both supporters of increased harmonization and regulatory competition theorists argue that their approaches will make markets work more efficiently and improve social welfare in the context of economic integration. Given that the policy implications of these two theories (one arguing for centralization and the other for decentralization of governmental activity) pull in opposite directions, at first blush, so it is argued,[101] it appears that one or the other approach must be wrong.[102] In recent years, however, several scholars have begun to develop more nuanced synthesis theories, demonstrating that this dichotomy need not be so sharp.[103] It can be referred in particular to Esty and Geradin's model of 'regulatory co-opetition'[104] and also to Deakin's theory of 'reflexive harmonization'.[105] A common policy goal emerges from the various 'synthesis' theories; in short, regulatory systems should be set up with enough interjurisdictional cooperation (or harmonization) to ensure that market failures are addressed, but with a sufficient degree of regulatory competition to prevent the resulting governmental structure from becoming untamed, overreaching, or inefficient.[106] The purpose of harmonization would not be to substitute for Member State level regulation; hence the Community rules would not operate to 'occupy the field' in the manner of a 'monopoly regulator'. Rather, Community rules would seek to promote regulatory competition.[107] In this way, far from suppressing regulatory competition, harmonization would aim to stimulate it.[108]

Focussing on 'constitutionality', the development of the debate thus may be characterized as follows. Initially, the relevant question was whether the principle of subsidiarity, in short, precludes the Community legislature from – wholly or partially – exercising its powers (in favour of regulatory competition). This question, incidentally, answered in the negative; as was shown, the principle of subsidiarity, does not hold a (or this specific) commitment to regulatory competition. Nowadays the issue seems more whether the Community legislature should, under the EC Treaty, use its powers to – actively – stimulate competition among

101. D.C. Esty & D. Geradin, 'Introduction', in Esty & Geradin, just cited, xx.
102. *Ibid.*
103. *Ibid.*, xx and xxiv.
104. Esty and Geradin propose that optimal governance requires a flexible mix of competition and cooperation between governmental actors as well as between governmental actors and non-governmental actors. They borrow the concept of 'co-opetition' from A.M. Brandenburg & B.J. Nalebuff, *Co-opetition* (New York: Doubleday, 1996). See Esty & Geradin, 'Regulatory Co-Opetition', in Esty & Geradin, just cited, 31.
105. Deakin argues in general terms that 'the harmonization of company law may represent the best chance of capturing beneficial aspects of regulatory competition'. More specifically, according to the theory of reflexive harmonization, harmonization should seek to underpin and encourage diverse, local-level approaches to regulatory problems by creating space for autonomous solutions to arise. In particular, mechanisms of group representation and participation should be supported. See Deakin, just cited, 192 and 211.
106. Esty & Geradin, 'Introduction', in Esty & Geradin, just cited, xxv.
107. Cf. Deakin, just cited, 211.
108. *Ibid.*, 213.

rules.[109] Such a general view, in my opinion, should be rejected. Where it is (or would be) based on the principle of subsidiarity, again this principle does not hold a commitment to (boost) regulatory competition.

At the risk of being repetitive, to briefly deal with the view that the Community legislature should use its powers to – actively – stimulate competition among rules: first of all, such a general view may from an economic viewpoint not necessarily be wise policy (see my remarks above); secondly, the individual legal bases, which are the point of departure for Community legislation (here in the field of company law),[110] do not as such contain a requirement to boost regulatory competition between Member States. As argued above, from the Court's remarks on harmonization in *Centros* and *Inspire Art* it follows that an interpretation of Article 44 EC as a guarantee for competition among rules, must be rejected;[111] thirdly, the *Protocol on the application of the principles of subsidiarity and proportionality* does not refer to regulatory competition, let alone that it contains the requirement under consideration; fourthly, such a view does not seem to fit well with the case-law of the Court of Justice on subsidiarity (see my remarks above). (Also, it must be realized in this connection, that it follows from the case-law of the Court of Justice, that the Community legislature has a broad discretionary power of a 'political nature'. The attribution of such a power is justified by the fact that the Community legislature is to balance various diverging interests.[112] A requirement to always stimulate regulatory competition could be argued to be at odds with this broad discretionary power). Finally, as an obiter remark, it should be noted that in particular in German literature, it is pointed out that the EC Treaty does not pursue competition among rules but competition between undertakings.[113]

In conclusion, both the view that the principle of subsidiarity, in short, amounts to a rule in favour of regulatory competition (a limit to or a prohibition for the Community legislature to exercise its powers (wholly or partially), in favour of regulatory competition), and the view that the Community legislature generally is required under the EC Treaty to use its powers to – actively – stimulate regulatory competition, must be rejected.

---

109. Both questions are not unrelated (as will also emerge from the main text below).
110. For these legal bases, see Chs 3 and 4.
111. See Ch. 3 (on the subject of regulatory competition).
112. See the Opinion of AG Léger in Case C-40/03 P, and 41/03 P, *Rica Foods* v *Commission* [2005] ECR I-6811 and [2005] ECR I-6875, pt. 45, which Opinion was entered into in Ch. 1.
113. See I.E. Schwartz, '30 Jahre EG-Rechtsangleichung', in *Eine Ordnungspolitik für Europa. Festschrift für Hans von der Groeben zu seinem 80. Geburtstag*, ed. E.-J. Mestmäcker, H. Möller & H.-P. Schwarz (Baden-Baden: Nomos, 1987), 357: 'Der EWG-Vertrag strebt nicht den Wettbewerb der Normen, Vorschriften und Rechtssysteme an, sondern der Unternehmen, ihrer Standorte und Erzeugnisse ohne künstliche, durch das Recht bedingte Verfälschungen'. For an assenting opinion: E.-J. Mestmäcker, 'Marktversagen und Staatsversagen in der Europäischen Union', in *Systembildung und Systemlücken in Kerngebieten des Europäischen Privatrechts*, ed. S. Grundmann (Tübingen: Mohr Siebeck, 2000), 62. This view fits in with the Freiburg or Ordoliberal School, which typically argues against a free choice of law and competition among rules; see further S. Lombardo, *Regulatory Competition in Company Law in the European Community* (Frankfurt am Main: Peter Lang, 2002), 70–71, about which: G.-J. Vossestein, 'Book reviews', *CML Rev.* 40 (2003): 1304–1306.

It must be emphasized that the rejection of this, in brief, general rule and requirement does not prevent the Community legislature – within the limits of the discretionary powers conferred on it – to take regulatory competition into consideration of its own free will or on its own initiative, as indeed the Commission did in its 2003 Action Plan on Modernising Company Law. One of the key policy objectives of the Action Plan is fostering efficiency and competitiveness of business. Business efficiency and competitiveness depend on many factors, one of which is a sound framework of company law.[114] In this connection, the Action Plan states:

> Key to the achievement of this objective is the setting up of a proper balance between actions at EU level and actions at national level. Some company law rules are likely to be best dealt with, and updated, more efficiently at national level, and some competition between national rules may actually be healthy for the efficiency of the single market.[115]

Regulatory competition has thus been incorporated into the EC's legislative policy. The political desirability of such a pro-regulatory competition policy, however, lacks a 'constitutional' dimension and is therefore outside the scope of this book.[116]

III. THE PROHIBITION OF ARTICLE 43 EC AS A LIMIT TO EC COMPANY LAW

A. Introduction

It is of regular occurrence that company law specialists contend that certain provisions of EC company law (Directives or Regulations) are in breach of Article 43 EC, which article prohibits – in short – restrictions on freedom of establishment. The reciprocity rule – included in the Directive on takeover bids – and the so-called 'real seat' arrangement adopted by the SE Regulation may be quoted as the most prominent examples of such provisions.[117]

This section deals with the applicability of Article 43 EC to Community legislation in general and with the contentions just referred to in particular.[118]

---

114. Action Plan, 9.
115. *Ibid.*
116. Incidentally, apart from regulatory competition, a (further) form of 'bottom-up' harmonization has been suggested and seems somewhat to develop in practice: initiatives for formulating non-binding rules or codes of conduct on certain areas within company law. I leave this aside, but refer to Wouters, just cited, 298, and in the area of contract law, e.g., U. Bernitz, *The Harmonisation of European Contract Law*, ed. S. Vogenauer & S. Weatherill (Oxford: Hart 2006), 191–193.
117. For the contentions at issue, see *inter al.*, J. Rickford, 'The Emerging European Takeover Law from a British Perspective', *EBLR* (2004): 1402 and 1408 (with regard to reciprocity); E. Wymeersch, 'The transfer of the company's seat in European company law', *CML Rev.* 40 (2003): 692–693 (with regard to the 'real seat' arrangement). See further s. D, *infra* for more references.
118. In light of these contentions, I will only deal with Art. 43 EC. (It should not be forgotten, however, that – as will be shown in the main text – the Community institutions are also bound by the other basic prohibitions of Art. 28 (free movement of goods), Art. 39 (free movement of workers), Art. 49 (freedom of services) and Art. 56 (free movement of capital). These

The structure of this section is as follows. First, the applicability of the basic prohibition of Article 43 EC to Community legislation is dealt with (s. B). Then it is argued that even though the Community is bound by Article 43 EC, the special character of Community legislation may influence the outcome of the test for compatibility with Article 43 EC (s. C). Section D, finally, contains an analysis of various provisions of EC company law in view of Article 43 EC.

B. Applicability of the Basic Prohibition of Article 43 EC to the Community Legislature

The applicability of Article 43 EC to measures adopted by the Community institutions can speedily be dealt with. In respect of the free movement of goods (Article 28 et seq. EC), it is settled case-law that although the basic prohibition of Article 28 EC applies primarily to unilateral measures adopted by the Member States, it also applies to the Community institutions.[119] Referring to several of these judgments in the field of free movement of goods, it is generally assumed by company law specialists, that also the Community legislature is simply bound by Article 43 EC, just like the Member States.[120]

It can be noted in this regard that indeed also with respect to freedom of establishment – for a relatively short time now – the Court has been prepared to test Community legislation for compatibility with Article 43 EC.[121] This follows

provisions may therefore also be of relevance for the compatibility of EC company law with the Treaty. Of these provisions, particularly Art. 56 EC may be relevant in this respect; Art. 28, 39, and 49 EC are less, if at all, related with the issue of EC company law).

119. See: Case 15/83 *Denkavit Nederland* [1984] ECR 2171, para. 15; Case C-51/93 *Meyhui* v *Schott Zwiesel Glaswerke* [1994] ECR I-3879, para. 11; Joined Cases C-427/93, C-429/93 and C-436/93 *Bristol-Myers Squibb a.O.* v *Paranova* [1996] ECR I-3457, para. 36; Case C-114/96 *Criminal proceedings against Kieffer and Thill* [1997] ECR I-3629, para. 27; Case C-341/95 *Bettati* v *Safety Hi-Tec* [1998] ECR I-4355, para. 61; Case C-169/99 *Schwarzkopf* [2001] ECR I-5901, para. 37; Case C-469/00 *Ravil* [2003] ECR I-5053, para. 86; Case C-108/01 *Consorzio del Prosciutto di Parma* [2003] ECR I-5121, para. 53; Case 434/02 *Arnold André* [2004] ECR I-11825, para. 57; Joined Cases C-154/04 and C-155/04 *Alliance for Natural Health* [2005] ECR I-6451, para. 47 ('It must be observed that by virtue of settled case-law the prohibition of quantitative restrictions and of all measures having equivalent effect, laid down in Article 28 EC, applies not only to national measures but also to measures adopted by the Community institutions'). Similarly, the prohibition of Art. 49 EC (freedom of services) also applies to measures adopted by the Community institutions: see Case C-56/01 *Inizan* [2003] ECR I-12403, paras 15–26.

120. See e.g., J. Rickford, 'Current Developments in European Law on the Restructuring of Companies: An Introduction', *EBLR* (2004): 1251; and F. Kainer, 'Binnenmarktrechtliche Grenzen des Übernahmerechts', *ZHR* 168 (2004): 562 (who, for instance, refers to Case C-284/95 *Safety Hi-Tech* v *S. & T.* [1998] ECR I-4301).

121. As to the issue of the addressees of Art. 43 EC, one can further raise the question whether the prohibition of Art. 43 EC also applies to conduct by private persons (the issue of the so-called horizontal direct effect). See on this issue extensively G. Kemperink & J. Stuyck, 'The Thirteenth Company Law Directive and competing bids', *CML Rev.* 45 (2008): 113–119. This issue is left aside here as we are primarily concerned with conduct of the Community legislature.

from two cases: *Luxembourg* v *Parliament and Council* of 2000,[122] and *Inasti* v *Hervein* of 2002.[123]

The first case, *Luxembourg* v *Parliament and Council*, concerned the compatibility of Articles 2, 5, and 11 of Directive 98/5 (which articles concern respectively the right of migrant lawyers to practise under their home-country professional title, their area of activity and joint practice of the profession) with the second paragraph of Article 43 EC. In the second, the *Hervein* case, the Court appraised the validity of Article 14c(b) of and Annex VII to Regulation No 1408/71 (concerning the coordination of rules on social security) in the light of, *inter alia*, Article 43 EC. Although the Court in these cases did not expressly address the question whether and why the Community legislature was bound by the basic prohibition of Article 43 EC, by, in fact, testing the various Community measures on their compatibility with Article 43 EC, it made clear that the prohibition of Article 43 EC (also) applies to measures adopted by the Community institutions. Incidentally, in both cases, the Court held that the Community legislation under consideration was *not* incompatible with Article 43 EC.

Now that the principle has been established that the Community legislature is indeed bound by Article 43 EC, in the next section I deal with the test for compatibility with Article 43 EC.

C. The Test for Compatibility with Article 43 EC

As has been established above, the prohibition of Article 43 EC also applies to measures adopted by the Community institutions. In order to usefully analyze below (s. D) several provisions of EC company law in view of Article 43 EC, I will now first briefly examine the different parts of the test for compatibility with Article 43 EC (*infra*, sub *a*). (As was explained,[124] the Court of Justice uses a three-part test: (i) Is Article 43 EC applicable? (ii) Is there a restriction? (iii) Is a restriction justified?). Next, I will show (*infra*, sub *b*) that the Court, particularly at the stage of the justification, arguably takes into account the special character of Community legislation.

a. The Court's test for compatibility with Article 43 EC comprises (up to) three stages. The Court first examines whether the Treaty provisions on freedom

122. Case C-168/98 *Luxembourg* v *Parliament and Council* [2000] ECR I-9131, paras 16 et seq.

123. Joined Cases C-393/99 and C-394/99 *Inasti* v *Claude Hervein a.O.* [2002] ECR I-2829, para. 42. In addition to this case-law, it can also be referred to certain provisions in Part One of the Treaty ('Principles'). According to Art. 2 EC, the *Community* pursues its objectives by establishing a common market. Art. 3(1) first words, and (c) EC states that the activities of the *Community* shall include, an internal market characterized by the abolition, as between Member States, of obstacles to the free movement of goods, persons, services, and capital. From these articles too, it may be concluded that the Community is bound by the free movement provisions (see J. Snell, *Goods and Services in EC Law. A Study of the Relationship Between the Freedoms* (Oxford: OUP, 2002), 160).

124. See Ch. 3.

of establishment apply.[125] The scope of these provisions (*ratione personae* and *materiae*) is extensively discussed in Chapter 3, to which I refer.

If this first question on the applicability of the Treaty provisions on freedom of establishment is answered in the affirmative, the second question is whether the measure under consideration constitutes a 'restriction' on freedom of establishment.

As to the notion of 'restriction', I recall two important sets of case-law which may be of importance for our analysis below of EC company law in view of Article 43 EC. While the first set of cases is specifically concerned with restrictions on the exercise of rights granted under Article 43 EC and Article 48 EC (in short: companies' freedom of establishment), the second set of cases has a more general import, in that these cases are not *specifically* (or 'exclusively') related to companies. I will not enter into the intricacies of these (sets of) cases, as many of these cases are already very widely debated and my purpose here is only to provide a short overview of the notion of 'restriction' in function of my later analysis of various EC company law Directives and Regulations.

In the first set of cases, concerning *Centros*, *Überseering*, *Inspire Art*, and various judgments in the field of taxation, the Court's reasoning as to the question whether certain conduct constitutes an obstacle to freedom of establishment, is premised on the rights granted by Article 43 EC and Article 48 EC to companies or firms formed in accordance with the law of another Member State. The Court observed on these rights as follows:

> the freedom of establishment, conferred by Article 43 EC on Community nationals, includes the right for them to take up and pursue activities as self-employed persons and to set up and manage undertakings under the same conditions as are laid down by the law of the Member State of establishment for its own nationals. Furthermore, according to the actual wording of Article 48 EC, companies or firms formed in accordance with the law of a Member State and having their registered office, central administration or principal place of business within the Community shall, for the purposes of the provisions of the Treaty concerning the right of establishment, be treated in the same way as natural persons who are nationals of Member States.
>
> The immediate consequence of this is that those companies or firms are entitled to carry on their business in another Member State. The location of their registered office, central administration or principal place of business constitutes the connecting factor with the legal system of a particular Member State in the same way as does nationality in the case of a natural person.[126]

125. If the applicability of the freedom of establishment is *in confesso*, the Court passes over this (first) part of the test.

126. *Überseering*, paras 56–57. See also: *Centros*, paras 19–20; *Inspire Art*, paras 97, 99–101; and in the field of taxation, similarly (but here explicitly referring to a right to exercise activity through a subsidiary, a branch or an agency): Case C-307/97 *Saint-Gobain* [1999] ECR I-6161, paras 34–35; Case C-446/03 *Marks & Spencer* [2005] ECR I-10837, para. 30; Case C-231/05 *Oy AA* [2007] ECR I-6373, paras 29–30 ('Freedom of establishment, which

On these premises, the Court then based its reasoning as to what constitutes a restriction. The Court thus qualified as a restriction, in short, the refusal by a Member State to register a branch of a company having its registered office in another Member State,[127] the refusal by a host Member State to recognize the legal capacity of a company formed in accordance with the law of another Member State,[128] and the subjection of the creation of a branch to certain rules provided for by that State in respect of the formation of a limited-liability company.[129] Further, in the field of taxation, the Court of Justice ruled, also based on the above premises, that discrimination based on the place where the registered office, central administration, or principal place of business of a company is situated, is prohibited.[130]

Article 43 EC grants to Community nationals and which includes the right to take up and pursue activities as self-employed persons and to set up and manage undertakings, under the conditions laid down for its own nationals by the law of the Member State where such establishment is effected, entails, in accordance with Article 48 EC, for companies or firms formed in accordance with the law of a Member State and having their registered office, central administration or principal place of business within the European Community, *the right to exercise their activity in the Member State concerned through a subsidiary, a branch or an agency*. With regard to companies, it should be noted that it is their registered office, central administration or principal place of business, within the meaning of Article 48 EC, that serves as the connecting factor with the legal system of a particular Member State, like nationality in the case of natural persons'; emphasis added).

127. *Centros*, para. 21 ('where the practice of a Member State, in certain circumstances, is *to refuse to register a branch of a company having its registered office in another Member State*, the result is that *companies formed in accordance* with the law of that other Member State *are prevented from exercising the freedom of establishment* conferred on them by Articles 43 and 48 of the Treaty'; emphasis added).

128. *Überseering*, paras 59 and 82 ('A necessary precondition for the exercise of the freedom of establishment is the recognition of those companies by any Member State in which they wish to establish themselves' (para. 59) and '*the refusal by a host Member State (B) to recognise the legal capacity of a company formed in accordance with the law of another Member State (A)* in *which it has its registered office* on the ground, in particular, that the company moved its actual centre of administration to Member State B following the acquisition of all its shares by nationals of that State residing there, with the result that the company cannot, in Member State B, bring legal proceedings to defend rights under a contract unless it is reincorporated under the law of Member State B, *constitutes a restriction on freedom of establishment* which is, in principle, incompatible with Articles 43 EC and 48 EC'; para. 82, emphasis added).

129. *Inspire Art*, para. 101 ('Creation of a branch in the Netherlands by companies of that kind is (. . .) subject to certain rules provided for by that State in respect of the formation of a limited-liability company. The *legislation* at issue in the case in the main proceedings, *which requires the branch of such a company formed in accordance with the legislation of a Member State to comply with the rules of the State of establishment on share capital and directors' liability, has the effect of impeding the exercise by those companies of the freedom of establishment conferred by the Treaty*'; emphasis added).

130. *Oy AA*, just cited, para. 30 ('With regard to companies, it should be noted that it is their registered office, central administration or principal place of business, within the meaning of Article 48 EC, that serves as the connecting factor with the legal system of a particular Member State, like nationality in the case of natural persons. To accept that the Member State of establishment may freely apply different treatment solely because the registered office,

A (further) explanation regarding this first set of cases, *Centros*, *Überseering* and *Inspire Art* in particular, seems to be implicit in the Court's recent *Cartesio* judgment. Let me briefly recall the Court's ruling in this case on cross-border conversion.[131] The Court decided that a Member State of incorporation may not prevent a company, by requiring its winding-up or liquidation, from converting into a company which is governed by the law of another Member State *to the extent that it is permitted under that law to do so*.[132] This would constitute a restriction on the freedom of establishment of the company concerned, which – unless it serves overriding requirements in the public interest – is prohibited under Article 43 EC.[133] In my view, Article 43 EC thus compels the Member State of incorporation *to recognize* the possibility of such a conversion under the law of another Member State (to which the company intends to move).

> The Court does not explicitly rule on an obligation for the Member State of relocation, in a situation in which the Member State of incorporation permits the company to convert itself into a company under the law of other Member States. It seems probable that in such a situation Article 43 EC also compels the Member State of relocation, to recognize the possibility of such a conversion under the law of the Member State of incorporation. Then, the Member State of relocation may, in particular, not refuse generally that the status of company under its law is obtained (and, in this sense, a company under its law will be incorporated). This view is also supported by the Court's observation in *Cartesio*, in paragraph 112, to the effect that national legislation on the *incorporation* and winding-up of companies does not enjoy immunity from the rules of the EC Treaty on freedom of establishment.

It is noteworthy that the Court, in *Cartesio*, seems to be bent on emphasizing the relevance of the issue of recognition to companies' freedom of establishment in general (so, not just in cases of cross-border conversion).

---

central administration or principal place of business of a company is situated in another Member State would deprive Article 43 EC of its substance (. . .). Freedom of establishment is thus designed to guarantee the benefit of national treatment in the host Member State, by prohibiting all discrimination based on the place where the registered office, central administration or principal place of business of a company is situated on the above cited premises'; emphasis added). See further: Case 270/83 *Commission* v *France* [1986] ECR 273, para. 18; Case C-330/91 *Commerzbank* [1993] ECR I-4017, para. 13; Case C-307/97 *Saint-Gobain* [1999] ECR I-6161, para. 35; Joined Cases C-397/98 and C-410/98 *Metallgesellschaft a.O.* [2001] ECR I-1727, para. 42; Case C-446/03 *Marks & Spencer* [2005] ECR I-10837, para. 37; and Case C-374/04 *Test Claimants in Class IV of the ACT Group Litigation* [2006] ECR I-11673, para. 43.

131. See further Ch. 3.

132. *Cartesio*, para. 112. Portugal and Luxembourg are examples of such other Member States which permit a cross-border conversion. For Portugal, see: S. Leible & J. Hoffmann, 'Cartesio – fortgeltende Sitztheorie, grenzüberschreitender Formwechsel und Verbot materiellrechtlicher Wegzugsbeschränkungen', *BB* (2009): 60; for Luxembourg, see: 'Impact assessment on the Directive on the cross-border transfer of registered office', SEC (2007) 1707 of 12 Dec. 2007, 23.

133. *Cartesio*, para. 113.

The Court in *Cartesio* underlines indeed that *the case which gave rise to the* judgment in *Sevic*:

> concerned the *recognition*, in the Member State of incorporation of a company, of an establishment operation carried out by that company in another Member State by means of a cross-border merger (. . .).[134] (emphasis added).

In *the Sevic judgment (itself)*, however, the Court had ruled that it was the difference in treatment between companies according to the internal or cross-border nature of the merger (which in itself is not related to recognition), which constituted a restriction on freedom of establishment.[135] The Court in *Cartesio* furthermore adds, that the situation considered in *Sevic* is 'similar to the situations considered in other judgments of the Court', in which connection the Court refers to *Centros*, *Überseering* and *Inspire Art*.[136] It is true that *Centros*, *Überseering*, and *Inspire Art* did concern (or may be argued to concern) the recognition of companies.[137]

Now, if it is assumed that in the above cases (*Centros*, *Überseering*, *Inspire Art*, *Sevic*, and *Cartesio*) the Court has (indeed) established mutual recognition as a (perhaps even the) criterion to determine whether there is a restriction on (companies') freedom of establishment, these cases, thus understood, seem to be primarily relevant for the issue of compatibility with Article 43 EC of diverging Member State legislation. On the basis of the criterion at issue, EC company law legislation – which applies Community wide – is unlikely to restrict freedom of establishment.

In a second set of cases, not specifically related to Article 48 EC, the Court further held, on the question whether certain conduct constitutes an obstacle to freedom of establishment, in settled case-law that:

> Article 43 EC requires the elimination of restrictions on the freedom of establishment. All measures which prohibit, impede or render less attractive the exercise of that freedom must be regarded as such restrictions.[138]

---

134. *Ibid.*, para. 122.
135. *Sevic*, paras 22–23.
136. *Cartesio*, para. 122.
137. See: *Überseering*, para. 82; *Inspire Art*, paras 99–101. (Both explicitly referring to recognition). In *Centros* it is not explicitly referred to it, but this judgment may be argued to concern recognition nevertheless. The Court ruled as follows: 'the refusal of a Member State to register a branch of a company formed in accordance with the law of another Member State in which it has its registered office on the grounds that the branch is intended to enable the company to carry on all its economic activity in the host State, with the result that the secondary establishment escapes national rules on the provision for and the paying-up of a minimum capital, is incompatible with Articles 52 and 58 of the Treaty, in so far as it prevents any exercise of the right freely to set up a secondary establishment which Articles 52 and 58 are specifically intended to guarantee'. See para. 30. This refusal could be argued to amount to the non-recognition of the company in question (cf. *Inspire Art*).
138. Case C-442/02 *CaixaBank France* [2004] ECR I-8961, para. 11; See further e.g., Case C-55/94 *Gebhard* [1995] ECR I-4165, para. 37, Case C-108/96 *Mac Quen a.O.* [2001] ECR I-837,

In this respect it remains necessary, however, to give actual shape to this concept of 'restriction' on freedom of establishment.[139] In this connection, Advocate General Poiares Maduro has, in his Opinion in *Marks & Spencer*, conveniently provided an overview of the principles established by the Court in interpreting 'the fundamental provisions of the Treaty' (i.e., free movement of goods, persons (including the right of establishment), services, and capital),[140] Article 43 EC in particular. With respect to the 'criteria applicable to restriction of freedom of establishment',[141] the Advocate General notes that the Court has established various criteria to determine whether there is a restriction on freedom of establishment:[142]

> [39] (. . .) the criterion of non-discrimination on the ground of nationality,[(44)] the criterion of additional costs imposed on Community nationals,[(45)] [and] the criterion of access to the market.[(46)]

Advocate General Poiares Maduro explains these criteria as follows:

> [39] [these criteria] (. . .) all spring from the same source of inspiration which appears to me to be to prevent Member States from creating or maintaining in force measures promoting internal trade to the detriment of intra-Community trade. *Such a restriction may take several forms. It may be the effect of discrimination in favour of nationals. It may be the consequence of a measure protecting positions acquired by economic operators established on the national market by restricting the entry of new operators. Such a restriction may further stem from legislation rendering trade between the Member States more difficult than internal trade within a Member State.* (footnote omitted; emphasis added).

---

para. 26, and Case C-79/01 *Payroll a.O.* [2002] ECR I-8923, para. 26. Note that the fact that a measure does not discriminate on grounds of nationality, does not exclude that it none the less constitutes a restriction within the meaning of Art. 43 EC. See: Case C-19/92 *Kraus* [1993] ECR I-1663, para. 32; Case C-299/02 *Commission* v *Netherlands* [2004] ECR I-9761, para. 15; Case C-140/03 *Commission* v *Greece* [2005] ECR I-3177, para. 27.

139. Opinion of AG Poiares Maduro in *Marks & Spencer*, just cited, pt. 35.
140. For this term, see Opinion, just cited, pt. 20. The Court itself refers to the four freedoms (or one of these) also as: 'fundamental freedom', 'one of the fundamental principles of the Treaty'; a 'fundamental Community provision' and 'one of the foundations of the Community', see P. Oliver & W.-H. Roth, 'The Internal Market and the Four Freedoms', *CML Rev.* 41 (2004): 407.
141. See the heading above pts. 41–55 of the Opinion, which reads 'Application of the *criteria applicable to restriction of freedom of establishment*' (emphasis added). See also the heading above pts. 37–40 which refers to 'criteria for restricting freedom of establishment'.
142. Opinion, pts. 37, 39, and 40.
    (44). See for example *Commission* v *France*, cited above at fn. 7 [of the Opinion].
    (45). See for example Case C-470/93 *Mars* [1995] ECR I-1923.
    (46). See for example *CaixaBank France*, cited above at fn. 39 [of the Opinion].

> [40] It seems to me that it is to such a restriction on Community trade which the Court is alluding when it seeks to pursue all measures prohibiting, impeding or rendering less attractive *the exercise of the freedoms of movement.*[143] (original emphasis).
> [28] (. . .) the task of the Court is not to engage in challenging every rule of State origin having an indirect or wholly uncertain effect on the exercise of the freedoms of movement. It is not for it to review the political choices made by the Member States.

Proceeding from this it can indeed be argued that the concept of restriction, which, as indicated above, encompasses 'all measures which prohibit, impede or render less attractive the exercise of that freedom', does not concern every rule of State origin having an indirect or wholly uncertain effect on the exercise of freedom of establishment.[144] What is more, it can be argued that the Court has established different criteria to determine whether there is a restriction on freedom of establishment: the criterion of non-discrimination on the ground of nationality,[145] the

---

143. Observe that AG Poiares Maduro in this Opinion, at pt. 40, further emphasizes that 'not every restriction on economic or commercial freedom is a restriction on the exercise of the freedoms of movement' (referring to Joined Cases C-267/91 and C-268/91 *Keck and Mithouard* [1993] ECR I-6097; Opinion of AG Tesauro in Case C-292/92 *Hünermund a.O.* [1993] ECR I-6787 and Opinion of AG Tizzano in *CaixaBank France*, just cited, pts. 62 and 63). While I agree with this statement, it should be noted, however, that the Court so far has not explicitly applied its ruling from *Keck and Mithouard* (as to what *(not)* constitutes a restriction) to the freedom of establishment.
144. See, to that effect, with regard to freedom of movement for workers, Case C-190/98 *Graf* [2000] ECR I-493, para. 25; with regard to freedom of goods, Case 69/88 *Krantz* v *Ontvanger der Directe Belastingen* [1990] ECR I-583, para. 11, and Case C-44/98 *BASF* [1999] ECR I-6269, paras 16 and 21; with regard to freedom of establishment, Opinion of AG Mischo in Case C-9/02 *de Lasteyrie du Saillant* [2004] ECR I-2409, pt. 43; Opinion of AG Léger in Case C-299/02 *Commission* v *Netherlands* [2004] ECR I-9761, pt. 43; and Opinion of AG Poiares Maduro in *Marks & Spencer*, just cited, pt. 28 (quoted in the main text). (I leave here aside the question whether the notion of 'indirect or wholly uncertain effect' is an autonomous criterion or an expression of the different criteria mentioned in the main text, and its relation with *Keck and Mithouard* mentioned in the previous fn.).
145. See e.g., Case C-453/04 *Innoventif* [2006] ECR I-4929, in which the Court, at para. 39, in an *obiter dictum* applies a non-discrimination test ('legislation which, in circumstances such as those in the main proceedings, requires the payment of an advance is not liable to place companies from other Member States in a less favourable factual or legal situation than companies from the Member State of establishment (see, to that effect, Case C-70/95 *Sodemare and Others* [1997] ECR I-3395, paragraph 33)'). See further e.g., Case C-383/05 *Talotta* [2007] ECR I-2555, para. 32 (legislation laying down minimum tax bases only for non-resident taxpayers constituting (indirect) discrimination on grounds of nationality); Case C-346/04 *Conijn* [2006] ECR I-6137, paras 24–25 (national provision which refuses to non-residents possibility to deduct costs incurred in obtaining tax advice as special expenditure is likely to operate mainly to the detriment of nationals of other Member States and therefore entails indirect discrimination on grounds of nationality).

criterion of additional costs imposed on Community nationals[146] and the criterion of access to the market.[147]

These criteria are also identified in the literature,[148] in which connection it incidentally is found that there is increasing case-law to suggest that *market access* is central to the scope of Article 43 EC.[149] It is noted further in the doctrine that 'the Court has not yet achieved sufficient clarity as to the circumstances under which

146. With respect to this criterion, AG Poiares Maduro refers in his Opinion in *Marks & Spencer*, just cited, to Case C-470/93 *Mars* [1995] ECR I-1923 (concerning the free movement of goods, in which the Court held that a prohibition relating to the marketing in a Member State of products bearing the same publicity markings as those lawfully used in other Member States, is by nature such to hinder intra-Community trade: 'it may compel the importer to adjust the presentation of his products according to the place where they are to be marketed and consequently to incur additional packaging and advertising costs'). E. Spaventa, 'From *Gebhard* to *Carpenter*: Towards a (Non-)Economic European Constitution', *CML Rev.* 41 (2004): 745–746 talks about 'the double burden theory', according to which the internal market requires not only the abolition of discrimination but also that, even lacking harmonization, only one set of rules should apply to those covered by the free movement provisions and that Member States must take into account the checks performed or qualifications acquired in other Member States. In this respect, one can refer as to the freedom of establishment to e.g., Case C-313/01 *Morgenbesser* [2003] ECR I-13467, para. 62 (holding that the exercise of the right of establishment is hindered if national rules fail to take account of learning, skills, and qualifications already acquired by the person concerned in another Member State, so that the competent national authorities must measure whether such factors sufficiently demonstrate that missing learning and skills have been acquired); similarly: Case C-340/89 *Vlassopoulou* [1991] ECR I-2357, paras 15 and 20 and Case C-234/97 *Fernández de Bobadilla* [1999] ECR I-4773, para. 33. Note finally that the double burden theory may overlap with the discrimination theory in that 'a rule which imposes a double burden is almost inevitably also indirectly discriminatory since it affects migrants or imported products more than it affects non-migrants or domestic products' (see Spaventa, just cited, 746).
147. With respect to this criterion, AG Poiares Maduro refers in his above cited Opinion in *Marks & Spencer* to *CaixaBank France*, just cited, in which – indeed – the Court observed that national legislation (prohibiting the payment of remuneration on sight accounts) made 'Access to the market (. . .) more difficult' and, subsequently, found such legislation in breach of Art. 43 EC. See also Case C-500/06 *Corporación Dermoestética*, judgment of 17 Jul. 2008, n.y.r., para. 33. According to the criterion of access to the market, (national) measures preventing or hindering market access constitute a 'restriction', irrespective of whether they actually discriminate against migrants. See e.g., C. Barnard, *The Substantive Law of the EU* (Oxford: OUP, 2004), 19. See further Spaventa, just cited, 747 who refers in this connection to barriers for economic actors to access the market. For an elaborate discussion of this market access test, see also Spaventa, 756–764.
148. See Spaventa, just cited, 744 with extensive references.
149. *Ibid.*, 756. For the relevance of the access to the market criterion to Art. 28 EC, see G. Straetmans, 'Selling arrangements, advertising rules and access to the market: Keck undone? (case-note on Case C-405/98, *Konsumentombudsmannen (KO)* v *Gourmet International Products AB (GIP)*, Judgment of the Court (Sixth Chamber) of 8 Mar. 2001)', *CML Rev.* 39 (2002): 1407–1421. Straetmans further notes that: 'the Court systematically underlines the similarity of the test to which restrictions on the fundamental freedoms are subject'. See G. Straetmans, 'Case-note on Case C-124/97, Läärä, Judgment of the Court of 21 Sep. 1999 and Case C-67/98, Zenatti, Judgment of the Court of 21 Oct. 1999, Full Court', *CML Rev.* 37 (2000): 999.

> *market access* is held to be impeded. Future case law will have to achieve the necessary legal certainty in this respect'.[150]

If there is indeed a restriction, the third question of the test for compatibility with Article 43 EC is whether the restriction can be *justified*, on one of the grounds set out in the Treaty (notably Article 46 EC) or, failing that, by an overriding reason relating to the public interest. With respect to these overriding reasons relating to the public interest, it is settled case-law, that national measures liable to hinder or make less attractive the exercise of fundamental freedoms guaranteed by the Treaty must, if they are to be justified, fulfil four conditions:[151] they must be applied in a non-discriminatory manner; they must (indeed) be justified by imperative requirements in the public interest;[152] they must be suitable for securing the attainment of the objective which they pursue, and they must not go beyond what is necessary in order to attain it.[153] The two conditions last mentioned are regarded as expressing a requirement of proportionality.[154]

b. In the above, I have established that the Community institutions are bound by the prohibition of Article 43 EC (s. B, *supra*) and briefly examined the content of this prohibition (the present s. C, *sub a*, *supra*). In the current subsection *b*, I will address an issue that amongst company lawyers, arguing that certain provisions of EC company law are contrary to Article 43 EC, has remained largely unobserved. More specifically, I will show that even though the Community institutions are bound by the prohibition of Article 43 EC, the Court, in examining whether acts of Community institutions are compatible with Article 43 EC, arguably may take into account the special character of Community legislation.

As repeatedly stated, the Court in determining whether Article 43 EC has been infringed, analyzes measures following a three-part standard approach (i.e., Is Article 43 EC applicable? Is there a restriction? Is a restriction justified?).[155] It is primarily in the third stage of the analysis, that is, the justification stage, that

---

150. P. Oliver & W.-H. Roth, 'The Internal Market and the Four Freedoms', *CML Rev.* 41 (2004): 414.
151. See e.g., Case C-55/94 *Gebhard* [1995] ECR I-4165, para. 37; *Centros*, para. 34; *Inspire Art*, para. 133.
152. It will be recalled that the Court of Justice has recognized as such imperative requirements, e.g., the protection of the interests of creditors, minority shareholders, and employees (see: *Überseering*, para. 92; *Sevic*, para. 28), and the preservation of the effectiveness of fiscal supervision and the fairness of commercial transactions (see: *Inspire Art*, para. 132; *Sevic*, para. 28).
153. See e.g., *Inspire Art*, para. 133. See also: *Gebhard*, just cited, para. 37; *Centros*, para. 34.
154. See Lenaerts & Van Nuffel, 198.
155. For recent cases following this approach as regards the compatibility of measures adopted by the Community legislature *vis-à-vis* Art. 28 EC, see *Arnold André* and *Alliance for Natural Health* and *vis-à-vis* Art. 49 EC *Inizan*: Case 434/02 *Arnold André* [2004] ECR I-11825, paras 57–59 (first observing that the prohibition of marketing tobacco products for oral use under Art. 8 of Directive 2001/37 constitutes one of the *restrictions* referred to in Art. 28 EC and subsequently holding that it is *justified* on grounds of the protection of human health); Joined Cases C-154/04 and C-155/04 *Alliance for Natural Health a.O.* [2005] ECR I-6451, paras 47–93 (first observing that by prohibiting the marketing in the Community of food supplements

the Court arguably takes into account the specific character of Community legislation. (The case-law of the Court in other areas (than freedom of establishment), in any case, seems to offer several indications in that direction, which I will address below).

As will be recalled, Article 43 EC does not preclude restrictions justified by an overriding reason relating to the public interest, under the condition that the restrictive measure meets the requirements of: (1) non-discrimination and (2) proportionality.

With respect to the first, *non-discrimination* requirement, it should be noted, that the objective of Community measures may be distinguished from that of Member State measures. Community measures are not prescribed by each Member State in order to protect some local interest of its own, but by the Community legislature (presumably) in the general interest of the Community.[156] In the absence of such an interest of its own, any discrimination on the part of the Community is less likely to occur.[157]

Still within the context of the condition of non-discrimination, I observe that it is recognized in the Court's case-law (on the general principle of non-discrimination) that difficulties for the Community legislature surrounding harmonization may be objective reasons justifying a difference in treatment.[158] That seems to be the case whether such difficulties result from the complexity and divergence of

---

containing vitamins and minerals, or vitamin and mineral substances, not included on the positive lists, the provisions of Art. 3 in conjunction with those of Art. 4(1) and 15(b) of Directive 2002/46 constitute a *restriction* covered by Art. 28 EC, and subsequently concluding that the restrictions are *justified* on grounds of protection of human health (paras 48, 51, 52–93)). (In both cases the Court did not explicitly address the first part of the standard test: the applicability of Art. 28 EC was not at issue); Case C-56/01 *Inizan* [2003] ECR I-12403, paras 15–25 (first observing that medical activities fell within the *scope* of Art. 50 EC, and subsequently examining in light of its case-law on Art. 49 EC whether the provision of Art. 22(1)(c)(i) of Regulation No 1408/71, which makes the grant of the benefits in kind to which it guarantees entitlement subject to prior authorization, constitutes a *restriction* (which is rejected as it rather helps to facilitate the free movement of insured persons; the question on the *justification* thus not arises)).

156. Cf. Case 46/76 *Bauhuis* [1977] ECR 5, para. 29. See also K. Mortelmans, 'The Relationship between the Treaty Rules and Community Measures for the Establishment and Functioning of the Internal Market – Towards a Concordance Rule', *CML Rev.* 39 (2002): 1333.
157. See also J. Snell, *Goods and Services in EC Law. A Study of the Relationship Between the Freedoms*, Oxford: OUP 2002, 164–165: 'the Community, unlike an individual Member State, usually has no incentive to adopt discriminatory measures. The interests of other Member States are not represented in a national political process. In the Community every Member State is heard'. Cf. H.D. Jarass, 'A Unified Approach to the Fundamental Freedoms', in *Services and Free Movement in EU Law*, ed. M. Andenas & W.-H. Roth (Oxford: OUP, 2002), 152 (arguing that the ambit of possible justifications available to the Community legislature most likely is wider than the justifications on which the Member States can rely, 'as it is unlikely that the Community would support the economy of one Member State at the cost of another, an aim that might not be too far off where a measure of a single Member State is concerned').
158. Tridimas, 97, who refers in particular to: Case C-63/89 *Assurances du Crédit* v *Council and Commission* [1991] ECR I-1799; Case C-479/93 *Francovich* v *Italy* [1995] ECR I-3843.

national laws (which e.g., may require a harmonization in phases, leading to a difference in treatment), or from policy disagreements within the level of the Community legislature (e.g., within the Council) which restrict the scope of application of a Community measure *ratione materiae* leading to a difference in treatment.[159] This might suggest how the special character of Community legislation may influence the outcome of the test for compatibility with Article 43 EC.

With respect to the second, *proportionality* requirement (is a Community measure proportionate in relation to an overriding reason relating to the public interest?) it can be referred to the *Alliance for Natural Health* case.[160] In this case, the Court held that in an area which entails political, economic, and social choices on the part of the Community legislature, and in which it is called upon to undertake complex assessments, the Community legislature must, with regard to judicial review of the proportionality requirement, be allowed a broad discretion.[161] The Court concluded in this regard that the legality of a legislative measure can be affected only if the measure is manifestly inappropriate having regard to the objective which the legislature is seeking to pursue.[162] Such manifest

159. Tridimas, 97. Cf. also Case C-233/94 *Germany* v *Parliament and Council* ('Deposit Guarantees') [1997] ECR I-2405, paras 42–43 (rejecting plea of infringement of Art. 57(2) EC Treaty (now, Art. 47(1) EC) observing that: 'When harmonization takes place, traders established in one Member State may lose the advantage of national legislation which was particularly favourable to them. [43] Second, it is true that the export prohibition is an exception to the minimum harmonization and mutual recognition which the Directive generally seeks to achieve. However, in view of *the complexity of the matter and the differences between the legislation of the Member States, the Parliament and the Council were empowered to achieve the necessary harmonization progressively*'; emphasis added). Cf. Case 37/83 *Rewe* [1984] ECR 1229, para. 20 (observing that 'in the exercise of the powers conferred on them in this respect by Articles 43 and 100 of the Treaty, the Community institutions have a discretion in particular with regard to the possibility of proceeding towards harmonisation *only in stages and of requiring only the gradual abolition* of unilateral measures adopted by the member states'. (emphasis added).
160. Joined Cases C-154/04 and C-155/04 *Alliance for Natural Health* [2005] ECR I-6451.
161. For the issue of judicial review (and the intensity of legal review), see Ch. 1.
162. See *Alliance for Natural Health*, just cited, para. 52. The Court refers in this connection to Case C-491/01 *British American Tobacco* [2002] ECR I-11453, para. 123. The observations in this latter case related to the general principle of proportionality, but apparently also apply in the context of a test for compatibility with a basic Treaty prohibition (Art. 28 EC in *Alliance for Natural Health*). It will be recalled that is settled case-law on the principle of proportionality, which is one of the general principles of Community law and which requires that measures adopted by Community institutions are appropriate for attaining the objective pursued and must not go beyond what is necessary to achieve, that as to judicial review of the conditions referred to, 'the Community legislature must be allowed a broad discretion in areas which involve political, economic and social choices on its part, and in which it is called on to undertake complex assessments. Only if a measure adopted in this field is manifestly inappropriate in relation to the objective which the competent institutions are seeking to pursue can the lawfulness of such a measure be affected' (see C-434/02 *Arnold André* [2004] ECR I-11825, para. 46); see also: Case C-114/96 *Criminal proceedings against Kieffer and Thill* [1997] ECR I-3629, para. 37 (noting that 'the Community legislature enjoys a discretion in the framework of its powers of harmonisation'); Case C-51/93 *Meyhui* v *Schott Zwiesel Glaswerke* [1994] ECR I-3879, para. 21.

inappropriateness was not present, incidentally, in *Luxembourg* v *Parliament and Council* of 2000, discussed in the previous section B, where the Court observed that: 'In making such a choice of the method and level of consumer protection and of ensuring the proper administration of justice, the Community legislature has not overstepped the limits of its discretion.'[163]

In addition to the above, I note that, in determining the compatibility of measures adopted by the Community with Article 43 EC, a role may also play the aim of the Community legislature to eliminate obstacles to intra-Community trade, posed by national measures which, in the absence of coordination at Community level, were justified in the public interest. In this regard, one can refer to *Bauhuis*.[164] Even though in this case the compatibility of a *national* measure with the Treaty was at issue and strictly speaking not a measure of a Community institution, it may nonetheless be noteworthy. In this case, the Court held that fees charged by national authorities for the veterinary and public health inspections prior to export, were not contrary to the prohibition on custom duties on exports and measures having an equivalent effect. The Court first observed that these health inspections were prescribed by a Directive with a *view to eliminating obstacles to intra-community trade* in bovine animals and swine, by substituting for the numerous traditional means of protection at the frontier a single system designed in particular to facilitate intra-community trade by imposing upon Member States exporting cattle the obligation to ensure compliance with certain veterinary and public health measures. It next reasoned that these health inspections were not prescribed by each Member State in order to protect some interest of its own, but by the Council *in the general interest of the Community*, and that they cannot be regarded as unilateral measures which hinder trade but rather as operations intended *to promote the free movement of goods*, in particular by rendering ineffective the obstacles to this free movement which might be created by the measures for veterinary and public health inspections adopted pursuant to Article 36 EEC (now Article 30 EC). In these circumstances, the Court held that the fees charged for the health inspections, which are prescribed by a Community provision, which are uniform and are required to be carried out before despatch within the exporting country, do not constitute charges having an equivalent effect to customs duties on exports, provided that they do not exceed the actual cost of inspection for which they were charged. It could be argued that under these circumstances, (also) the Community provision prescribing health inspections on exports would not be prohibited. Indeed, in its cases *Rewe*[165] and

163. Case C-168/98 *Luxembourg* v *Parliament and Council* [2000] ECR I-9131, para. 44.
164. Case 46/76 *Bauhuis* [1977] ECR 5.
165. Case 37/83 *Rewe* [1984] ECR 1229 (holding that a provision in a Directive permitting phytosanitary inspections by sampling on up to one-third of consignments of fruit on their importation, complied with (now) Art. 28 EC (para. 20). This Directive sought the gradual *removal of obstacles to and checks on intra-Community-trade*, by substituting the plant-health inspections carried out at both the export and import country, with a system in which the latter checks were gradually abolished and the former checks were rendered more stringent (para. 14). The Court then noted that the Directive at issue: 'is *not intended to hinder intra-Community trade*. On the contrary it seeks to achieve the gradual abolition of measures which were adopted unilaterally by the Member States and were, at the time, justified in principle by Article 36 of the Treaty [now, after amendment, Art. 30 EC] (. . .)' (para. 19; emphasis added). At the same time, the Directive seeks to *strengthen, in the general interest of the Community,*

Luxembourg v *Parliament and Council*,[166] the Court, for its holding that provisions of measures adopted by the Community institutions complied with respectively Article 28 EC and Article 43 EC, somewhat similarly mentioned: (i) the aim of the Community to eliminate obstacles to intra-Community trade, posed by national measures which, in the absence of coordination at Community level, sought to protect the public interest; and (thus) (ii) the aim to facilitate trade (rather than to hinder trade); (iii) as well as the (strengthened level of) protection of public interest by the Community. In addition, in these cases the Court refers to the discretion for the Community legislature as to the stages of harmonization and the level of protection of the public interest.[167]

To conclude, even though the Community institutions are bound by the prohibition of Article 43 EC, the Court, in determining whether measures adopted by the Community legislature are compatible with Article 43 EC, arguably takes into account the specific character of Community legislation.

D. Analysis of Provisions of EC Company Law in View of Article 43 EC

1. Introduction

This section contains an analysis in view of Article 43 EC of various provisions of EC company law which in particular have been argued to be incompatible with this article:[168] first, the minimum legal capital requirement of the Second Directive

---

the protection of agricultural products against the substantial damage which may be caused by harmful organisms (para. 19). The Court finally noted that: 'in the exercise of the powers conferred on them in this respect by Articles 43 and 100 of the Treaty, the Community institutions have a discretion in particular with regard to the possibility of proceeding towards harmonisation *only in stages and or requiring only the gradual abolition* of unilateral measures adopted by the member states' (para. 20; emphasis added)).

166. Case C-168/98 *Luxembourg* v *Parliament and Council* [2000] ECR I-9131 (holding that various provisions in a Directive did not contravene (now) Art. 43 EC, referring to, *inter al.*, the *barriers posed to freedom of movement by national measures* which, in the absence of coordination at Community level, protect consumers, and next noting that the Community legislature, with a view to *making it easier* for a particular class of migrant lawyers to exercise the fundamental freedom of establishment, has chosen, in preference to a system of *a priori* testing of qualification in the national law of the host Member State, a plan of action combining *inter al.* consumer information and restrictions on the extent to which or the detailed rules under which certain activities of the profession may be practised, releasing the migrant lawyer from the obligation to prove that knowledge in advance, allowing, in some circumstances, gradual assimilation of knowledge through practice. The Court finally noted that in making such a choice of the method and *level of consumer protection* and of ensuring the proper administration of justice, the Community legislature has not overstepped the limits of its *discretion*).

167. See further the Opinion of AG Geelhoed in Case C-491/01 *British American Tobacco* [2002] ECR I-11453, pt. 106, which is dealt with in Ch. 3.

168. Or – to be precise – these provisions have been argued to constitute a *restriction* on freedom of establishment, in which case it must be considered whether the provision in question can be

(s. 2) (while this is an older Directive, it plays a role in the modernization debate[169]); next, the reciprocity rule, included in the Directive on takeover bids (s. 3); and, finally, several provisions of the SE Regulation (s. 4).

2. The Minimum Capital Requirement of the Second Directive

Article 6(1) of the Second Directive, which applies to public companies, provides that:

> The laws of the Member States shall require that, in order that a company may be incorporated or obtain authorization to commence business, a minimum capital shall be subscribed the amount of which shall be not less than 25 000 ecus.[170]

Is the minimum capital requirement of the Second Directive compatible with the freedom of establishment guaranteed by Article 43 EC?

Let me first discuss the judgment of the Court of Justice in *Inspire Art*, as on the basis of this judgment it has been argued in the literature – in sweeping terms – that rules on minimum share capital in general constitute a 'restriction' on freedom of establishment within the meaning of Article 43 EC.[171]

This interpretation of the Court's ruling must, in my view, be dismissed. *Inspire Art* does not concern relations between a company and the Member State under the laws of which it has been incorporated. More specifically, *Inspire Art* does not relate to legislation of a Member State requiring 'its own' companies, that is, companies formed under the law of that State, to have a certain minimum capital.[172] The compatibility with Article 43 EC of such a requirement was not at issue and was not dealt with by Court. The (only) thing at issue in *Inspire Art* was that a Member State's company law rules on minimum capital provided for in domestic law in respect of company formation were applied mandatorily to *foreign* companies when they carried on their activities exclusively, or almost exclusively,

justified on one of the grounds set out in Art. 46 EC or, failing that, by an overriding reason relating to the public interest.

169. On the desirability of the minimum capital requirement from a company law *policy* perspective. See e.g., L. Enriques & J.R. Macey, 'Creditors versus Capital Formation: The Case Against the European Legal Capital Rules', *Cornell L. Rev.* 86 (2001): 1184–1189; G. Hertig & H. Kanda, 'Creditor Protection', in *The Anatomy of Corporate Law. A Comparative and Functional Approach*, ed. R. Kraakman et al. (Oxford: OUP, 2004), 84; J. Rickford (ed.), 'Reforming Capital. Report of the Interdisciplinary Group on Capital Maintenance (Apr. 2004)', *EBLR* 15 (2004): 926 in particular; W. Schön, 'The Future of Legal Capital', *EBOR* 5 (2004): 436–438.

170. The Second Directive was amended in Oct. 2006. The amending Directive did not provide for an amendment or withdrawal of the minimum capital requirement of Art. 6.

171. See e.g., W.-H. Roth, 'Niederlassungs- und Dienstleistungsfreiheit', in *Handbuch des EU-Wirtschaftsrechts*, ed. M.A. Dauses (Munich: C.H. Beck, 2006), 43 (no. 89).

172. See *Inspire Art*, para. 103.

in that Member State.[173] In fact, such rules in respect of *company* formation were imposed on the setting-up of a *branch*.[174] This – very specific – legislation, constituted a (non-justifiable) restriction on freedom of establishment as guaranteed by Article 43 EC, said the Court.[175]

For the same reason, the contentions that: the Court would have suggested in *Inspire Art* 'that substantial rules on legal capital requirements are generally unnecessary';[176] the Court would have decided that legal capital rules are not 'a meaningful way of responding to the policy problems concerning non-adjusting creditors',[177] and that 'for the protection of contractual creditors, the ECJ considers material minimum capital requirements to be unnecessary',[178] must also be dismissed. *Inspire Art*, it bears repeating, does not concern minimum capital requirements in general,[179] it only relates to, in short, a minimum capital requirement for specific foreign companies.

A similar reasoning, finally, applies – I would argue – with respect to minimum capital requirements laid down in Community legislation (as opposed to Member State legislation), such as the Second Directive.[180] Article 6 of the Second Directive concerns, in short, the minimum capital required of a Member State's 'own' companies. Therefore, it cannot be argued *on the basis of Inspire Art* (which concerns 'foreign' companies, as explained) that such a requirement constitutes a restriction on freedom of establishment (or would be in breach of Article 43 EC).[181]

---

173. *Ibid.*, para. 100. In terms of methods of exercising freedom of establishment, *Inspire Art* concerns (the setting up of) a branch (as opposed to, for instance, the participation in the incorporation of a company – in another Member State). See paras 101 and 105 of the judgment.
174. See *Inspire Art*, paras 101 and 105.
175. *Ibid.*, paras 104–105. In this context, it must further be noted that in examining a possible justification for this restriction (protection of creditors), the Court explicitly rules (at para. 135) that there is 'no need for the Court to consider whether the rules on minimum share capital constitute in themselves an appropriate protection measure'.
176. W. Schön, 'The Future of Legal Capital', *EBOR* 5 (2004): 433.
177. J. Armour, 'Legal Capital: An Outdated Concept?', *EBOR* 7 (2006): 25.
178. H. Merkt, 'Creditor Protection and Capital Maintenance from a German Perspective', *EBLR* (2004): 1048. See also 1053. See, finally (for a similar comment), H. Merkt, 'Creditor Protection through Mandatory Disclosure', *EBOR* 7 (2006): 105: 'In *Inspire Art*, [fn. omitted] the Court favored the idea of creditor protection via capital market disclosure and information, as opposed to the company law concept of statutory regulation of capital maintenance.'
179. Let alone legal capital rules or capital maintenance rules (of which minimum capital requirements are a part).
180. Article 4 of the SE Regulation also includes a minimum capital requirement. It states that: '[1.] The capital of an SE shall be expressed in euro. [2.] The subscribed capital shall not be less than EUR 120 000. [3.] (. . .)'.
181. See, in this connection, finally, A. Looijestijn-Clearie, 'Have the dikes collapsed? Inspire Art a further breakthrough in the freedom of establishment of companies?', *EBOR* 5 (2004): 416, who remarks: 'in *Inspire Art* [fn. omitted] the ECJ carefully avoids becoming entangled in the question as to whether requirements with regard to minimum share capital are a suitable or proportionate way of protecting the interests of creditors, leaving this presumably for the Community legislator to decide'.

This being so, the question remains whether the minimum capital requirement of the Second Directive is perhaps incompatible with the freedom of establishment guaranteed by Article 43 EC on some other ground (than, in short, *Inspire Art*).

As was explained, the issue of compatibility must be solved by means of the three part standard test discussed above. With respect to, first, the question of whether the Treaty provisions on freedom of establishment *apply*, it must be reiterated that the participation in the incorporation of a company (in another Member State) may be considered as a method for exercising freedom of establishment.[182] Since the event giving rise to the minimum capital requirement is a company's incorporation or the commencement of its business, it may be assumed that the Treaty provisions on freedom of establishment apply.

Then, with respect to the subsequent question, whether there is a *restriction* within the meaning of Article 43 EC, I recall as a preliminary remark that the underlying rationale of the case-law on the notion of restriction, as sketched above by Advocate General Poiares Maduro is preventing 'Member States from creating or maintaining in force measures promoting internal trade to the detriment of intra-Community trade' and that such restrictions may take several forms: (i) it may be the effect of discrimination in favour of nationals; (ii) it may be the consequence of a measure protecting positions acquired by economic operators established on the national market by restricting the entry of new operators; and it (iii) may further stem from legislation rendering trade between the Member States more difficult than internal trade within a Member State.

Examining the minimum capital requirement of the Second Directive in this light, it does not in my view constitute a restriction within the meaning of Article 43 EC. This requirement does not promote internal trade within a Member State to the detriment of intra-Community trade: it does not discriminate in favour of nationals, it does not protect national incumbent operators by restricting market access, nor does it render intra-Community trade more difficult than internal trade. As to the issue of market access, a similar view is held by Leible, who notes:

> Erlässt die Gemeinschaft – wie etwa in der Kapitalrichtlinie – eine Regelung, die für bestimmte Gesellschaftsformen gemeinschaftsweit ein Mindestkapital festschreibt, kann dies niemals zu einer Beschränkung der Niederlassungsfreiheit führen. *Eine spezifische Marktzutrittsbehinderung begründet eine solche Anforderung nicht*, da in der Gemeinschaft überhaupt nur Gesellschaften errichtet werden dürfen, die den Vorgaben der Kapitalrichtlinie entsprechen.[183] (emphasis added).

According to Leible, therefore, a Community minimum capital requirement does not constitute a restriction on freedom of establishment for the reason that this requirement does not form a specific impediment to market access, referring in

182. See Ch. 3.
183. S. Leible, 'Niederlassungsfreiheit und Sitzverlegungsrichtlinie', *ZGR* (2004): 542.

particular to the fact that the same minimum capital requirement applies to all (public limited) companies Community wide.

In conclusion, the minimum capital requirement of the Second Directive does not seem to constitute a restriction on freedom of establishment. Absent such a restriction on freedom of establishment, it must be concluded that Article 6(1) of the Second Directive, in which the minimum capital requirement is laid down, cannot be considered, in all probability, as incompatible with freedom of establishment as guaranteed by the Treaty.[184]

184. Article 6 of the Second Directive concerning the minimum capital, therefore does not require any justification (the third part of the standard test discussed above).

If, for the sake of argument, the issue of justification is entered upon, it can be referred to High Level Group Report II, where it is stated at 82, that: 'The Group has reached the conclusion that the only function of the minimum capital requirement is to deter individuals from lightheartedly starting a public limited company. We are not convinced that minimum capital, at its present levels, performs any other useful functions, *but there is no evidence that it constitutes a hurdle to business activity either.* It is probably wise not to spend much time on minimum capital in a reform to make the current system more efficient, and to direct attention to issues which are more relevant. The minimum capital requirement should not be removed, nor increased.' The function of the minimum capital referred to by the High Level Group, is also recognized in the doctrine, where it is pointed out that 'it [minimum capital] ensures that a corporation with limited liability is usually only formed by founders who have more or less serious entrepreneurial intentions for it'. See H. Eidenmüller, B. Grunewald & U. Noack, 'Minimum Capital in the System of Legal Capital', in *Legal Capital in Europe* (ECFR special vol. 1), ed. M. Lutter (Berlin: De Gruyter, 2006), 30.

As was explained in the previous s. C, a restriction can be justified by an overriding reason (or imperative requirement) relating to the public interest. With respect to these overriding reasons, it is settled case-law, as was also explained above, that national measures, if they are to be justified, must be applied in a non-discriminatory manner and must be proportionate in relation to the overriding reason.

First, the issue of the overriding reason or imperative requirement. The minimum capital requirement at issue is included in the Second Directive to 'ensure' the protection of creditors. See, to this effect, Opinion of AG La Pergola in *Centros*, pt. 21 (who refers in this connection to the fourth recital in the preamble to the Second Directive). The protection of the interests of creditors has been recognized as such an imperative requirement in the case-law of the Court of Justice. See *Überseering*, para. 92. The function of the minimum capital requirement 'to deter individuals from lightheartedly starting a public limited company' could also be regarded as an 'overriding reason' in its own right; as I explained above, it is probable that the ambit of possible justifications available to the Community is wider than the justifications on which the Member States can rely.

Assumed that the (second) condition of non-discrimination is also met, the minimum capital requirement must finally be proportional in relation to the overriding reason (creditor protection). In this connection it must be reiterated that the Court has held that with regard to judicial review of the proportionality condition, the Community legislature must be allowed a broad discretion and has concluded that the legality of a legislative measure can be affected only if the measure is *manifestly inappropriate* having regard to the objective which the legislature is seeking to pursue. Such manifest inappropriateness does not seem to be present where the minimum capital requirement is concerned.

3. The Reciprocity Rule of the Directive on Takeover Bids

The Directive on takeover bids allows Member States *not to require* companies established within their territories *to apply* the provisions of the Directive: (1) limiting the powers of the board of an offeree company[185] during the time allowed for the acceptance of a bid (the so-called anti-frustration rule, laid down in Article 9); and (2) rendering ineffective barriers, provided for in the articles of association or in specific agreements (the so-called breakthrough rule of Article 11).[186] In case of such a Member State opt-out, the Member States nevertheless must allow companies established within their territories to make the choice, which must be reversible, to apply those provisions (the anti-frustration rule and/or breakthrough rule). In other words, companies must be allowed an opt-in.[187] Member States, finally, are allowed *not to require* companies which apply those provisions (in accordance with the optional arrangements) *to apply* them, when they become the subject of offers launched by companies which do not apply the same provisions (as a consequence of the use of those optional arrangements).[188] This is called the reciprocity rule.

It is sometimes contended in the literature that the reciprocity rule constitutes a (non-justifiable) restriction of freedom of establishment within the meaning of Article 43 EC.[189] What to think of the compatibility of the reciprocity rule with Article 43 EC?

As was explained, the issue of compatibility, here of the reciprocity rule, with freedom of establishment within the meaning of Article 43 EC, must be answered by means of the three-part standard test discussed above.

---

185. 'Offeree company' is defined in Art. 1(b) of the Directive as 'a company, the securities of which are the subject of a bid'.
186. See Art. 12(1) Directive on takeover bids.
187. See Art. 12(2) Directive on takeover bids.
188. See Art. 12(3) Directive on takeover bids in connection with recital 21 in the preamble to the Directive. For an in-depth discussion of the question against whom exactly an offeree ('target') company may reciprocate, see, *inter al.*, S. Simpson, M. Berkner & L. Corte, 'The Effect of the 13th Directive on US bidders', *IFLR* (2004) (Apr. suppl.): 233–234; B.J. Drijber, 'De dertiende richtlijn tussen Europese politiek en Europees recht', *Ondernemingsrecht* (2004): 377–378; J. Winter, 'EU Company Law on the Move', *LIEI* 31 (2004): 112–113; C.H. Seibt & K.J. Heiser, 'Analyse der EU-Übernahmerichtlinie und Hinweise für eine Reform des deutschen Übernahmerechts', *ZGR* (2005): 234–235; M. Menjucq, 'The European Regime on Takeovers', *ECFR* (2006): 233; G. Kemperink & J. Stuyck, 'The Thirteenth Company Law Directive and competing bids', *CML Rev.* 45 (2008): 111.
189. See e.g., J. Rickford, 'The Emerging European Takeover Law from a British Perspective', *EBLR* (2004): 1402 and 1408; Drijber, just cited, 378. For a further critical analysis of the reciprocity rule (however, not on grounds of EC law), see J. Winter, 'Level playing fields forever', in *De nieuwe macht van de kapitaalverschaffer*, ed. H. Beckman et al. (Deventer: Kluwer, 2007), 123–124. For a discussion, finally, of whether 'the national implementation of the reciprocity rule' would be in breach of Art. 56 EC (on free movement of capital), see P. Werdmuller, 'Compatibility of the EU Takeover Bid Directive Reciprocity Rule with EU Free Movement Rules', *Bus.L.R* (2006): 64–69.

Consequently, first it must be established whether the Treaty provisions on freedom of establishment *apply*. In this connection, it can be noted that the acquisition of shares in a company which shareholding confers a definite influence over the company's decisions and allows the shareholder to determine its activities, constitutes a method of exercise of the freedom of establishment.[190] It is typically in such a takeover situation that the reciprocity rule comes up. The Treaty provisions on freedom of establishment, so it may be assumed, therefore do apply here.

The second part of the test, then, is whether the reciprocity rule constitutes a *restriction* within the meaning of Article 43 EC. Again recall that the underlying rationale of the case-law on the notion of restriction, as sketched above by Advocate General Poiares Maduro, is preventing 'Member States from creating or maintaining in force measures promoting internal trade to the detriment of intra-Community trade' and that such restrictions may take several forms: (i) it may be the effect of discrimination in favour of nationals; (ii) it may be the consequence of a measure protecting positions acquired by economic operators established on the national market by restricting the entry of new operators; and it (iii) may further stem from legislation rendering trade between the Member States more difficult than internal trade within a Member State.

Now, the reciprocity rule does not seem to discriminate in favour of nationals[191] (it may be reciprocated against both foreign and national bidders). On the other hand, at first sight, the rule may seem to protect national incumbent operators by restricting market access; the reciprocity rule could then be argued to form a restriction on freedom of establishment.

Let us have a closer look at the issue of the existence of a restriction (in connection with market access). Does the rule indeed *restrict* freedom of establishment? In this connection, I recall, to begin with, that it is widely believed that (most) barriers to takeover bids[192] do not fall within the scope of the prohibition of Article 43 EC for the reason that they are not created by the Member States, but by private persons on the basis of regular national company or contract law.[193] Now,

190. See Ch. 3.

191. See (however, not within the context of the existence of a *restriction*, but within that of a possible *justification*), J.N. Schutte-Veenstra, 'Europeesrechtelijke aspecten van de dertiende richtlijn', in *Handboek openbaar bod*, ed. M.P. Nieuwe Weme et al. (Deventer: Kluwer, 2008), 134.

192. Including the restrictions and rights which have been made the subject of the breakthrough rule of Art. 11 of the Directive on takeover bids.

193. See further Ch. 3. For a recent discussion of the applicability of Art. 43 EC to barriers to takeovers, see G. Kemperink & J. Stuyck, 'The Thirteenth Company Law Directive and competing bids', *CML Rev.* 45 (2008): 113–119 (who caution that 'the attribution of direct horizontal effect of the freedom of establishment to corporate action and particularly in relation to defensive measures against takeover bids may have far-reaching consequences. Accordingly, such attribution of direct horizontal effect to the freedom of establishment should be very well thought over. As a matter of fact, companies cannot rely on the exceptions of Article 46 EC relating to i.e., public policy and public security. Also the possibility for private operators to rely on the rule of reason, as developed in case-law, and relating to justification of the restriction of fundamental freedoms on grounds of general interest that are not mentioned in the Treaty, would seem far from obvious. It would seem inappropriate for a private company

where a Member State makes use of the optional arrangement of 'reciprocity', bidders (companies wishing to acquire control and exercise their rights of establishment) are, then, not made worse off: whereas before adoption of the Directive on takeover bids, this Member State's regular company law or contract law could enable companies to put up barriers against *any bidder*,[194] the reciprocity rule – if indeed opted for by a Member State – is less far-reaching (i.e., less of an obstacle to takeovers) in that it only allows for (certain) barriers to takeover bids put up against, in short, *bidders not open to a bid themselves*.[195] This, in itself, raises doubts as to the question of whether the reciprocity rule 'restricts' freedom of establishment.

Moreover, for other reasons, I think, it may be argued that the reciprocity rule in fact contributes to attainment of freedom of establishment. First, it cannot be excluded that without the reciprocity rule, companies would not be inclined at all, or less inclined, to make use of the (then across the board) opt-in in the first place. To put it differently, the existence of a reciprocity rule may offer an incentive for companies to opt-in, the rule would thus facilitate, not restrict, freedom of establishment.[196]

Secondly, the reciprocity rule may also contribute to the attainment of freedom of establishment in that companies that want to be players on the takeover market rather than targets, must first accept the takeover facilitating rules to apply to themselves.[197] As Bartman has aptly put it:

> The effect [of the reciprocity rule] may be that an OOC [opted out company] may decide at any time to become an OIC [opted in company] after all, since the position of an OOC on the takeover market, that is to say as an acquirer, has

---

to legitimize its private action which would restrict the fundamental freedom, by invoking the general interest').

194. Which is, incidentally, still possible under the Member State opt-out of the Directive.

195. It must further be realized that these protected bidders can opt-in and thus easily avoid invocation of the reciprocity rule against them. Moreover, the reciprocity rule is of a supplementary or optional nature (i.e., not mandatory): Member States are *allowed* to apply a reciprocity rule, *not required* to do so.

196. There may be various incentives for companies to opt-in: see J. Winter, 'EU Company Law on the Move', *LIEI* 31 (2004): 112, who refers to market pressure; see also S.M. Bartman, 'Crack the OOC-Code!', *ECL* (2006): 162–163, who refers to national law, as for instance the Netherlands inquiry proceedings, which may function 'as a sort of crowbar to remove unjustified defensive constructions'; and S. Bartman, 'The EC Directive on Takeover Bids: Opting in as a Token of Good Corporate Governance', in *European Company Law in Accelerated Progress*, ed. S. Bartman (Alphen aan den Rijn: Kluwer Law International, 2006), 1–7.

197. For this – second – effect of the reciprocity rule, see: M.M. Siems, 'The Rules on Conflict of Laws in the European Takeover Directive', *ECFR* (2004): 460; J. Winter, 'We all want to go to heaven but nobody wants to die', *ECL* (2004): 1; J. Winter, 'You must be joking', *Ondernemingsrecht* (2004): 368; S. Maul & A. Kouloridas, 'The Takeover Bids Directive', *German L.J.* 5 (2004): 360; M. Gatti, 'Optionality Arrangements and Reciprocity in the European Takeover Directive', *EBOR* 5 (2005): 575; Department of Trade and Industry, Company law implementation of the European Directive on takeover bids. A Consultative Document, Jan. 2006, 28, <www.berr.gov.uk/index.html>.

> deteriorated. Since every target company may be a (potential) acquirer in the various phases of its existence, it may be wise for (. . .) the desirable or even necessary expansion to assume the status of OIC.[198]

In support of the above, it may further be pointed out that the reciprocity rule is part of a provision (Article 12) which is inextricably bound up with the anti-frustration and breakthrough rule, of which the objective is the facilitation of takeovers (and freedom of establishment).[199] In view of this, it seems justified that the reciprocity rule should not be considered in isolation, but in the context of the Directive provisions of which it thus forms a part. The impact of the reciprocity rule should consequently be assessed in the light of the overall thrust of the Directive in this respect.[200] Let me remark in this connection that it was already established in Chapter 3 that the breakthrough rule contributes to the attainment of freedom of establishment within the meaning of Article 44 EC (and the arguments underlying this conclusion seem to apply to the anti-frustration rule as well).[201]

In conclusion, for various reasons it seems questionable that the reciprocity rule constitutes a restriction on freedom of establishment. (This conclusion, incidentally, shows how the special character of Community legislation may influence the outcome of the test for compatibility with Article 43 EC; an individual Member State reciprocity rule, probably, would have formed a (non-justified) restriction[202]). If it is assumed that (indeed) there is no restriction of freedom of establishment, it must be concluded that Article 12(3) of the Directive on takeover bids, in which the reciprocity rule is laid down, cannot be considered as incompatible with freedom of establishment as guaranteed by the Treaty.[203]

4. Various Provisions of the SE Regulation

a. Introduction

This section deals with the compatibility of various provisions of the SE Regulation with Article 43 EC. First, the rules for, in short, 'the incorporation and functioning' of the SE will be discussed jointly (s. b). Next, the 'real seat' arrangement of

198. S.M. Bartman, 'Analysis and consequences of the EC Directive on takeover bids', *ECL* (2004): 7.
199. For this objective, see also recital 19 in the preamble to the Directive on takeover bids. See further Ch. 3.
200. For a similar test, cf. Case C-233/94 *Germany* v *Parliament and Council* ('Deposit Guarantees') [1997] ECR I-2405, para. 44; Opinion of AG Léger in this case, pt. 104, and further on this case: W.-H. Roth, 'Case-note Case C-233/94', *CML Rev.* 35 (1998): 464.
201. For the conclusion that the Directive may increase the number of takeover bids overall, see G. Hertig & J.A. McCahery, 'An Agenda for Reform: Company and Takeover Law in Europe', in *Reforming Company and Takeover Law in Europe*, ed. G. Ferrarini et al. (Oxford: OUP, 2004), 44.
202. See in this connection B.J. Drijber, 'De dertiende richtlijn tussen Europese politiek en Europees recht', *Ondernemingsrecht* (2004): 378.
203. The reciprocity rule therefore does not require any justification (the third part of the standard test discussed above).

Article 7 will be entered into (s. c). The issue of the personal scope of freedom of establishment, which is discussed in Chapter 3, will be shown to play an important role in both sections. Then, the head office requirement for formation of the SE of Article 2 will be examined (s. d). Here the so-called real and continuous link requirement, discussed above,[204] turns out to be of relevance. Finally, Article 8(14), which contains an authorization procedure for transfer of the registered office of the SE, will be tested for compatibility with Article 43 EC (s. e).

b. *Rules for the Incorporation and Functioning of the SE*

The issue of compatibility (here: of the rules for the incorporation and functioning of the SE) with Article 43 EC must be solved by means of the three-part standard test dealt with above.

With respect to the question whether the Treaty provisions on freedom of establishment apply *ratione personae* (the first part of the test), it is reiterated that Article 48 EC, which defines the class of persons to whom the provisions on the right of establishment apply,[205] is generally assumed to also include Community legal forms (as, for instance, the SE).[206] This means that a violation of Article 43 EC may concern also *the Community legal form's (the SE's)* right of establishment. It must be realized, however, that Article 48 EC does lay down certain (additional) conditions for a company to qualify as a beneficiary of the right of establishment.[207] Of relevance here is that the company must be 'formed in accordance with the law of a Member State'.

The requirement that a company must be 'formed in accordance with the law of a Member State' is entered into in more detail in Chapter 3, where the personal scope of freedom of establishment is discussed. It is concluded there that Article 48 EC leaves it, in principle, to the Member States to lay down rules for the incorporation and functioning of its own (national) companies. If a company does not respect these (mandatory) rules, it has no access to freedom of establishment to begin with. Moreover, so it could be argued, forming a precondition for a company to have access to freedom of establishment, the rules at issue cannot be in breach of *that company's* right of establishment (as it does not have such a right yet).[208] The Court's recent judgment in *Cartesio*, as was explained,[209] may be argued to confirm this conclusion.

For the SE, where the requirement would be that it is 'formed in accordance with (secondary) Community law', the conclusion should be similar: Article 48 EC

204. See Ch. 3.
205. See Case C-70/95 *Sodemare a.O.* [1997] ECR I-3395, para. 25.
206. See Ch. 3.
207. See Ch. 3. Cf. also *Cartesio*, para. 109, which is dealt with in more detail in the next section.
208. Even though Art. 43 EC prohibits not only restrictions on the freedom of establishment (in another Member State) on the part of *the host State*, but also those restrictions which are attributable to *the State of origin* the Treaty rules on freedom of establishment just do not (yet) apply; the company is not (yet) within the personal scope of those rules, as it is not (yet) formed in accordance with the law of a Member State.
209. See Ch. 3.

leaves it, in principle, to the Community legislature to lay down rules for the incorporation and functioning of its own (Community) companies (here: the SE). If these rules are not observed, the SE – should it have come into being – has no access to freedom of establishment. Moreover, so it could also be argued here, forming a precondition for an SE to have access to freedom of establishment, the rules at issue cannot be in breach of *that company's* (the SE's) right of establishment (as it does not have such a right yet).

Many of the provisions of the SE Regulation presumably concern, in short, what was just referred to as the incorporation and functioning of the SE: for example, Article 2 (formation); Article 4 (minimum capital); Article 12 (registration); and Articles 38–60 (structure of the SE).[210] (In this connection, I think, it may be pointed out that the official title of the SE Regulation is 'Council Regulation *on the Statute* for a European company (SE)' (emphasis added). Under Member State law, the term *statute* (company statute or internal statute) is often used to indicate the set of rules concerning in particular the issues in question[211]).

Even though, as was just mentioned, the provisions under consideration here will not be in breach of the *SE's* right of establishment, in theory the rules under consideration could be in breach of *other persons'* right of establishment (notably national forms of company), that is, those companies interested in establishing themselves through an SE in another Member State.[212]

---

210. The provisions concerning the incorporation and functioning of the SE do not seem to include the provisions regulating a facility the SE, once it exists, may use, such as transfer of the registered office of the SE. Therefore, the authorization procedure for transfer of the registered office of the SE could (as opposed to the provisions concerning the incorporation and functioning of the SE) be argued to be in violation of the SE's own right of establishment under Art. 43 EC (see for this: s. e, *infra*).

    In this connection, two further remarks could be made. Firstly, transfer of the registered office of the SE is not related to 'incorporation' of an SE (which already exists; nor does it lead to incorporation of a new SE). Secondly, a transfer of the registered office of the SE could be argued not to concern the 'functioning' of the SE either. This 'functioning' remains as it is in case of a transfer; the SE Regulation does not provide for alterations in this respect. This finding does not seem to be affected by the fact that the SE Regulation does not lay down exhaustively all of the rules applicable to SEs and that, for certain matters, it refers to the law of the Member State in the territory of which the SE has its registered office, since that referral is – as the Court has put it – of a subsidiary nature; cf. Case C-436/03 *Parliament* v *Council* ('SCE Regulation') [2006] ECR I-3733, para. 45.

211. For French law, see M. Menjucq, *Droit international et européen des sociétés* (Paris: Montchrestien, 2001), 97–99; for Netherlands law, see J.M.M. Maeijer, *Mr. C. Asser's handleiding tot de beoefening van het Nederlands burgerlijk recht. Vertegenwoordiging en rechtspersoon. De naamloze en de besloten vennootschap* (Deventer: W.E.J. Tjeenk Willink, 2000), no. 27. For a discussion of the US internal affairs doctrine, finally, see J.A. McCahery & E.P.M. Vermeulen, 'Understanding Corporate Mobility in the EU. Towards the Foundations of a European Internal Affairs Doctrine', Working Paper Prepared for the European Company Law and Corporate Governance Conference in Berlin on 27–28 Jun. 2007, <www.bdi.eu/company-law-conference2007>.

212. Cf. also *Cartesio*, paras 110–113, where the Court observes, in short, that legislation on the incorporation of companies does not enjoy an immunity from the rules of the EC Treaty on freedom of establishment.

As to the applicability *ratione materiae* of the Treaty provisions on freedom of establishment in such a situation, the method for exercising freedom of establishment most likely (least unlikely) to be considered here is that of 'taking part in the incorporation of a company'.[213] This method can be assumed to also include participation in *the formation of an SE*.[214]

Do the provisions at issue, concerning the incorporation and functioning of the SE constitute a *restriction* on freedom of establishment?

These provisions do not, so it may be argued, discriminate in favour of nationals, do not protect national incumbent operators by restricting market access, or render intra-Community trade more difficult than internal trade. In this light, it is unlikely the provisions at issue can be considered to form a *restriction* within the meaning of Article 43 EC.[215] (The criteria the Court has established to determine whether there is a restriction on freedom of establishment, against which the SE provisions are thus tested, were dealt with more extensively above). As regards specifically the provisions concerning the functioning of the SE,[216] as for instance, the Articles 38–60 SE Regulation on the structure of the SE, it is, incidentally, also improbable that there is a restriction in view of the fact that these specific provisions do not or not directly affect participation in the incorporation – that is, the method for exercising freedom of establishment – itself (which may even raise doubts about the *applicability* of the Treaty provisions on freedom of establishment in the first place).

As to the specific question of whether the minimum subscribed capital requirement of Article 4 of the SE Regulation, which is EUR 120,000, is compatible with Article 43 EC, let me further note this. A similar question in respect of the minimum capital requirement of the Second Directive was discussed above. As the answer with regard to the SE is similar, I can be brief. The Treaty provisions on freedom of establishment *apply*, since the event giving rise to the minimum capital requirement is a company's incorporation or the commencement of its business, that is, a form of establishment. On the question of whether the requirement constitutes a *restriction* on freedom of establishment, it was pointed out, in short, that it does not discriminate in favour of nationals, does not protect national incumbent operators by restricting market access, or render intra-Community trade more difficult than internal trade. This seems to apply *mutatis mutandis* to the minimum subscribed capital requirement of Article 4 of the SE Regulation, so that it, too, cannot be considered as restricting freedom of establishment.

---

213. It seems unlikely that the SE provisions at issue constitute impediments to other methods of establishment. For 'taking part in the incorporation of a company' and the other methods for exercising freedom of establishment, see Ch. 3.

214. For this view, see also Timmermans, 10. Participation in the formation of an SE, incidentally, is assumed here to also include the cross-border merger as a means of formation of an SE.

215. It is reiterated, moreover, in this connection, see s. C, that AG Poiares Maduro in his Opinion in Case C-446/03 *Marks & Spencer* [2005] ECR I-10837, pt. 40, emphasized that: 'not every restriction on economic or commercial freedom is a restriction on the exercise of the freedoms of movement' (referring to Joined Cases C-267/91 and C-268/91 *Keck and Mithouard* [1993] ECR I-6097).

216. I.e., as opposed to the provisions concerning the incorporation of the SE.

In conclusion, the provisions at issue, concerning the incorporation and functioning of the SE, will – in principle – not be in breach of Article 43 EC. (An exception may be Article 2 of the Regulation on formation of the SE. This, however, as will be shown, is connected with the real and continuous link requirement of Article 43 EC in particular, which requirement is discussed in Chapter 3. It will, therefore, be dealt with separately, in section d, below).

c. The 'Real Seat' Arrangement of the SE Regulation

Article 7 of the SE Regulation provides that the registered office of an SE must be located in the same Member State as its head office. The preamble to the Regulation refers in this connection to the 'real seat' arrangement.[217] An SE which does not comply with this requirement may be liquidated.[218]

The prevailing view, among company law specialists, is that the arrangement in question forms a restriction on freedom of establishment which is in breach of Article 43 EC.[219] The supporters of this view generally refer to the Court's decision in *Überseering*, which, in some way, would recognize the right under Article 43 EC to a free transfer of a company's head office to another Member State.

In my view, this interpretation of *Überseering* is not correct.[220] After all, in that judgment the Court clearly ruled that: 'the question whether a company formed in accordance with the legislation of one Member State [can] transfer its (...) actual centre of administration to another Member State without losing its legal personality under the law of the Member State of incorporation and, in certain circumstances, the rules relating to that transfer [are] determined by the national law in accordance with which the company [has] been incorporated'. The conclusion to be drawn from *Überseering* is, therefore, that a Member State – on the contrary – *may* prescribe that a company (incorporated under its law) cannot

217. Recital 27 in the preamble to the SE Regulation.
218. See Art. 64 SE Regulation.
219. See e.g., C.R. Huiskes, *De Europese vennootschap. Enkele beschouwingen omtrent het ontwerp-Statuut (1991) voor een Europese vennootschap* (Zwolle: W.E.J. Tjeenk Willink, 1993), 91; J. Rickford, 'An Overview of the Conference – Three Big Questions', and E. Wymeersch, 'Cross-Border Transfer of the Seat of a Company – Recent EU Case Law and the SE Regulation', both in Rickford, 127 and 91 resp. (see, however, J. Rickford, 'Current Developments in European Law on the Restructuring of Companies: An Introduction', *EBLR* (2004): 1250 noting that: 'in the present state of the law, as currently declared by the ECJ, the real seat status of the SE is valid'); E. Wymeersch, 'The transfer of the company's seat in European company law', *CML Rev.* 40 (2003): 692–693. G.J.H. van der Sangen & W. Mulder, 'The European Company and Cross-Border Reorganisations', in *The European Company*, ed. S.H.M.A. Dumoulin et al. (The Hague: Boom, 2005), 109–110; E. Werlauff, 'The SE as a Legal Form for Financial Companies', in *European Company Law in Accelerated Progress*, ed. S. Bartman (Alphen aan den Rijn: Kluwer Law International, 2006), 169. See, however: W.-G. Ringe, *Die Sitzverlegung der Europäischen Aktiengesellschaft* (Tübingen: Mohr Siebeck, 2006), 99, who is of the opinion that Art. 7 is not in violation of the freedom of establishment.
220. See already my case note on *Inspire Art*, *JOR* 2003/249.

transfer its real seat (head office) to another Member State ('without losing its legal personality under the law of the Member State of incorporation').[221] The Court has confirmed this, recently, in its *Cartesio* judgment, where it ruled that: Articles 43 EC and 48 EC do not preclude legislation of a Member State under which a company incorporated under the law of that Member State may not transfer its seat (head office) to another Member State whilst retaining its status as a company governed by the law of the Member State of incorporation.[222] The idea that in view of *Überseering* the real seat arrangement of the SE Regulation (after the alleged example of such arrangements for national forms of company) would be in breach of (the SE's rights[223] under) Article 43 EC is therefore to be rejected.

The Court's judgment in *Cartesio* could also otherwise be advanced in support of the real seat arrangement of the Community legal form of the SE: Although the ruling in *Cartesio* concerned a national form of company, the underlying observations seem to be relevant to Community legal forms, too. I shall not reiterate these observations, which were dealt with above, to which I refer,[224] but what they amount to, in essence, is this: In the absence of a uniform Community law definition of the companies which may enjoy the right of establishment, the question whether a company is faced with a restriction on the freedom of establishment, within the meaning of Article 43 EC, can arise only if it has been established, in the light of the conditions laid down in Article 48 EC, that the company actually has a right to that freedom. Within the context of this preliminary matter, the Court concludes, in short, that a *Member State* may define the connecting factor and preclude a cross-border transfer of the seat. The case which gave rise to *Cartesio*, of course, concerned such Member State legislation. However, on the basis of the above, it could similarly be concluded, so it seems, that the *Community legislature* may define the connecting factor for Community legal forms and preclude these entities a cross-border transfer of seat (with no change as regards the national law applicable to the legal form).[225] Recall that in this connection, Article 48 EC, which defines the class of persons to whom the provisions on the right of

---

221. *Überseering*, para. 70.
222. *Cartesio*, para. 124.
223. A violation of Art. 43 EC may, admittedly, concern *the SE's* right of establishment. (After all, Art. 48 EC, which defines the class of persons to whom the provisions on the right of establishment apply (see Case C-70/95 *Sodemare a.O.* [1997] ECR I-3395, para. 25), is generally assumed to also include Community legal forms. See further s. b, *supra*, and Ch. 3). However, such a violation does not occur here, as explained in the main text. Incidentally, also in view of the broad terms in which *Daily Mail*, *Überseering* and *Cartesio* are formulated, it may neither be assumed that a real seat arrangement such as that under discussion, violates *other beneficiaries'* right of establishment (notably national companies participating in the formation of an SE).
224. These observations of *Cartesio* were dealt with in more detail in the discussion of the personal scope of freedom of establishment. See Ch. 3.
225. It is noted that an SE may transfer its real seat *with an attendant change as regards the national law applicable*. See Art. 7 to 9(1)(c)(ii) SE Regulation and for a discussion of such a transfer (as opposed to that without any change as to the national law applicable), *Cartesio*, paras 114–120.

establishment apply, is generally assumed to also include Community legal forms (as, for instance, the SE).

In conclusion, the view that in consideration of *Überseering* the real seat arrangement of the SE Regulation would be in breach of Article 43 EC must be rejected. It may further be argued, in my opinion, on the basis of *Cartesio* in particular, that – having regard to the Court's interpretation there of Article 48 EC – the question whether the SE is faced with a restriction on the freedom of establishment does not even arise here, and consequentially the real seat arrangement at issue cannot be held to be in violation of Article 43 EC.[226]

d. The Head Office Requirement for Formation of the SE

Under Article 43 EC companies formed in accordance with the law of a Member State with their registered, but not their head office or main establishment within the Community, can nevertheless invoke the right of establishment (which includes the participation in the incorporation or formation of a company), provided that they have, what is called, a 'real and continuous link' with the economy of a Member State.[227] This right of companies with 'only' their registered office (and in this connection the 'real and continuous link' requirement) was entered into in more detail in Chapter 3, where the personal scope of freedom of establishment was discussed.

Recital 23 in the preamble to the SE Regulation links up with this requirement. It reads as follows:

> A company the head office of which is not in the Community should be allowed to participate in the formation of an SE provided that company is formed under the law of a Member State, has its registered office in that Member State and has a real and continuous link with a Member State's economy according to the principles established in the 1962 General Programme for the abolition of restrictions on freedom of establishment. Such a link exists in particular if a company has an establishment in that Member State and conducts operations therefrom.

---

226. Well before *Cartesio*, Timmermans had already similarly contended (in respect of the real seat arrangement of the SE), that he did not think that 'this choice for the real seat approach is contrary to the Treaty as some have argued. The Community legislator has chosen one of the connecting factors which the EC Treaty has allowed under Article 48'. See C.W.A. Timmermans, *Neue Rechtsprechung des Gerichtshofs der EG zum Europäischen Gesellschaftsrecht* (Zentrum für Europäisches Wirtschaftsrecht. Vorträge und Berichte, no. 132) (Bonn: The members of the Zentrum, 2003), 19.

227. Cf. Timmermans, 9–10. To be precise, the 'real and continuous link' is required in a case in which a Member State company that wants to set up *agencies, branches, or subsidiaries* only has its registered office within the Community. To avoid unnecessary complication, it is not distinguished in the main text between the forms of establishment just mentioned (which require the link at issue) and other forms, which, arguably, include the *participation in the incorporation of a company* (or here: the *formation of an SE*). See Ch. 3. The fact is that the arguments put forward in the main text (in short, against the head office requirement) seem to apply similarly (if not *a fortiori*) in case of these other forms of establishment.

According to Article 2 of the SE Regulation, however, an SE may only be formed by companies with their registered offices *and* head offices within the Community. So, a registered office, together with a real and continuous link, does not suffice. This raises the question of whether the requirement of the head office is compatible with Article 43 EC.[228]

There is certainly a case for incompatibility, in my view. As stated, companies formed in accordance with the law of a Member State and having their registered office within the Community have under Article 43 EC a right of establishment (which includes the participation in the incorporation of a company)[229] provided that they have a real and continuous link with the economy of a Member State. In light of this, the head office requirement comes within the scope (*ratione personae* and *materiae*) of freedom of establishment. This is, of course, the first part of the test for compatibility with Article 43 EC. The second part of the test then, is whether there is a restriction on freedom of establishment. This question, in my opinion, is to be answered in the affirmative: a specifically defined group of persons explicitly entitled to benefit from Article 43 EC,[230] namely companies with 'only' their registered office within the Community, are simply excluded from exercising their right of establishment (by means of formation of an SE). 'Simply', because of a circumstance (i.e., the lack of a head office within the Community; or having 'only' the registered office within the Community) which precisely characterizes this group of beneficiaries (or distinguishes it from the other beneficiaries).

> In this connection, the specific character of the SE as an *extra facility* available for businesses on top of national legal forms does not, in my view, exclude the possibility of there being a restriction (within the meaning of Article 43 EC).
>
> The SE Regulation has as its purpose the creation of a new, European public limited-liability legal form (see Article 1(1) SE Regulation) in addition to the – 27 – national forms of public limited-liability companies. See Recitals 6 and 7 in the preamble to the SE Regulation and cf. Case C-436/03 *Parliament* v *Council* ('SCE Regulation') [2006] ECR I-3733, para. 44. The SE coexists with (public limited-liability) companies under national law (cf. *Parliament* v *Council*, just cited, para. 43), and may thus be characterized as a 28th (public limited-liability) company form, an *extra facility* available for businesses on top of national legal forms. In view of the specific character of the SE as an *extra facility* available for businesses on

228. Timmermans, 9–10, remarks that: 'One would expect such a company being a beneficiary of the right of establishment to be entitled to participate in the formation of a European company. (. . .) However, and strangely enough, Article 2, paragraph 5, provides this only as an option for the Member States.'
229. Let me emphasize that 'taking part in the incorporation of a company' constitutes a method for exercising freedom of establishment and that this method can be assumed to also include participation in the formation of an SE. See also Timmermans, previous fn.
230. See the 1961 'General Programme for the abolition of restrictions on freedom of establishment', (the relevance of) which was discussed in Ch. 3. The other category (categories) of persons also entitled to benefit from Art. 43 EC are, in short, the companies formed under the law of a Member State having their head office or their main establishment within the Community.

top of national legal forms, which leaves unchanged the different national laws already in existence, one might be of the opinion that the SE Regulation or specific provisions thereof, cannot be regarded as *restricting* (national companies') freedom of establishment.

The correctness of this opinion, however, must – I think – be questioned. The fact that a (Community) measure is to be characterized as (such) a facility does, as stated, not exclude the possibility of there being a restriction (within the meaning of Article 43 EC). The Court's *Sevic* ruling provides an example, albeit in a different context, which also concerned a facility offered to companies and firms, particularly the form of merger. Whilst being a facility, the Court ruled that the national rules at issue were incompatible with Article 43 EC. I refer to paras 22–23 of that judgment:

> In so far as, under national rules, recourse to such a means of company transformation is not possible where one of the companies is established in a Member State other than the Federal Republic of Germany, German law establishes a difference in treatment between companies according to the internal or cross-border nature of the merger, which is likely to deter the exercise of the freedom of establishment laid down by the Treaty. [23] Such a difference in treatment constitutes a restriction within the meaning of Articles 43 EC and 48 EC (...).

In My view then, the requirement of the head office laid down in Article 2 of the SE Regulation is tantamount to an outright negation of the freedom of establishment conferred on companies by Articles 43 EC and 48 EC, for which objectives as protection of the interests of creditors, minority shareholders, employees, and the taxation authorities do not provide a justification, and must therefore be regarded as (directly) in breach of Article 43 EC.[231]

Furthermore, I note that the requirement of the head office impedes or renders less attractive the exercise of the freedom of establishment, in that a company (validly incorporated under the law of, and having its registered office in a Member State and having a real and continuous link with a Member State) that wishes to participate in the formation of an SE but that does not satisfy the requirement under consideration, must (this is the only course of action available) first transfer its head office to the Community. Such a transfer may entail serious disruption within a company (recruitment policies, for instance) and also may require the completion of numerous formalities which have financial consequences, impeding *market access* of companies with only their registered office within the Community.[232]

---

231. Cf. *Überseering*, paras 81 and 93.
232. Cf. Case C-299/02 *Commission* v *Netherlands* [2004] ECR I-9761, para. 19. As explained, 'market access' is an important criterion to determine whether there is a restriction on freedom of establishment. Of relevance to the issue of *market access* (and thus the restriction on freedom of establishment) is also that the Statute for an SE is intended, particularly, to remove barriers to cross-border cooperation of companies and to contribute to the possibilities for reorganization (in the sense of adaptation of the structures of production to the Community dimension). See recital 1 in the preamble to the SE Regulation and cf. also Case C-436/03 *Parliament* v *Council* ('SCE Regulation') [2006] ECR I-3733, para. 2.

> The head office requirement furthermore establishes a difference in treatment between companies according to the connecting factor with the legal system of a particular Member State, this while, according to the Court in *Daily Mail:* 'In defining, in Article 58 (now Article 48 EC), the companies which enjoy the right of establishment, the Treaty places *on the same footing*, as connecting factors, the registered office, central administration and principal place of business of a company'[233] (emphasis added). Indeed, the Court of Justice has regularly held that: 'To accept that the Member State of establishment may freely apply different treatment solely because the registered office, central administration or principal place of business of a company is situated in another Member State would deprive Article 43 EC of its substance.'[234] In view of this, too, it may be argued that the head office requirement of Article 2 SE Regulation is to be regarded as constituting a restriction on freedom of establishment within the meaning of Article 43 EC.
>
> Such a restriction could, in principle, be justified, but the problem with that is, that the Community legislature has not provided any insight into the (general interest) objective it seeks to pursue with the head office requirement, let alone whether such a requirement would be suitable for securing the attainment of the objective it pursues and would not go beyond what is necessary in order to attain it. It is, consequently, by no means clear whether the head office requirement may be justified.

In conclusion, in view of – in short – the issue of the beneficiaries of Article 43 EC, the requirement that the founders of an SE have their head offices within the Community can be argued to be in breach of Article 43 EC. Even apart from this specific issue of the beneficiaries, however, the head office requirement seems to constitute a restriction on freedom of establishment, to which I must add that is by no means settled that it is justified by an imperative requirement in the public interest.

e. *The Authorization Procedure for Transfer of the Registered Office of the SE*

On the basis of Article 8 of the SE Regulation, an SE may transfer its registered office to another Member State. Let me briefly recall some key provisions in this regard. Such a transfer must be accompanied, in view of Article 7 of the SE Regulation,[235] with a transfer of the head office.[236] The transfer of the registered office does not result in the winding up of the SE or in the creation of a new legal person.[237] Member States may, on the basis of Article 8, paragraph 14 of the SE Regulation, provide that, as regards SEs registered in that Member State, the

233. *Daily Mail,* para. 21.
234. Case C-231/05 *Oy AA* [2007] ECR I-6373, para. 31, with further references ('In effect, acceptance of the proposition that the Member State in which a company seeks to establish itself may freely apply to it a different treatment solely by reason of the fact that its registered office is situated in another Member State would deprive Article 43 EC of all meaning').
235. Article 7 SE Regulation was discussed in s. c, *supra.*
236. See also Art. 64 SE Regulation.
237. Article 8(1), *in fine*, SE Regulation.

transfer of a registered office (which results in a change of the law applicable)[238] shall not take effect if any of that Member State's competent authorities opposes it.[239] Such opposition may, also according to Article 8(14), be based only on grounds of public interest.

Timmermans has commented that Article 8(14) of the SE Regulation deserves a discussion of its compatibility with the provisions of the EC Treaty on the right of establishment.[240] He observed in this connection:

> the possible transfer of the seat of a SE, which is to be regarded as an exercise of the right of establishment, can be vetoed by the Member State where the SE is registered on grounds of public interest without any indication of what such public interest may imply. [fn.: Article 8, paragraph 14 of the Statute] In the past the European Commission has launched infringement procedures against Member States attacking similar clauses under national law, for instance, in national merger regulations, as contrary to the Treaty (Crédit Lyonnais case).[241]

Timmermans, thus, feels dubious about the compatibility of the authorization procedure of Article 8(14) with the EC Treaty. May Article 8(14) be considered to violate Article 43 EC?

The first question to be answered in this connection is whether the Treaty provisions on freedom of establishment *apply* in respect of the authorization procedure. In my view, this is indeed the case. As I argued above, transfer of the registered office (conversion) is within the substantive scope of freedom of establishment.[242] As to the personal scope of freedom of establishment (the beneficiaries), it is pointed out next that in case of the transfer of the registered office, the right of establishment is exercised *by the SE* itself. The SE now, as I have argued above, is indeed a beneficiary of the freedom of establishment.[243]

---

238. Article 8(14) speaks of 'the transfer of a registered office which would result in a change of the law applicable'; the Court of Justice, however, has stated that a transfer of the registered office 'necessarily entails a change as regards the national law applicable to the entity making such a transfer', in which connection it referred to Art. 7 to 9(1)(c)(ii) of the SE Regulation. See *Cartesio*, paras 117–119.
239. Article 68(2) SE Regulation adds in this regard: 'Each Member State shall designate the competent authorities within the meaning of Articles 8, (. . .). It shall inform the Commission and the other Member States accordingly.'
240. See Timmermans, 9–10.
241. *Ibid.*, 10.
242. See Ch. 3. To be precise, the Court made clear in *Cartesio* that cross-border conversion is within the substantive scope of freedom of establishment. In view of the fact that transfer of the registered office is very similar to cross-border conversion, it may be argued, it seems, that it, too, is within the substantive scope of freedom of establishment. This is also Timmermans' view, as appears from the quotation in the main text.
243. Article 48 EC, which defines the class of persons to whom the provisions on the right of establishment apply (See Case C-70/95 *Sodemare a.O.* [1997] ECR I-3395, para. 25), is generally assumed to also include Community legal forms. See also Ch. 3. See further s. c, *supra* (fn. text on this issue).

The question of applicability (*ratione materiae* and *personae*) of the Treaty provisions on freedom of establishment must therefore be answered in the affirmative.

The subsequent question is whether the authorization procedure constitutes a *restriction* on freedom of establishment.

> In *Cartesio*, as explained, the Court gave a ruling on, *inter alia*, cross-border conversion of a company governed by the law of a Member State. Such a conversion entails a change as regards the national law applicable to the company concerned.[244] Transfer of the registered office (of Community legal forms) may be considered as the counterpart of cross-border conversion (of national legal forms). Such a transfer of the registered office also necessarily entails a change as regards the national law applicable to the entity making such a transfer.[245]
>
> It may be inferred from *Cartesio* that in case of impediments to cross-border conversions (transfers of the registered office), the question arises indeed whether the company at issue is faced with a *restriction* on its right of establishment.[246] (In case of cross-border transfer of the seat (with no change as regards the law which governs that company), it is rather the preliminary question whether the company concerned may be regarded as a company which possesses the nationality of the Member State of incorporation).[247]
>
> The Court decided in *Cartesio*, in short, that a Member State of incorporation may not prevent a company *by requiring its winding-up or liquidation* from converting itself (i.e., with a change as regards the national law applicable to the company) into a company governed by the law of another Member State.[248] *Such a barrier* to conversion of a company constitutes a *restriction* on freedom of establishment.[249] The Court did not rule on an *authorization requirement for conversion (or transfer of the registered office)*, so the question whether such a requirement forms a restriction remained unanswered there.

To return to the question just raised, does the authorization procedure constitute a *restriction* on freedom of establishment? Under the above Article 8(14), Member States are entrusted with broad powers. They may provide that, as regards SEs registered in that Member State, the transfer of a registered office shall not take effect if any of that Member State's competent authorities opposes it. Such opposition may, also according to Article 8(14), be based on (all) 'grounds of public interest'. Now, of particular relevance here, I would argue, is the risk that the broad powers conferred on the Member State's competent authorities may be used arbitrarily, perhaps even in a protectionist way.[250] In view of this, the authorization

244. *Cartesio*, paras 111–113.
245. See *Cartesio*, paras 117–119, in which connection the Court refers to Art. 7 to 9(1)(c)(ii) of the SE Regulation.
246. *Cartesio*, paras 111–113 and para. 123.
247. *Ibid.*, paras 109–110 and paras 121–123.
248. *Ibid.*, para. 112.
249. *Ibid.*, para. 113.
250. The question whether this (also) constitutes a restriction on freedom of establishment by the *Member State* in which the SE has its registered office, will not be considered here.

procedure of Article 8(14) itself could be regarded as liable to deter SEs from transferring their registered offices (i.e., exercising their right of establishment). In this connection, I further recall that the underlying rationale of the case-law on the notion of restriction, as sketched above by Advocate General Poiares Maduro is preventing 'Member States from creating or maintaining in force measures promoting internal trade to the detriment of intra-Community trade.' This now, the promotion of internal trade to the detriment of intra-Community trade, may thus precisely be the consequence of Article 8(14). In view of all this, it may be concluded, it seems, that the authorization procedure of Article 8(14) constitutes a restriction on freedom of establishment indeed.

Finally, as to the issue of *justification* of the restriction, it can be referred to, *inter alia*, the golden share case *Commission* v *Spain*,[251] which case concerned an authorization procedure rather similar to that of Article 8(14) of the SE Regulation (and to the national procedures Timmermans refers to). As regards the – (also) restrictive – authorization procedure at issue in that case,[252] the Court held that the procedure, to be justified, had to be proportionate to the (public interest) aim pursued, inasmuch as the same objective could not be attained by less restrictive measures. In this connection, the Court emphasized that the authorization procedure had to be based on objective, non-discriminatory criteria which are known in advance to the undertaking(s) concerned, and that all persons affected by a restrictive measure of that type must have a legal remedy available to them.[253] The authorization procedure of *Commission* v *Spain*, incidentally, did not meet the criteria just referred to and was held to be in breach of the Treaty, more particularly Article 56 EC (free movement of capital).[254]

Examining Article 8(14) of the SE Regulation in light of the criteria of *Commission* v *Spain* and assuming that the (so) generally described 'grounds of public interest' as such, qualify as an overriding reason relating to the public interest, the procedure of Article 8(14) does not seem proportionate, as interpreted by the Court, in that it does not lay down objective, non-discriminatory criteria which are known in advance (to the SEs concerned). Even though the Community legislature has discretionary powers in areas which require complex political, economic assessments, it would seem to me that the Community legislature has overstepped this discretion by enacting the procedure at issue which lacks specified criteria. As a consequence, the authorization procedure

251. Case C-463/00 *Commission* v *Spain* [2003] ECR I-4581, para. 74.
252. Spanish law submitted to the approval of the national authorities specific decisions of certain commercial undertakings. The Court of Justice held that the national provisions in question constituted a restriction on free movement of capital.
253. *Commission* v *Spain*, just cited, para. 69. As regards the legal remedy, it must be admitted that Art. 8(14), third section of the SE Regulation stipulates, that: 'Review by a judicial authority shall be possible.'
254. *Commission* v *Spain*, just cited, in particular paras 76, 80, and 84. For a discussion of authorization procedures in the financial services sector, see Commission Communication 'Intra-EU investment in the financial services' sector', OJ 2005 C 293, 2–7.

of Article 8(14) of the SE Regulation may be argued to be in breach of the Treaty, Article 43 EC in particular.

IV. CONCLUDING REMARKS

The previous two chapters were about the *competence* or *powers* of the EC in the field of company law. This chapter was about the requirements for the lawful *exercise* of these powers. More specifically, it was about the principle of subsidiarity and the observance of Article 43 EC. The following conclusions can be drawn.

The principle of subsidiarity is set out in the second paragraph of Article 5 EC, according to which, in areas which do not fall within its exclusive competence, the Community is to take action only if and in so far as the objectives of the proposed action cannot be sufficiently achieved by the Member States and can therefore, by reason of the scale or effects of the proposed action, be better achieved at Community level. Most Community competences, including those in the field of company law, are non-exclusive. Accordingly, the exercise of these competences must comply with the principle of subsidiarity.

One should, however, not overestimate the limits subsidiarity places on the Community legislature. From the case-law of the Court of Justice, it follows that where the objectives of a Community measure seek to eliminate the barriers raised by the differences which exist between the Member States' laws, the requirements of the subsidiarity principle will be readily met.

It is occasionally claimed in the literature that the principle of subsidiarity holds a commitment to regulatory competition, in the sense that *as a rule regulatory competition* between Member States is the means to achieve the goals of the proposed action (or even that the Community legislature, in view of subsidiarity, would be (generally) required to use its powers to – actively – stimulate regulatory competition). This view, however, (i) may from an economic viewpoint not necessarily be wise policy; (ii) does not find support in the *Protocol on the application of the principles of subsidiarity and proportionality*, which expressly allows Community action within the limits of its powers to be *expanded* where *circumstances so require* and conversely, to be *restricted* or discontinued where it is no longer justified; (iii) does not seem to fit well with the case-law of the Court of Justice in *Centros* and *Inspire Art* and in its case-law on subsidiarity.

Article 43 EC, which prohibits – in short – restrictions on freedom of establishment, not only applies to the *Member States* but, as an analysis of the case-law of the Court of Justice shows, also applies to the *Community* legislature. It is of regular occurrence that company law specialists contend that certain provisions of EC company law are in breach of Article 43 EC. The reciprocity rule – included in the Directive on takeover bids – and the so-called 'real seat' arrangement adopted by the SE Regulation may be quoted as the most prominent examples of such provisions. Also, the minimum capital requirement of the Second Directive is believed to constitute a restriction on freedom of establishment. Whereas the correctness of the above prevailing views on the reciprocity rule and 'real seat' arrangement, as well as that on the minimum capital requirement must be seriously questioned, other provisions of EC company law (do) seem to be contrary to Article 43 EC, namely the head office requirement for formation of an SE and the authorization procedure for transfer of the registered office of an SE.

Chapter 6
Conclusion

1. This book is about the modernization of European (EC) company law and corporate governance. More particularly, it addresses two main questions: (1) to what extent does the European Community enjoy legislative competence in the field of company law and corporate governance and, once this competence has been established; (2) which – legal – limits apply to the exercise of this competence. Immediate cause for raising these two questions is the European Commission's *Action Plan on Modernising Company Law and Enhancing Corporate Governance* which aims to bring about thoroughgoing, especially legislative changes concerning a broad range of subjects in the field of company law.

2. The main conclusions may be summarized as follows. First as to the *competence* of the European Community, Article 44(1) EC and 44(2)(g) EC, the principal legal bases used for EC action in the field of company law, do not provide a general power to adopt EC company law instruments.[1] The power conferred is of a functional nature; it is conferred for the purpose of attaining freedom of establishment. Attainment of freedom of establishment may encompass, in short, the elimination of restrictions and other impediments (not being restrictions within the meaning of Article 43 EC) and the facilitation of the effective exercise of the right of establishment.

3. Both the Commission (in its 2003 *Action Plan on Modernising Company Law and Enhancing Corporate Governance*) and the Community legislature, however, arguably fail to explain (frequently) how Company Law Directives based on Article 44 EC (or 44(1) EC and 44(2)(g) EC) contribute to the attainment of freedom of establishment. In fact, in its Action Plan the Commission identifies two policy objectives that modern company law actions at the European level *should* seek as

1. A similar conclusion holds as regards Art. 95 EC and Art. 308 EC, two other legal bases that have been used for EC action in the field of company law (See Ch. 4).

much as possible to meet – (1) fostering efficiency and competitiveness of business, and (2) strengthening shareholders rights and third party protection –, but it does not reveal any close attention being paid to the prior question whether the Community legislature is *competent* to pursue these modernization objectives in the first place. Article 44(1) EC and 44(2)(g) EC, however, do not confer the power to act for purposes of fostering efficiency and competitiveness of business and strengthening shareholders rights *per se*,[2] without a contribution to attainment of freedom of establishment.

4. The legal basis for the *Directive on takeover bids* is formed by Article 44(1) EC *juncto* Article 44(2)(g) EC. This Directive contains a mandatory bid rule: when a person or entity acquires control of a listed company as a result of an acquisition of securities, minority shareholders are protected, for the mandatory bid rule requires that person or entity to address a bid to all holders of securities, for all their holdings, at an equitable price.

Article 44(2)(g) EC carefully defines the 'addressee' of the safeguards which may be harmonized on the basis of that provision: companies (or firms). Outside the scope are therefore, safeguards required of others, for example shareholders. The mandatory bid rule is a case in point. It is addressed to ('controlling') shareholders (of companies), not to companies themselves. In view of this, Article 44(2)(g) EC may not be used to harmonize rules with respect to the mandatory bid. This is, however, what may have happened. The legal basis for the Directive on takeover bids is formed by Article 44(1) EC *juncto Article 44(2)(g) EC. Article 44(1) EC*, by contrast, does seem to provide a legal basis for adoption of a mandatory bid rule, both as regards the requirement it entails for EC companies (as shareholders) to make a bid as well as for third country companies (as shareholders).

5. The *Directive on shareholder rights* has a double legal basis: Article 44 EC (concerning freedom of establishment) and Article 95 EC (concerning, *inter alia*, free movement of capital). It is not evident that the Community legislature has sufficiently established a link between the Directive and freedom of establishment. Even if it is established that the Directive contributes to the attainment of freedom of establishment, there are various indications that contribution to free movement of capital seems to be the main or predominant purpose or component of the Directive. If this is the main or predominant purpose or component indeed, the Community legislature has, in short, incorrectly based the Directive on shareholder rights also on Article 44 EC (instead of just Article 95 EC). (The incorrect reference to Article 44 EC as a (second) legal basis for the Directive, arguably, is a 'purely formal defect', which does not render the Directive invalid).

2. *Ibid.*

6. Second, as to limits applying to the *exercise* of the competence of the European Community, this exercise in the field of company law of the Community competences under Articles 44, 95 and 308 EC, must be in keeping with in particular the principle of subsidiarity and with Article 43 EC. The principle of subsidiarity is set out in the second paragraph of Article 5 EC, according to which, in areas which do not fall within its exclusive competence, the Community is to take action only if and in so far as the objectives of the proposed action cannot be sufficiently achieved by the Member States and can therefore, by reason of the scale or effects of the proposed action, be better achieved at Community level. Most Community competences, including those in the field of company law, are non-exclusive. Accordingly, when these competences are exercised, the principle of subsidiarity must be complied with.

One should not overestimate the limits subsidiarity places on the Community legislature. From the case-law of the Court of Justice, it follows that where the objectives of a Community measure seek to eliminate the barriers raised by the differences which exist between the Member States' laws, the requirements of the subsidiarity principle will be readily met.

It is regularly claimed in the literature that the principle of subsidiarity holds a commitment to regulatory competition, in the sense that *as a rule regulatory competition* between Member States is the means to achieve the goals of the proposed action. This view, however: (i) may from an economic viewpoint not necessarily be wise policy; (ii) does not find support in the *Protocol on the application of the principles of subsidiarity and proportionality*, which expressly allows Community action within the limits of its powers to be *expanded* where *circumstances so require* and conversely, to be *restricted* or discontinued where it is no longer justified; (iii) does not seem to fit well with the case-law of the Court of Justice in *Centros* and *Inspire Art* and in its case-law on subsidiarity.

7. In the exercise of its powers, the Community legislature is further bound by Article 43 EC. This article prohibits – in short – restrictions on freedom of establishment and not only applies to the *Member States* but (as an analysis of the case-law of the Court of Justice shows) also applies to the *Community* legislature as well. It is of regular occurrence that company law specialists contend that certain provisions of EC company law are in breach of Article 43 EC. The reciprocity rule – included in the Directive on takeover bids – and the so-called 'real seat' arrangement adopted by the SE Regulation may be quoted as the most prominent examples of such provisions. Also, the minimum capital requirement of the Second Directive is believed to constitute a restriction on freedom of establishment. Whereas the correctness of the above prevailing views on the reciprocity rule and 'real seat' arrangement, as well as that on the minimum capital requirement, must be seriously questioned, other provisions of EC company law (do) seem to be contrary to Article 43 EC, namely the head office requirement for formation of an SE and the authorization procedure for transfer of the registered office of an SE.

Annex I

Pre-action Plan Company Law Instruments

This Annex contains an overview of the pre-Action Plan company law instruments, meaning EC company law instruments which already existed or which had been proposed at the time of publication of the Commission's Action Plan, in May 2003. The Action Plan itself, conveniently, contains a 'List of Existing and Proposed European Company Law Instruments'. This 2003 list is brought up to date in this Annex. Where an instrument has been repealed, this is indicated. As regards, specifically, the proposed company law instruments just referred to, it is noted that they have actually been adopted. These meanwhile adopted company law instruments are: (1) the Council Regulation on a statute for a European Cooperative Society; (2) the Directive of the European Parliament and of the Council amending Council Directive 68/151/EEC, as regards disclosure requirements in respect of certain types of companies; and (3) the Directive of the European Parliament and of the Council on takeover bids. There are two exceptions: proposed company law instruments which have not been adopted, namely: (1) the Amended Proposal for a Council Regulation on a statute for a European Association and (2) the Amended Proposal for a Council Regulation on a statute for a European Mutual Society. These instruments, however, have been incorporated in the Action Plan.[1] Consequently, they are not dealt with here, but are dealt with in Annex II.

Following the 'List of Existing and Proposed European Company Law Instruments', on which this Annex is based, publication references concern, the original regulation or directive (or recommendation), and not any subsequent amending acts. The amendments or even consolidated text versions of the EC company law instruments can be found on the 'Eur-Lex' website: <http://eur-lex.europa.eu>.

1. See Action Plan, *sub* 3.6.

First, regulations will be dealt with, then directives, and finally recommendations. Within this categorization, specific instruments are arranged in chronological order.

I. REGULATIONS

- *Regulation on the European Economic Interest Grouping (EEIG)* (1985),[2] based on Article 235 EC Treaty (now Article 308 EC). The EEIG is an EC legal form of association. Even though an EEIG has the capacity, in its own name, to have rights and obligations of all kinds, to make contracts or accomplish other legal acts, and to sue and be sued,[3] the Member States had to determine, through implementing legislation, whether or not EEIGs were to have legal personality.[4]
- *Regulation on the Statute for a European company (SE)*[5] and the accompanying *Directive supplementing the SE with regard to the involvement of employees* (2001),[6] both based on Article 308 EC. The SE forms an(other) EC legal form of enterprise. The SE has legal personality.[7] An SE can be set up, *inter alia*, by merger of two or more existing public limited companies from at least two different Member States.[8] The Regulation thus provides for the possibility of cross-border mergers. The Regulation contains another facility: it allows an SE registered in Member State A to move its registered office to Member State B without having to wind up the company in Member State A and re-register it in Member State B.[9]

  Under the accompanying Directive on employee involvement, the creation of an SE requires negotiations on the involvement of employees with a body representing all employees of the companies concerned. If it proves impossible to negotiate a mutually-satisfactory arrangement then a set of standard principles applies, the exact nature of which depends on the format for worker participation in the companies concerned before the SE was set up.[10]

---

2. Council Regulation (EEC) No. 2137/85 of 25 Jul. 1985 on the European Economic Interest Grouping (EEIG), OJ 1985 L 199, 1.
3. Article 1(2) EEIG Regulation.
4. Article 1(3) EEIG Regulation.
5. Council Regulation (EC) No. 2157/2001 of 8 Oct. 2001 on the Statute for a European company (SE), OJ 2001 L 294, 1.
6. Council Directive 2001/86/EC of 8 Oct. 2001 supplementing the Statute for a European company with regard to the involvement of employees, OJ 2001 L 294, 22.
7. Article 1(3) SE Regulation.
8. Article 2(1) *jo*. Art. 17–31 SE Regulation.
9. Article 8 SE Regulation; see further MEMO/01/314 of 8 Oct. 2001 (The European Company – Frequently Asked Questions).
10. See, for this abstract, IP/04/1195 of 8 Oct. 2004 (Company law: European Company Statute in force, but national delays stop companies using it).

- *Regulation on the application of international accounting standards* (2002),[11] based on Article 95 EC. This Regulation, which forms part of the 1999 Financial Services Action Plan,[12] requires listed companies, including banks and insurance companies, to prepare their consolidated accounts in accordance with international accounting standards (IAS and IFRS) from 2005 onwards.[13] Member States have the option of extending the requirements of this Regulation to unlisted companies and to the production of individual accounts.[14]
- *Regulation on the Statute for a European Cooperative Society (SCE)*[15] and the accompanying *Directive supplementing the Statute for a European Cooperative Society with regard to the involvement of employees* (2003),[16] both based on Article 308 EC. Both instruments are broadly based on those relating to the European Company (SE), with the changes required by the specific characteristics of cooperative societies.[17] An SCE, which has legal personality, should have as its principal object the satisfaction of its members' needs and/or the development of their economic and/or social activities, in particular through the conclusion of agreements with them to supply goods or services or to execute work of the kind that the SCE carries out or commissions.[18]

---

11. Regulation (EC) No. 1606/2002 of the European Parliament and of the Council of 19 Jul. 2002 on the application of international accounting standards, OJ 2002 L 243, 1. See also Commission Regulation (EC) No. 1126/2008 of 3 Nov. 2008 adopting certain international accounting standards in accordance with Regulation (EC) No. 1606/2002 of the European Parliament and of the Council, OJ 2008 L 320, 1.
12. Financial Services: Implementing the Framework for financial markets – Action Plan, Communication of the Commission, COM (1999) 232 of 11 May 1999 (hereinafter also: FSAP).
13. The IAS were issued by the International Accounting Standards Committee (IASC); the IFRS are issued by the International Accounting Standards Board (IASB), the successor of the IASC. See the seventh recital in the preamble to Regulation 1606/2002 and further the so-called Tenth Progress Report, 3. Since adoption of the FSAP (see previous fn.), the Commission has reported biannually to the Council on the progress on the implementation of the FSAP. The Tenth Progress Report just referred to is of Jun. 2004. Art. 2 of Regulation 1606/2002 provides that for the purposes of the Regulation: '"international accounting standards" shall mean International Accounting Standards (IAS), International Financial Reporting Standards (IFRS) and related Interpretations (SIC-IFRIC interpretations), subsequent amendments to those standards and related interpretations, future standards and related interpretations issued or adopted by the International Accounting Standards Board (IASB)'.
14. Article 5 Regulation 1606/2002. See also IP/02/827 of 7 Jun. 2002 (Agreement on IAS will help investors and boost business in EU).
15. Council Regulation (EC) No. 1435/2003 of 22 Jul. 2003 on the Statute for a European Cooperative Society (SCE), OJ 2003 L 207, 1. This is an EC company law instrument which had only been proposed (not adopted) at the time of publication of the ACTION PLAN.
16. Council Directive 2003/72/EC of 22 Jul. 2003 supplementing the Statute for a European Cooperative Society with regard to the involvement of employees, OJ 2003 L 207, 25.
17. Council Press Release 11598/03 (Presse 215), 2524th Council Meeting (Agriculture and fisheries) of 22 Jul. 2003, IX. For a survey of these specific characteristics, see recitals 7–9 in the preamble to the SCE Regulation.
18. Article 1(3) SCE Regulation.

II. DIRECTIVES[19]

- The *First Directive* (1968) concerns the disclosure, the power of representation of the organs, the validity of transactions entered into by, and the nullity of companies with limited liability.[20] This Directive was amended soon after publication of the Action Plan.[21]
- The *Second Directive* (1976) concerns the formation of public limited liability companies and the maintenance and alteration of their capital.[22]
- The *Fourth Directive* (1978) relates to the presentation and content of annual accounts and annual reports of companies with limited liability, to the valuation rules, and to the publication of the annual reports and annual accounts; it furthermore provides for a system of auditing.[23]
- The *Third Directive* (1978) concerns mergers between public limited liability companies from the same Member State.[24]
- The *Sixth Directive* (1982) concerns divisions involving public limited liability companies from the same Member State.[25] This Directive does not carry with it a compulsory introduction into the law of the Member States of the restructuring facility of 'division'.[26]

19. Unless stated otherwise, these Directives are based on Art. 54(3)(g) of the EC Treaty.
20. First Council Directive (EEC) 68/151 of 9 Mar. 1968 on coordination of safeguards which, for the protection of the interests of members and others, are required by Member States of companies within the meaning of the second paragraph of Art. 58 of the Treaty, with a view to making such safeguards equivalent throughout the Community, OJ 1968 L 65, 8.
21. See Directive 2003/58/EC of the European Parliament and of the Council of 15 Jul. 2003 amending Council Directive 68/151/EEC, as regards disclosure requirements in respect of certain types of companies, OJ 2003 L 221, 13. This amending Directive is an EC company law instrument which had only been proposed (not adopted) at the time of publication of the ACTION PLAN. For an overview of the amendments brought about by the Directive, see IP/03/828 of 11 Jun. 2003 (Company law: Commission welcomes Council adoption of a Directive simplifying and modernising the provision of company information).
22. Second Council Directive (EEC) 77/91 of 13 Dec. 1976 on coordination of safeguards which, for the protection of the interests of members and others, are required by Member States of companies within the meaning of the second paragraph of Art. 58 of the Treaty, in respect of the formation of public limited liability companies and the maintenance and alteration of their capital, with a view to making such safeguards equivalent throughout the Community, OJ 1977 L 26, 1.
23. Fourth Council Directive (EEC) 78/660 of 25 Jul. 1978 based on Art. 54(3)(g) of the Treaty on the annual accounts of certain types of companies, OJ 1978 L 222, 11.
24. Third Council Directive (EEC) 78/855 of 9 Oct. 1978 based on Art. 54(3)(g) of the Treaty concerning mergers of public limited liability companies, OJ 1978 L 295, 36.
25. Sixth Council Directive (EEC) 82/891 of 17 Dec. 1982 based on Art. 54(3)(g) of the Treaty, concerning the division of public limited liability companies, OJ 1982 L 378, 47.
26. See Art. 1 Sixth Directive and, in this connection, the ninth recital in the preamble to the Directive, which states: 'Whereas the protection of the interests of members and third parties requires that the laws of the Member States relating to divisions of public limited liability companies be coordinated where the Member States permit such operations.'

- The *Seventh Directive* (1983) coordinates national laws on consolidated accounts (i.e., group accounts) of companies with limited liability.[27]
- The *Eighth Directive* (1984) deals primarily with the approval of statutory auditors in Member States.[28] This Directive has been repealed (and replaced by Directive 2006/43/EC of the European Parliament and Council of 17 May 2006, see Annex II).
- The *Eleventh Directive* (1989) concerns disclosure requirements imposed in a Member State in respect of branches of companies with limited liability governed by the law of another State, in order to provide an equivalent level of protection for shareholders and third parties.[29]
- The *Twelfth Directive* (1989), which is based on Article 54 of the EC Treaty, concerns single-member private limited liability companies.[30] A (private limited liability) company may have a sole member when it is formed and also when all its shares come to be held by a single person (single-member company). The Directive contains specific disclosure and recording requirements.[31]
- The *Directive on takeover bids* (2004)[32] is based on Article 44(1) EC.[33] This Directive, which forms part of the 1999 Financial Services Action Plan,[34] pursues the general objectives of integrating European markets in line with the Financial Services Action Plan just mentioned and of undertaking

---

27. Seventh Council Directive (EEC) 83/349 of 13 Jun. 1983 based on the Art. 54(3)(g) of the Treaty on consolidated accounts, OJ 1983 L 193, 1.
28. Eighth Council Directive (EEC) 84/253 of 10 Apr. 1984 based on Art. 54(3)(g) of the Treaty on the approval of persons responsible for carrying out the statutory audits of accounting documents, OJ 1984 L 126, 20.
29. Eleventh Council Directive (EEC) 89/666 of 21 Dec. 1989 concerning disclosure requirements in respect of branches opened in a Member State by certain types of company governed by the law of another State, OJ 1989 L 395, 36.
30. Twelfth Council Company Law Directive (EEC) 89/667 of 21 Dec. 1989 on single-member private limited liability companies, OJ 1989 L 395, 40.
31. The Directive is also applicable where a Member State allows single-member companies in the case of public limited companies (Art. 6).
32. Directive 2004/25/EC of the European Parliament and of the Council of 21 Apr. 2004 on takeover bids, OJ 2004 L 142, 12. This is an EC company law instrument which had only been proposed (not adopted) at the time of publication of the Action Plan.
33. Note that its preamble (first recital) also refers to Art. 44(2)(g) EC. This Directive on takeover bids is often, but mistakenly, referred to as the Thirteenth Directive on Company Law. This has its origins, presumably, in the legislative history of the Directive. Originally, the Commission had presented proposals for a 'Thirteenth Directive' concerning takeover bids. The proposal which has led to the Directive now in force, however, did no longer provide for a numbered directive. It should further be noted, that the words 'company law' do not feature in the title of any of the Directives just dealt with, with the exception of the 'Twelfth Council Company Law Directive.'
34. The fact that the Directive under consideration has its origins in the Financial Services Action Plan ('Financial Services: Implementing the Framework for financial markets – Action Plan, Communication of the Commission', COM (1999) 232 of 11 May 1999) is explicitly confirmed in: Commission Proposal for a Directive of the European Parliament and of the Council on takeover bids, OJ 2003 C 45 E, 1 (Explanatory Memorandum, *sub* 1).

harmonization conducive to corporate restructuring, it sets out to strengthen the legal certainty of cross-border takeover bids in the interests of all concerned and to ensure protection for minority shareholders in the course of such transactions.[35]

III. RECOMMENDATIONS

The 2003 Action Plan referred to three (then already existing) Recommendations. The Recommendations are all in the field of 'Financial Reporting' (accounting and auditing).[36]

- *Recommendation on quality assurance for the statutory audit in the European Union* (2000),[37] based on Article 221, second indent EC.
- *Recommendation on the recognition, measurement, and disclosure of environmental issues in the annual accounts and annual reports of companies* (2001),[38] based on Article 221 EC.
- *Recommendation on statutory auditors' independence* (2002),[39] based on Article 221, second indent EC.

---

35. Proposal, just cited, (Explanatory Memorandum, *sub* 1); IP/02/1402 of 2 Oct. 2002 (Company law: Commission proposes a transparent framework for takeover bids), 2.
36. Just to be clear, it is noted that the first and third Recommendation listed below have not been repealed by Directive 2006/43/EC on statutory audits. Recital 4 in the preamble to this Directive (even) refers to the first and third Recommendations. See further recital 11.
37. Commission Recommendation 2001/256/EC of 15 Nov. 2000 on quality assurance for the statutory audit in the European Union: minimum requirements, OJ 2001 L 91, 91. See also Commission Recommendation 2008/362/EC of 6 May 2008 on external quality assurance for statutory auditors and audit firms auditing public interest entities, OJ 2008 L 120, 20. In recital 5 in the preamble to this latter Recommendation, it is stated that: 'it is appropriate to provide for a new Recommendation which is more in line with the current state of affairs than Recommendation 2001/256/EC and which takes into account new international trends as well as specific needs of the Member States'. The Recommendation, however, does not contain a provision which withdraws Recommendation 2001/256/EC.
38. Commission Recommendation 2001/453/EC of 30 May 2001 on the recognition, measurement, and disclosure of environmental issues in the annual accounts and annual reports of companies, OJ 2001 L 156, 33.
39. Commission Recommendation 2002/590/EC of 16 May 2002, Statutory Auditors' Independence in the EU: A Set of Fundamental Principles, OJ 2002 L 191, 22. See further IP/02/723 of 16 May 2002 (Auditing: Commission issues Recommendation on independence of statutory auditors).

Annex II
Action Plan Company Law Instruments

This Annex provides an overview of EC company law instruments which are part of the Action Plan. First, in section I, the instruments which have been adopted will be dealt with. Initiatives for company law instruments in respect of which the Commission has decided that there will be no (further) action are included at the end of the section. Then, in section II, the still remaining actions for which implementation has begun, but is not yet completed, will be examined.

As in Annex I, publication references concern the original directive or recommendation and not any subsequent amending acts. The amendments or even consolidated text versions of the EC company law instruments can be found on the 'Eur-Lex' website: <http://eur-lex.europa.eu>.

I. ADOPTED COMPANY LAW INSTRUMENTS

A. Directives

- The *Directive on cross-border mergers* (2005), based on Article 44 EC.[1] In the Action Plan, the Commission made clear its intention to present in the short term (2003–2005) a proposal for a Directive on cross-border mergers.[2] Already in November 2003, the Commission offered its proposal.[3] The proposed Directive was the first measure which was presented

1. Directive 2005/56/EC of the European Parliament and of the Council of 26 Oct. 2005 on cross-border mergers of limited liability companies, OJ 2005 L 310, 1–9.
2. Action Plan, *sub* 3.4. (Corporate restructuring and mobility) and 25.
3. Proposal for a Directive of the European Parliament and of the Council on cross-border mergers of companies with share capital, COM (2003) 703 of 18 Nov. 2003.

under the Action Plan.[4] The Directive covers all 'limited liability companies'.[5] The basic principle underlying the cross-border merger procedure is that – save as otherwise provided by the Directive for reasons to do with the cross-border nature of the merger – each company remains subject to its national law on domestic mergers. In other words, each company taking part in a cross-border merger will do so in accordance with the laws of its own Member State.[6] One of the main issues at stake during the adoption process was the provision on employee participation, given the widely diverging systems in force in Member States, and the related question of how to deal with cross-border mergers implying a loss or a reduction of employee participation. This issue, incidentally, had led to deadlock over an earlier (1984) proposal. Under the adopted Directive, employee participation schemes should apply to cross-border mergers where at least one of the merging companies already operates under such a scheme. Employee participation in the newly created company will be subject to negotiations based on the model of the European Company Statute.[7]

- The *Directive on statutory audits* (2006), based on Article 44(2)(g) EC.[8] The Action Plan regards as an initiative related to, but not a part of, the Action Plan itself 'The Communication on the priorities for the statutory audit in the EU.' This Communication covers various issues, including the modernization of the Eighth Company Law Directive into a comprehensive principles-based approach.[9] From this perspective, the Directive too might be regarded as not an Action Plan company law instrument. The Directive, however, does also contain some amendments to EC company law instruments.

  The objectives of this Directive are: requiring the application of a single set of international auditing standards, the updating of the educational requirements, the definition of professional ethics, and the technical implementation of the cooperation between competent authorities of Member States and between those authorities and the authorities of third countries, in order further to enhance and harmonize the quality of statutory audit in the

4. IP/03/1564 of 18 Nov. 2003 (Company law: Commission proposes Directive on cross-border mergers). There was no consultation on the planned measure. In this context, the following observation by the Commission deserves mentioning: 'In the light of this state of affairs and of the fact that the parties have had an opportunity to comment on the broad lines of the proposal, both as part of the consultations carried out by the High Level Group of Company Law Experts and as part of those on the above-mentioned Commission communication of 21 May 2003, further consultations and impact assessment on the present proposal, the speedy adoption of which is wished for by the interests concerned, have not been considered necessary.' See the Explanatory Memorandum to the proposal, 3.
5. See Art. 1.
6. Article 4.
7. Article 16, about which IP/05/1487 of 29 Nov. 2005 (Company law: cross-border mergers Directive adopted and published), 1.
8. Directive 2006/43/EC of the European Parliament and Council of 17 May 2006 on statutory audits of annual accounts and consolidated accounts, amending Council Directives 78/660/EEC and 83/349/EEC and repealing Council Directive 84/253/EEC, OJ 2006 L 157, 87–107.
9. See ACTION PLAN, 4.

Community and to facilitate cooperation between Member States and with third countries so as to strengthen confidence in the statutory audit.

With a view to rendering the relationship between the statutory auditor or audit firm and the audited entity more transparent, Directives 78/660/EEC (i.e., the *Fourth Directive*) and 83/349/EEC (i.e., the *Seventh Directive*) are amended to require disclosure of the audit fee and the fee paid for non-audit services in the notes to the annual accounts and the consolidated accounts.

Directive 84/253/EEC (i.e., the *Eighth Directive*) is repealed because it lacks a comprehensive set of rules to ensure an appropriate audit infrastructure, such as public oversight, disciplinary systems, and systems of quality assurance, and because it does not provide specifically for regulatory cooperation between Member States and third countries.

- The *Directive Amending the Fourth and Seventh Directive* (2006), based on Article 44(1) EC.[10] The Action Plan designated as short-term priorities (2003–2005), *inter alia*, to: (1) confirm the collective responsibility of board members;[11] (2) increase transparency in transactions with related parties,[12] and (3) improve disclosure about corporate governance practices applied in a company.[13] The Commission originally intended to propose three separate proposals.[14] Because of the close 'interlinkage' between the three initiatives and in order to ensure coherence, however, it decided that it would make one comprehensive proposal.[15] Before it presented the proposal, the Commission carried out an open consultation on the planned measures in spring 2004.[16] The adopted Directive indeed (1) confirms the collective responsibility of board members for drawing up and publishing annual accounts and annual reports;[17] (2) increases transparency

10. Directive 2006/46/EC of the European Parliament and Council of 14 Jun. 2006 amending Council Directives 78/660/EEC on the annual accounts of certain types of companies, 83/349/EEC on consolidated accounts, 86/635/EEC on the annual accounts and consolidated accounts of banks and other financial institutions and 91/674/EEC on the annual accounts and consolidated accounts of insurance undertakings, OJ 2006 L 224, 1–7.
11. Action Plan, *sub* 3.1.3 (Modernising the board of directors) and 24.
12. Action Plan, *sub* 3.1.1 (Enhancing Corporate Governance disclosure – Annual Corporate Governance Statement, in particular *sub* d and e); Action Plan, *sub* 3.3 (Groups & Pyramids, *sub* Financial and non-financial information).
13. Action Plan, *sub* 3.1.1 (Enhancing Corporate Governance disclosure) and 24.
14. See the questionnaire drawn up by the Commission with a view to the consultation on the proposed measures. The questionnaire can be found at: <http://ec.europa.eu/internal_market/>.
15. See questionnaire, just cited.
16. That is to say, a consultation on the basis of an on-line, largely multiple-choice questionnaire, just cited. The consultation was launched on 22 Apr. 2004 and closed on 4 Jun. 2004. The responses to this consultation were published in (according to Explanatory Memorandum to the proposal, 3) Sep. 2004. For these responses, see: European Commission Internal Market DG Financial Markets, Accounting and auditing, G5 D(2004), 'Synthesis of the Ipm-Consultation, including substantiated comments received beyond', which document can be downloaded from: <http://ec.europa.eu/internal_market/>.
17. See e.g., Art. 1(8).

in transactions with related parties and off-balance-sheet arrangements;[18] and (3) improves disclosure about corporate governance practices applied in a company (the annual corporate governance statement).[19] Note, finally, that the 2006 Directive is based on Article 44(1) EC, whereas the original (amended) Directives had been based on Article 54(3)(g) EEC (now Article 44(2)(g) EC). The Community legislature does not provide an explanation for this.

- The *Directive amending the Second Directive* (2006), based on Article 44(1) EC.[20] The Second Directive[21] of 1976 coordinates national provisions on the formation of public limited liability companies, minimum share capital requirements, distributions to shareholders, and increases and reductions in capital. The Directive establishes the conditions to ensure that the capital of the company is maintained in the interest of creditors. Furthermore, it protects minority shareholders and states the principle that all shareholders who are in the same position should be treated equally.[22] In its Action Plan, the Commission considered simplification of the Second Directive as a priority for the short term (2003–2005).[23] To realize this priority, the Commission presented a proposal for a Directive in October 2004.[24]

  The Directive was adopted in September 2006. Under the amended Directive, Member States are able to permit public limited liability companies to allot shares for consideration other than in cash without requiring them to obtain a special expert valuation in cases in which there is a clear

18. See e.g., Art. 1(6).
19. See e.g., Art. 1(7).
20. Directive 2006/68/EC of the European Parliament and Council of 6 Sep. 2006 amending Council Directive 77/91/EEC as regards the formation of public limited liability companies and the maintenance and alteration of their capital, OJ 2006 L 264, 32–36.
21. See Annex I.
22. See, for this abstract, IP/04/1334 of 29 Oct. 2004 (Company law: Commission proposes to simplify the formation, maintenance and alteration of companies' capital).
23. Action Plan, *sub* 3.2 (Capital Maintenance and Alteration); Action Plan, *sub* 3.4 (Corporate restructuring and mobility, *sub* squeeze-out rights and sell-out rights) and 24.
24. Proposal for a Directive of the European Parliament and of the Council amending Council Directive 77/91/EEC, as regards the formation of public limited liability companies and the maintenance and alteration of their capital, COM (2004) 730 of 29 Oct. 2004 (see OJ 2005 C 24, 8). The full text of the proposal and a working document containing further detailed information are available at the Commission's Internal Market website: <http://ec.europa.eu/internal_market/>. See further IP/04/1334, just cited.

    The proposal was not preceded by a consultation. It may, however, be referred to the proposals for reform at EU and UK level of the law of capital maintenance by the Interdisciplinary Group on Capital Maintenance of Jun. 2004. This Group was established by J. Rickford (Director of the Company Law Centre, The British Institute of International and Comparative Law) and M. Keegan (Chairman of the Accounting Standards Board). See J. Rickford (ed.), 'Reforming Capital. Report of the Interdisciplinary Group on Capital Maintenance (Jun. 2004)', *EBLR* 15 (2004): 919–1027.

point of reference for the valuation of such consideration.[25] Member States may permit public limited liability companies to acquire their own shares up to the limit of the company's distributable reserves. Also, the period for which such an acquisition may be authorized by the general meeting is increased so as to enhance flexibility and reduce the administrative burden for companies which have to react promptly to market developments affecting the price of their shares.[26] Member States may permit public limited liability companies to grant financial assistance with a view to the acquisition of their shares by a third party up to the limit of the company's distributable reserves (so as to increase flexibility with regard to changes in the ownership structure of the share capital of companies). This possibility is subject to safeguards, having regard to the Directive's objective of protecting both shareholders and third parties.[27]

Note, finally, that – as with the Directive amending the Fourth and Seventh Directive – the 2006 Directive is based on Article 44(1) EC, whereas the original (amended) Directive had been based on Article 54(3)(g) EEC (now Article 44(2)(g) EC). The Community legislature does not provide an explanation for this.

– The *Shareholder Rights Directive* (2007), based on Article 44 EC and Article 95 EC.[28] In the Action Plan on company law, it was announced that improving the rights of shareholders of companies across the Member States was a priority for the short term (2003–2005). This would include (1) the right to ask questions, (2) the right to table resolutions, (3) the right to vote in absentia and (4) the right to participate in general meetings via electronic means. These facilities should be offered to shareholders across the EU and specific problems relating to cross-border voting should be solved. The Commission considered that the necessary framework should be developed in a Directive.[29]

In implementation of the Action Plan, the Commission launched a public consultation on facilitating the exercise of basic shareholders' rights in company general meetings and solving problems in the cross-border exercise of such rights, particularly voting rights.[30] The Commission's

25. See Art. 10A and 10B.
26. See Art. 19(1).
27. See Art. 23(1).
28. Directive 2007/36/EC of the European Parliament and of the Council of 11 Jul. 2007 on the exercise of certain rights of shareholders in listed companies, OJ 2007 L 184, 17–24.
29. Action Plan, *sub* 3.1.2 ('Strengthening shareholders' rights', *sub* 'Other shareholders' rights') and 24. Here 'Other shareholder rights' means other than access to information rights, which are dealt with under the preceding heading, still *sub* 3.1.2. With respect to this latter category, it can be referred to Directive 2004/109/EC of the European Parliament and of the Council of 15 Dec. 2004 on the harmonisation of transparency requirements in relation to information about issuers whose securities are admitted to trading on a regulated market and amending Directive 2001/34/EC, OJ 2004 L 390, 38.
30. IP/04/1107 of 16 Sep. 2004 (Corporate governance: Commission consults on shareholders' rights).

consultation paper 'Fostering an appropriate regime for shareholders' rights'[31] gave first indications as to the possible future EU regime on shareholders' rights in listed companies.

The consultation started in September and closed in December 2004.[32] The Commission indicated to take the results of the consultation into account in a forthcoming proposal for a Directive.[33] In April 2005, the Commission published a report summarizing the responses to the consultation.[34]

In light of the responses to the consultation,[35] the Commission decided to launch a second public consultation.[36] For the purpose of the consultation, a second (consultation) paper was published.[37] The objective of this second consultation was 'to prompt comments on specific potential follow-up measures in the areas covered by the first consultation document, with a special emphasis on cross-border voting'.[38]

The consultation started in May and closed in July 2005.[39] Again, the Commission indicated to take the results of the consultation into account in a (then) forthcoming proposal for a Directive.[40] The Commission came forward with a proposal in January 2006; the Directive was adopted in July 2007. The Directive establishes requirements in relation to the exercise of certain shareholder rights attaching to voting shares in relation to general meetings of companies which have their registered office in a Member State and whose shares are admitted to trading on a regulated market situated or operating within a Member State. The Directive contains provisions on: (1) equal treatment of shareholders (Article 4); information prior to the general meeting (Article 5); the right to put items on the agenda of the general meeting and to table draft resolutions (Article 6); requirements for participation and voting in the general meeting (Article 7); participation in the general meeting by electronic means (Article 8); the right to ask questions (Article 9); proxy voting (Article 10); voting by correspondence

---

31. The consultation paper is available at the Commission's Internal Market website: <http://ec.europa.eu/internal_market/>.
32. IP/04/1107, just cited, 2; consultation paper, just cited, 4.
33. IP/04/1107, just cited, 1.
34. Synthesis of the comments on the consultation document of the services of the Internal Market Directorate-General 'Fostering an appropriate regime for shareholders' rights'. A working document of DG Internal Market (Apr. 2005). The synthesis is published on the Commission's Internal Market website: <http://ec.europa.eu/internal_market/>.
35. Consultation paper (13 May 2005), cited below, 3.
36. IP/05/561 of 13 May 2005 (Corporate governance: Commission consults on minimum standards that should apply to shareholders' rights).
37. Consultation paper 'Fostering an Appropriate Regime for Shareholders' Rights. Second consultation by the Services of the Internal Market Directorate General' (13 May 2005). The consultation paper is published on the Commission's Internal Market website: <http://ec.europa.eu/internal_market/>.
38. Consultation paper (13 may 2005), just cited, 3.
39. See IP/05/561, just cited.
40. *Ibid.*

(Article 12); the removal of certain impediments to the effective exercise of voting rights (Article 13); and, voting results (Article 14).

- The *Directive amending the Third and Sixth Directive* (2007), based on Article 44(2)(g) EC.[41] The High Level Group of Company Law Experts had made various recommendations relating to restructuring transactions, including that some of the requirements foreseen by the Third Company Law Directive (mergers of public limited liability companies) and by the Sixth Company Law Directive (division of such companies) should be relaxed in specific cases which make them superfluous. In its 2003 Action Plan, the Commission considered that the simplification of restructuring transactions pursued by this proposed relaxation of some of the requirements foreseen by the Third Directive and the Sixth Directive was desirable insofar as the necessary safeguards were ensured. The Commission noted that this simplification was not perceived by the High Level Group as an immediate priority, and therefore the Commission intended to take the necessary initiatives in the medium term (2006–2008).[42]

  In November 2007, the Directive was adopted. The changes made by this Directive were inspired by the Directive on cross-border mergers of limited liability companies. This latter Directive provides for an exemption from the obligation to have the draft terms of merger examined by independent experts and a report drawn up by such experts for the shareholders of the companies involved in the merger, if all the shareholders agree that such a report is not needed. The Third Directive concerning mergers of public limited liability companies did not contain any similar exemption in respect of the draft terms of merger, while the Sixth Directive concerning the division of public limited liability companies left it to the Member States whether or not to provide for such an exemption in respect of the draft terms of division. According to the Community legislature of the Directive amending the Third and Sixth Directive, there is no reason to require such an examination by an independent expert for the shareholders if all the shareholders agree that it may be dispensed with. The Third and Sixth Directive were therefore amended accordingly.

B. Recommendations

- *Recommendation on directors' remuneration* (2004), based on Article 221 EC.[43] In its Action Plan, the Commission had stated that

41. Directive 2007/63/EC of the European Parliament and of the Council of 13 Nov. 2007 amending Council Directives 78/855/EEC and 82/891/EEC as regards the requirement of an independent expert's report on the occasion of merger or division of public limited liability companies, OJ 2007 L 300, 47–48.
42. See Action Plan, 21 and 26.
43. Commission Recommendation 2004/913/EC of 14 Dec. 2004, fostering an appropriate regime for the remuneration of directors of listed companies, OJ 2004 L 385, 55. Agreement on this

shareholders should be able to appreciate fully the relation between the performance of the company and the level of remuneration of directors, both *ex ante* and *ex post*, and that they should be able to make decisions on the remuneration items linked to the share price. To this end, a Commission Recommendation should be adopted. The Commission regarded this action as key to the restoration of confidence and intended to adopt such a Recommendation in the short term (2003–2005).[44] The Recommendation on directors' remuneration was then adopted in December 2004.

The non-binding Recommendation invites Member States to adopt measures in four areas. First, the remuneration policy should be considered. All listed companies should release a statement of their policy on directors' remuneration for the following year. It should include information on the breakdown of fixed and variable remuneration, on performance criteria and on the parameters for annual bonus schemes or non-cash benefits. It should also explain the company's contract policy. The company should not have to disclose commercially-sensitive information.[45]

Second, the shareholders meeting should be considered. Remuneration policy for directors should be on the agenda of the shareholders' general meeting. In order to increase accountability, the remuneration policy should be submitted to a vote which may be either binding or advisory. An advisory vote would require neither the directors' contractual entitlement nor the remuneration policy to be amended.[46]

Third, disclosure of the remuneration of individual directors should be considered. This should include detailed information about the remuneration and/or emoluments of individual directors; the shares or rights to share options granted to them; their contribution to supplementary pension schemes; and any loans, advances, or guarantees to each director.[47]

Fourth, approval of share and share option schemes should be considered. Variable remuneration schemes under which directors are paid in shares, share options, or any other right to acquire shares should be subject to prior approval of the annual general meeting of shareholders. The approval relates to the system of remuneration and the rules applied

---

Recommendation was reached in Oct. 2004. See IP/04/1183 of 6 Oct. 2004 (Directors' pay – Commission sets out guidance on disclosure and shareholder control). See also MEMO/04/231 of 6 Oct. 2004 (European Commission Recommendations on directors' remuneration and the role of non-executive and supervisory directors – frequently asked questions). For a discussion of a draft version of the Recommendation, see S. Maul & G. Lanfermann, 'Europäische Corporate Governance – Stand der Entwicklungen', *BB* (59) 2004, 1866–1867.

44. See Action Plan, 16 and 24.
45. Recommendation, pt. 3.
46. *Ibid.*, pt. 4.
47. *Ibid.*, pt. 5.

to establish individual remuneration under the scheme. It would not relate to the individual remuneration of directors.[48]

- *Recommendation on the role of non-executive and supervisory directors* (2005), based on Article 221 EC.[49] According to the Action Plan, in key areas where executive directors clearly have conflicts of interests, decisions in listed companies should be made exclusively by non-executive or supervisory directors who are in the majority independent. Certain minimum standards of what cannot be considered to be independent should be established at EC level. Moreover, minimum standards applicable to the creation, composition, and role of the nomination, remuneration, and audit committees should be defined. The Commission regarded these measures as key to the restoration of confidence in the markets and therefore intended to adopt a Commission Recommendation to this effect in the short term (2003–2005).[50] The Commission then adopted the Recommendation on the role of non-executive and supervisory directors in February 2005.

  The non-binding Recommendation concentrates on the role of non-executive or supervisory directors in areas where executive or managing directors may have conflicts of interest. It includes minimum standards for the qualifications, commitment, and independence of non-executive or supervisory directors.

  The main principles in the Recommendation may be summarized as follows. First, the administrative, managerial and supervisory bodies should include overall an appropriate balance of executive/managing and non-executive/supervisory directors so that no individual or small group can dominate decision-making.[51]

  Second, boards should be organized so that a sufficient number of independent non-executive or supervisory directors play an effective role in defining and dealing with potential conflicts of interest. To this end, nomination, remuneration, and audit committees should normally be created within the (supervisory) board. The Recommendation defines minimum standards for the creation, composition, and role of those committees.[52]

---

48. *Ibid.*, pt. 6. Summary taken from IP/04/1183, just cited.
49. Commission Recommendation 2005/162/EC, on the role of non-executive or supervisory directors of listed companies and on the committees of the (supervisory) board of 15 Feb. 2005, OJ 2005 L 52, 51. Agreement on this Recommendation was reached in Oct. 2004. See IP/04/1182 of 6 Oct. 2004 (Corporate governance: Commission urges Member States to ensure a strong role for independent directors). See also MEMO/04/231 of 6 Oct. 2004 (European Commission Recommendations on directors' remuneration and the role of non-executive and supervisory directors – frequently asked questions). For a discussion of a draft version of the Recommendation, see Maul & Lanfermann, just cited, 1861–1865.
50. See Action Plan, 15 and 24.
51. Recommendation, pt. 3.1.
52. *Ibid.*, pt. 5.

Third, a director is considered independent when free from any business, family, or other relationship – with the company, its controlling shareholder or the management of either – which might jeopardize his or her judgment.[53]

Fourth, the (supervisory) board should be composed of members who, taken together, have the diversity of knowledge, judgment, and experience to properly complete their tasks.[54]

Fifth, all directors should devote to their duties the necessary time and attention. When the appointment of a director is proposed, his or her other significant professional commitments should be disclosed.[55]

C. Community Bodies

- *European Corporate Governance Forum.* In October 2004, the Commission set up the *European Corporate Governance Forum* to coordinate corporate governance efforts of Member States.[56] The creation of this Forum was one of the short-term initiatives (2003–2005) of the 2003 Action Plan to Modernise Company Law.[57] The Forum is discussed in Chapter 1, to which I refer here.
- *Group of Non-Governmental Experts on Corporate Governance and Company Law.* In April 2005, the Commission set up the Group of Non-Governmental Experts on Corporate Governance and Company Law.[58] The creation of this Group is an initiative not explicitly laid down in the Action Plan. The Group has been established in view of the fact that 'the Action Plan recognises the importance of expert and public consultation as an integral part of the development of company law and corporate governance at Community level'.[59] The Group is discussed in Chapter 1, to which I refer here.

D. No Action

- *European Association and European Mutual Society.* The Commission in its 2003 Action Plan made clear its intention 'to actively support the ongoing legislative process engaged on (. . .) statutes [for a Societas Cooperativa Europaea (SCE), a European Association and a European Mutual

53. *Ibid.*, pt. 13.1.
54. *Ibid.*, pt. 11.1.
55. *Ibid.*, pts. 12.1 and 12.2. Summary taken from IP/04/1182, just cited.
56. Commission Decision 2004/706/EC of 15 Oct. 2004, establishing the European Corporate Governance Forum, OJ 2004 L 321, 53.
57. Action Plan, 24.
58. Commission Decision 2005/380/EC of 28 Apr. 2005, establishing a group of non-governmental experts on corporate governance and company law, OJ 2005 L 126, 40.
59. See the second recital in the preamble to the Decision just cited.

Society]'.[60] This support was (also) in response to the explicit desire expressed by the European Parliament for giving significant attention to the development of new European legal forms of enterprises.[61] In addition to this, the Commission observed that a majority of the responses received in the consultation organized by the High Level Group expressed positive views on the usefulness of these statutes.[62] The statute for a European Cooperative Society was adopted in 2003.[63] The proposals for a Regulation on the statute for a European Association and for a Regulation on a statute for a European Mutual Society, by contrast, were withdrawn in March 2006.[64]

Withdrawal took place following a screening exercise of pending proposals undertaken as part of the Commission's effort for better regulation ('in the framework of the Partnership for Growth and Jobs in the European Union').[65] Withdrawal concerned certain proposals – 68 in total – on which the legislature had not yet reached a decision and which were found not to be consistent with the 'Lisbon and Better Regulation criteria', unlikely to make further progress in the legislative process or found to be no longer topical for objective reasons.[66] Remarkable is that the proposals in question were withdrawn during the public *Consultation on Future Priorities for the Action Plan on Modernising Company Law and Enhancing Corporate Governance in the European Union.*[67] One of the objectives of this consultation was to clarify and evaluate precisely the 'added value of modernising and simplifying European Company Law, *with particular regard to the Better Regulation initiative*'.[68] (emphasis added).

60. Action Plan, 23, *sub* 3.6 (The European Cooperative Society and other EU legal forms of enterprises); and 25.
61. *Ibid.*
62. *Ibid.*
63. See Annex I.
64. 'Withdrawal of Commission proposals following screening for their general relevance, their impact on competitiveness and other aspects', OJ 2006 C 64, 3. The date of publication in the Official Journal (Mar. 2006, as mentioned) may be assumed to be the date of withdrawal. This date, in any case, is (roughly) confirmed in 'A strategic review of better regulation in the European Union' (Commission communication to the European Parliament, the Council, the European Economic and Social Committee, and the Committee of the Regions), COM (2006) 689 of 14 Nov. 2006, 8: 'That is why, upon taking office at the end of 2004, this Commission decided to screen proposals adopted by the previous Commission, pending before the Council and the European Parliament to see if they aligned with the Growth and Jobs priority and met better regulation standards. *68 pending proposals were withdrawn in early 2006.*' (emphasis added).
65. See 'Withdrawal of Commission proposals', just cited.
66. *Ibid.*
67. On this Consultation: IP/05/1639 of 20 Dec. 2005 (Company Law and Corporate Governance: Consultation on Future Priorities for Action Plan).
68. See IP/05/1639, just cited.

– A *Directive on Transfer of the Registered Office*. The Commission, in its Action Plan on company law, undertook to adopt a proposal for a Directive on the cross-border transfer of a company's seat, considering this to be one of its short-term priorities (2003–2005).[69]

In February 2004, the Commission launched an open consultation[70] on an outline of the planned proposal for a 'Directive on the right of limited companies to transfer their registered office from one Member State to another.'[71] The consultation closed in April 2004.[72]

The planned Directive would enable companies to transfer their registered office from the Member State where they are registered (the 'home' Member State) to another Member State (the 'host' Member State). A company transferring its registered office would be registered in the host Member State and would acquire a legal identity there, while at the same time being removed from the register in its home Member State and giving up its legal identity there.[73] If necessary, companies would have to adapt their structures and assets in order to meet the substantive and formal conditions required for registration in the host Member State. However, they would not be obliged to go through liquidation proceedings in their home Member State or to create a new company in the host Member State.[74]

The results of the consultation have been published on the Commission's Internal Market website.[75] The Commission expected to be able to present its proposal for a Directive in September 2004.[76]

However, the Commission decided not to proceed with the Directive in October 2007.[77] In December 2007, the Commission published an impact assessment on the Directive on the cross-border transfer of registered office. The document presents the pros and cons of possible policy actions, also including an evaluation of the consequences of not undertaking any regulatory action in this field. The impact assessment has been validated by the Commission's impact assessment board. Having weighed the arguments advanced, Commissioner McCreevy has decided, as mentioned, that

69. ACTION PLAN, *sub* 3.4 (Corporate Restructuring and Mobility) and 25.
70. That is to say, a consultation on the basis of an on-line, largely multiple-choice questionnaire.
71. IP/04/270 of 26 Feb. 2004 (Company law: Commission consults on the cross border transfer of companies' registered offices). The outline was not laid down in a separate consultation document. The outline was only published as an integrated part of the Commission's Internal Market website: <http://ec.europa.eu/internal_market/>.
72. IP/04/270, just cited.
73. *Ibid.*
74. *Ibid.*
75. See <http://ec.europa.eu/internal_market/>. More detailed qualitative analyses of the results (of the consultation) would be available at a later date. See IP/04/270, just cited. As far as I am able to ascertain, these analyses have not been made public. It can, of course, be referred to the impact assessment on the draft proposal, see fns below.
76. IP/04/270, just cited.
77. SPEECH/07/592 of 3 Oct. 2007 (Speech by Commissioner McCreevy at the European Parliament's Legal Affairs Committee, Brussels).

there is no need for action at EU level on this issue. DG Internal Market and Services has therefore stopped work in this area.[78]

- *'One share, one vote'*. The Commission considered in the Action Plan that there was a strong medium- to long-term case for aiming to establish a real shareholder democracy in the EU.[79] The Commission nevertheless observed that any initiative which would give further effect to the principle of proportionality between capital and control advocated by the High Level Group in its First Report on issues related to takeover bids, required prior study.[80] The Commission therefore intended to undertake a study, in the short to medium term,[81] on the consequences which such an approach would entail.[82]

  The Commission published the external study on the question of proportionality between ownership and control in EU listed companies in June 2007. The study finds that, on the basis of the academic research available, there is no conclusive evidence of a causal link between deviations from the proportionality principle and either the economic performance of listed companies or their governance. However, there is some evidence that investors perceive these mechanisms negatively and consider more transparency would be helpful in making investment decisions.[83] The study was carried out by Institutional Shareholder Services Europe (ISS Europe), the European Corporate Governance Institute (ECGI) and the law firm Shearman & Sterling LLP.[84]

  In October 2007, the Commission decided that 'on the issue of one-share, one vote, there will be no action'.[85] In December 2007, the Commission published an impact assessment on the question of proportionality between capital and control in listed companies (commonly referred as to the 'one share, one vote' problem). The document presents the pros and cons of possible policy actions, also including an evaluation of the consequences of not undertaking any regulatory action in this field. The impact assessment has been validated by the Commission's impact assessment board. Having weighed the arguments advanced, Commissioner

78. See Impact assessment on the Directive on the cross-border transfer of registered office, SEC (2007) 1707 (Commission Staff Working Document) of 12 Dec. 2007. See further G.-J. Vossestein, 'Transfer of the registered office. The European Commission's decision not to submit a proposal for a Directive', *UL Rev.* (2008): 53–65.
79. Action Plan, 14.
80. *Ibid.*
81. *Ibid.* The list of actions attached to the Action Plan categorizes this study, however, as a medium-term initiative (2006–2008).
82. Action Plan, 14 and 25.
83. See IP/07/751 of 4 Jun. 2007 (Commission publishes external study on proportionality between capital and control in EU listed companies).
84. The study is available at the Commission's Internal Market website: <http://ec.europa.eu/internal_market/>.
85. SPEECH/07/592 of 3 Oct. 2007 (Speech by Commissioner McCreevy at the European Parliament's Legal Affairs Committee, Brussels).

McCreevy has, as mentioned, decided there is no need for action at EU level on this issue. DG Internal Market and Services has therefore stopped work in this area.[86]

- *Amendment of the Second Directive.* The High Level Group of Company Law Experts had suggested that adequate protection of shareholders and creditors might be achieved, possibly even more effectively, with the introduction of an alternative regime which would not be based on the concept of legal capital.[87] The Commission considered in its 2003 Action Plan that, before deciding to introduce an alternative regime further work was needed as to both the exact characteristics of a possible alternative regime and its ability to achieve an effective protection of shareholders and third parties. The Commission then proposed to carry out, as a medium-term priority (2006–2008), a study into the feasibility of an alternative to the capital maintenance regime.[88] This study was commissioned in October 2006. It was delivered in January 2008.[89] In the light of the conclusions of the external study, the view of the Commission was that 'the current capital maintenance regime under the Second Company Law Directive does not seem to cause significant operational problems for companies'.[90] Therefore, no follow-up measures or changes to the Second Company law Directive are foreseen in the immediate future, says the Commission.[91]

II. FURTHER INITIATIVES

- Proposal for a Council Regulation on the *Statute for a European private company.*[92] The High Level Group had noted that the Societas Europaea (SE),

86. Impact Assessment on the Proportionality between capital and control in listed companies, SEC (2007) 1705 (Commission Staff Working Document) of 12 Dec. 2007.
87. See: High Level Group Report II, 87; Action Plan, 18.
88. Action Plan, 18 and 25. For alternative studies, see: J. Rickford (ed.), 'Reforming Capital. Report of the Interdisciplinary Group on Capital Maintenance', *EBLR* 15 (Jun. 2004): 919–1027; H. Boschma, M.-L. Lennarts & H. Schutte-Veenstra, *Alternative Systems for Capital Protection* (Deventer: Kluwer, 2005); M. Lutter (ed.), *Legal Capital in Europe* (European Company and Financial Law Review, Special Vol. 1) (Berlin: De Gruyter, 2006).
89. 'Feasibility study on an alternative to the capital maintenance regime established by the Second Company Law Directive 77/91/EEC of 13 Dec. 1976 and an examination of the impact on profit distribution of the new EU-accounting regime', KPMG, *sine loco et anno.* The study is available at the Commission's Internal Market website: <http://ec.europa.eu/internal_market/>.
90. See 'Results of the external study on the feasibility of an alternative to the Capital Maintenance Regime of the Second Company Law Directive and the impact of the adoption of IFRS on profit distribution', 2. This document is available at the Commission's Internal Market website: <http://ec.europa.eu/internal_market/>.
91. *Ibid.*
92. Proposal for a Council Regulation on the Statute for a European private company, COM (2008) 396 of 25 Jun. 2008.

adopted in October 2001, may not meet all expectations of the business community, in particular SMEs, and referred to the development, from a private initiative, of a 'European Private Company' which, as a new legal form at EU level, would primarily serve the needs of SMEs which are active in more than one Member State.[93] Against this background, the Commission in its Action Plan, announced to launch a feasibility study in the short term (2003–2005), with a view to presenting a proposal for an EPC statute ('if the feasibility study confirms the need for such an initiative') in the medium term (2006–2008).[94] In June 2008, the Commission put forward the proposal.

The proposal is based on Article 308 EC. Article 308 EC is also the legal basis of the existing European company forms, that is, the European Company, the European Economic Interest Grouping and the European Cooperative Society.[95] The European Private Company is referred to as 'SPE' after its Latin name *Societas Privata Europaea* that allows the use of the abbreviation SPE without needing to translate it to national languages.

- A *European Foundation.* With respect to the possible development of a proposal for a Regulation on a European Foundation, the Action Plan merely conveyed the Commission's intention to launch a study before it would decide to submit a proposal. The study should be aimed at assessing in depth the feasibility of a statute for a European Foundation. Such an assessment would, in the view of the Commission, have to take account of 'the lessons to be drawn from the adoption and use of the other European statutes', so that it should best take place in the medium term (2006–2008).[96] In October 2007, the Commissioner for the Internal Market Charlie McCreevy informed the European Parliament that work on the European Foundation Statute was at an early stage and that the Commission would shortly engage a contractor to work on a feasibility study, the results of which were expected in mid-2008.[97] These results (or feasibility study) have (has) not been published to date.

93. ACTION PLAN, 21.
94. *Ibid.*
95. According to the 'Citizens' summary – European Commission proposes the creation of a European Private Company (SPE)' (this summary was published simultaneously with the proposal and is available at the Commission's Internal Market website: <http://ec.europa.eu/internal_market/>) the proposed SPE Regulation will have to be adopted by a unanimous decision of the Member States in the Council of Ministers of the European Union and it will also require the approval of the European Parliament. The reference to approval of the European Parliament is remarkable, I would think, now that Art. 308 EC does not require approval, but a mere consultation of the European Parliament.
96. ACTION PLAN, 23, *sub* 3.6 (The European Cooperative Society and other EU legal forms of enterprises) and 26.
97. SPEECH/07/592 of 3 Oct. 2007 (Speech by Commissioner McCreevy at the European Parliament's Legal Affairs Committee).

Annex III
Table of Equivalence

This Annex contains an overview of the new numbering of selected EC Treaty provisions, after the entry into force of the Treaty of Lisbon.[1]

Old numbering of the Treaty establishing the European Community (EC)	*New numbering of the Treaty on the Functioning of the European Union (TFEU)*
PART ONE – PRINCIPLES	PART ONE – PRINCIPLES
Article 2 (repealed)[2]	
Article 3, paragraph 1 (repealed)[3]	
Article 3, paragraph 2	Article 8
Article 5 (replaced)[4]	
Article 7 (repealed)[5]	
Article 12 (repealed)	Article 18
Article 14 (moved)	Article 26
PART TWO – CITIZENSHIP OF THE UNION	PART TWO – NON-DISCRIMINATION AND CITIZENSHIP OF THE UNION
Article 18	Article 21

1. See Consolidated versions of the Treaty on European Union and the Treaty on the Functioning of the European Union, OJ 2008 C 115, 1–388.
2. Replaced, in substance, by Art. 3 of the Treaty on the European Union (TEU).
3. Replaced, in substance, by Art. 3–6 of the Treaty on the Functioning of the European Union (TFEU).
4. Replaced, in substance, by Art. 5 TEU.
5. Replaced, in substance, by Art. 13 TEU.

Old numbering of the Treaty establishing the European Community (EC)	New numbering of the Treaty on the Functioning of the European Union (TFEU)
PART THREE – COMMUNITY POLICIES	PART THREE – POLICIES AND INTERNAL ACTIONS OF THE UNION
Title I – Free movement of Goods	*Title II – Free movement of Goods*
Chapter 2 – Prohibition of quantitative restrictions between Member States	Chapter 3 – Prohibition of quantitative restrictions between Member States
Article 28	Article 34
Article 29	Article 35
Article 30	Article 36
Title III – Free movement of persons, services and capital	*Title IV – Free movement of persons, services and capital*
Chapter 1 – Workers	Chapter 1 – Workers
Article 39	Article 45
Chapter 2 – Right of Establishment	Chapter 2 – Right of Establishment
Article 43	Article 49
Article 44	Article 50
Article 45	Article 51
Article 46	Article 52
Article 47	Article 53
Article 48	Article 54
Chapter 3 – Services	Chapter 3 – Services
Article 49	Article 56
Article 55	Article 62
Chapter 4 – Capital and Payments	Chapter 4 – Capital and Payments
Article 56	Article 63
Title IV – Visas, asylum, immigration and other policies related to free movement of persons	*Title V – Area of freedom, security and justice*
	Chapter 1 – General provisions
Article 61	Article 67
	Chapter 3 – Judicial cooperation in civil matters
Article 65	Article 81
Article 67 (repealed)	

Old numbering of the Treaty establishing the European Community (EC)	*New numbering of the Treaty on the Functioning of the European Union (TFEU)*
Title VI – Common rules on competition, taxation and approximation of laws	*Title VII – Common rules on competition, taxation and approximation of laws*
Chapter 3 – Approximation of laws	Chapter 3 – Approximation of laws
Article 94 (moved)	Article 115
Article 95 (moved)	Article 114
Title XI – Social policy, education, vocational training and youth	*Title X – Social policy*
Chapter 1 – Social provisions (repealed)	
Article 136	Article 151
Article 137	Article 153
Title XIII – Public health	*Title XIV – Public health*
Article 152	Article 168
Title XVI – Industry	*Title XVII – Industry*
Article 157	Article 173
PART FIVE – INSTITUTIONS OF THE COMMUNITY	PART SIX – INSTITUTIONAL AND FINANCIAL PROVISIONS
Title I – Institutional provisions	*Title I – Institutional provisions*
Chapter 1 – The institutions	Chapter 1 – The institutions
Section 3 – The Commission	Section 4 – The Commission
Article 211 (repealed)[6]	
Section 4 – The Court of Justice	Section 5 – The Court of Justice of the European Union
Article 220 (repealed)[7]	
Article 225	Article 256
Article 226	Article 258
Article 230	Article 263
Article 231	Article 264
Article 234	Article 267
Chapter 2 – Provisions common to several institutions	Chapter 2 – Legal acts of the Union, adopted procedures and other provisions

6. Replaced, in substance, by Art. 17, para. 1 TEU.
7. Replaced, in substance, by Art. 19 TEU.

Old numbering of the Treaty establishing the European Community (EC)	*New numbering of the Treaty on the Functioning of the European Union (TFEU)*
	Section 1 – The legal acts of the Union
Article 249	Article 288
Article 251	Article 294
Article 253	Article 296
PART SIX – GENERAL AND FINAL PROVISIONS	PART SEVEN – GENERAL AND FINAL PROVISIONS
Article 288	Article 340
Article 293 (repealed)	
Article 294 (moved)	Article 55
Article 308	Article 352

List of References

Alpa, G. 'The Meaning of "Natural Person" and the Impact of the Constitution for Europe on the Development of European Private Law'. *ELJ* 10 (2004): 734–750.

Andenas, M. & W.-H. Roth (eds). *Services and Free Movement in EU Law*. Oxford: OUP, 2002.

Andenas, M. 'Free Movement of Companies'. *LQR* 119 (2003): 221–222.

Armour, J. 'Legal Capital: An Outdated Concept?' *EBOR* 7 (2006): 5–27.

Barnard, C. *The Substantive Law of the EU*. Oxford: OUP, 2004.

Bartman, S.M. 'Minderheidsaandeelhouders tussen exit en zorgplicht'. In *Concernverhoudingen*, edited by L. Timmerman et al. Deventer: Kluwer, 2002, 29–45.

Bartman, S.M. 'Analysis and Consequences of the EC Directive on Takeover Bids'. *ECL* (2004): 5–8.

Bartman, S.M. 'Crack the OOC-Code!' *ECL* (2006): 162–163.

Bartman, S.M. 'The EC Directive on Takeover Bids: Opting in as a Token of Good Corporate Governance'. In *European Company Law in Accelerated Progress*, edited by S. Bartman. Alphen aan den Rijn: Kluwer Law International, 2006, 1–7.

Bartman, S.M. (ed.). *European Company Law in Accelerated Progress*. Alphen aan den Rijn: Kluwer Law International, 2006.

Basedow, J. 'The Communitarization of the Conflict of Laws under the Treaty of Amsterdam'. *CML Rev*. 37 (2000): 687–708.

Basedow, J. 'Codification of Private Law in the European Union: The making of a Hybrid'. *ERPL* 1 (2001): 35–49.

Bauman, J.D. *Corporations and Other Business Associations: Statutes, Rules and Forms. 2001 edition*. St. Paul (Minnesota): West Group, 2001.

Baums, T. 'European Company Law Beyond the 2003 Action Plan'. *EBOR* 8 (2007): 143–160.

Bebchuk, L.A. 'Federalism and the Corporation: The Desirable Limits on State Competition in Corporate Law'. *Harv. L. Rev.* 105 (1992): 1435–1510.

Bebchuk, L.A. 'Efficient and Inefficient Sales of Corporate Control'. *QJE* 109 (1994): 957–993.

Beckman, H., et al. (eds). *De nieuwe macht van de kapitaalverschaffer*. Deventer: Kluwer, 2007.

Beitzke, G. 'Anerkennung und Sitzverlegung von Gesellschaften und juristischen Personen im EWG-Bereich'. *ZHR* (1965): 1–47.

Bellingwout, J.W. *Zetelverplaatsing van rechtspersonen*. Deventer: Kluwer, 1996.

Bisacre, J. 'The Migration of Companies within the European Union and the Proposed Fourteenth Company Law Directive'. *ICCLJ* (2001): 251–270.

Boschma, H., H. Schutte-Veenstra & M.-L. Lennarts. *Alternative Systems for Capital Protection*. Deventer: Kluwer, 2005.

Boschma, H., L. Lennarts & H. Schutte-Veenstra. 'The Reform of Dutch Private Company Law: New Rules for the Protection of Creditors'. *EBOR* 8 (2007): 856–604.

Brandenburg, A.M. & B.J. Nalebuff. *Co-opetition*. New York: Doubleday, 1996.

Bratton, W.W. & J. McCahery. 'Fiscal Federalism, Jurisdictional Competition, and Tax Coordination: Translating Theory to Policy in the European Union'. In *Regulatory Competition and Economic Integration*, edited by D.C. Esty & D. Geradin. Oxford: OUP, 2001, 157–189.

Bratton, W.W., J.A. McCahery & E.P.M. Vermeulen. 'How Does Corporate Mobility Affect Lawmaking? A Comparative Analysis'. Amsterdam Center for Law & Economics Working Paper no. 2008-01, <http://ssrn.acle.nl>.

Bröhmer, J. 'Artikel 48'. In *Kommentar des Vertrages über die Europäische Union und des Vertrages zur Gründung der Europäischen Gemeinschaft – EUV/EGV –*, edited by C. Calliess & M. Ruffert. Neuwied – Kriftel: Luchterhand, 2002.

Bulterman, M.K. & P.J. Slot. 'Harmonisatie van wetgeving betreffende migrerende EU-burgers en derdelanders: op weg naar een uniform toetsingskader?' *SEW* (2005): 346–362.

Bungert, H. 'Grenzüberschreitende Verschmelzungsmobilität – Anmerkung zur Sevic-Entscheidung des EuGH'. *BB* (2006): 53–56.

Buxbaum, R.M. & K.J. Hopt. *Legal Harmonization and the Business Enterprise*. Berlin/New York: De Gruyter, 1988.

Cary, W.L. 'Federalism and Corporate Law: Reflections Upon Delaware'. *Yale L.J.* 83 (1974): 663–705.

Craig, P. & G. de Búrca. *EU Law*. Oxford: OUP, 2003.

Dashwood, A. 'The Relationship Between the Member States and the European Union/European Community'. *CML Rev* 41 (2004): 355–381.

Davies, G. 'Can Selling Arrangements be Harmonized?' *ELRev.* 30 (2005): 370–385.

Davies, G. 'Subsidiarity: The Wrong Idea, in the Wrong Place, at the Wrong Time'. *CML Rev.* 43 (2006): 63–84.

Davies, P.L. *Introduction to Company Law*. Oxford: OUP, 2002.

Davies, P.L. *Gower and Davies' Principles of Modern Company Law*. London: Sweet & Maxwell, 2003.

Davies, P.L. 'Employee Involvement in the European Company'. In *The European Company. Developing a Community Law of Corporations*, edited by J. Rickford. Antwerp: Intersentia, 2003, 67–82.

Deakin, S. 'Regulatory Competition versus Harmonization in European Company Law'. In *Regulatory Competition and Economic Integration*, edited by D.C. Esty and D. Geradin. Oxford: OUP, 2001, 190–217.

de Búrca, G. 'The Tobacco Advertizing Saga: Political Aspirations and Constitutional Constraints'. CELS Occasional Paper no. 5 (Jul. 2001, Cambridge), <www.cels.law.cam.ac.uk/>.

de Groot, C. *Bescherming en breakthrough bij overname*. Amsterdam: Rozenberg, 2004.

de Kluiver, H.J., et al. *De Europese vennootschap (SE)* (preliminary report Vereeniging 'Handelsrecht' 2004). Deventer: Kluwer, 2004.

Demaret, P. 'A Short Walk in the Realm of Subsidiarity'. In *European Economic and Business Law*, edited by R.M. Buxbaum et al. Berlin: Walter de Gruyter, 1996, 13–31.

Diephuis, J.H. & C.W.A. Timmermans. *Erkenning van vreemde vennootschappen en rechtspersonen* (Preadviezen). The Hague: Mededelingen van de Nederlandse Vereniging voor Internationaal Recht (no. 81), 1980.

Diez de Velasco Vallego, M. & J.M. Sobrino Heredia. 'El control jurisdiccional del principio de subsidiaridad en la Unión Europea'. In *Une communauté de droit-Festschrift für Gil Carlos Rodríguez Iglesias*, edited by N. Colneric et al. Berlin: BWV, 2003, 581–589.

Dodd, P. & R. Leftwich. 'The Market for Corporate Charters: "Unhealthy Competition" versus Federal Regulation'. *J. Bus.* 53 (1980): 259–283.

Dorresteijn, A.F.M. 'Xenophobia or Competition'. *ECL* (2004): 152.

Dorresteijn, A.F.M. & C. de Groot. 'Corporate Governance Codes: Origins and Perspectives'. In *European Company Law in Accelerated Progress*, edited by S. Bartman. Alphen aan den Rijn: Kluwer Law International, 2006, 31–57.

Dortmond, P.J. & M.J.G.C. Raaijmakers. *De juridische fusie naar wordend recht* (preliminary report Vereeniging 'Handelsrecht' 1980). Zwolle: Tjeenk Willink, 1980.

Dortmond, P.J. 'De Europese vennootschap en juridische fusie'. *Ondernemingsrecht* (2001): 190–193.

Drijber, B.J. 'De dertiende richtlijn tussen Europese politiek en Europees recht'. *Ondernemingsrecht* (2004): 375–380.

Drijber, B.J. 'De interstatelijkheid voorbij: een slotbeschouwing'. In *De EU: de interstatelijkheid voorbij?*, edited by E. Manunza & L. Senden. Nijmegen: Wolf Legal Publishers, 2006, 191–206.

Dyrberg, P. 'Full Free Movement of Companies in the European Community at Last'. *ELRev* 28 (2003): 528–537.

Easterbrook, F.H. 'Federalism and European Business Law'. In *European Economic and Business Law*, edited by R.M. Buxbaum et al. Berlin: Walter de Gruyter, 1996, 1–11.

Ehlermann, C.D. 'Compétition entre systèmes réglementaires'. *RMCUE* (1995): 220–227.

Eidenmüller, H., B. Grunewald & U. Noack. 'Minimum Capital in the System of Legal Capital'. In *Legal Capital in Europe* (ECFR special Vol. 1), edited by M. Lutter. Berlin: De Gruyter, 2006, 17–41.

Enriques, L. & J.R. Macey. 'Creditors versus Capital Formation: The Case Against the European Legal Capital Rules'. *Cornell L. Rev.* 86 (2001): 1165–1204.

Enriques, L. 'EC Company Law and the Fears of a European Delaware'. *EBLR* (2004): 1259–1274.

Enriques, L. 'Schweigen ist Gold: Die Europäische Aktiengesellschaft als Katalysator für regulative Arbitrage im Gesellschaftsrecht'. *ZGR* (2004): 735–759.

Enriques, L. 'The Mandatory Bid Rule in the Proposed EC Takeover Directive: Harmonization as Rent-Seeking?' In *Reforming Company and Takeover Law in Europe*, edited by G. Ferrarini et al. Oxford: OUP, 2004, 767–795.

Enriques, L. & M. Gelter. 'How the Old World Encountered the New One: Regulatory Competition and Cooperation in European Corporate and Bankruptcy Law'. ECGI-Law Working Paper no. 63/2006, Feb. 2006, <www.ecgi.org/wp/>.

Esty, D.C. & D. Geradin (eds). *Regulatory Competition and Economic Integration*. Oxford: OUP, 2001.

Esty, D.C. & D. Geradin. 'Introduction'. In *Regulatory Competition and Economic Integration*, edited by D.C. Esty & D. Geradin. Oxford: OUP, 2001, xix–xxxi.

Esty, D.C. & D. Geradin. 'Regulatory Co-Opetition'. In *Regulatory Competition and Economic Integration*, edited by D.C. Esty & D. Geradin. Oxford: OUP, 2001, 30–46.

Ferrarini, G., et al. (eds). *Reforming Company and Takeover Law in Europe*. Oxford: OUP, 2004.

Fleischer, H. 'Case note' (Case C-367/98. *Commission of the European Communities v. Portuguese Republic* (Golden shares); C-483/99. *Commission of the European Communities v. French Republic* (Golden shares); and C-503/99. *Commission of the European Communities v. Kingdom of Belgium* (Golden shares). Judgments of the Full Court of 4 June 2002). *CML Rev.* 40 (2003): 493–501.

Garrido, J. 'Company Law and Capital Markets'. In *The European Company. Developing a Community Law of Corporations*, edited by J. Rickford. Antwerp: Intersentia, 2003, 95–111.

Gatti, M. 'Optionality Arrangements and Reciprocity in the European Takeover Directive'. *EBOR* 5 (2005): 553–579.

Geelhoed, L.A. 'Het subsidiariteitsbeginsel: een communautair principe?' *SEW* 39 (1991): 422–435.

Geens, K. 'Beschermingsconstructies: enkele recente evoluties'. In *Openbaar bod en beschermingsconstructies*, edited by Jan Ronse Instituut. Kalmthout: Biblo, 1990, 77–118.

Geens, K. & M. Wyckaert. 'Cross-border Mergers and Minority Protection. An open-ended Harmonization'. *UL Rev.* (2008): 43–56.

Gerard, D. & K. Lenaerts. 'The Structure of the Union According to the Constitution for Europe: The Emperor is Getting Dressed'. *ELRev.* 29 (2004): 289–322.

Gevurtz, F.A. *Corporation Law*. St. Paul (Minnesota): West Group, 2000.

Goldman, B. 'The Convention between the Member States of the European Economic Community on the Mutual Recognition of Companies and Legal Persons'. *CML Rev.* 6 (1968–1969): 104–128.

Gormley, L.W. 'Competition and Free Movement: Is the Internal Market the Same as a Common Market?' *EBLR* (2002): 517–522.

Grossfeld, B. 'Die Anerkennung der Rechtsfähigkeit Juristischer Personen'. *RabelsZ* 31 (1967): 1–50.

Grossfeld, B. 'Zur Geschichte der Anerkennungsproblematik bei Aktiengesellschaften'. *RabelsZ* 38 (1974): 344–371.

Grundmann, S. 'Wettbewerb der Regelgeber im Europäischen Gesellschaftsrecht – jedes Marktsegment hat seine Struktur'. *ZGR* (2001): 783–832.

Grundmann, S. & F. Möslein. 'Die Goldene Aktie. Staatskontrollrechte in Europarecht und wirtschaftspolitischer Bewertung'. *ZGR* (2003): 317–366.

Grundmann, S. *Europäisches Gesellschaftsrecht*. Heidelberg: C.F. Müller, 2004.

Halbhuber, H. 'National Doctrinal Structures and European Company Law'. *CML Rev.* 38 (2001): 1385–1420.

Hamilton, R.W. *The Law of Corporations*. St. Paul (Minnesota): West Group, 2000.

Hansen, L.L. 'Employee Involvement and the Formation of a European Company'. *ECL* (2004): 126–130.

Hansmann, H. & R. Kraakman. 'What is Corporate Law?' In *The Anatomy of Corporate Law. A Comparative and Functional Approach*, edited by R. Kraakman et al. Oxford: OUP, 2004, 1–19.

Hartkamp, A.S., C.H. Sieburgh & L.A.D. Keus (eds). *De invloed van het Europese recht op het Nederlandse privaatrecht*. Deventer: Kluwer, 2007.

Heine, K. & W. Kerber. 'European Corporate Laws, Regulatory Competition and Path Dependence'. *Eur. J. of L. and Econ* 13 (2002): 47–71.

Heine, K. *Regulierungswettbewerb im Gesellschaftsrecht*. Berlin: Duncker & Humblot, 2003.

Hertig, G. & J.A. McCahery. 'Company and Takeover Law Reforms in Europe: Misguided Harmonization Efforts or Regulatory Competition'. *EBOR* 4 (2003): 179–211.

Hertig, G. & J.A. McCahery. 'An Agenda for Reform: Company and Takeover Law in Europe'. In *Reforming Company and Takeover Law in Europe*, edited by G. Ferrarini et al. Oxford: OUP, 2004, 21–45.

Hertig, G. & H. Kanda. 'Creditor Protection'. In *The Anatomy of Corporate Law. A Comparative and Functional Approach*, edited by R. Kraakman et al. Oxford: OUP, 2004, 71–99.

Heslinga, S.F. 'Survey of Legislation'. *ECL* (2007): 43.

Hijmans van den Bergh, L.J. & G. van Solinge. *Implementatie van de Dertiende Richtlijn. Een terreinverkenning* (preliminary report Vereeniging 'Handelsrecht' 2000). Deventer: Kluwer, 2000.

Hirte, H. 'The Takeover Directive – A Mini-Directive on the Structure of the Corporation: Is it a Trojan Horse?' *ECFR* (2005): 1–19.

Hopt, K.J. *Company Law in the European Union: Harmonization or Subsidiarity* (Saggi, conferenze e seminari, No. 31). Rome: Centro di studi e ricerche di diritto comparato e straniero, 1998.

Hopt, K.J. & E. Wymeersch (eds). *Capital Markets and Company Law*. Oxford: OUP, 2003.

Hopt, K.J. & E. Wymeersch (eds). *European Company and Financial Law. Texts and Leading Cases*. Oxford: OUP, 2007.

Huiskes, C.R. *De Europese vennootschap. Enkele beschouwingen omtrent het ontwerp-Statuut (1991) voor een Europese vennootschap*. Zwolle: W.E.J. Tjeenk Willink, 1993.

Iber, A. 'ECJ Judgment on the New Tobacco Directive'. *LIEI* 30 (2002): 167–177.

Jarass, H.D. 'A Unified Approach to the Fundamental Freedoms'. In *Services and Free Movement in EU Law*, edited by M. Andenas & W.-H. Roth. Oxford: OUP, 2002.

Kainer, F. 'Binnenmarktrechtliche Grenzen des Übernahmerechts'. *ZHR* 168 (2004): 542–576.

Kanda, H. & G. Hertig. 'Creditor Protection'. In *The Anatomy of Corporate Law. A Comparative and Functional Approach*, edited by R. Kraakman et al. Oxford: OUP, 2004, 71–99.

Kemperink, G. & J. Stuyck. 'The Thirteenth Company Law Directive and Competing Bids'. *CML Rev.* 45 (2008): 93–130.

Kieninger, E.-M. *Wettbewerb der Privatrechtsordnungen im Europäischen Binnenmarkt*. Tübingen: Mohr Siebeck, 2002.

Klinke, U. 'European Company Law and the ECJ: The Court's Judgements in the Years 2001 to 2004'. *ECFR* (2005): 270–321.

Körber, T. *Grundfreiheiten und Privatrecht*. Tübingen: Mohr Siebeck, 2004.

Lamandini, M. 'Report from Italy'. *ECL* (2006): 31–32.

Lauwaars, R.H. & J.M. Maarleveld. *Harmonisatie van wetgeving in Europese organisaties*. Deventer: Kluwer, 1987.

Leible, S. 'Niederlassungsfreiheit und Sitzverlegungsrichtlinie'. *ZGR* (2004): 531–558.

Leible, S. & J. Hoffmann. 'Cartesio – fortgeltende Sitztheorie. grenzüberschreitender Formwechsel und Verbot materiellrechtlicher Wegzugsbeschränkungen'. *BB* (2009): 58–63.

Lenaerts, K. & P. van Ypersele. 'Le principe de subsidiarité et son contexte: étude de l'article 3b du Traité CE'. *CDE* (1994): 3–85.

Lenaerts, K. & J. Vanhamme. 'Procedural Rights of Private Parties in the Community Administrative Process'. *CML Rev.* 34 (1997): 531–569.

Lenaerts, K. & M. Desomer. 'New Models of Constitution-making in Europe: The Quest for Legitimacy'. *CML Rev.* 39 (2002): 1217–1253.

Lennarts, M.-L., 'Company Mobility within the EU, Fifty Years on. From a Non-issue to a Hot Topic'. *UL Rev.* 4 (2008): 1–6.

Lombardo, S. *Regulatory Competition in Company Law in the European Community*. Frankfurt am Main: Peter Lang, 2002.

Looijestijn-Clearie, A. 'Have the Dikes Collapsed? Inspire Art a Further Breakthrough in the Freedom of Establishment of Companies?' *EBOR* 5 (2004): 389–418.

Lutter, M. (ed.). *Legal Capital in Europe* (European Company and Financial Law Review, Special Vol. 1). Berlin: De Gruyter, 2006.

Maeijer, J.M.M. *Mr. C. Asser's handleiding tot de beoefening van het Nederlands burgerlijk recht. Vertegenwoordiging en rechtspersoon. De naamloze en de besloten vennootschap*. Deventer: W.E.J. Tjeenk Willink, 2000.

Maul, S. & A. Kouloridas. 'The Takeover bids Directive'. *German L.J.* 5 (2004): 355–366.

Maul, S. & G. Lanfermann. 'Europäische Corporate Governance – Stand der Entwicklungen'. *BB* 59 (2004): 1861–1868.

McCahery, J.A. & E.P.M. Vermeulen. 'The Changing Landscape of EU Company Law'. TILEC discussion paper. DP 2004–023 (Tilburg University, 2004), <http://ssrn.com>.

McCahery, J.A. & E.P.M. Vermeulen. 'Does the European Company prevent the "Delaware Effect"?' TILEC Discussion Paper, Mar. 2005, <http://ssrn.com>.

McCahery, J.A. *Harmonisatie in het Europese vennootschapsrecht: de politieke economie van economische integratie* (preliminary report Nederlandse Juristenvereniging 2006). Deventer: Kluwer, 2006, 157–205.

McCahery, J.A. & E.P.M. Vermeulen. 'Understanding Corporate Mobility in the EU. Towards the Foundations of a European Internal Affairs Doctrine'. Working Paper Prepared for the European Company Law and Corporate Governance Conference in Berlin on 27–28 Jun. 2007, <www.bdi.eu/company-law-conference2007>.

Menjucq, M. *Droit international et européen des sociétés*. Paris: Montchrestien, 2001.

Menjucq, M. 'The European Regime on Takeovers'. *ECFR* (2006): 222–236.

Merkt, H. 'Creditor Protection and Capital Maintenance from a German Perspective'. *EBLR* (2004): 1045–1057.

Merkt, H. 'Creditor Protection through Mandatory Disclosure'. *EBOR* 7 (2006): 95–122.

Mestmäcker, E.-J. 'Marktversagen und Staatsversagen in der Europäischen Union'. In *Systembildung und Systemlücken in Kerngebieten des Europäischen Privatrechts*, edited by S. Grundmann. Tübingen: Mohr Siebeck, 2000, 53–65.

Moloney, N. 'New Frontiers in EC Capital Markets Law: From Market Construction to Market Regulation'. *CML Rev.* 40 (2003): 809–843.

Moloney, N. *EC Securities Regulation*. Oxford: OUP, 2008.
Mortelmans, K. 'The Common Market, the Internal Market and the Single Market: What's in a Market?' *CML Rev.* 35 (1998): 101–136.
Mortelmans, K. 'Towards Convergence in the Application of the Rules on Free Movement and on Competition?' *CML Rev.* 38 (2001): 613–649.
Mortelmans, K. 'The Relationship Between the Treaty Rules and Community Measures for the Establishment and Functioning of the Internal Market – Towards a Concordance Rule'. *CML Rev*. 39 (2002): 1303–1346.
Mortelmans, K. 'Verslag van de discussie'. In *De EU: de interstatelijkheid voorbij?*, edited by E. Manunza & L. Senden. Nijmegen: Wolf Legal Publishers, 2006, 207–213.
Mucciarelli, F.M. 'The Transfer of the Registered Office and Forum-Shopping in International Insolvency Cases: an Important Decision from Italy – Case Note on the Decision "B & C" of the Italian Corte di Cassazione'. *ECFR* (2005): 512–533.
Nieuwe Weme, M.P. *Het verplicht bod op effecten*. Deventer: Kluwer, 2004.
Nieuwe Weme, M.P., et al. (eds). *Handboek openbaar bod*. Deventer: Kluwer, 2008.
Noack, U. 'Moderne Kommunikationsformen vor den Toren des Unternehmensrechts'. *ZGR* (1998): 592–616.
Oliver, P. & W.-H. Roth. 'The Internal Market and the Four Freedoms'. *CML Rev*. 41 (2004): 407–441.
Omar, P.J. 'The Convergence of Company and Insolvency Initiatives within the European Union'. *ECL* (2005): 59–65.
Prechal, S. & R.H. van Ooik. 'Het institutionele recht van de Europese Unie en de Nederlandse rechter: het acquis in een notendop'. *SEW* (2003): 348–352.
Prechal, S. *Directives in EC Law*. Oxford: OUP, 2005.
Raaijmakers, M.J.G.C. 'Sevic: grensoverschrijdende fusie binnen de EU'. *AA* 55 (2006): 628–634.
Rammeloo, S.F.G. *Corporations in Private International Law: A European Perspective*. Oxford: OUP, 2001.
Rammeloo, S.F.G. 'The Long and Winding Road Towards Freedom of Establishment for Legal Persons in Europe'. *MJ* (2003): 169–197.
Rammeloo, S.F.G. 'Vrij verkeer van rechtspersonen in Europa na HvJ EG Inspire Art Ltd.: zetelleercontroverse beslecht!' *NIPR* (2004): 283–295.
Reich, N. 'Competition Between Legal Orders: A New Paradigm?' *CML Rev*. 29 (1992): 861–896.
Reichert, J. 'Experience with the SE in Germany'. *UL Rev*. (2008): 23–34.
Renauld, J.G. *Droit européen des sociétés*. Brussels: Bruylant, 1969.
Rickford, J. 'Foreword'. In *The European Company. Developing a Community Law of Corporations*, edited by J. Rickford. Antwerp: Intersentia, 2003, 3–11.
Rickford, J. 'An Overview of the Conference – Three Big Questions' In *The European Company. Developing a Community Law of Corporations*, edited by J. Rickford. Antwerp: Intersentia, 2003, 123–131.

Rickford, J. 'Current Developments in European Law on the Restructuring of Companies: An Introduction'. *EBLR* (2004): 1225–1258.
Rickford, J. (ed.). 'Reforming Capital. Report of the Interdisciplinary Group on Capital Maintenance'. *EBLR* 15 (June 2004): 919–1027.
Rickford, J. 'The Emerging European Takeover Law from a British Perspective'. *EBLR* (2004): 1379–1421.
Ringe, W.-G. *Die Sitzverlegung der Europäischen Aktiengesellschaft*. Tübingen: Mohr Siebeck, 2006.
Roe, M.J. 'Regulatory Competition in Making Corporate Law in the United States – and its Limits'. *Oxf. Rev. Econ. Policy* 21 (2005): 232–242.
Rohe, M. 'Binnenmarkt oder Interessenverband?' *RabelsZ* 61 (1997): 1–85.
Roth, W.-H. 'Case-note Case C-233/94'. *CML Rev.* 35 (1998): 459–479.
Roth, W.-H. 'Case-note on *Centros*'. *CML Rev.* 37 (2000): 147–155.
Roth, W.-H. 'From *Centros* to *Überseering*: Free Movement of Companies, Private International Law, and Community Law'. *ICLQ* 52 (2003): 177–208.
Roth, W.-H. 'Niederlassungs- und Dienstleistungsfreiheit'. In *Handbuch des EU-Wirtschaftsrechts*, edited by M.A. Dauses. Munich: C.H. Beck, 2006.
Schall, A. 'European Framework for the Mobility of Companies'. In *European Corporate Law*, edited by K. Van Hulle & H. Gesell. Baden-Baden: Nomos, 2006, 3–24.
Schön, W. 'Gesellschaftsrecht nach Maastricht – Art. 3b EGV und das europäische Gesellschaftsrecht'. *ZGR* (1995): 1–38.
Schön, W. 'Mindestharmonisierung im europäischen Gesellschaftsrecht'. *ZHR* 160 (1996): 221–249.
Schön, W. 'The Free Choice Between the Right to Establish a Branch and to Set-up a Subsidiary – a Principle of European Business Law'. *EBOR* 2 (2001): 339–364.
Schön, W. 'The Future of Legal Capital'. *EBOR* 5 (2004): 429–448.
Schön, W. 'Playing Different Games? Regulatory Competition in Tax and Company Law Compared'. *CML Rev* 42 (2005): 331–365.
Schön, W. 'The Mobility of Companies in Europe and the Organizational Freedom of Company Founders'. *ECFR* (2006): 122–146.
Schutte-Veenstra, J.N. 'Europeesrechtelijke aspecten van de dertiende richtlijn'. In *Handboek openbaar bod*, edited by M.P. Nieuwe Weme et al. Deventer: Kluwer, 2008, 123–143.
Schwartz, I.E. '30 Jahre EG-Rechtsangleichung'. In *Eine Ordnungspolitik für Europa. Festschrift für Hans von der Groeben zu seinem 80. Geburtstag*, edited by E.-J. Mestmäcker, H. Möller & H.-P. Schwarz. Baden-Baden: Nomos, 1987, 333–368.
Seibt, C.H. & K.J. Heiser. 'Analyse der EU-Übernahmerichtlinie und Hinweise für eine Reform des deutschen Übernahmerechts'. *ZGR* (2005): 200–251.
Seidel, M. 'Präventive Rechtsangleichung im Bereich des Gemeinsamen Marktes'. *EuR* (2006): 26–45.
Siems, M.M. 'The Rules on Conflict of Laws in the European Takeover Directive'. *ECFR* (2004): 458–476.

Simpson, S., M. Berkner & L. Corte. 'The Effect of the 13th Directive on US bidders'. *IFLR* (2004) (Apr. suppl.): 233–234.

Slot, P.J. 'Harmonisation'. *ELRev.* 21 (1996): 378–387.

Slot, P.J. 'A Contribution to the Constitutional Debate in the EU in the Light of the Tobacco Judgment'. *EBLR* (2002): 3–27.

Slot, P.J. & G. Straetmans. 'Harmonisatie van wetgeving in de EG', *TPR* (2003): 691–833.

Snell, J. *Goods and Services in EC Law. A Study of the Relationship Between the Freedoms*. Oxford: OUP, 2002.

Snell, J. 'Who's Got the Power? Free Movement and Allocation of Competences in EC Law'. *YEL* 22 (2003): 323–351.

Spaventa, E. 'From Gebhard to Carpenter: Towards a (non-)economic European Constitution', *CML Rev.* 41 (2004): 743–773.

Stein, E. *Harmonization of European Company Laws. National Reform and Transnational Coordination*, Indianapolis: The Bobbs-Merrill Company, 1971.

Steindorff, E. 'Konzentrationskontrolle und Niederlassungsfreiheit. Ein Beitrag zur Konsultationspflicht der Staaten nach Art. 5 EWGV'. In *Festschrift zum 125jährigen Bestehen der Juristischen Gesellschaft zu Berlin*, edited by D. Wilke. Berlin/New York: De Gruyter, 1984.

Straetmans, G. *Consument en markt: onderzoek naar de rechtspositie van de consument op de Europese interne markt.* Deurne: Kluwer Rechtswetenschappen België, 1998.

Straetmans, G. 'Case-note on Case C-124/97, Läärä, Judgment of the Court of 21 Sep. 1999 and Case C-67/98. Zenatti, Judgment of the Court of 21 Oct. 1999, Full Court'. *CML Rev.* 37 (2000): 991–1005.

Straetmans, G. 'Selling Arrangements, Advertising Rules and Access to the Market: Keck undone? (case-note on Case C-405/98, *Konsumentombudsmannen (KO) v. Gourmet International Products AB (GIP).* Judgment of the Court (Sixth Chamber) of 8 Mar. 2001)'. *CML Rev.* 39 (2002): 1407–1421.

Strese, J. *Die Kompetenzen der Europäischen Gemeinschaft zur Privatrechtsangleichung im Binnenmarkt.* Baden-Baden: Nomos, 2006.

Stuyck, J. 'Zetelverplaatsing en vrije vestiging van vennootschappen in de EEG (noot bij Daily Mail)'. *TVR* (1989): 198–203.

Stuyck, J. 'Patterns of Justice in the European Constitutional Charter: Minimum Harmonisation in the Field of Consumer Law'. In *Law and diffuse Interests in the European Legal Order: Liber Amicorum Norbert Reich*, edited by L. Krämer et al. Baden-Baden: Nomos Verlag, 1997.

Stuyck, J. 'Libre circulation et concurrence: les deux piliers du Marché commun'. In *Mélanges en hommage à Michel Waelbroeck* (Vol. II), edited by M. Dony & A. De Walsche. Brussels: Bruylant, 1999, 1477–1498.

Stuyck, J. 'European Consumer Law after the Treaty of Amsterdam: Consumer Policy In or Beyond the Internal Market?' *CML Rev.* 37 (2000): 367–400.

Stuyck, J., E. Terryn & T. Van Dyck. 'Confidence through Fairness? The New Directive on Unfair Business-to-Consumer Commercial Practices in the Internal Market'. *CML Rev.* 43 (2006): 107–152.

Szyszczak, E. 'Golden Shares and Market Governance'. *LIEI* (2002): 255–284.

Teichmann, C. 'Law as a Product – Regulatory Competition in the Common Market and the European Private Company'. In *European Company Law in Accelerated Progress*, edited by S. Bartman. Alphen aan den Rijn: Kluwer Law International, 2006, 145–157.

Teichmann, C. *Binnenmarktkonformes Gesellschaftsrecht*. Berlin: De Gruyter, 2006.

Tiebout, C. 'A Pure Theory of Local Expenditures'. *J. of Pol. Econ.* 64 (1956): 416–424.

Tilleman, B. 'Een kritische kijk op de law & economics-benadering van onvriendelijke overnamebiedingen'. In *Openbaar bod en beschermingsconstructies*, edited by Jan Ronse Instituut. Kalmthout: Biblo, 1990, 243–304.

Tillotson, J. & N. Foster. *Text, Cases and materials on European Union Law*. London: Cavendish Publishing, 2003.

Timmerman, L. 'Wat hebben de Europese Richtlijnen in ons vennootschapsrecht aangericht?' *AA* (1996): 23–28.

Timmerman, L. 'Kleine gebeurtenissen'. *Ondernemingsrecht* (2001): 413.

Timmerman, L. 'Van digitaal naar analoog vennootschapsrecht en de gevolgen daarvan voor de concurrentie tussen vennootschapssystemen'. *Ondernemingsrecht* (2003): 38–42.

Timmerman, L. 'Some Thoughts on the Impact of Fundamental Rights on Dutch Company Law'. In *Constitutionalisation of Private Law*, edited by T. Barkhuysen & S. Lindenbergh. Leiden/Boston: Martinus Nijhoff, 2006, 23–32.

Timmerman, L. 'Mensenrechten van minderheidsaandeelhouders: voice, exit of gelijke behandeling'. In *De nieuwe macht van de kapitaalverschaffer*, edited by H. Beckman et al. Deventer: Kluwer, 2007, 31–42.

Timmermans, C.W.A. 'De Harmonisatie van nationale voorschriften op het gebied van het vennootschapsrecht' (preliminary report Netherlands Association for European Law 1971). *SEW* 19 (1971): 608–640.

Timmermans, C.W.A. 'Het Verdrag van 29 februari 1968 inzake de onderlinge erkenning van vennootschappen en rechtspersonen. Enkele Europeesrechtelijke kanttekeningen'. In *Erkenning van vreemde vennootschappen en rechtspersonen* (Preadviezen), edited by J.H. Diephuis & C.W.A. Timmermans. The Hague: Mededelingen van de Nederlandse Vereniging voor Internationaal Recht (no. 81), 1980, 37–78.

Timmermans, C.W.A. 'De tweede golf: de Europese onderstroom'. *TVVS* (1983): 166–169.

Timmermans, C.W.A. 'Die europäische Rechtsangleichung im Gesellschaftsrecht'. *RabelsZ.* 48 (1984): 1–47.

Timmermans, C.W.A. 'Ontwerp EEG-Richtlijn over internationale fusies'. *TVVS* (1985): 98–99.

Timmermans, C.W.A. 'Europeesrechtelijke erkenning van pseudo-buitenlandse vennootschappen'. In *Tot vermaak van Slagter*, edited by J.H. Christiaanse et al. Deventer: Kluwer, 1988, 321–331.

Timmermans, C.W.A. 'Voorstel dertiende EEG-Richtlijn vennootschapsrecht betreffende het openbare bod'. *TVVS* (1989): 149–150.
Timmermans, C.W.A. (case note Daily Mail). *SEW* (1991): 69–73.
Timmermans, C.W.A. 'Methods and Tools for Integration'. In *European Business Law. Legal and Economic Analyses on Integration and Harmonization*, edited by R.M. Buxbaum et al. Berlin/New York: De Gruyter, 1991, 129–166.
Timmermans, C.W.A. 'Chapter Ten (Takeovers-Discussion)'. In *European Business Law. Legal and Economic Analyses on Integration and Harmonization*, edited by R.M. Buxbaum et al. Berlin/New York: De Gruyter, 1991, 375–391.
Timmermans, C.W.A. 'De joint venture naar komend EG-recht'. In *Grensoverschrijdende samenwerking van ondernemingen*, edited by H.J.M.N. Honée et al. Deventer: Kluwer, 1992, 63–75.
Timmermans, C.W.A. 'Community Directives Revisited'. *YEL* (1997): 1–28.
Timmermans, C.W.A. 'Subsidiarity and Transparency'. *Fordham Int'l L.J.* 22 (1999): 106–127.
Timmermans, C.W.A. 'Europees vennootschapsrecht'. *SEW* (2002): 248–252.
Timmermans, C.W.A. 'Harmonization in the Future of Company Law in Europe'. In *Capital Markets and Company Law*, edited by K.J. Hopt & E. Wymeersch. Oxford: OUP, 2003, 623–637.
Timmermans, C.W.A. 'Lifting the Veil of Union Citizen's Rights'. In *Une communauté de droit. Festschrift für Gil Carlos Rodríguez Iglesias*, edited by N. Colneric et al. Berlin: Berliner Wissenschafts-Verlag, 2003, 195–206.
Timmermans, C.W.A. *Neue Rechtsprechung des Gerichtshofs der EG zum Europäischen Gesellschaftsrecht* (Zentrum für Europäisches Wirtschaftsrecht. Vorträge und Berichte, no. 132). Bonn: The members of the Zentrum, 2003.
Timmermans, C.W.A. 'La justiciabilité de la subsidiarité'. In *Festskrift til Claus Gulmann. Liber Amicorum*, edited by B. Vesterdorf et al. Copenhagen: Forlaget Thomson, 2006, 450–459.
Timmermans, C.W.A. 'Is het subsidiariteitsbeginsel vatbaar voor rechterlijke controle?' *SEW* (2007): 224–230.
Troberg, P. & J. Tiedje, 'Artikel 43 EG'. In *Kommentar zum Vertrag über die Europäische Union und zur Gründung der Europäischen Gemeinschaft*, edited by H. von der Groeben & J. Schwarze. Baden-Baden: Nomos, 2003.
Usher, J.A. 'Annotation, Case C-376/98, *Germany v. European Parliament and Council* (*tobacco advertising*). Judgment of the Full Court of 5 October 2000, [2000] ECR I-8419'. *CML Rev.* 38 (2001): 1519–1543.
Vaccaro, E. 'Transfer of Seat and Freedom of Establishment in European Company Law'. *EBLR* (2005): 1348–1365.
Van den Bergh, R. 'Towards an Institutional Legal Framework for Regulatory Competition in Europe'. *Kyklos* 53 (2000): 435–466.
van den Braak, S.M. 'Grensoverschrijdende omzetting van rechtspersonen'. *WPNR* (2007): 688–693.
van der Grinten, W.C.L. 'Erkenning van vennootschappen en rechtspersonen in de Europese Economische Gemeenschap'. *SEW* (1966): 201–210.

van der Grinten, W.C.L. 'Europese n.v.?' In *Grensoverschrijdend privaatrecht* (liber amicorum Van Rijn van Alkemade). Deventer: Kluwer, 1993, 109–117.

van der Sangen, G.J.H. & W. Mulder, 'The European Company and Cross-Border Reorganisations'. In *The European Company*, edited by S.H.M.A. Dumoulin et al. The Hague: Boom, 2005, 95–132.

van Gerven, W. 'Harmonization of Private Law: Do we Need it?' *CML Rev.* 41 (2004): 505–532.

van Gerven, W. 'Bringing (Private) Laws Closer to Each Other at the European Level'. In *The Institutional Framework of European Private Law*, edited by F. Cafaggi. Oxford: OUP, 2006, 37–77.

Van Hulle, K. 'European Corporate Law: United in Diversity'. In *European Corporate Law*, edited by K. Van Hulle & H. Gesell. Baden-Baden: Nomos, 2006, 1–2.

Van Ommeslaghe, P. 'La première directive du conseil du 9 mars 1968 en matière de sociétés'. *CDE* (1969): 495–563.

van Ooik, R.H. *De keuze der rechtsgrondslag voor besluiten van de Europese Unie*. Deventer: Kluwer, 1999.

van Solinge, G. *Grensoverschrijdende juridische fusie*. Deventer: Kluwer, 1994.

Ventoruzzo, M. 'Cross-border Mergers, Change of Applicable Corporate Laws and Protection of Dissenting Shareholders: Withdrawal Rights under Italian Law'. *ECFR* (2007): 47–75.

Vermeulen, E.P.M. *The Evolution of Legal Business Forms in Europe and the United States*. The Hague/London/New York: Kluwer Law International, 2003.

Villiers, C. *European Company Law: Towards Democracy?* Aldershot: Ashgate Publishing, 1998.

Vogenauer, S. & S. Weatherill (eds). *The Harmonisation of European Contract Law: Implications for European Private Laws, Business and Legal Practice*. Oxford: Hart Publishing, 2006.

von Bogdandy, A. & J. Bast. 'The European Union's Vertical Order of Competences: The Current Law and Proposals for its Reform'. *CML Rev.* 39 (2002): 227–268.

von der Groeben, H. & J. Schwarze (eds). *Kommentar zum Vertrag über die Europäische Union und zur Gründung der Europäischen Gemeinschaft*. Baden-Baden: Nomos, 2003.

Vossestein, G.-J. 'De bevoegdheid van de Europese Gemeenschap tot regeling van het vennootschapsrecht'. *WPNR* (2002): 247–253.

Vossestein, G.-J. 'Gouden aandelen'. *WPNR* (2002): 807–812.

Vossestein, G.-J. 'Book Reviews' (S. Lombardo, *Regulatory Competition in Company Law in the European Community*, Frankfurt am Main: Peter Lang 2002). *CML Rev.* 40 (2003): 1304–1306.

Vossestein, G.-J. 'Capital and Companies: On the Move!' *ECL* (2006): 124.

Vossestein, G.-J. 'Companies' Freedom of Establishment after *Sevic*'. *ECL* (2006): 177–182.

Vossestein, G.-J. 'Exit Restrictions on Freedom of Establishment after Marks & Spencer'. *EBOR* 7 (2006): 863–878.

Vossestein, G.-J. 'De invloed van de EG op het vennootschapsrecht. Concurrentie tussen lidstaten: het Nederlandse beleid'. In *De invloed van het Europese recht op het Nederlandse privaatrecht* (Vol. II), edited by A.S. Hartkamp et al. Deventer: Kluwer, 2007, 397–428.

Vossestein, G.-J. 'Transfer of the Registered office. The European Commission's Decision not to Submit a Proposal for a Directive'. *UL Rev.* (2008): 53–65.

Vossestein, G.-J. 'Volkswagen: The State of Affairs of Golden Shares, General Company Law and European Free Movement of Capital'. *ECFR* (2008): 115–133.

Weatherill, S. 'The European Commission's Green Paper on European Contract Law: Context, Content and Constitutionality'. *JCP* 24 (2001): 339–399.

Weatherill, S. 'The Commission's Options for Developing EC Consumer Protection and Contract Law: Assessing the Constitutional Basis'. *EBLR* (2002): 497–515.

Weatherill, S. *Cases and Materials on EU Law*. Oxford: OUP, 2003.

Weatherill, S. 'Why Object to the Harmonization of Private Law by the EC?' *ERPL* (2004): 633–660.

Weatherill, S. 'The Constitutional Competence of the EU to Deliver Social Justice'. *ERCL* (2006): 136–158.

Weatherill, S. 'European Private Law and the Constitutional Dimension'. In *The Institutional Framework of European Private Law*, edited by F. Cafaggi. Oxford: OUP, 2006, 79–106.

Weatherill, S. 'Constitutional Issues – How Much is Best Left Unsaid?' In *The Harmonisation of European Contract Law: Implications for European Private Laws, Business and Legal Practice*, edited by S. Vogenauer & S. Weatherill. Oxford: Hart Publishing, 2006, 89–103.

Weatherill, S. *Cases and Materials on EU law*. Oxford: OUP, 2007.

Weiss, W. 'The Chapter II on Establishment in the Europe Agreements'. *E.For. Aff.Rev.* 6 (2001): 234–281.

Werdmuller, P. 'Compatibility of the EU Takeover Bid Directive Reciprocity Rule with EU Free Movement Rules'. *Bus.L.R* (2006): 64–69.

Werlauff, E. 'The SE as a Legal Form for Financial Companies'. In *European Company Law in Accelerated Progress*, edited by S. Bartman. Alphen aan den Rijn: Kluwer Law International, 2006, 159–174.

Werlauff, E. & T. Rønfeldt. 'Merger as a Method of Establishment: On Cross-border Mergers, Transfer of Domicile and Divisions, Directly Applicable under the EC Treaty's Freedom of Establishment'. *ECL* (2006): 125–129.

Werlauff, E. 'Relocating a Company within the EU'. *ECL* (2008): 136–139.

Wessels, B. 'The Insolvency Regulation: Three Years in Force'. *ECL* (2005): 50–58.

Winter, J. 'De Europese vennootschap als sluis voor in- en uitvoer van vennootschapsrecht'. *NJB* (2002): 2034–2040.

Winter, J. 'Thalassa! Thalassa! – The SE as a glimpse of the future?' In *The European Company. Developing a Community Law of Corporations*, edited by J. Rickford. Antwerp: Intersentia, 2003, 113–122.

Winter, J. 'EU Company Law at the Cross-Roads'. In *Reforming Company and Takeover Law in Europe*, edited by G. Ferrarini et al. Oxford: OUP, 2004, 3–20.

Winter, J. 'We all want to go to Heaven but Nobody Wants to Die'. *ECL* (2004): 1.

Winter, J. 'EU Company Law on the Move'. *LIEI* 31 (2004): 97–114.

Winter, J. 'You Must be Joking'. *Ondernemingsrecht* (2004): 367–368.

Winter, J. 'Level Playing Fields Forever'. In *De nieuwe macht van de kapitaalverschaffer*, edited by H. Beckman et al. Deventer: Kluwer, 2007, 121–138.

Woolcock, S. 'Competition among rules in the single European Market'. In *International Regulatory Competition and Coordination. Perspectives on Economic Regulation in Europe and the United States*, edited by W. Bratton et al. Oxford: Clarendon Press, 1996, 289–321.

Wouters, J. 'Het wetsvoorstel beschermingsconstructies in Europees perspectief'. In *Het wetsvoorstel beschermingsconstructies* (preliminary report Vereeniging 'Handelsrecht' 1998). Deventer: W.E.J. Tjeenk Willink, 1998, 65–135.

Wouters, J. 'European Company Law: *Quo Vadis*?' *CML Rev.* 37 (2000): 257–307.

Wyatt, D. 'Community Competence to Regulate Medical Services'. In *Social Welfare and EU Law*, edited by E. Spaventa & M. Dougan. Oxford/Portland: Hart Publishing, 2005, 131–143.

Wyatt, D. 'The Growing Competence of the European Community'. *EBLR* (2005): 483–488.

Wyatt, D. 'Community Competence to Regulate the Internal Market', Working Paper no. 9/2007 (Jul. 2007, University of Oxford Faculty of Law Legal Studies Research Paper Series), <http://ssrn.com>.

Wymeersch, E. 'The Use of ICT in Company Law Matters'. In *Capital Markets in the Age of the Euro. Cross-Border Transactions, Listed Companies and Regulation*, edited by G. Ferrarini, K.J. Hopt & E. Wymeersch. The Hague: Kluwer Law International, 2002, 469–501.

Wymeersch, E. 'Cross-border transfer of the Seat of a Company – Recent EU case law and the SE Regulation'. In *The European Company. Developing a Community Law of Corporations*, edited by J. Rickford. Antwerp: Intersentia, 2003, 83–94.

Wymeersch, E. 'The Transfer of the Company's Seat in European Company Law'. *CML Rev.* 40 (2003): 661–695.

Wymeersch, E. & K.J. Hopt (eds). *Capital Markets and Company Law*. Oxford: OUP, 2003.

Wymeersch, E. & K.J. Hopt (eds). *European Company and Financial Law. Texts and Leading Cases*. Oxford: OUP, 2007.

Wymeersch, E. 'Is a Directive on Corporate Mobility Needed?' *EBOR* 8 (2007): 161–169.

Index

EUROPEAN COMPANY LAW SERIES

. Steef M. Bartman (ed.), *European Company Law in Accelerated Progress*, 2006 (ISBN 978-90-411-2529-3).

. Karen Vandekerckhove, *Piercing The Corporate Veil: A Transnational Approach*, 2007 (ISBN 978-90-411-2591-0).

. Beate Sjåfjell, *Towards a Sustainable European Company Law: A Normative Analysis of the Objectives of EU Law, with the Takeover Directive as a Test Case*, 2009 (ISBN 978-90-411-2768-6).

. Cornelis de Groot, *Corporate Governance as a Limited Legal Concept*, 2009 (ISBN 978-90-411-2873-7).

. Adriaan Dorresteijn, Tiago Monteiro, Christoph Teichmann & Erik Werlauff, *European Corporate Law*, Second Edition, 2009 (ISBN 978-90-411-2484-5).

. Gert-Jan Vossestein, *Modernization of European Company Law and Corporate Governance: Some Considerations on its Legal Limits*, 2010 (ISBN 978-90-411-2592-7).

www.ingramcontent.com/pod-product-compliance
Lightning Source LLC
Chambersburg PA
CBHW071240230926
51849CB00001B/177
9789041125927